THE LANGUAGE OF MUSIC

By

KLAUS LIEPMANN

DIRECTOR AND ASSOCIATE PROFESSOR OF MUSIC
MASSACHUSETTS INSTITUTE OF TECHNOLOGY

THE RONALD PRESS COMPANY · NEW YORK

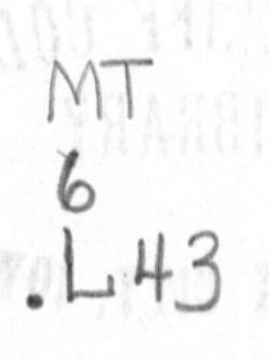

Library of Congress Catalog Card Number: 52–12521

PRINTED IN THE UNITED STATES OF AMERICA

Preface

This book is a practical guide to the enjoyment of music. An outgrowth of the author's long experience as a music educator, it is designed for the music lover who, whether attending concerts or listening to broadcasts and recordings, desires a better understanding of what he hears. The chapters embody a method of going to the art of music itself for information. The reader gains a more direct and rewarding access to music by being shown what music is and how it is expressed.

It is my firm belief that everyone has a sort of music instinct, latent or apparent, and that it can be fostered and nourished. I have tried to explain the basic principles of the language of music in terms that require open-minded enthusiasm but no previous training. The reader need only concede that music has its own signs and symbols which can become as familiar as numbers or letters are. Once he makes the initial effort to acquire this familiarity, many facets of the language of music—at least as far as its rudiments are concerned—can be systematically illustrated, discussed, and mastered. As the reader learns how musical fundamentals are the foundation on which more complicated structures are built, many of the eternal and major intentions of composers can be meaningfully communicated to him.

We never cease to learn from a masterpiece; each hearing, each examination, discloses new subtleties, new relationships, new significance. Hence, it is futile for us to try to capture any "essence" which presumably is the core of a musical composition. Instead, we should proceed to a discussion of the behavior of the materials and the formative principles of music as they have developed in history and as they apply to almost *all* music. In this book, then, the problems of rhythm, melody, harmony, tonality, tone color, expression, texture, form, and style are treated in the way they have occupied the thought and imagination of all composers; that is, as evolving out of historical preferences and the abiding concerns of musicians. And to keep the discussion concrete and practical, the reader is instructed in ear training, musical theory and analysis, and score reading.

Some may feel that a thorough acquaintance with details—or with what are often condescendingly called "technicalities"—obscures the sweep and flight of imagination. I believe, however, that the vision of great composers and the impact and logic of their masterworks rest on these very details of craftsmanship and ingenuity.

Obviously, it is impossible in a book such as this to examine all rhythmic, melodic, harmonic points of interest and significance in a symphony or to analyze "all that can be explained" in a sonata. But if, on the other hand, certain fundamental musical phenomena are studied thoroughly and practically, this knowledge and experience can be fruitfully and cumulatively applied to other musical works. Thus the reader is introduced to a process of understanding which he himself can develop without limit. The many musical examples in this book and the many compositions which are mentioned by title only are meant to induce the reader to explore on his own the world of music. Likewise it is hoped that the introduction to problems in the theory, history, and aesthetics of music, and in acoustics, may lead him to further study in these fascinating subjects.

I have the pleasant duty to thank a number of friends and colleagues who have helped me greatly during the time of preparing this book. Especially, I want to express my gratitude to Professor Theodore Wood, Jr., of the Department of English and History at the Massachusetts Institute of Technology, who has been of immeasurable help in advising me on matters dealing with the organization and presentation of the material. Thanks are also due to Professor Gregory Tucker who collaborated from the very beginning in the presentation of the M. I. T. humanities courses, "Introduction to Music," and "Western Music from the Middle Ages to the Present"; to Mr. John Kessler who advised me in acoustical matters; and to the following members of the Boston Symphony Orchestra who contributed suggestions to the section on instruments: Eugen Lehner, Rosario Mazzeo, Georges Moleux, Ernst Panenka, James Pappoutsakis, Charles Smith, Louis Speyer, Willem Valkenier, and Josef Zimbler. For their assistance in preparing the manuscript and in the checking of references, music examples, etc., I am deeply grateful to the Music Librarian at M. I. T., Mrs. Duscha Scott, and to Mrs. Esther Phillips and Miss Mary Torrey.

KLAUS LIEPMANN

Cambridge,
December, 1952

Contents

The Language of Music

1

Orientation

THERE are literally inexhaustible treasures to be found in the realm of music. This timeless art flourishes not in a secret world, yet in one which is unique. It does not "come to you," however—you have to enter it by yourself. Many different approaches have been suggested by commentators and writers, yet there are still the strangest misconceptions and prejudices abroad which withhold from the adult layman much of the greatest music in existence. Let us, then, by way of introduction, try to reach common ground in outlook and attitude so that we may start from the same point of departure toward the common goal of a better relationship between our lives and music.

What Is Music?

Today, music surrounds us everywhere, and it is safe to assume that since very early in the history of mankind no day has passed without some sort of music having been produced in this world. It has been said that music is a language. This seems sufficiently inclusive if one remembers that every language serves to communicate human experiences and aspirations. But just as verbal concepts do not mean the same thing to everyone, so music "means" different things to different persons at different times. And exactly as language has developed from the communication of simple needs to that of complex and sophisticated meanings, so music has progressed from the conveying of primitive ideas to the expression of subtle shadings of emotions and thoughts. Let us examine some of the changes which the language of music has undergone during its history.

Starting with tribal incantations and war dances, music developed into mystic worship songs and work songs and later into organized church music and sung poetry. Through many centuries music was dominated and directed by the church, so that even dance music (which was originally improvised like the "jam sessions" of today) became stylized under the influence of complicated church music. Later, dances were further developed by the artful playfulness of operas, ballets, and instrumental and vocal virtuosi.

It was after 1600 that the dividing line between spiritual and worldly values became gradually obscured. The Renaissance (*c.* 1400–1600), with its revival of Greek mythology, the Reformation and Counter-Reformation, and finally the French Revolution with its freeing of the individual man—all these great movements resulted ultimately in the acknowledgment of spiritual values independent of the church. Consequently, in the Classic Era (*c.* 1750–1820) we find among composers an increased concern with abstract ideas and structural principles, directed especially toward instrumental music—independent of the word, the church, the drama, or the ballet.

Later in the nineteenth century the language of music became the very personal expression of individuals, and today we are still in the midst of this romantic era of highly developed individual communication, which flourishes, strangely enough, in an age of mechanical reproduction.

Even a rapidly drawn rough sketch of the history of music shows that the functions which music fulfils differ greatly. For that reason we must not expect to hear pretty music-hall tunes in a church, or Bach chorales in a music hall. Furthermore, how the same functions of, let us say, worship, entertainment, and dance are fulfilled varies from one period to the next. Unless we insist on being surrounded by period furniture exclusively, we do not expect to find a horse and buggy in our garage, nor do we demand that our average dance bands play a minuet or a chaconne. It would hardly be necessary to mention these obvious facts were it not for our modern concert life which for variety's sake juxtaposes music of entirely different vintage and function in one program. The listener, therefore, in his imagination must transport himself rapidly from a Protestant church service in 1720 to an aristocratic after-dinner entertainment of the late eighteenth century, to a nineteenth-century "séance" by a demonic virtuoso, to a seventeenth-century opera house, and possibly to the Broadway of 1920.

Besides serving functions of the era in which he lives, the work of the composer shows influences of his religion, his philosophy, his political beliefs, his audience, and his performers. For example, it is significant that Palestrina and Bach strove for "Glory to God Only" within their respective churches, while Beethoven and Wagner, on the other hand, tried to change history. The fact that Haydn was an obedient and satisfied employee in the household of Count Esterhazy and that Beethoven a few years later rebelled against the stuffiness of his aristocratic hosts can at times be sensed in their music. If Händel's opera company had not failed in 1737 in London, we might today be without many of his greatest oratorios—including the *Messiah.* And finally, the quantity and quality of the performers who were available have both inspired and limited the creative output of composers in many instances.

But these varying factors in music—its original function, the composer's philosophy and social position, the reaction of his first audience, and the number and skill of the contemporary musicians and singers—are no indication of the value of the music nor do they necessarily help us come nearer to the content of a composer's message. At best they will put the listener into a sympathetic frame of mind and perhaps cure him of the popular illusion that all music was created to please and "entertain" present-day audiences.

"Good" and "Bad" Music

To learn to discriminate between valuable and worthless music is a most difficult task. First of all, good and bad music are not confined to categories. Remember, there are well-constructed kitchen tables as well as dining-room tables. Each kind is well constructed if it fulfils its function. They cannot and should not be exchangeable—if you have a separate kitchen and dining room. Aesthetically, each piece of furniture should harmonize with the surroundings and, in its construction, contemporary skill in treating and shaping materials should show. A table which is artificially made to look antique is a copy and therefore does not contribute to the history or development of furniture; it is characteristic of its time only in so far as it indicates lack of originality. In similar fashion, a great composer will use previously developed methods of dealing with musical materials, but he will also introduce new ways of handling them rather than copy old masterpieces. It is entirely immaterial in this connection whether the result of his labors happens to be a march or a symphony. Familiarity with many different categories and styles of music will help the layman to discern skill and ingenuity in a composer. However, to pass judgment on unfamiliar music is better left to musicians, historians, and other "experts" —although all of them have been wrong many times. Frequently, their misjudgment has resulted from the common procedure of trusting inherently only in that which has survived and applying the yardstick of the old to the new.

Besides craftsmanship, we seek in a great piece of music that indefinable "message" which we perceive sometimes but which escapes us frequently. To evaluate this message is far more difficult than to judge technical skill of construction. An added complication is that sometimes a piece of music is so well made that the beauty of craftsmanship overshadows the message. In such a case an aesthetic pleasure of functional attractiveness may be derived from a piece of music similar to the exciting emotional effect produced by a beautiful bridge. However, if you abandon preconceptions and prejudices and remain as receptive to the message as an unexposed photographic film is to light, you will receive an impression, more or less accurate, of the composer's intentions.

We can all sense the distinction between good and bad music when we listen to one of the ever-present commercial songs about "love and the silver moon" and compare it to one of the Schubert songs about love. We may assume that both are composed with technical skill, yet one strikes us as sugary, sentimental, pretentious, insincere, superficial, and the other moves us deeply. On the other hand, many folk tunes and every once in a while popular songs ring just as true as any Schubert song. Although these reactions are real, what evokes them can rarely be identified. The main difference between a "polluted" and a genuine musical essence seems to lie not so much in competence and genius or in style of composing but rather in the attitudes of composers. Some are looking for earthly goods and personal power only, and others are grasping for eternal values. One sets out to write a "hit" and the other to pour out his heart. The listener will have to approximate the outlook of the composer if he wants to be receptive to his message.

Popular and "Classical" Music

It should be clear after the foregoing that a "popular" song is not necessarily limited in scope or in value. The distinction between popular and "classical" music creates considerable confusion. The reasons for this are first of all that popularity is hard to measure exactly, and secondly that the word "classical" is used in three different meanings.

In the exact historical sense the Classic Era is the time of Haydn, Mozart, and the early Beethoven. The word "classical" is also used for the description of an ideal and the tendency to approach that ideal in one's style. In this sense "classical" means the revival of the striving of the ancient Greeks for the "beautiful and the good." It specifies that the form, clearly defined through well-organized lines, shapes, and colors, should become all-important as a setting for good material. In music this kind of classic ideal is often mentioned as opposed to the "romantic" ideal of *Sturm und Drang,* the individualistic expression of personal thoughts and feelings which create their own less obvious forms, depending on the state of passion or quiet inner reflection to be expressed. Classical and romantic tendencies, however, are not confined to the two chief historic eras which bear these labels; both occur all through history in a sort of huge pendulum movement and even within the work of single composers.

Commonly, the term "classical" is also supplied to any "serious" or "highbrow" music and to any music which has lasted and survived the popular acclaim or the disapproval of its own time. Popular music, on the other hand, is supposedly created for amusement only; it is considered functional (written for dancing or shows) and is expected to last generally for a few seasons only.

Now, much concert music was originally written for festive functions of its time, much contains popular tunes of its day, and some of it has, though "classical," become popular. Consequently, the terms have lost their original meaning and frequently have become entangled. We speak, therefore, sometimes of a "popular classic," and recognize an older popular tune as a popular song which has become a "classic." (One term which should be avoided is the hybrid "semi-classical." It is of no help as a definition and is an insult to both popular and classical music, analogous to calling someone a "semi-lady.")

The terms "classical" and "popular" should, therefore, never be used as an evaluation of music. All one can say is that popularity in music is no guarantee of lasting value or of any value for that matter except a commercial one, and that "classical" music is neither always popular nor necessarily valuable. It seems advisable to limit the use of the term "classical" to the description of the *Classic Era* in music and the *classic tendencies in style* which appear in many eras. The expression "popular music" may be used in the usual sense as meaning simply a dance, song, or musical show tune which has been whistled, hummed, sung, and played by many persons at any one time.

Who Is "Musical"?

Another controversial term is the word "musical." If music is an eternal human expression, it should be accessible to every human being. And so it is. The expression "musical" is commonly used in order to describe someone who can carry a tune or who plays an instrument or who goes to many concerts and operas. The "unmusical" ones are those who are "tone-deaf," who have had music lessons for twelve years in their youth but are now unable to play a Christmas carol with or without music, and finally those who are dragged to concerts and especially operas for social reasons and are bored and puzzled by what they are supposed to enjoy. How many, then, must necessarily remain "unmusical"? The answer is, practically none. Music educators and psychologists generally agree that incurable tone-deafness occurs only among a negligible number of persons, and that practically anyone can be taught, within a varying time limit for instruction, to carry a tune, to read and to memorize music, and to enjoy concerts, if he makes the effort.

On the other hand, few of those whom we think of as "musical" have more than a nodding acquaintance with a handful of favorite pieces of music. To have been drilled to play or sing a few tunes fairly well does not develop familiarity with the literature of great music, nor does frequent listening to concerts and records guarantee an extensive knowledge of what has been produced in music throughout history. If one defines "musical" in the most general way as meaning to be able, ready, and accustomed to receive impressions from music, then practically every human being is potentially musical. Keeping this in mind, it can be fairly stated that it seems desirable for everyone not to by-pass the opportunity so readily offered nowadays to partake in the thoughts and feelings expressed by great men in that untranslatable medium of music.

"Background Music"

It is true that people have at all times had the bad habit of eating, talking, sleeping, while music is played. In order to do justice to music, however, it will not suffice to degrade it to background music for conversation, meals, reading, working, and the like. Nobody would dream of painting a copy of the "Mona Lisa" on a shopping bag and then proclaiming himself a connoisseur and lover of art, yet almost everyone nowadays commits a comparable crime against music. Whoever is reproached for reading or knitting while "listening" to the *B Minor Mass* by Bach, always answers: "I can concentrate perfectly well on the music while doing something else." To ask these persons whether they would like to have their wedding guests read or knit during the ceremony is usually considered in bad taste. Yet to do this, or to read your favorite newspaper or magazine while attending a performance of a play by Shakespeare, is no more indecent than to listen with half an ear to a symphony. Every ounce of one's concentration is needed if one wants even to begin to do justice to a great work of music. To approach music in an appropriate frame of mind and under the most favorable circumstances means preserving the very minimum of respect for the better manifestations of the human race.

The Music's the Thing

If, in addition to bringing a concentrated readiness to music, we want to prepare ourselves more thoroughly, we have several ways in which we can do so. We have said that the historical approach to music has certain advantages; however, it also has many limitations. To become familiar with the original function of a piece of music, with the life of its composer and the character of his first audience, with events in the physical and spiritual contemporary world, all this is not only valuable but necessary as an important step in understanding music. Yet to do nothing else might obscure the real significance of the composer's music, which is his way of crystallizing and transmitting the experience of his life and his time in his own medium of organized tones which cannot be "retranslated." The life of a composer is never "mirrored" in his music. It is preposterous to assume that a composer writes "sad" music whenever a tragic event occurs in his life. Mozart and Beethoven wrote some of their most joyful and carefree masterworks in their darkest hours. A great novelist does not describe dramas of love or passionate crimes because he is in love or has murdered his sweetheart. Great masters draw from deeper sources than day-to-day experiences; their vision of human motivation and destiny reaches far beyond self-pity and personal failure.

Another popular approach to music is to hunt for a "story" which may be hidden in it. Actually, compared with the total available body of music, the cases where a composer has started the process of creating music with a story (a literary program) are negligible. Besides, if what we call "program music" were to convey no more than its verbal content, the music would be superfluous. In a good piece of program music, the music stands in its own right and the program is left far behind in the role of the rudimentary initial impetus for the creation of the music.

Finally, there is what we might call the "idiomatic" approach to music, that is, going to the music itself. It should not be assumed that meeting music "on its own terms" as a living thing in itself is always easy. Sometimes music employs an intricate musical syntax and vocabulary which might be comparable to the complexities of Chaucer or Joyce.

Here there is only one thing to do: in order to become increasingly familiar with the language of music, we must study its grammar and its old and new idiomatic expressions. The best way to learn a language is to converse in it with others. And indeed the best and quickest way to become familiar with music is to sing and play a great deal of the music of all eras in choral groups, orchestras, and chamber-music groups. The next best way is to listen to live performances, undistorted by frequency limitations, and to be exposed to the true sound sources rather than to one, two, or five loud-speakers. Finally, you may listen to recordings. This, although passive and once removed from life, does have the great advantage over listening to the radio, and even to live performances, that you can choose your own music when you want it, repeat sections at will, and consult the score of the music before and after the music has been played.

While there are many avenues of approach to music which have been suggested in the present chapter, we shall devote this book to the attempt to assist the reader to develop an intensified and more impressionable attitude toward music by becoming more familiar with the idiomatic use of the language of music by composers throughout history. We shall endeavor to have a close look at the elements of music itself—rhythm, melody, harmony—and to learn how their properties were discovered through centuries of music. We shall investigate how these elements are used in creating various musical forms, and while doing so we shall become familiar with the symbols commonly used in writing and reading music.

Our Method of Procedure

In trying to fulfil this task we will have to choose among several methods: (1) the all-inclusive total approach, (2) the reduction in scale to miniature proportions, and (3) the microscopic analysis of one detail after another.

The first method would show all that can be shown in music on one single example. As a prominent composer once said, one could learn all about harmony by studying the first few measures of Mozart's C Major (the "dissonant") Quartet. Unfortunately, this procedure would make too heavy a demand on the endurance and concentration of the average person.

The second approach may be explained by using the less polite terms of baby talk or sugar-coating. To reduce every symphony to the scale of "Three Blind Mice" is obviously neither very flattering to the symphony nor to an audience of adults (or of children, for that matter).

The third procedure, the microscopic analysis of one musical problem after another, is attempted here. This method can work only with the help of an active collaboration on the part of the reader.

Because we must of necessity convert the simultaneous happenings in a piece of music into a successive order, our information gathered and our experience gained must operate in a cumulative way. That is to say that we will, for example, fail to comprehend the concept of tonality unless we retain throughout the discussion a vivid and active understanding of the problems of harmony (which are discussed before the chapters on tonality). On the other hand, the examples which are found in the chapters on rhythm will demand a concentration on rhythmical problems and will exclude, as far as possible, melodic and harmonic problems which are to be discussed later.

The technical details of musical notation are presented in the same progressive and cumulative order: while discussing rhythm we will consider the rhythmic aspect only of the notes; during the chapters on melody, the melody aspect; and so forth.

The reader will do well, in listening to the music which surrounds him or which he chooses from the examples and the "Suggestions for Listening" in this book, to concentrate successively and cumulatively on the various elements and aspects of music as they will be dealt with. Rhythm should be in the foreground when rhythm is under discussion, melody plus rhythm while the spotlight is turned on melody, etc. It is hoped that in this way any adult layman may, without previous musical training, approach the complex field of musical notation, the elements of musical theory and ear-training, and the expressive force of musical masterpieces and their structural components in many small and accurately measured and directed steps.

The road to music is long and unending. There are no short cuts, and ultimately it has to be walked over—not driven along—by each individual for himself. The fastest and most rewarding progress will be made by those who start out with an attitude of searching determination, not by those who are forgetful and wander dreamingly and aimlessly in circles.

It is the common procedure to approach art or literature in general outlines at first and later gradually to fill in the details. In music, however, we must start with the details and build up a total conception gradually. Only when we have learned what to listen for and what to retain in our memory will the general impression of a piece of music "make sense" to us. The reason for this is that music is *time bound*; it is unique among all the arts in this respect. You cannot slow down music in order to investigate, nor can you compress a symphony of thirty minutes' duration into a "Listener's Digest" of five minutes. In any piece of music of more than a minute's duration there will be repetitions and cross references which combine into an over-all structural framework. However, this framework unfolds only bit by bit while the music moves on. The casual listener will be unable to follow the ground plan even at repeated hearings because music flows and there are no cross glimpses possible to him as in reading a novel or looking at a painting. Let us assume that you commute in a train which passes by a treasure of architecture—say a Gothic cathedral. The train never stops at the cathedral, nor do you have the time to make a special trip to it by car. Yet you become increasingly interested in its beauty and curious about its layout and detail in workmanship. Would it not help to have a ground plan available at home and to check further information gathered from it at every consecutive trip? Even a layman can make out certain distinct features from an architect's blueprint. Similarly, a nonmusician can learn quite a bit from the reading of musical scores, which are nothing but the composer's blueprint for his music.

Suggestions for Listening [1]

Bach	Chorale Preludes
Beethoven	String Quartet in E Minor, Op. 59, No. 2
	Symphony No. 6 ("Pastorale")
Gershwin	*An American in Paris*
	Porgy and Bess
Händel	*Water Music*
Haydn	String Quartet, Op. 74, No. 3 ("The Horseman")
Liszt	Piano Concerto No. 1 in E♭ Major
Lully	Opera overtures
Mozart	*Eine Kleine Nachtmusik*, K. 525
Schubert	Songs: "Gretchen am Spinnrade," "Der Doppelgänger," "Ständchen"
Strauss, J.	*The Blue Danube*
	Die Fledermaus
Tchaikovsky	Piano Concerto No. 1 in B♭ Minor

[1] These suggestions refer to points which are made earlier in the chapter. Frequently they extend an example which occurs in the text. It is strongly recommended that the reader listen to all movements of a piece, even if only one measure of it may have been discussed or reproduced.

2

Time Factors in Music

THE THREE basic elements of music are *rhythm, melody*, and *harmony*. Of these, rhythm alone can be isolated for separate consideration without losing its character. Both melody and harmony appear nebulous and unconvincing when stripped of rhythm. A popular game among musicians and music lovers consists of "tapping the rhythm" of a well-known musical excerpt and letting others guess the title of the piece from which the excerpt was taken. It is considerably more difficult to identify the same excerpt if only its melody or its harmony is presented without any rhythmic shape.

The term *rhythm* as used in the above context will probably cause no misunderstanding. However, should we ask ten musicians and laymen to give a definition of rhythm, we would be sure to hear ten widely varying answers. The reason for this prevailing confusion about the exact meaning of the word is that rhythm has fulfilled various functions throughout history and therefore has acquired several meanings through the gradual development of music and its notation. An all-inclusive definition of rhythm would have to run somewhat like this: rhythm is the pattern of long and short, regular and irregular, accentuated and unaccentuated sounds and silences. We shall attempt to separate the various components of rhythm by recalling their appearance in history and the means by which they are indicated in modern notation.

Quantitative Rhythm

During the Second World War the opening of Beethoven's Fifth Symphony was used by the BBC as a call signal because it resembles the letter *V* (for victory) in Morse code: . . . —.

Let us pursue this analogy for a moment and assume that in tapping rhythms we ignore differences in intensity and instead try to re-create musical patterns through various combinations of long and short sounds. We thus imitate ancient Greek and Latin, which distinguished between syllables according to their length, not according to stress or accent as we do in modern languages. Much of the music of the Middle Ages and the Renaissance was written under the influence of ancient Greece and Rome, and tried to re-create the ancient word rhythms of short and long syllables through patterns of long and short tones.[1]

At first there was no need to indicate the exact duration of tones. As long as people sang and chanted poetry and psalms in unison (which they did as far as we know until about A.D. 850) they could stay together by following the rhythms of the poem or by watching the hand signs of their priest or choir master. Even later, in two- or three-part harmony, as long as an entire chorus moved simultaneously from one tone to the next, the duration of each tone was determined rather arbitrarily by tradition, experience with the rhythms of poetry, or by simple signs from the choir leader. Only when the various voices sang different parts and words at the same time did it become necessary to measure the duration of the various tones exactly. Therefore, in the thirteenth century "measured music" was introduced, a system which determined the exact duration of each tone symbol in connection with all others. Our present system of determining the duration of tones relative to each other is still basically the same.

To become acquainted with the shape and the meaning of these time symbols of music is as important to the serious music lover as is familiarity with numbers and letter equations for those who consider arithmetic and mathematics.

Rhythmic Symbols

A whole note 𝅝 equals in duration two half notes 𝅗𝅥 𝅗𝅥, or four quarter notes ♩ ♩ ♩ ♩, or eight eighth notes ♫♫ ♫♫, and so forth.

[1] The fact that the ancient languages emphasized syllables by a rising inflection of the voice, as expressed in the "speech accents" of the Greeks, belongs in the field of melody rather than in that of rhythm.

1. TABLE OF NOTE VALUES

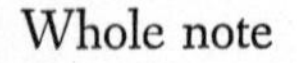

Whole note

Half notes

Quarter notes

Eighth notes

Sixteenth notes

Thirty-second notes

Note: single eighth or sixteenth notes are written thus:

or and or

Groups of two:

or and or

Mixed groups:

(=)

It will be seen from the above table that it provides only for the division of each note value by two. In order to make possible a division by three, so-called *triplets* are used. An arc and/or a superimposed number indicate that 3 equals in duration, etc.

2. TABLE OF TRIPLETS

3 equals and in duration

equals and in duration 3

Multiplication by three is attained through the use of the *prolongation dot* which prolongs the note after which it appears for half the duration of the original value.

3. TABLE OF PROLONGATION

𝅝. = 𝅝 + 𝅗𝅥	♩. = ♩ + ♪
𝅗𝅥. = 𝅗𝅥 + ♩	♪. = ♪ + 𝅘𝅥𝅯

With the help of these symbols any one of the ancient Greek poetic rhythms could fairly accurately be reproduced and synchronized with another. One or more voices could now combine various rhythms without abandoning the customary ternary[2] division of time; they could "recite" different "rhythmic modes" and still "stay together" once they had agreed upon the duration of the smallest time symbol (a quarter note in the following table), which served as counting unit.

4. THE RHYTHMIC MODES

I. Trochee	– ⏑	= 𝅗𝅥 ♩ |
II. Iamb	⏑ –	= ♩ 𝅗𝅥 |
III. Dactyl	– ⏑ ⏑	= 𝅗𝅥. | ♩ 𝅗𝅥
IV. Anapaest	⏑ ⏑ –	= ♩ 𝅗𝅥 | 𝅗𝅥.
V. Spondee	– – –	= 𝅗𝅥. | 𝅗𝅥. | 𝅗𝅥.
VI. Tribrach	⏑ ⏑ ⏑	= ♩ ♩ ♩ |

[2] During the age of "Measured Music" (*c.* 1250–1600), ternary (three-unit) rhythms were at first preferred to binary (two-unit) rhythms, as can be seen from the very terms used: *tempus perfectum* (our three-four), and *tempus imperfectum* (our two-four). By far the greatest part of written music in the Middle Ages was liturgical music, and, because it mostly used *tempus perfectum*, ternary rhythm was conceived to be related to the Holy Trinity.

For those cases where one voice remained temporarily silent, symbols had to be introduced which determined the duration of silences or "rests" exactly in relation to the duration of sounds.

5. TABLE OF RESTS AND THEIR EQUIVALENTS IN NOTES

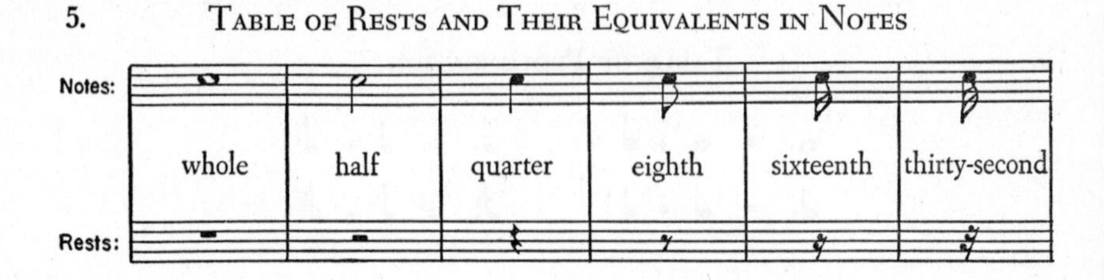

Examples of Quantitative Rhythm

Once we get used to recognizing, while reading and listening to music, the existence of "long-short" (trochaic) and other patterns, much of the "mystery" of medieval, Renaissance, and more recent music will disappear, inasmuch as the rhythmic idea which the composer had in mind reveals itself to us. What is more, the structure of a piece may become more convincing to us if we observe its rhythmical components. For example:

1. A repeated rhythmic pattern may create unity within a piece of music.

6. DOMINATOR—ECCE—DOMINO (Motet)
School of Notre Dame (c. 1225)

Source: Davison and Apel, *Historical Anthology of Music*, I, 25.

7. SYMPHONY NO. 7 (Second movement)
Ludwig van Beethoven (1770–1827)

2. Or a change of pattern may add variety within the line of a song or melody.

8. ECCO L'AURORA CON L'AURATA FRONTE
Andrea Gabrieli (*c.* 1510–1586)

Source: A. Einstein, *The Golden Age of the Madrigal,* p. 32.

3. Symmetry may be obtained by the repetition of mixed patterns.

9. MY BONNY LASS (Ballet)
Thomas Morley (1557–1603)

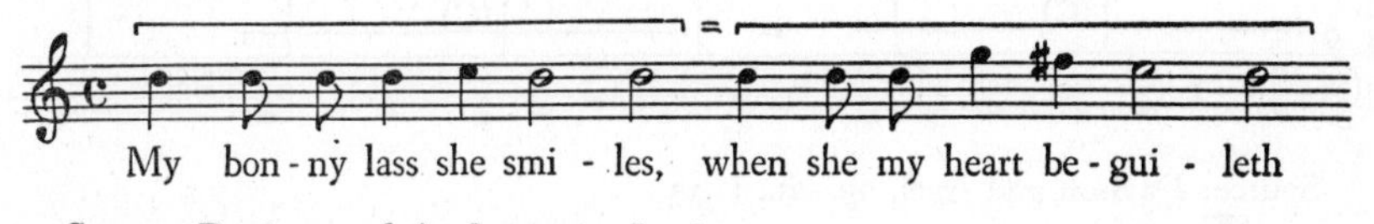

Source: Davison and Apel, *op. cit.,* I, 180.

10. SYMPHONY NO. 40 IN G MINOR, K. 550 (First movement)
Wolfgang Amadeus Mozart (1756–1791)

11. SYMPHONY NO. 2 IN D MAJOR, OP. 43 (First movement)
Jan Sibelius (1865-)

4. And finally, in a piece for several voices, both unity and variety may be achieved through rhythmical repetition and cross references.

12. MOTET

Anonymous (13th century)

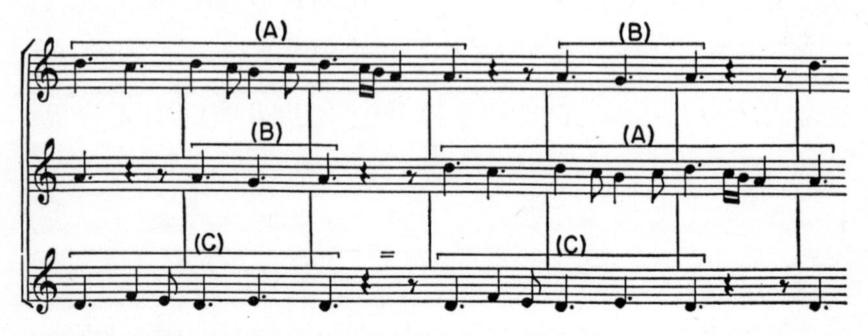

Source: Davison and Apel, *op. cit.*, I, 35.

Note: In the above example the upper voice sings the two rhythmic (and melodic) patterns which we have marked by letters in the order *A, B,* while the middle voice sings them in reverse order *B, A.* This exchange of voices ("*Stimmtausch*") was a much favored device of medieval music. Today, we use the same principle whenever we sing "Rounds."

"Playing with Rhythms"

Playing with rhythms is one of the things the composer does in creating music. It is for this reason that the importance of rhythmical perception in listening to music can hardly be exaggerated. The time and effort spent on concentrating on and analyzing rhythms—for a few weeks at least—will be amply repaid by the resulting increase of musical discrimination. Let us consider therefore at this point a complete piece of music from the point of view of rhythm only. We will have to remember of course that rhythm is not all, that, in addition, melody, harmony, and tone color will play an important part in almost all music which sounds familiar to us.

However, concentrating on rhythm for a while will help us eventually to discern these other musical factors as well. We will gradually be able to hear melodies (which depend on rhythm for their existence) more clearly. Secondly, whenever a particular instrument enunciates a rhythm, tone color will be brought into relief with the help of this very rhythm. And finally, if we want eventually to observe how harmonies underline or counteract melodic rhythms, or else create their own (harmonic) rhythm, we will have to become intimately acquainted with rhythm per se.

Schubert's String Quartet in D Minor is often called "Death and the Maiden" because the composer used the melody of his song of that title for the second movement of the quartet. The form of the piece is that of a theme (the "given" melody) with five variations. If the reader will provide himself with a pocket score of the work and a recording he may be able to partake substantially of Schubert's imagination and artistic skill merely by analyzing the rhythms which are employed and combined in this piece.

The theme—and consequently each variation—consists of two parts, each of which is repeated separately (as indicated by the signs 𝄆 𝄇 which frame the section which is to be repeated). Even a mere glance at the score will furnish us with a few important rhythmical points in preparation for the listening which should follow later:

1. The theme and the end (or *coda*) of the piece employ the long–short–short or dactyl rhythm in all instruments simultaneously.
2. This principal rhythm occurs in at least one instrumental voice throughout all five variations.
3. A rhythmical diminution of the dactyl occurs twice. That is to say, 𝅗𝅥 ♩ ♩ becomes ♪ 𝄾 ♫ (which is almost equivalent to ♩ ♫) in the viola part in variation *two*, and it becomes further diminished to ♪ ♬ in all instruments during the greater part of variation *three*.

A closer inspection will reveal that a great many additional rhythms are employed and set against each other. The variations reveal so much which is of rhythmical interest that we are reminded of the fact that Schubert's theme is characteristic in its rhythm (and harmony) rather than in its melody. Whenever we want to quote the theme we find its harmonies and rhythm more essential for identification than its melody. Because in this particular composition each instrument continues pretty much with its own rhythm throughout an entire variation, it will suffice to note here only the beginning of each section of the piece.

13. ANDANTE FROM QUARTET IN D MINOR ("Death and the Maiden")

Franz Schubert (1797–1828)

If we have the patience to postpone the hearing of the piece in question still further, we can indulge in an experiment which may prove to us that familiarity with the rhythms involved will bring us decidedly nearer to the essence of a composition. If we bring all available hands to tap the various rhythms, first of one, then of two, three, and finally of all four instruments involved, the subsequent repeated hearing of the piece will seem like a meeting between old friends—music and listeners will appear to meet on common physical and mental grounds.

There is much music which could be investigated merely in regard to its rhythm in a similar fashion, and to good advantage for the ambitious listener. This could for instance be done with the other movements of the Schubert D Minor Quartet and with the Allegretto of Beethoven's Seventh Symphony (see Fig. 7). As a matter of fact, all movements of Beethoven's First, Second, Fourth, Seventh, and Eighth Symphonies, especially, and many quartets and symphonies by Haydn and Mozart will reveal rhythmically significant principles and intricacies even to the layman's eyes and ears as soon as he tries in the least to discover them.

Suggestions for Listening

Beethoven — Symphony No. 5 in C Minor, Op. 67
Symphony No. 7 in A Major, Op. 92
LeJeune, Claude — Psalms and songs
Gabrieli, A. — Instrumental music
Morley — "My Bonny Lass"
Mozart — Symphony No. 40 in G Minor, K. 550
Music from the School of Notre Dame (13th century)
Schubert — "Death and the Maiden" (song)
String Quartet No. 14 in D Minor ("Death and the Maiden")
Sibelius — Symphony No. 2 in D Major, Op. 43

Also: Beethoven Symphonies No. 1, 2, 4, and 8; and additional quartets and symphonies by Haydn and Mozart.

←——In Fig. 13:

A: principal rhythm.

B: means continue the same rhythm (here).

C: derived from principal rhythm.

3

Time Factors in Music
(*Continued*)

Qualitative Rhythm

It would be simple indeed if one could call the foregoing a complete, if rapid, recounting of the story of rhythm and its symbols in music. However, people have not only chanted and sung prayers and songs of worship and love; they have, since the dawn of human culture, danced and marched and accompanied their work with songs. And for dances and work songs, cyclic patterns or regularly repeated "beats" in groups of two (rather than three) are needed which can be adjusted to the rhythm of the human pulse and breathing. When we march, we conceive the endlessly repeated left–right steps as *left*–right, *left*–right, *left*–right; or if we choose, we may instantaneously switch our minds so as to conceive a pattern of left–*right*. However, we do not stamp one foot more violently than the other, we do not always accentuate physically, but we do mentally register repetitive motion in shorter patterns of *down*–up or *left*–right. Similarly, in dancing we perceive an emphasis on the first of two (or sometimes three) dance steps. It is of the utmost importance, though, to remember that this emphasis is inherently felt and mentally perceived and not necessarily physically stressed. Let us illustrate this. The following series of dots represent a number of equally strong tones which are repeated at regular time intervals:

o o o o o o o o o o

Reading this pattern from left to right, its image will vary considerably depending on whether we perceive the dots in groups of two or of three.

1 2 1 2 1 2 1 2 1 2
o o o o o o o o o o

1 2 3 1 2 3 1 2 3 1
o o o o o o o o o o

We notice that, invariably, the beginning of a new group is felt as a significant new cycle. The same phenomenon occurs when we count people, strokes of church bells, etc., in quantities of two or three—each new group is conceived as an important new entry of time. Because the "one," the first "beat" of each group, assumes a special quality distinct from the other beats, we call this kind of rhythmic conception *qualitative* rhythm to differentiate it from the *quantitative* rhythm which we discussed above. We see, then, that quantitative rhythm which grew out of the *word* became enriched by and intertwined with qualitative rhythm which developed out of repetitive *action*.

This network of beats marking identical time intervals and their pulsating quality we call, in music, *meter*. Just as in poetry meter consists of a certain number of word rhythms, so in music meter contains a certain number of beats. Because music may subdivide some of the beats and combine others, meter and rhythm are seldom identical for any length of time, except in simple dances and marches. Meter, then, we shall call the network on which qualitative rhythm is based, and *metric accent* the inherent stress which we perceive on the first of a group of regularly recurring beats. If in the two examples which follow we tap each tone and observe the relative duration of the various notes, a pulsating pattern will result. Careful analysis will show that the metric accents, besides dividing and ordering the melody, help it along in its onward flow.

14. ENTRANCE HYMN FOR THE EMPEROR

Chinese (1000 B.C.)

Source: Davison and Apel, *op. cit.*, I, 3.

15. SONG OF THE ASS

Latin lyric from a liturgical play (*c.* 12th century)

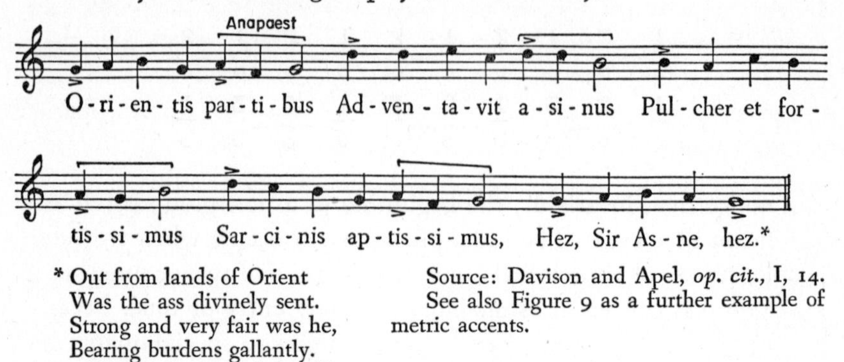

* Out from lands of Orient
Was the ass divinely sent.
Strong and very fair was he,
Bearing burdens gallantly.
Heigh, Sir Ass, oh heigh!

Source: Davison and Apel, *op. cit.*, I, 14.
See also Figure 9 as a further example of metric accents.

Emphasis of Meter

The metric accent may be emphasized by a sharp attack, or by an increase in volume produced by added instruments, in other words by a *dynamic accent*. However, to do this continuously is as primitive and monotonous as scanning poetry or stamping every first beat when dancing. Yet, as everybody knows, music which is played for marching or dancing does emphasize the "beat" and helps us to "keep time." Instead of using a repetitive dynamic reinforcement, this emphasis may be achieved by various other means. At "strategic moments," that is, simultaneously with the metric accent, significant changes in the melody or harmony may occur (this happens, for example, in the melodies and harmonies of the excerpts from compositions by Mozart, Beethoven, Schubert, and Sibelius which were quoted in the preceding chapter). Or a longer ("stretched") duration of tones may be substituted for dynamic, melodic, or harmonic accents. In the following example, which uses ancient dactyl verse rhythm for a dance tune, the metric accent is underlined by the regular recurrence of long notes:

16. ENGLISH DANCE (Estampie)

Anonymous (13th century)

Source: Davison and Apel, *op. cit.*, I, 43.

Here, force may be added through increased tone volume or through drums at the beginning of each rhythm group, but it is not necessary. If one compares the speech of a Southerner with that of a New Englander, one realizes that the percussive staccato of the latter is, in regard to emphasis, fully matched by the smooth stretching of syllables of the former. This fact, that emphasis, accents, stress may be obtained through quantitative as well as through varying qualitative treatment in language and music, has caused endless scholarly disputes about the correct interpretation of medieval music. To complicate matters further, it is known that in the fifth century dynamic differentiations and forceful accents rather than quantitative patterns came progressively into use in Latin. This is the reason why there are to this day various schools of thought about the correct rendition of Gregorian Chant, i.e., the official music of the Catholic Church, based on the collection of ancient chants instituted by Gregory the First (Pope, 590–604).

While we may leave the ultimate solution of these historical problems safely in the hands of the musicologists, we can nevertheless derive some benefit for our daily listening if we keep in mind that both quantitative and qualitative rhythm exist. Because frequently several rhythmical factors collaborate or even conflict with each other, the order of our investigation should always be as follows:

1. Recognize and mark quantitative patterns.
2. Perceive in listening and reading dynamic accents (*sf* or *fz* = suddenly loud, etc.).
3. Observe significant melodic and/or harmonic changes and determine whether they reinforce or contradict a previously established rhythm.
4. Determine whether a metric accent is involved and, if so, what the meter is.

The last-mentioned step, i.e., the recognition of the metric accent, has been made much easier through a development in rhythmical notation which we shall discuss presently.

Notation of Meters Through Measures

When, in the seventeenth century, with the development of opera and instrumental music the melodies became more florid and fluid, when each "beat" was subdivided into continuously varying rhythms, a clearer system of marking time in the notation of music became necessary. Bar lines came into general use at that time as "measuring rods," occurring regularly after a fixed number of beats and indicating the regular "pulse" or meter of a piece. Since then and to this day, all music, vocal as well as instrumental, has been written down in *measures,* enclosed by bar lines. Simultaneously, *time signatures,* which had been ambiguous and cumbersome through the Middle Ages, became clarified and standardized. In order to indicate the number and kind of counting units or beats in each measure, the time signature is placed at the beginning of a piece, explaining for example that each measure will contain two quarter notes ($\frac{2}{4}$ meter or time) *or its equivalent.* In another case three eighth notes ($\frac{3}{8}$ meter) may be indicated, and so forth.

The most important aspect of this use of bar lines is not, however, their measuring function, but rather the fact that they indicate the inherently felt metric accent or strong pulse which occurs immediately after each bar line with the beginning of a new measure. The notation of meter through measures, then, means the ordering of music into measures of equal duration and the rationalizing of the regular pulse of music. Now it becomes clear in notation whether, for example, a dynamic accent is meant to coincide with the metric accent:

17. HUNGARIAN DANCE NO. 5

Brahms-Joachim

Or whether the metric accent is "emphasized by negation," by a rest (see Fig. 18), or a sudden softness (Fig. 19).

18. SYMPHONY NO. 3 IN E♭ MAJOR, OP. 55 ("Eroica," first movement)

Ludwig van Beethoven (1770–1827)

19. STRING QUARTET IN B♭ MAJOR, OP. 130

Beethoven

The most common meters are duple, triple, and quadruple. A duple meter divides music into measures which each contain two beats. Similarly, triple meters contain three, and quadruple meters four beats per measure. These meters are indicated by the following time signatures:

Duple meters: $\frac{2}{2}$ $\frac{2}{4}$ $\frac{2}{8}$
Triple meters: $\frac{3}{2}$ $\frac{3}{4}$ $\frac{3}{8}$
Quadruple meters: $\frac{4}{2}$ $\frac{4}{4}$ $\frac{4}{8}$

The time signatures $\frac{2}{2}$ and $\frac{4}{4}$ are sometimes indicated by signs which are vestiges of medieval time signatures: ¢ = $\frac{2}{2}$, and **C** = $\frac{4}{4}$.[1] Whenever we find the fraction $\frac{2}{4}$ at the beginning of a piece of music it means that each measure will contain the equivalent of two quarter notes. For example, it may contain measures of the following kind:

20. RHYTHMIC SCHEME, BEETHOVEN'S STRING QUARTET IN D MAJOR, OP. 18, NO. 3, SECOND MOVEMENT (measures 1–14)

The above example might serve us well as a means to clarify the difference between *meter* and *rhythm* once for all. If we tap with our right hand each note according to its proportional duration (♩ = ♫, ♬♬ = ♩, etc.) we reconstruct the rhythm of

[1] The sign **C** is sometimes mistaken for the letter *C*, supposedly standing for Common Time ($\frac{4}{4}$). In reality, however, it is derived from the medieval symbol for *tempus imperfectum*—an uncompleted circle C. See footnote on page 17.

the piece. By tapping out with our other hand the two beats of each measure in regular succession, we mark the meter. We might emphasize the metric accent dynamically by tapping the first beat of each measure louder than the second.

Again it must be said that spending a little time on experiments of this sort is anything but a waste of time. On the contrary, it helps produce that state of physical and mental alertness and co-ordination which is so essential for the enjoyment of music. Once more the reader may have immediate proof of this whenever he follows up his tapping exercises with a rehearing of the piece in question.

Whether a composer chooses 2, or 4, or 8 as the *denominator* in his time signature, that is, as the basic counting unit, depends solely on factors of legibility in connection with the speed of the piece.

21.

In the above example the first kind of notation is best fitted for a moderate, the second for a very fast, and the third for a very slow rate of counting.

On the other hand, the choice of the *numerator* in the time signature is not just a question of expediency. In a 4/4 measure, for instance, two metric accents are perceived—a principal one on the first, and a secondary, or weaker one, on the third beat—while in a 2/4 meter one metric accent of constant strength occurs throughout the piece once in each measure.

22.

> = Principal metrical accent
> = Secondary metrical accent

The famous melody from the Finale of Beethoven's Ninth Symphony would appear quite different if we were to change its time signature from the original 4/4 to 2/4. The uniform metric accent which the 2/4 signature implies would add a pedestrian jerkiness to the tune which the unequal metric accents of the original avoid. Even without the use of dynamic stresses, the melody changes its character according to whether one thinks of 2/4 or 4/4 time while singing or hearing it.

23. SYMPHONY NO. 9 IN D MINOR, OP. 125 (Last movement)

Ludwig van Beethoven (1770–1827)

When several identical metrical units are combined within one measure—as, for instance, two duple meters in one quadruple measure (twice 2/4 in one 4/4 measure)—we speak of a *compound meter.* We could consequently call a "simple quadruple" meter also a *compound* (2 × 2) *duple meter.*

However, common usage prefers to speak of compound meters especially when groups of three are involved. Let us assume, for example, that we have three measures of 3/8 time:

3/8

In this case the first note of each measure receives the metric accent. If, on the other hand, we want to combine these three measures into *one* measure, we will have one principal triple meter superseding three (submerged) secondary triple meters.

9/8

In this case the time signature would be 9/8 and the measure would contain one principal metric accent (the first note) and three additional secondary metric accents (on the first, fourth, and seventh notes of the measure).

Should we prefer to combine $\frac{6}{8}$ in one measure, we would obtain duple time consisting of two beats, each subdivided into a secondary triple meter.

$\frac{6}{8}$

Here the first note would contain the principal metric accent and the first and fourth notes additional, secondary ones.

Finally, compound quadruple meter substitutes for each quarter note in our previous example (Figure 22) groups of three eighth notes.

$\frac{12}{8}$

In this case, we would have one major principal accent on *one* and a minor principal accent on *seven,* plus secondary accents on *one, four, seven,* and *ten.*

Let us not be unduly disturbed by the seemingly complicated aggregation of metric accents in compound meters. In most cases, composers will assist the listener by reinforcing metrical accents through dynamic, melodic, or harmonic accents.

24. CONCERTO GROSSO NO. 8 IN G MINOR ("Christmas Concerto," Pastorale)

Archangelo Corelli (1653–1713)

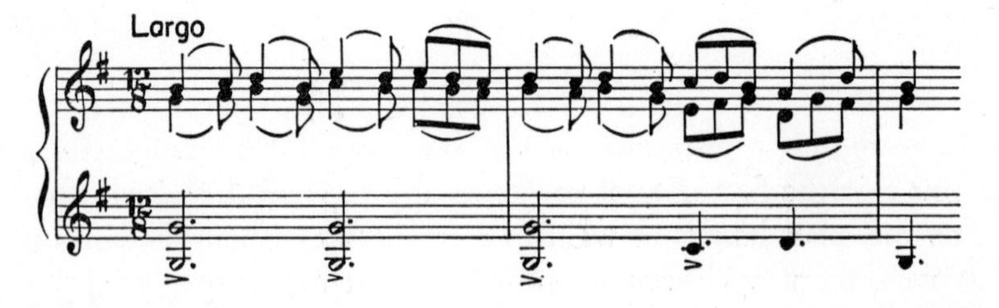

One should simply remember that compound meters are time signatures that consist in most cases of "submerged" triple meters (groups of threes) which are ordered into duple, triple, or quadruple measures, i.e.:

$\frac{6}{8}$ = compound duple meter, consisting of twice $\frac{3}{8}$
$\frac{9}{8}$ = compound triple meter, consisting of three times $\frac{3}{8}$
$\frac{12}{8}$ = compound quadruple meter, consisting of four times $\frac{3}{8}$

There is an easy way of acquiring a better awareness of meter in music: guessing the time signature of any music which you hear during the period of, let us say, a month, and checking your estimate against the score whenever possible. There will be many mistakes made in the beginning, and of the denominator in the time signature one may never be sure; yet a fairly clear perception of duple and triple meter is imperative for an intelligent approach to music. A short time of listening conscientiously for the meter in music will suffice to awaken the power of metric perception. When that state of alertness is reached one had better let the question of meter sink back into an attitude of subconscious readiness—else one might hear in the first and third movements of Beethoven's "Eroica" nothing but "$\frac{3}{4}$ time."

Examples of Various Rhythms Based on Meter

It would seem that a network of equal beats and regularly recurring metric accents would invite monotony. And indeed what the time-beating "jitterbugs" and foot-tapping concertgoers catch is little more than the bare rudiments of metric music, which in themselves have little interest. However, once a composer has decided on a meter, he has countless possibilities for rhythmical variety. The examples which follow should be sufficient proof of the fact that there is endless variety contained within the uniformity of meter.

An Excerpt from Brahms' *Requiem*

Even the mere inspection of the rhythmical proceedings will help in coming closer to the second movement of Brahms' *Requiem.* If there were no bar lines we might be in doubt whether the continuous rhythm of the bass line (bassoons, celli, string basses) ♩ 𝅗𝅥 ♩ 𝅗𝅥 ♩ 𝅗𝅥 ♩ 𝅗𝅥 is meant to be iambic or trochaic. This question, of whether to perceive the basic rhythmic chain link as ♩ 𝅗𝅥 or as 𝅗𝅥 ♩, can be solved by considering the melody and harmony, or by consulting the words (either in the original German or in translation) which the chorus sings later to the same rhythm. Another, perhaps quicker, if somewhat mechanical, way is to consider the place of the bar lines, and to remember that the metric accent occurs at the first beat of each measure. Accordingly, the piece and the chorus start with an incomplete trochee and the correct articulation for the instruments as well as for the voices is of course Be - hold and not Be - hold.

The major portion of the movement (up to the Allegro non troppo and its slower introduction) consists of this basic rhythm and derivations of it which are recited by the chorus and various instrumental groups. Thus:

25.

Timpani (kettledrums)

Oboes

Flutes, clarinets, violins, violas

Piccolo, oboe, violins, violas (later)

And the horns, trumpets, and harp mark the second beat of each measure

Because each instrument goes on repeating its particular rhythm with hardly any changes, we might do well to tap and memorize each pattern so as to perceive in listening as much of the actual score as possible.

When the text expresses a new thought the rhythm of the chorus changes to:

For lo, the grass with' - reth

And in the short interlude ("Etwas bewegter" = a little more lively) which brings the admonition, "Now therefore be patient," the entire fabric of orchestra and chorus changes to the following rhythm:

Now, there - fore, be pa - tient, O — my breth - ren,

We might also observe the expressive qualities of the long drawn-out note values to the words:

And hath long pa - - - - - - - - tience for it,

and the light flute and harp rhythm (introduced first by plucked celli and violas) which precedes the mentioning of the "rain of the morn" and the "rain of the eve":

26.

Flute and harp

Violas

Celli

From here on the reader should be able to proceed on his own in an investigation of the rhythms which are employed, repeated, varied, combined. A practical way to improve one's facility in recognizing and memorizing rhythms consists of these four steps:

1. Make a table of the various rhythms found in the score.
2. Number each rhythm according to importance and indicate the instruments, voices, and text fragments involved.
3. Determine and point out interrelationships between rhythms by naming derivations from "rhythm number one" (I), Ia, Ib, Ic, etc.
4. Identify each rhythm by number while listening.

An Excerpt from Haydn's String Quartet in D Major, Op. 20, No. 4

Not always do all instruments involved articulate as clearly and with as much conformity to one basic rhythm as in our excerpt from the Brahms' *Requiem*. Sometimes the metric accent is camouflaged or contradicted by one or more voices. Friction might arise between the meter, rhythm, harmony, or melody of various voices, one seemingly progressing in $\frac{2}{4}$, another in $\frac{3}{4}$, one accenting the metric accent, another an "offbeat" (i.e., beats two or three in $\frac{3}{4}$ or beats two or four in $\frac{4}{4}$). If the music seems off balance at times until the customary musical solution restores balance, the keen listener will experience a certain physical and mental excitement; his curiosity and patience, his power of musical judgment, are being taxed.

Let us suppose that we hear the first violin part only of the Minuet from Haydn's Quartet in D Major, Op. 20, No. 4, and that by some queer accident the score has come to us without bar lines and time signature (forget also that you ever knew the characteristic meter of every minuet which was ever danced or composed).

27. STRING QUARTET IN D MAJOR, OP. 20, NO. 4, (Third movement)

Joseph Haydn (1732–1809)

If we assume that the dynamic accents (marked *fz*) reinforce the metric accent, and if we insert accordingly the missing bar line before each of these accents, we will be led to believe that the meter is $\frac{2}{4}$.

28.

The cello and viola parts considered in a similar fashion seem to move in $\frac{4}{4}$ time:

29.

Only the three measures which follow and which contain nowhere a dynamic accent will indicate to the more experienced listener the true state of affairs, through an observation of the harmonic happenings. The end of the "cadence" (see p. 135) indicates the metric accent unmistakably.

30.

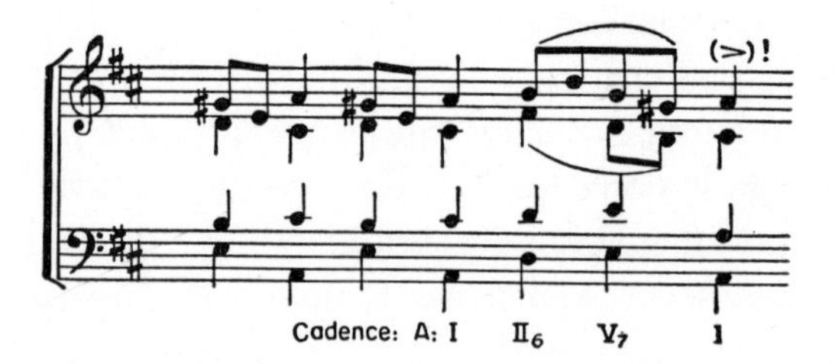

We shall not pause to clarify this at this point. For the moment it will suffice to understand the principle; what has been heard for five measures becomes belatedly clear at measure eight, and when the entire eight measures are repeated, as required by the composer, the metric and rhythmical structure appears as clear as daylight in spite of the *fz* accents. The rhythm in the first full measure of the first violin is an iamb and the meter is $\frac{3}{4}$.

31.

Summary and Additional Examples

Before we proceed with a discussion of the third time factor in music, *tempo,* it might be worth while to study a few more examples of similar rhythmical complications. A little concentration now on a few bars of a minuet might later serve to disclose many similar measures in a symphony or opera even upon a first hearing. For those who would like to explore further the rhythmical possibilities inherent in music, let us summarize and enumerate a few of the principles which we have encountered so far, and additional ones which we are apt to find in use upon closer inspection.

1. We have said that only in the simplest kind of music will the rhythm coincide with the meter for any length of time. In that case, there will obviously be no quantitative rhythm present. Yet even so—limiting our raw material for rhythm to three quarter notes in $\frac{3}{4}$ meter, let us say—we will be able to express three distinct rhythms.

$\frac{3}{4}$ | ♩ ♩ ♩ | ♩ | ♩ ♩ 𝄽 | ♩ ♩ | ♩ 𝄽 𝄽 |

Analogous word rhythms would be:

a) *Cy*–clo–tron   b) di–*ver*–gent   c) un–a–*dorned*

2. Frequently, a regular meter is established by the composer only to be counteracted by sudden "displaced" dynamic accents which stress usually light "syllables."

32. SYMPHONY NO. 1 IN C MAJOR, OP. 21 **(Menuetto)**
Ludwig van Beethoven (1770–1827)

3. At other times a metric accent is swallowed up by its preceding beat. In such a case we speak of *syncopation* (literally "cutting up" of beats or proportions).

33. THE BARTERED BRIDE **(Overture)**
Bedřich Smetana (1824–1884)

(See also the last three measures of Fig. 32 above.)

4. In the following example, the hearer is left in the dark at first as to the meter of the piece.

34. SYMPHONY NO. 5 IN C MINOR, OP. 67 **(First movement)**
Ludwig van Beethoven (1770–1827)

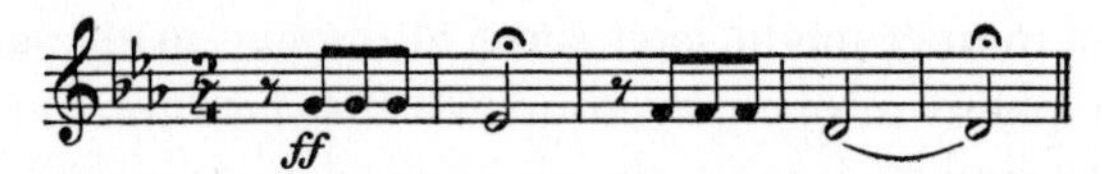

5. A subdivision of single beats may produce a sort of rhythmical diminution giving a microscopic version of a previous rhythm.

35. STRING QUARTET, OP. 77, NO. 2 **(First movement)**
Joseph Haydn (1732–1809)

6. By combining several measures in a kind of rhythmical augmentation the effect of a compound meter is sometimes obtained.

36. QUARTET IN E♭ MAJOR, OP. 74 **(Third movement)**
Ludwig van Beethoven (1770–1827)

Si ha s'immaginar la battuta di $\frac{6}{8}$ (*one should imagine a beat as in* $\frac{6}{8}$).

7. Irregular and changing meters have been employed for centuries, but most frequently they occur in the modern era of music. Tchaikovsky, for example, in the famous Allegretto of his "Pathétique" Symphony uses $\frac{5}{4}$ time, a compound of $\frac{2}{4}$ plus $\frac{3}{4}$ time.

37. SYMPHONY NO. 6 IN B MINOR ("Pathétique," Second movement)

Peter Ilyitch Tchaikovsky (1840–1893)

Ravel subdivides an $\frac{8}{8}$ measure into a compound of 3 plus 2 plus 3 beats.

38. PIANO TRIO IN A MINOR

Maurice Ravel (1875–1937)

Stravinsky especially employs rapid changes of meters which suspend the regularity of pulse and any anticipation of the metric accent.

39. HISTOIRE DU SOLDAT (from "Marche Royale")

Igor Stravinsky (1882–)

8. When several sharply contrasting rhythms are expressed simultaneously, without a change of meter, we speak of *polyrhythm*.

40. SONATA NO. 1 IN G MAJOR FOR VIOLIN AND PIANO, OP. 78 (First movement)

Johannes Brahms (1833–1897)

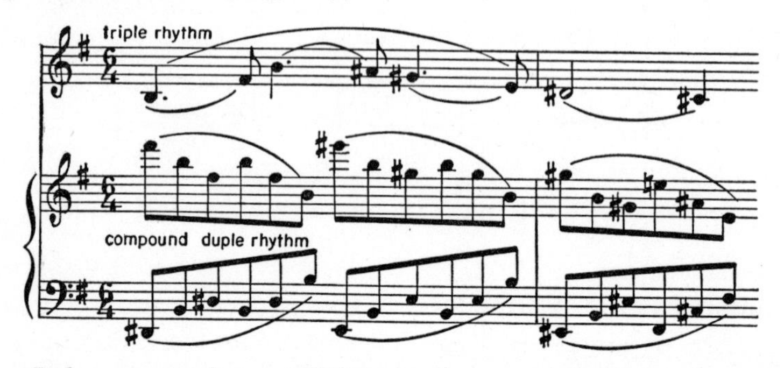

9. *Polymeter* is the simultaneous playing of different meters. For example, in Mozart's *Don Giovanni* the following three dances are played at the same time:

41. DON GIOVANNI (Act I, Finale)

Wolfgang Amadeus Mozart (1756–1791)

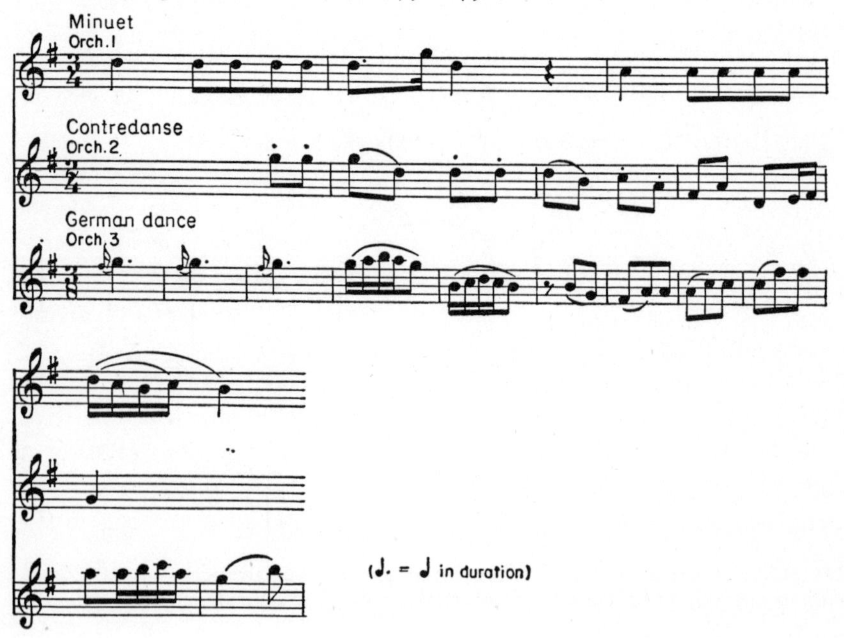

Should these examples seem bewildering at first, let us remember this: the whole problem of rhythm and meter is so complicated and controversial that it has taken centuries to express even a few of the countless variations inherent in them. Of the two basic approaches, the quantitative or the qualitative conception of rhythm, both have been used at different times in history separately or combined, with or without dynamic or other reinforcements. So endless seem the possibilities that the limits of using new patterns of time in connection with sound and silences will perhaps never be reached.[2]

Tempo

The third time factor in music, tempo, is the speed of the succession of counting units. Through the Middle Ages and the Renaissance, only custom or functional use determined the time interval from one counting unit to the next. Starting in the seventeenth century, inexact general hints came gradually into use as tempo indications: *Allegro* (gay, fast, light), *Adagio* (slow), *Allegretto* (slower than Allegro), *Andante* (faster than Adagio but slower than Allegretto), etc. Finally, in 1816, the invention of the *metronome* made it possible to indicate through a mechanically adjustable pendulum the exact rate of the succession of beats. For example, ♩ = MM 60 means that in the piece in question, the quarter-note beat should recur at the rate of 60 oscillations per minute on Maelzel's metronome; in other words, one quarter note should have the duration of one second in this case.

The tempo of a piece, even when a metronome speed is indicated, is a favorite subject of dispute among musicians and laymen. Metronomes, at least before the invention of the modern electronic instruments and the watchlike pocket devices, have frequently been unreliable, and furthermore, composers have always had a habit of changing their minds about the "ideal" tempo. The size of the concert hall, the weather which affects the instruments, the mood of the players or of the conductor, and many other imponderables will affect the choice of the "right" tempo, so that the disputable character description of a piece, "Allegro molto con brio" (Allegro with much spirit), may in the end be more satisfactory than MM = 138. Beethoven had this to say

[2] New experiments with rhythm are at present being made by several French composers, led by Messiaen. Cf. *Musical Quarterly*, Vol. XXXVI, No. 2 (April, 1950), pp. 259–68.

in connection with a metronome mark: "100 according to Maelzel; but this must be held applicable to only the first measures, for the feeling also has its tempo and this cannot entirely be expressed in this figure [i.e., 100]."[3] In another context Beethoven recommended using metronome figures in addition to character designations, a custom which has become more and more popular among composers of today.

> . . . what, for instance, can be more nonsensical than *Allegro*, which always means *merry* and how often are we so far from this conception of time that the piece says the very *opposite of the designation*. As regards these 4 chief speeds [Allegro, Andante, Adagio, Presto] which by no means have the correctness or truthfulness of the chief winds, we gladly allow that they be put aside, it is a different matter with the words used to designate the character of the composition, these we cannot give up, since time is really more the body while these have reference to the spirit.[4]

The task of the performer—to find the tempo which is best suited for the "right" spirit of a piece—is not an easy one. He has to avoid the two extremes: mechanical inhuman precision on the one hand, and individualistic license on the other. Among instrumentalists, professional musicians sometimes let their well-trained fingers run away with speed and amateurs slow down when they arrive at a technically difficult spot. Both instrumentalists and singers at times prolong a "good" tone beyond its prescribed duration. In all these cases the personality of the performer gets in the way of the composer's intentions.

Even the universal custom of slowing down at the end of a piece may not always be appropriate. The musical terms indicating gradual changes of tempo, e.g., a slowing down, "rallentando," and a speeding up, "stringendo," came into use only in the Classic Era. Even so, it is safe to assume that musicians of *all* times emphasized the end of a piece in one way or another. Here, as so often in music, taste and common sense will have to make the decision about the "right" relationships between the length and character of a piece and its ending. Sometimes the music may end abruptly or race dramatically toward the end. At other times it may linger over new or dreamingly repeated thoughts, or die out, slowly losing its momentum.

The intelligent and sensitive listener will become gradually aware of the precise and yet lifelike personal expression inherent in the time

[3] A. W. Thayer and H. E. Krehbiel, *The Life of Ludwig van Beethoven*, II, 386.
[4] *Ibid.* The italics are Beethoven's.

factors in music: rhythm, meter, and tempo. He will become increasingly responsive to the duration of sounds, their proportional relationships. He will feel the pulse, the meter of a piece of music, and recognize how the composer underlines, counteracts, combines, or subdivides the beats of this pulsating meter. Finally, the tempo will make him realize that time becomes truly relative in the hands of a great composer; minutes may reveal microscopic time and stress proportions, or they may combine many rapid glances at vast stretches of territory.

Suggestions for Listening

Bartok	*Mikrokosmos* (for piano)
Beethoven	Piano Concerto No. 5 in E♭ Major, Op. 73 ("Emperor")
	String Quartet in D Major, Op. 18, No. 3
	String Quartet in E♭ Major, Op. 74
	String Quartet in B♭ Major, Op. 130
	Symphony No. 1 in C Major, Op. 21
	Symphony No. 3 in E♭ Major, Op. 55 ("Eroica")
	Symphony No. 9 in D Minor, Op. 125
Brahms	*A German Requiem*, Op. 45
	Hungarian Dance No. 5
	Sonata No. 1 in G Major for Violin and Piano, Op. 78
Bruckner	Symphony No. 4 in E♭ Major
Copland	*Nocturne for Violin and Piano*
Corelli	Concerto Grosso No. 8 in G Minor ("Christmas Concerto")
Dances of the 13th Century	
Haydn	String Quartet in D Major, Op. 20, No. 4
	String Quartet, Op. 77, No. 2
Liszt	*Dante Symphony*
Mozart	*Don Giovanni*
Ravel	Trio in A Minor for Violin, Cello, and Piano
Schubert	Duo in A Major for Piano and Violin, Op. 162
Smetana	Overture to *The Bartered Bride*
Stravinsky	*Histoire du Soldat*
Tchaikovsky	Symphony No. 6 in B Minor ("Pathétique")

4

Melody

For most people melody is a "pretty" or "catchy" tune which falls "easily on the ear." Bach and many contemporary composers are frequently accused of having "no melodies at all." In these and similar cases, it is best to let Bach and some of the contemporary composers rest their defense on their own music. Two facts, though, may help to convert the skeptics: first, not all art aims to entertain in a pleasant fashion—think of the great tragedies of world literature and of the tremendous riches of architecture and the fine arts which have religious themes; secondly, preferences in the tone materials chosen and methods of using them change throughout history. Great music goes beyond fashion and temporary pleasure—it is not written for any one generation, but for eternity, regardless of a timebound function which may have occasioned its creation. It is true that "melody" will sometimes be the outstanding element of a piece of music; however, we must never forget that some of our greatest inheritance in music has other merits than just that. It might be more rewarding to observe how the composer develops a mere fragment or "motif" of a melody into a symphonic movement. At other times the rhythmic force of a piece may fascinate us beyond anything else. Nevertheless, a principal melodic outline will be present even in these cases, although at times it will be hidden by harmonic and rhythmic intricacies and its continuity and direction will occasionally be obscured.

Let us define melody, then, in inclusive terms as a single curve of tones which are arranged in a certain order with regard to pitch. That rhythm must play an important part in any melody is obvious—any succession of tones will create a certain pattern of time. However, in this chapter we shall ignore the time or stress relationships and for simplicity's sake consider only the melodic outline which is a result of changing pitch levels in music. That melody can exist independently of harmony (accompaniment) is proved by the fact that practically all music before the ninth century and most folk tunes are originally *monophonic*, i.e., one-voiced, consisting of a single melodic curve sung by one singer or by many singers who sing in unison. We will therefore limit our discussion of melody to those melodies which can stand by themselves, without added voices or harmonies.

Once we have gained an insight into what constitutes a single melody, we will be able to apply our experience to that music which combines several melodies simultaneously (*polyphony*). And finally, after a discussion of harmony, we may be able to do better justice to those melodies which are underlined, carried, and interpreted through accompanying harmony (*homophony*).

First, in order to become more familiar with the material of which melodies are made, it will be best to recall some of the important steps in the evolution of pitch relationships.

The Evolution of Scaled Pitch

In the most primitive stage of pitch relationships, changes occur on a sliding scale. Just as in nature the storm howls through trees with gliding variations of pitch, rising with the force of the wind and falling with recurring calm, so the child and the primitive man cry and shout, raising the pitch with increased excitement and gradually lowering it when peace returns. Usually these gradations in pitch are accompanied by dynamic fluctuations. It is characteristic that in describing dynamic variations we use terms which are related to pitch, i.e., we speak of the lowering or raising of voices when we mean getting softer or louder. Yet, even without any coincident increase or decrease in tone volume, we perceive rising pitch as striving, exciting, and tense, and falling pitch as relaxed, calm, and quiet. The starting pitch is immaterial in this connection; it is the direction and rate, the tendency of the changing pitch level, which produces these elemental reactions. Whether a high-voiced child or a low-voiced man talks to a dog, each will slide up in pitch while warning or commanding, and slide down while trying to "calm down" his pet.[1]

The next step in the evolution of melody is to fix a central starting point from which the singing or chanting voice rises or falls and to

[1] The habit of some performers of music of accompanying indiscriminately every rising melody with an increase in emotional excitement, with increased volume of tone, and often with an increase in tempo (and the opposite procedure in the case of a falling melody), is therefore a reversion to the most primitive stage of human communication.

which it returns. Even if the amount of rise and fall is still indefinite, the central tone has to be fixed in our throat (physically) and imagined (mentally) at all times if we want to remain aware of the sensation of change and the amount of deviation.

42.

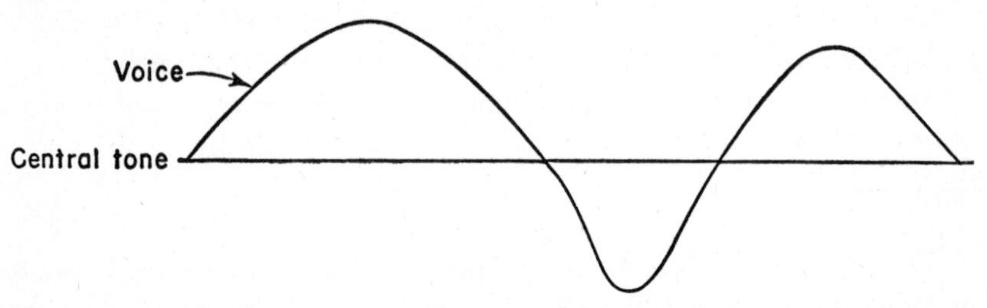

If we want, furthermore, to chart exactly the rise and fall of pitch above and below a central tone, we must obtain measurements for these distances at any given moment in the flow of the melody. By converting the curve into a chain of steps,

43.

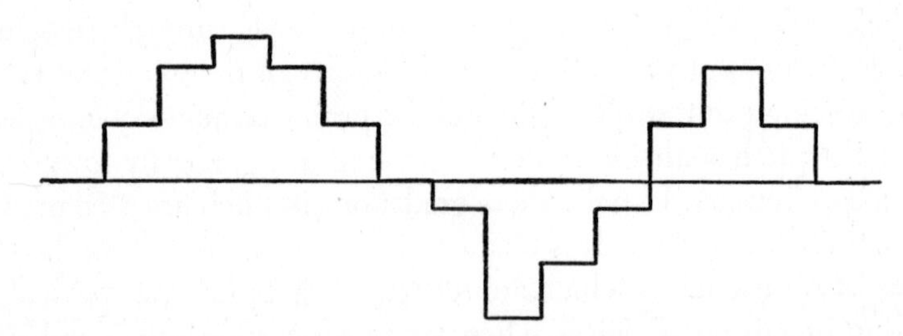

we lose the innumerable and infinitesimal shades of pitch, but on the other hand we gain a clearer graphic picture. In order now to make it possible to reproduce the melody repeatedly in the same fashion, it is necessary to introduce a measuring unit which may yield a frame of reference for pitch.

Intervals

The distance from one pitch level to another we call an *interval.* The smallest interval commonly used in our music is the so-called *semitone* or *half step* (any two adjacent keys on our modern piano keyboard, regardless of whether they are white or black).[2]

[2] Smaller intervals, quarter tones, etc., have been and are being used in Oriental, American Indian, and Negro music and in folk music of the Near East. For a time they were also part of the ancient Greek music theory and since the First World War several European and American composers have experimented with them.

44.

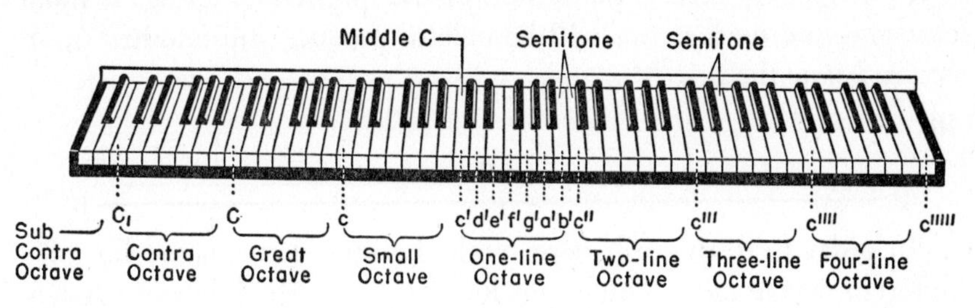

Semitones are combined into larger units, the largest of which is called the *octave,* consisting of twelve half steps. We might compare the unit of the octave to the foot—as distinguished from the semitone, which would constitute one inch.

It was Pythagoras who (*c.* 550 B.C.) discovered a basic physical law underlying differences in pitch.[3] As a measuring instrument, he used the ancient "monochord," which consists of a single string stretched between rigid supports over a movable bridge, which rests on a sounding board. The length of the vibrating part of the string can be altered by moving the bridge. With this instrument, he found that the tone which could be heard when the entire string (*XZ*) of the monochord was set in motion sounded strangely similar (closely related) to the higher tone produced by half of the string (*XY* or *YZ*).[4]

45.

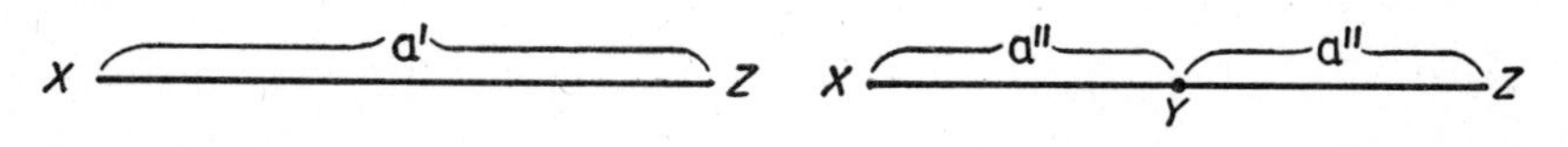

It is this interval, the distance between these two tones, which today we call an octave. Supposing that the entire string is tuned to a tone A′, we perceive its higher octave as so closely related to it, as so nearly the same tone, that we call it by the same name—simply another A (A″). In the "Star Spangled Banner," for example, the two tones on the words *say* and *see* are an octave apart, and have consequently the same letter name.

[3] In scientific terms, the word "pitch" is restricted to the subjective reaction to a tone, while "frequency" is used to describe its physical nature. In our musical terminology, no such clear distinction exists.

[4] Tones are produced by vibrating air columns or tense strings. A shorter (or tighter) string will vibrate faster than a longer (or looser) one; the higher the rate of vibration (the "frequency"), the higher the pitch of the tone produced, and vice versa.

If we exactly double the length of the monochord string, without changing the tension, we will be able to produce still another A, an octave *below* the first A′.

46.

v a w

In order to distinguish notes with the same letter name but of a different octave range (higher or lower C, etc.) the following system is used (see Fig. 44):

All tones from "middle C" to the next higher B are considered as belonging to the "one-line octave" and designated thus by adding one line to the letter (e.g., c′, d′, e′, etc.). Tones which belong to the higher "two-line," "three-line," etc., octaves are indicated accordingly. For the spelling of the tones of the "small octave"—which lies below the "one-line octave"—small letters are used; for members of the next lower "great octave," capital letters; and finally, for the still lower "contra octave," capital letters with the added numeral "1": C_1, D_1, E_1, etc.[5]

TABLE OF OCTAVE PITCH-DESIGNATIONS

Contra Octave	Great Octave	Small Octave	One-Line Octave
C_1, D_1, . . ., B_1	C, D, . . ., B	c, d, . . ., b	c′, d′, . . ., b′

Two-Line Octave	Three-Line Octave
c″, d″, . . . b″	c‴, d‴ . . . b‴

The close relationship of tones exactly one or more octaves apart can be experienced whenever a mixed group sings the same tune "in unison,"[6] starting on tones with identical letter names and singing from there along the melodic line in parallels—the children, women, and men each moving within the range which is most convenient. The principle which Pythagoras discovered, then, was that the relation-

[5] This system, however, is customarily adhered to only when it becomes imperative to specify an exact octave range. Generally, A, B, etc., means A, B of any convenient pitch, not specifically the A and B of the "great octave."

[6] Although singing in "unison" means literally the singing of one (identical) pitch or tune by several voices, it is also commonly used for tones one or more octaves apart (and sounded simultaneously).

ship between the lower and higher tones of an octave is 2 : 1 in terms of the length of the vibrating string. Other scientists found later that the ratio of vibration between a tone and its higher octave is 1 : 2. If, for example, we fix arbitrarily the frequency of our first tone, A′, as 100 vibrations per second, its higher octave (A″) will vibrate twice as fast (200 times per second). In other words, the frequency ratio between two tones varies inversely as to their string lengths as long as the tension of the string remains constant.

The ear learns very readily to detect the interval of an octave as a pleasing and "natural" sound and consequently any octave which is out of tune, as "false." Since this is the case, and since the range of the developed singing voice is approximately two octaves, it is only natural that the octave has served and is serving as a frame of reference for most melodies which are known today.

From our modern instruments and through our acquaintance with the music of the modern era we know that the octave contains today twelve semitones. However, in the music of former eras this was not always so. Traditionally, seven tones were selected as musical building stones, the eighth being the octave—as its name implies—and, as such, conceived as a higher (or lower) repetition of the first tone. Our names for intervals are derived from this tradition, the second, third, fourth, fifth, and so forth being the second, third, etc., tones within one octave. The fact that there are twelve, not seven, tones within one octave makes it necessary to establish additional kinds of intervals (major, minor, augmented, diminished) in our terminology. Similarly, we use only seven letters of the alphabet when we name the tones contained within each octave, and in order to account for additional possibilities, we have to add "sharps" or "flats" to the letters. (We shall discuss the major and minor intervals as well as sharps and flats in Chapter 5.)

Other intervals besides the octave which were considered by the Greeks and their medieval imitators as basic and "natural" are the *fifth* and the *fourth*. These intervals may be reproduced by singing the beginning of a nursery tune and a melody by Wagner. In "Baa, Baa, Black Sheep" a fifth occurs between the notes of the second and third words, and in the Wedding March from *Lohengrin*, a fourth between the first two tones. Let us see what the proportional relationships are which the fifth and the fourth contain. If we divide the string into three equal parts, one third of the string will produce a tone which sounds higher than the tone produced by one half of the original string.

47.

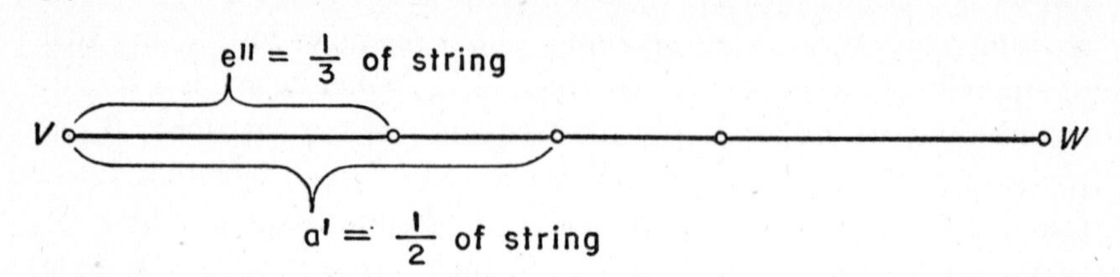

The two tones are traditionally considered to be five tones apart; the relationship of the upper tone to the lower is ⅓ : ½ or 2 : 3 in terms of string length and 3 : 2 in terms of frequencies. If, as in our case, the basic tone is called A, the letter name of the higher tone will be the fifth after A, namely E.

Setting one fourth of the string into motion will give another A (A″), a tone which is higher than the last E. This interval of two tones, the relationship of which is ¼ : ⅓ or 3 : 4 as far as string lengths are concerned, and 4 : 3 in regard to their frequencies, is called a *fourth.*

a'' = 1/4 of string

V W

e'' = 1/3 of string

It is most likely that these intervals were sung and played instinctively first and later fixed exactly, and that the numerical simplicity of the string length (or frequency) ratios was recognized afterwards by Pythagoras and his successors. The fact that the three intervals (the octave, the fifth, and the fourth) which can be expressed in the simplest of number relationships have played the principal role in the music of all times can be understood as deriving from the Greek ideal of "beauty and order." We must remember that in ancient Greece and again in the Middle Ages the mystery of numbers was believed to contain the secret of life and beauty, and that the universe was believed to be constructed as a "music of the spheres." Science and art, mathematics and imagination, arithmetic and music were therefore considered inseparable by the Greeks, all tending toward the same goal, an (ethically) good and (artistically) beautiful life. Leisure and the pursuit of the arts were felt as integrated parts of the education and the life of a human being—unless he was a slave or artisan of the lowest class. The important three intervals, the octave, the fifth, and the fourth, served first as range limits for scales and later in the Middle Ages as "perfect consonances," that is to say, as tone combinations which blended well when heard together. Even today, practically all melodies consider these intervals as structural beams, as proportions which add character, stability, and direction.

Further subdivisions of the string yielded the interval of the third, and subtraction and addition of previously established intervals produced the second, the sixth, and the seventh. Finally, another so-called *minor* second, our semitone, was found by splitting the difference between the intervals of a fifth and a fourth. In using these names (second, third, fourth, etc.) for intervals, we must remember that they do not represent fractions (½, ⅓, ¼, etc.) but are instead derived from their ascending position within a basic octave. Only the semitone or half step carries in its very name a correct fractional implication: ½ step plus ½ step = 1 whole step, or in interval language, two *minor seconds* constitute one so-called *major second* in our system of tuning.

Ear-Training in Intervals

It would be an excellent help toward the more articulate hearing of melodies if the reader would at this point train his ear to distinguish between the intervals of a third, a fourth, etc. This might be done by analyzing a well-known song in regard to its melodic interval structure and using it as a frame of reference for the intervals of other tunes. The first four measures of the "Star Spangled Banner," for example, contain the following intervals: four seconds, five thirds, one fourth, and one sixth.[7]

49.

We have now found examples for all intervals except for the seventh.[8] This is an interval which is difficult to sing and therefore rarer in

[7] No distinction should be made at this stage between major and minor thirds, etc., except for major and minor seconds, which should be recognized and designated as whole and semitones.

[8] Intervals which are larger than an octave are called *ninth, tenth,* etc. For all practical purposes, they are considered as "an octave plus a *second*," etc.

songs than in music for instruments. We can find an example in the above excerpt if we skip a few intervening tones, just as we did previously in trying to recognize an octave (p. 47). If we skip in the "National Anthem" the tones between "can" and "the" (dawn's), *thinking* of the intervening tones only, and singing aloud the fourth and the eighth tones of the song, we may learn to perceive and to sing the interval of a seventh after a few attempts. Having thus become familiar with the sound of a seventh, we will enjoy better the awkwardly stuttering behavior of the deadly frightened Leporello in Mozart's *Don Giovanni* when the statue of the murdered Comthur seems to move.

50. DON GIOVANNI (No. 24)

Wolfgang Amadeus Mozart (1756–1791)

"X-raying" the melodic components of a few well-known songs in this manner on paper, and with our minds and ears, is anything but detrimental to the pleasure which we might derive from a melody. Let us not forget that the composer writes various intervals in the hope that the listener may be able to distinguish between them. If a fourth and a third sound the same to us, we lose an important point which the composer wants to make. Therefore, consciously analyzing and naming the intervals which we hear will train us within a short period of time to perceive melodies much more accurately than if we are satisfied with a state of passively drifting along the seemingly nebulous contours of music.

Scales

Let us now return to our problem of fixing graphically the shape of a melody. We have the central tone, which we had chosen preferably in the middle of our voice range, so as to be able to wander above and below it. Charting semitones as well as multiples of them, we will be able to indicate exactly how far we want to digress from this central tone.

51. MY COUNTRY 'TIS OF THEE

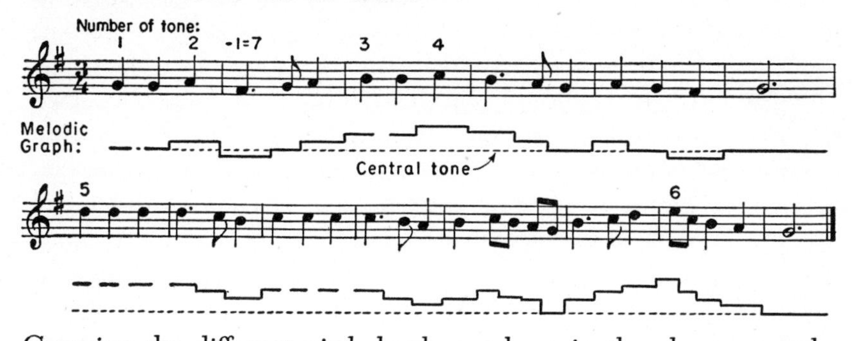

Counting the different pitch levels, we have in the above example five steps above and one below the central tone. It is customary to number the central tone "one" or "eight." Consequently, the step below the central tone, i.e., the tone below "one" or "eight" is called "seven" (instead of "minus one"); the tone which lies two steps below "one" or "eight" is called "six," and so forth. This is done not only for simplicity's sake but also in order to stress the fact that in a melody the central tone is really its most important one, its "number one" tone, and that, regardless of octave pitch, tones three, four, five, and seven, etc., stand in a characteristic relationship to the central tone, as we shall see later.

In order, then, to get a clearer picture of all the tones used in a melody it is best to compress them into the range of a single octave. By *"transposing"* into a higher octave all tones which are lower than the central tone, so that they may appear above the central tone, we may survey at a glance all the building blocks of our melody. Thus ordered, all tones will appear in a simple ascending scale and we will be able to determine the exact intervals, inasmuch as only semitones and their multiples are used.

52.

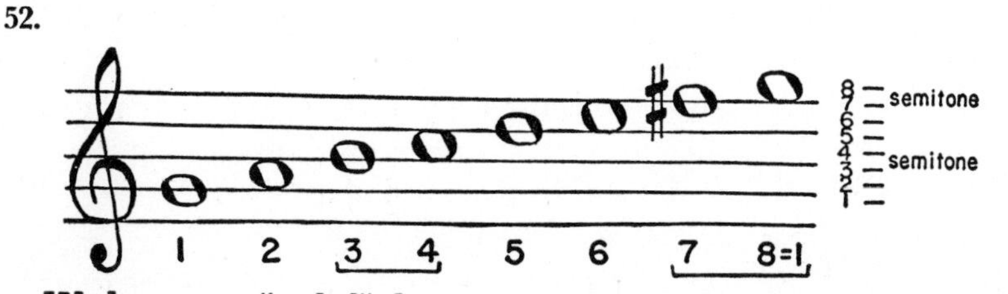

We have now "scaled" the interval steps and have analyzed how the semitones and whole tones are arranged in this particular melody: half steps (or semitones) occur between tones 3 and 4 and between

7 and 8 in our scale, and all other steps are whole steps (or whole tones).[9] Should we have chosen another voice range or central tone, the same pattern could be repeated with other tones. Here we simply think of our graph appearing in identical shape but higher or lower in space according to our choice of a higher or lower pitch for the central tone. The manner or fashion of the melody in question, the kind of its tone material as far as proportions of pitch are concerned, its "profile," remain the same in each case.

We can draw two conclusions from our experiment in building and analyzing a melody: (1) Because it is most convenient to order tone material according to pitch, it is best to use ascending octave *scales* for the measuring of the basic melodic material. (2) The way a scale is constructed, that is, how the various semitones and whole tones follow each other, will determine the "profile" of a melody.

Finding the Central Tone of a Melody

We have seen that it is essential to find and to be aware of the central tone of a melody. The central tone does not always appear in the center of the range of a melody, nor do all melodies start with the central tone. Moreover, frequently the middle part of a song will use a different central tone, and therefore a new basic scale altogether. However, the great majority of those songs which "make musical sense" without an accompaniment—that is, those which need no clarification or interpretation through added harmonies—will end on the central tone. If the reader will once more survey mentally or in singing, whistling, playing, or listening to the nursery tunes, folk songs, or Christmas carols which he knows best, he will find the central tone of each tune quite easily by concentrating on the last tone of a song and by asking himself whether it provides a satisfactory completion. If it does, the tune will be found to end on its central tone.

The opposite sensation may be experienced at the end of "The First Noel." The refrain "Born is the King of Israel" regularly suggests that there are more verses to come. The reason for this is that the last tone of the song is tone three of its basic scale instead of tone one: [10]

[9] The intricacies of our musical notation in regard to half and whole steps are purposely reserved for the next chapter. At the present stage the reader is supposed to become aware only of the *sound* of various melodies and their basic scales.

[10] When sung "in harmony" by several voices or with an accompaniment the song ends perfectly satisfactorily because the central tone is furnished by the bass line.

53.

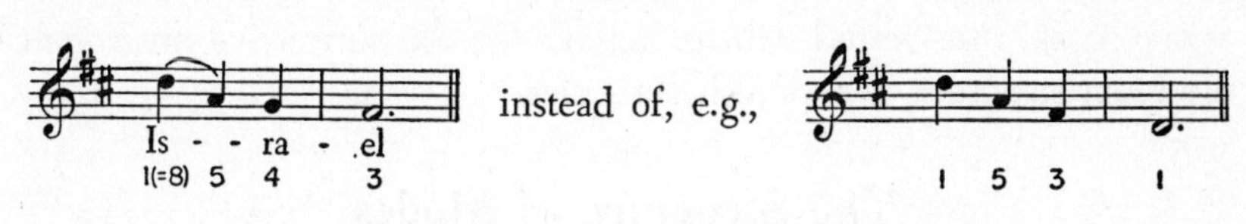

Once the central tone of a song is marked (preferably by underlining all syllables which are sung to it), the remaining tones may be ordered above it in scale form either on graph or on music paper, as shown in the following example:

54. DECK THE HALLS

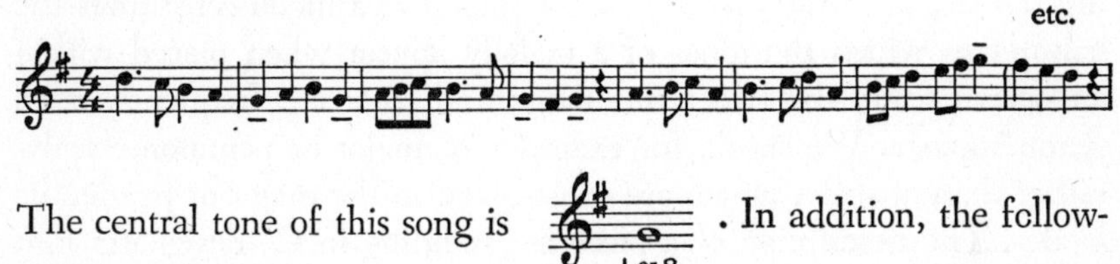

The central tone of this song is [1 or 8]. In addition, the following tones are used:

2 3 4 5 6 (-1)=7 7 8 = 1

When represented graphically and in ascending order, the tones which were used in this tune represent the picture of a staircase:

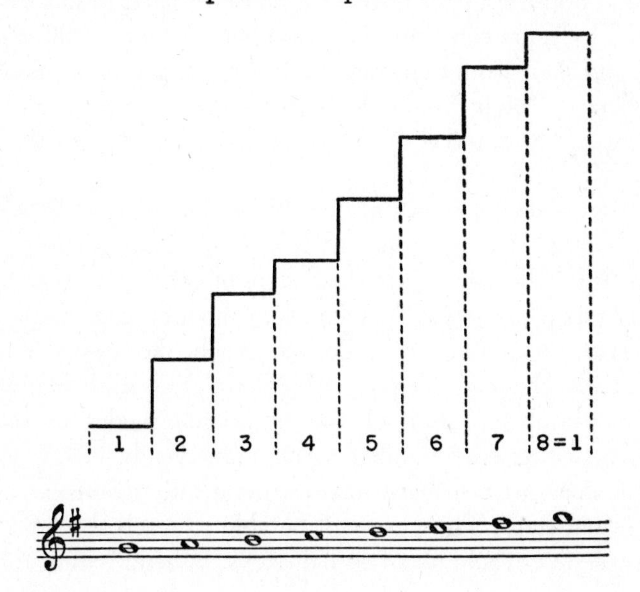

Our facility in distinguishing between whole steps and semitones in the scales thus found will be helped considerably if we investigate the exact structure of several basic scales.

The Structure of Modes

The manner in which a scale is constructed—its pattern—we call its *mode*. A great many different modes have been used throughout history. Most of them take the range of an octave as outer frame and distinguish seven degrees or tones within that space (the eighth being the octave to the first tone). Inasmuch as a mode constitutes the manner in which the tones of a melody appear when placed within an octave scale, the two terms *mode* and *scale* are frequently used synonymously. We speak, for example, of major or pentatonic scales rather than of scales which are constructed in the major or pentatonic modes. The description of a piece as "standing in C" designates that the central tone is C; it does not indicate the mode which is being utilized—whether the C major or the C minor scale or another kind of scale provides the basic material for the piece in question.

It will help us see the difference in the structure of various modes if we visualize the scales as representing stairs leading from one floor to the next. In that case, the first tone and its octave would represent the ground and the upper floors of a house—a fixed distance which is connected by stairs consisting of a number of steps of different sizes. The ground floor would be "one" of our scale, the upper floor or the higher octave, "eight." The level of our first step would be the equivalent of the interval of a second in relationship to the ground floor ("one"), and so forth.

We know that the octave as divided by the music of Western culture contains twelve semitones or half steps. Consequently, we can reach the upper floor in twelve small steps of equal size (the chromatic scale) or in six whole steps (the whole-tone mode or scale) (see Fig. 55).

However, in neither case do we reach the upper floor (the octave) with the eighth tone, which we had said was the customary procedure in most of the traditional modes or scales. In order to arrive at tone number seven immediately before we reach the upper floor, we will have to construct a rather unusual stair, one with unequal steps. Thus, we will be able to reach the next floor in seven steps—five whole plus two half steps. Where, within the octave

55. Chromatic and Whole-Tone Stairways (Scales)

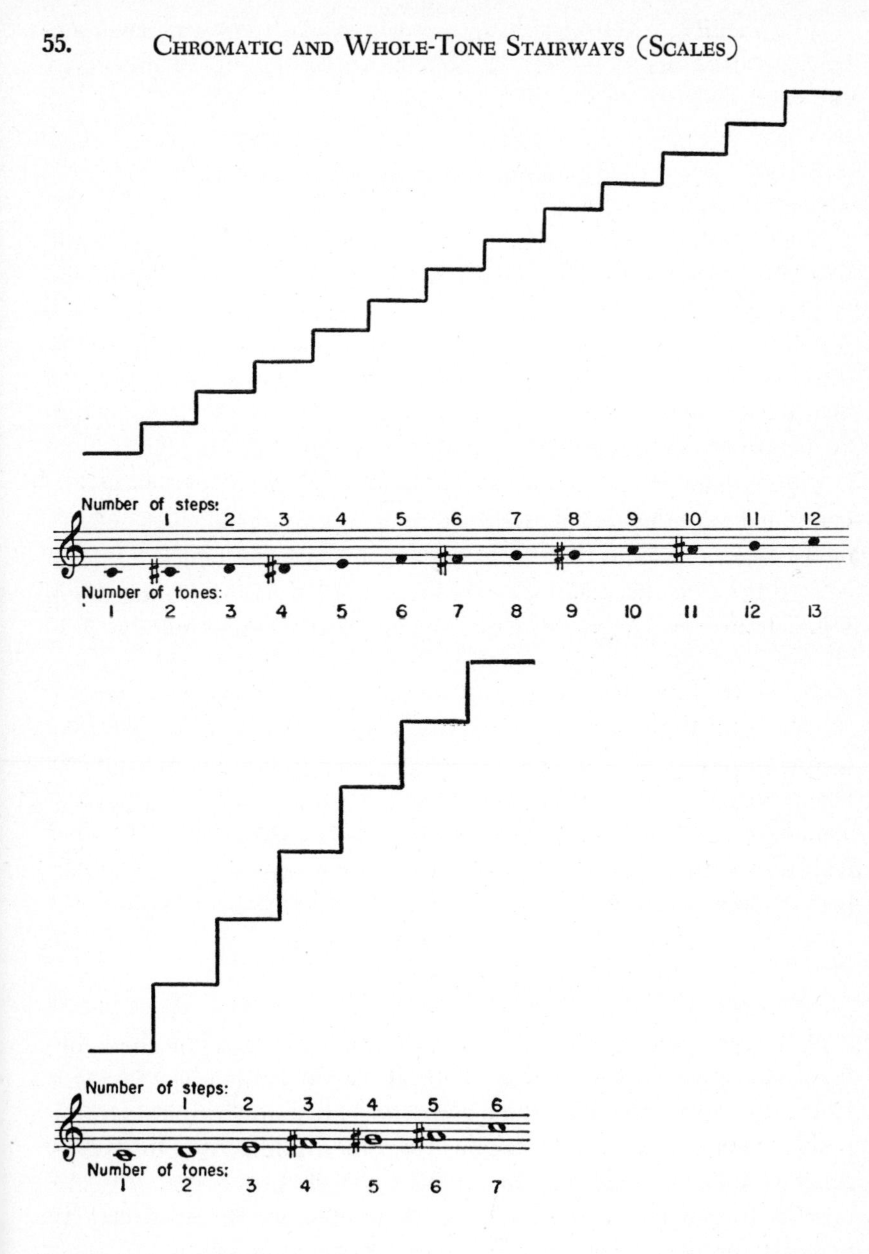

space, these two small (half) steps occur constitutes the sole difference between the many modes: ancient, ecclesiastical, and our major and minor.

We may safely skip a discussion of the ancient Greek modes, inasmuch as less than a dozen fragments of Greek music have come to us—which, to make things worse, cannot even be accurately deciphered. While the scientific data, philosophies, literature, and sculpture of ancient Greece have influenced Western culture profoundly, ancient Greek music has for more than two thousand years been nothing but one long frustrating field day for treasure-hunting historians and theorists. This is the more regrettable as we know from many authentic literary sources that music played an essential part in the artistic and festive life of ancient Greece.

All we know of the Greek music, besides the meager fragments, is contained in theoretical writings about music by ancient and medieval scholars and their successors. The confusion which has been created through speculation, errors in translation, and misunderstanding of terms can be grasped if we imagine that by an atomic accident all music of the twentieth century were lost and only the writings *about* music by music commentators, educators, music theorists, historians, philosophers, mathematicians, and musicologists were preserved. Would anyone two thousand years from now be able to reconstruct the sounds of our present-day music from the most erudite, complete, and utterly contradictory descriptions of the music of Debussy, R. Strauss, Sibelius, Reger, Ravel, Bartok, Stravinsky, Prokofieff, Hindemith, Gershwin, Copland, and so on?

Gregorian Modes

The Gregorian (or ecclesiastic or church) modes, on the other hand, are with us in the music of the Catholic church and in many of the hymns of the Protestant churches. They are furthermore the basis for many secular compositions from the Middle Ages to modern times (sections which are composed in one of the Gregorian modes may be found in the music of Beethoven, Bartok, Brahms, Chopin, Debussy, Franck, Gershwin, Hindemith, Liszt, Moussorgsky, Sibelius, Stravinsky, Tchaikovsky, Wagner, Vaughan Williams, and others). Let us therefore try to become more sensitive to music which is composed in modes other than the usual major and minor.

1. The Dorian (or First Gregorian) Mode. Here is a well-known hymn which is composed in the Dorian mode:

56. COMMIT THOU ALL THY GRIEFS (Dorian mode)

Ravenscroft Psalter (1621)

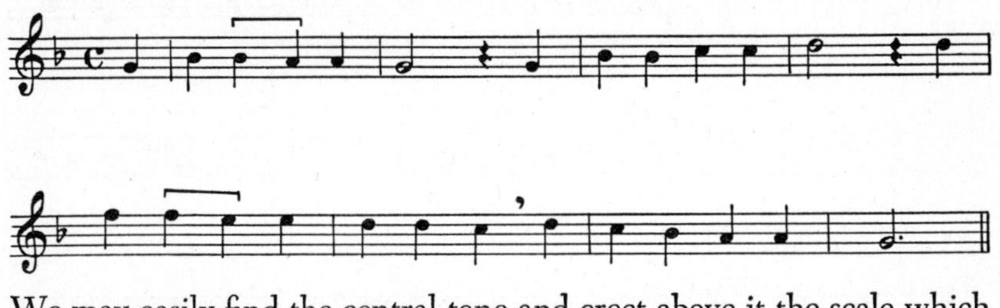

We may easily find the central tone and erect above it the scale which contains all the tones of the melody:

57.

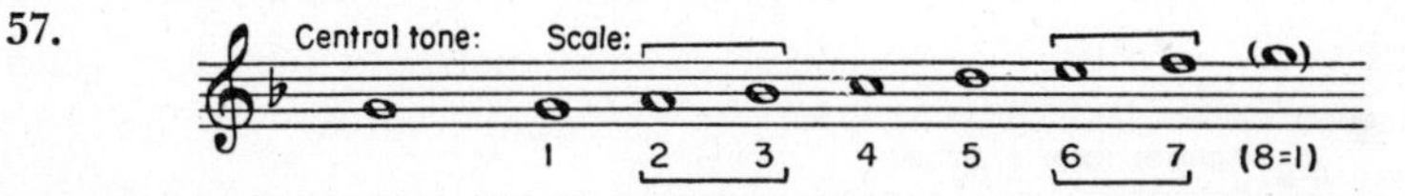

By carefully observing the steps of the melodic line we may recognize that the third and fourth tones of the melody are only a semitone apart. In our Dorian scale they are tones number two and three. Another half step occurs between the fifteenth and the sixteenth tones of our melody. These notes we will find in the scale numbered as tones six and seven. Let us remember, then, that in the Dorian scale half steps occur between the second and third, and between the sixth and seventh tones (all other steps being whole steps).

The profile of a Dorian scale is:

58.

8=1 7 6 5 4 3 2 1

Profile:

Halfsteps: between 2 and 3, and 6 and 7.

Other modes may be investigated in the same manner.

2. The Aeolian (Ninth Gregorian) Mode.

59. VENI EMMANUEL (Aeolian mode)

See also "The Agincourt Tune."

3. The Mixolydian (Seventh Gregorian) Mode. An example of this mode may be found in the "Song of the Ass" (Fig. 15, p. 26). Following our usual procedure in establishing the basic scale, the reader will find that in the Mixolydian mode half steps occur between tones three and four and between six and seven.

4. The Phrygian (Third Gregorian) Mode.

61. CHRISTUM WIR SOLLEN LOBEN SCHON (In Thankful Praise Sing Everyone to Christ) (Phrygian mode)

(Harmonized by Johann Sebastian Bach (1685–1750) in his Cantata No. 121)

Major and Minor Modes

1. The Major Mode. The major mode, which was derived from the ancient Ionian or Eleventh Gregorian Mode, has half steps between the third and fourth and between the seventh and eighth tones of its scale (see Fig. 63).

63.

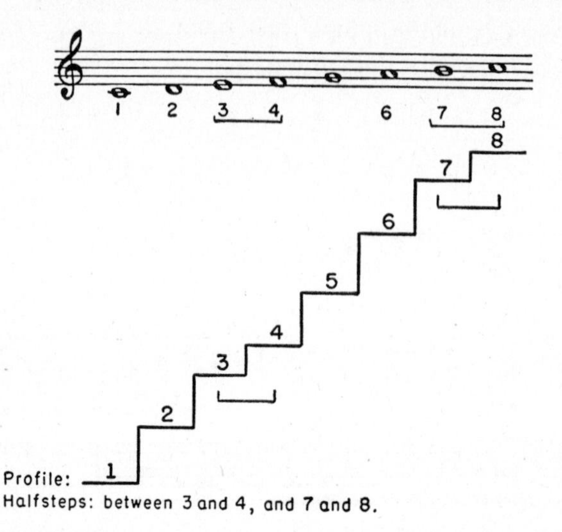

2. The Minor Mode. The minor mode is unusual in so far as it is based on a variable scale. We distinguish between three different minor scales. While the first five scale tones are the same in all versions, tones six and seven may be adjusted (raised or lowered) according to melodic or harmonic requirements in the so-called *melodic* or *harmonic* minor scales.

A. *The Natural or Unaltered Minor Scale* is the rarest of the three versions of the minor mode. It is identical with the scale of the Aeolian or Ninth Gregorian Mode.

64. WE THREE KINGS OF ORIENT ARE (Natural or unaltered minor)

J. H. Hopkins (written 1857)

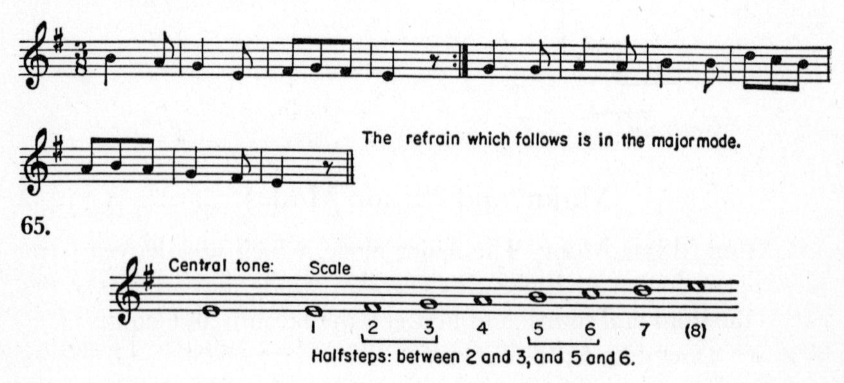

65.

B. *The Harmonic Minor Scale* adds another half step, one between the seventh and eighth tones, thus becoming more similar to the major mode. However, an important difference between the two modes remains in that the major mode has half steps between three and four, while the minor mode has them between two and three (besides the harmonic minor half step between five and six).

66. THE WILD HORSEMAN, OP. 68, NO. 8 (Harmonic minor)

Robert Schumann (1810–1856)

C. *The Melodic Minor Scale* came into being because the large step between steps six and seven of the harmonic minor scale was difficult to sing and pulled the flow of minor mode melodies too violently up or down when a smooth progression was desired. The half step between tones five and six was therefore eliminated by raising tone six while going upward. This diminished the distance between tones six and seven to the more normal size of one whole step instead of the one and a half steps of the harmonic minor scale. Instead of

68.

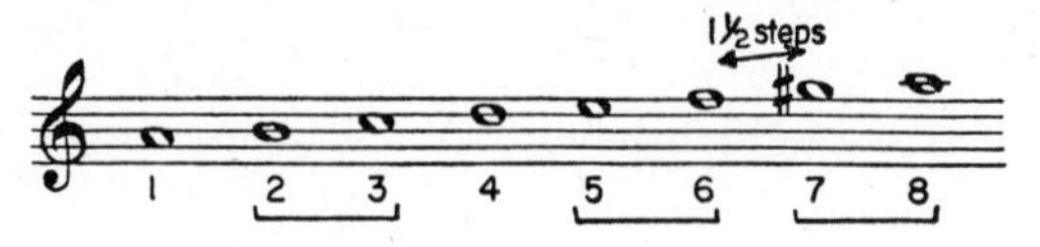

the melodic minor scale uses

69.

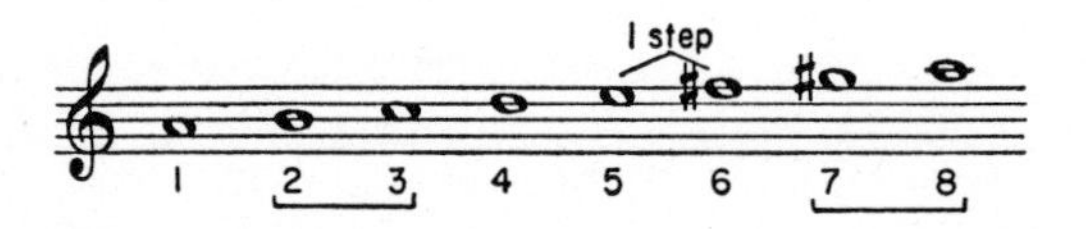

whenever the melody tends in a general upward direction.

However, going downward the same way would make the melodic minor scale appear to be a major scale as far down as from tones eight to four. Therefore, whenever a melodic minor melody tends downward, it reverts to the natural or unaltered minor scale:

70.

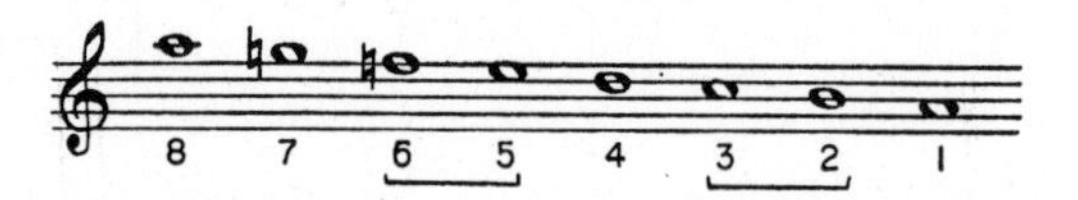

71. "WITH DROOPING WINGS" (DIDO AND AENEAS) (Melodic minor)

Henry Purcell (*ca.* 1659–1695)

The melodic minor scale, then, changes tones six and seven depending on whether it goes up or down.

72.

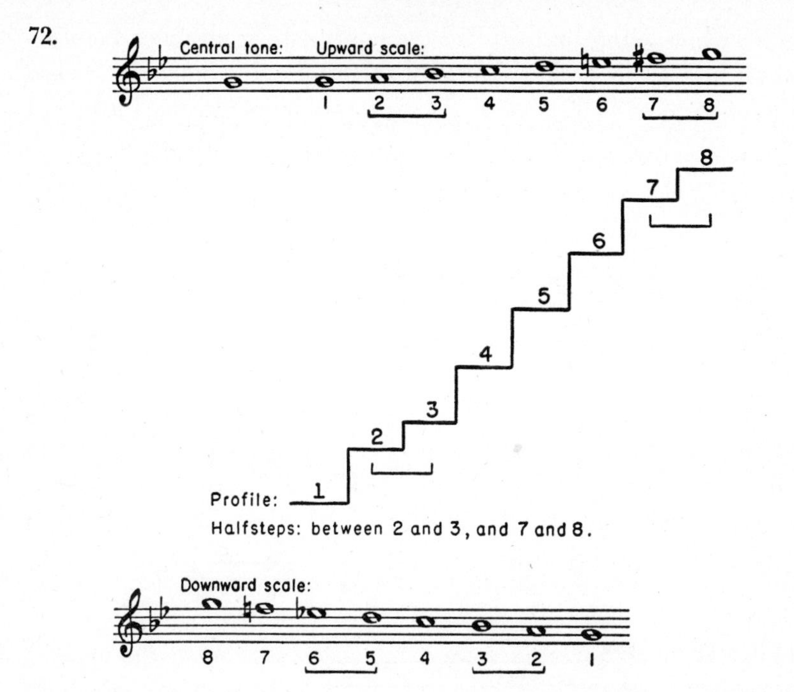

While these different versions of the minor mode may seem complicated at first, when explained theoretically, they will in actual listening experience rarely interfere with our clear distinction between major and minor modes. Let us keep in mind that the crucial difference between the two modes lies in the third tone of the scale. In the major mode, tone three is farther away from the central tone than in the minor mode. Anticipating our detailed discussion of intervals (p. 109), we might become aware of the fact that the distance from tones one to three is a *major third* in the major, and a *minor third* in the minor mode.

Remembering this rule the reader will have no difficulties in judging whether a melody is in major or in minor, provided that he proceeds in the following manner:

1. Select a melody from the musical literature which seems well defined as to beginning and end.
2. Visualize and chart the scale.
3. Find out whether the step between tones two and three is a whole step or a half step, or—what amounts to the same thing—whether the interval between tones one and three is a major or a minor third.

Additional Modes

In trying to determine the mode of the music which we sing and hear we might find very frequently a melody which will not fit into any of the scale patterns which were described so far. Three examples follow.

1. The Pentatonic Mode.

73. AULD LANG SYNE

Scottish song

Compare also the songs, "Speed, Bonnie Boat, Like a Bird in the Wind," and the French nursery tune, "*Il Etait une Bergère.*"

We see that the famous "Auld Lang Syne" is built on a scale of five (instead of seven) tones, and that it contains no half step at all. We may of course insert the missing semitones (which is done occasionally in "arrangements") and declare that the song is based upon a major scale. However, a moment's deliberation will tell us that just those tones which are characteristic of the major mode are omitted. Therefore, we may conclude that we deal with a specially designed mode which has its own particular melodic flavor. And indeed, the pentatonic mode (so called because its scale consists of five tones—the sixth tone being the higher octave of tone one) is found in many Scottish and Irish folk songs. It is also found—and this attests to its Oriental origin—in China, in Africa, and among American Indians.

Besides singing pentatonic songs you can use the piano in recreating the pentatonic mode; playing exclusively on the black keys will give a good idea of how it sounds.

2. THE GYPSY MODE.

74. VIOLIN CONCERTO IN D MAJOR, OP. 77 (First movement)

Johannes Brahms (1833–1897)

3. THE WHOLE-TONE MODE. The whole-tone mode or scale will be found frequently in the music of Debussy.

75. IBERIA (First movement)

Claude Debussy (1862–1918)

Fluctuating Modes

An entire piece of music will not always adhere to one mode throughout. Composers will, for example, not only use different versions of the minor mode in a single piece, but they will in a symphony "in the minor mode" include entire movements in the major, and vice versa. In listening to Beethoven's Fifth and to Brahms' First Symphonies we will find that their final movements are in C major—in spite of the fact that we designate both symphonies as standing "in C minor." Even within a single movement modes will frequently change from major to minor. In some of our modern music there will be found sections in the pentatonic and others in the whole-tone mode, and so forth. These changes are brought about by using "extra" tones which do not occur in the basic scale which is used for the beginning of the piece in question. Let us take as an example the excerpt from the Brahms Violin Concerto (Fig. 74). The principal mode of the first movement is major. However, at the indicated point the solo violin enters with a scale which is typical for the "gypsy" mode, while the orchestra sustains at the same time a chord in the *minor* mode.

We see, then, that besides changing the mode, the composer may also superimpose different modes. This led in the nineteenth century especially to the inclusion of so many extra tones (or *chromatic* tones, as they are called in musical terminology), that neither the central tone nor the mode could always be determined with certainty. The result was a fluctuation between major and minor modes which produced a "tendency of the two modes to merge into what one is finally tempted to call a chromatic mode," as Walter Piston says.[11]

The famous Shepherd's melody from Wagner's *Tristan* may be explained by conventional school harmony methods, retracing frequent momentary changes of the central tone and the mode. But the perceptive and unpedantic listener will hear the tune as the aimless, dreamingly restless, and frantic call—without a stable central tone or mode—which it was probably intended to be.

76. TRISTAN UND ISOLDE (Introduction to Act III)

Richard Wagner (1813–1883)

This "mystification" of traditional modes and central tones may be experienced in a more advanced state in the music of the modern school of Arnold Schoenberg. We could, theoretically at least, come much nearer to the music of Schoenberg and his followers if we would conceive of their music as being composed in various "chromatic modes." The "Twelve-Tone Row" principle of this modern school (which is frequently given the misleading name of "Atonalism"), takes the twelve half steps of the octave and arranges them in an order which is especially designed for each particular piece. While

[11] Piston, *Harmony*, p. 39.

this procedure does not recognize a central tone, it does use basic scale patterns as musical raw material—just as the modes do.

Here we have a modern melody reduced to its basic scale:

77. PIERROT LUNAIRE ("Colombine")

Arnold Schoenberg (1874–1951)

The "Character" of Modes

Just as we describe a piece in the pentatonic mode as typically Scottish, Irish, or Oriental, and a piece in the whole-tone mode as sounding like Debussy, even if it is written by another composer, so the Greeks gave names such as Dorian, Aeolian, Phrygian, etc., to tonal combinations which were popular among the Dorian, Aeolian, and Phrygian peoples. Whenever there was a special national character attached to the peoples, as fierce, warlike, romantic, sentimental, the respective modes were consciously or unconsciously related to those characteristics. The Greek philosophers, who were also mathematicians and musicians, evolved elaborate systems and characterized the modes as manly, languid, sensual, purifying, etc. Plato especially prescribed which modes and rhythms were educationally sound, dangerous, appropriate for heroic themes or for funerals, etc. Similarly, the Gregorian modes are supposed to have various expressive qualities which make certain modes more appropriate than others for particular parts of the Roman Catholic liturgy. We even have certain meanings attached to our major and minor modes—such as manly, vigorous, joyful for the former; and feminine, subdued, sad for the latter. These theories, that a mood is automatically presented whenever a certain musical mode is being used in a piece of music are of doubtful value. Frequently, pieces in the minor mode are pleasantly gay and those in the major are serious or even tragic (investigate for example the mode of "The Loreley," Schubert's "Ave Maria," "Silent Night," and the Cemetery Scene (Act II, No. 24) in *Don Giovanni*). Furthermore, descriptions like the ones just used are necessarily inaccurate and disputable as definitions. The Greeks had the opposite impression—our major they considered effeminate, and our (unaltered) minor as worthy of a free and noble man.[12] And finally, even if we should all agree on one kind of impression made on us by a piece of music, this effect would be more the result of *how* a composer uses his material than *what* he uses. We must never forget that the melodies came first and the scales afterward. Only after certain tunes became traditional did the theorists try to find a common descriptive denominator for all those melodies which were composed with the same kind of melodic raw material.

During the past a great many different melodic (and harmonic) patterns and traditional formulas have been created with tone combinations which might be conveniently summarized by various kinds of scales. However, it will be impossible ever to describe in one word the endless varieties of expression which are inherent in any mode.

When a composer creates music in the Dorian, pentatonic, major, or minor mode he does so because he is familiar with a great body of music written in these melodic styles. They have influenced the creative musician through the living sound; he is not inspired—and neither will the listener be helped—by rules, theories, or aesthetic impressions of philosophers, mathematicians, music theorists, or musicologists.

Let us consider one final example. When Beethoven wrote above the third movement of his String Quartet, Op. 132, "Song of Thanksgiving to the Deity on recovery from an illness, written in the Lydian mode," he meant that he had used the ecclesiastical, not the ancient Greek Lydian, mode for this piece. The Fifth Gregorian or medieval Lydian mode is characterized by the fact that its scale has half steps between tones four and five and between seven and eight.

78.

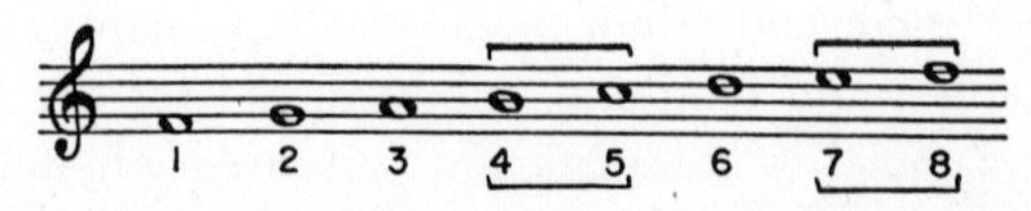

[12] Cf. Hermann Abert, *Die Lehre vom Ethos in der griechischen Musik* (Leipzig, 1899), p. 94.

Should we attempt, in addition, to find out before hearing the piece what associative meanings have been attached to the term *Lydian mode* throughout history, we would encounter an utterly confusing picture. An authority on Gregorian Chant describes this mode as resembling our major mode.[13]

What the medieval church fathers and Beethoven thought of as Lydian is in tonal structure equivalent to the ancient Greek Hypolydian. This mode, in turn, was characterized by Plato and Aristotle as producing a bacchanal ecstasy, a delirious orgy similar to or caused by drunkenness.[14] The Lydian mode of the Greeks, on the other hand, was used for music in memory of the dead,[15] and later for the accompaniment of poetry of naïve and graceful tenderness.

It seems best, then, to be conscious of the existence of modes other than the more common major and minor of our days, but for their expressive impact to consult the music directly before preconceived book-learning prejudices us about what "mood" to attach to a musical mode, especially when, as in the above case, the composer himself has indicated what kind of feelings he wants to express.

Suggestions for Listening

Bach	Cantata No. 121, "*Christum wir sollen loben schon*"
Beethoven	String Quartet in A Minor, Op. 132
Berg	Violin Concerto
Brahms	Symphony No. 1 in C Minor, Op. 68
	Violin Concerto in D Major, Op. 77
Debussy	*Pelleas and Melisande*
	Iberia
Gregorian Chant	
Mozart	*Don Giovanni*
Purcell	*Dido and Aeneas*
Reger	*Variations on a Theme by Mozart* (for orchestra)
Schoenberg	*Pierrot Lunaire*
Schubert	*"Ave Maria"*
Schumann	*"Wilder Reiter"* (from *Album für die Jugend*, Op. 68)
Strauss, R.	*Der Rosenkavalier*
Wagner	*Lohengrin*
	Tristan und Isolde

[13] Prunières, *A New History of Music*, p. 13.
[14] Abert, *op. cit.*, p. 94.
[15] *Ibid.*, pp. 78 and 92.

5

Melody
(*Continued*)

Notation of Pitch

THE GRAPHIC picture of absolute and relative pitch in our present notation of music is the result of a long development which included Greek and Roman letters and symbols derived from speech accents and choir-leader signs (so-called *neumes*.) Finally, someone drew a horizontal line depicting the basic pitch and soon two, three, and four lines were added to indicate the "steps" in sung melodies, or the fingering to be used on string instruments. Since about A.D. 1200 our *staff*, consisting of five horizontal lines and enclosing four spaces, has been in use.[1] By placing notes which designate duration of sound on the lines and spaces of the staff, we may express both duration and pitch simultaneously. Nine different pitches can thus be illustrated:

79.

and a few more if we use the space above and below the staff and draw *leger lines* which function as temporary extensions of the staff:

80.

Yet even nineteen or twenty notes are only a fraction of the range of tones represented by an orchestra or by a four-part chorus.

[1] The *four*-line staff which is still used today for the notation of Gregorian Chant dates from the year 1000. Its invention is ascribed to Guido of Arezzo (see Apel, *Harvard Dictionary of Music*, p. 709).

Clefs

In order to notate the entire range of instruments and voices, which has increased ever since harmony (the sounding of different tones simultaneously) came into being, *clefs* are used. The G (violin, or treble) clef 𝄞 serves for the notation of soprano voices or instruments of a similar range (flute, oboe, violin, the right-hand part of the piano score, etc.), and the F, or bass, clef, for the voices and instruments with bass range (cello, bassoon, the left-hand part of a piano score, etc.)[2] The two staves meet as far as pitch is concerned at middle C, which may either be written on the first leger line below the treble clef staff or on the first leger line above the bass clef staff.

81.

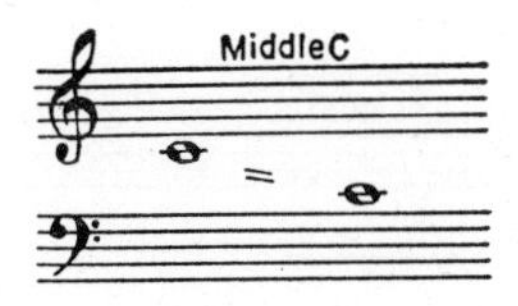

Naming the Notes

As we mentioned earlier, the first seven letters of the alphabet are used as names for our notes, starting again with the first letter when another octave is reached. Keeping this in mind, we are now able to name each note on the two staves.

82.

Half Steps

We have also seen above (p. 56) that in order to reach an octave after seven steps, five of the intervals of our scales must consist of a whole step each and two of half steps. Based on an age-old custom (going back again to the medieval theorists and their attempt to revive the ancient Greek system of scales), the half steps in the scale A–B–C–

[2] For additional clefs see p. 184.

D–E–F–G–(A) occur between B–C and between E–F. A look at our list of modes (p. 62) will show us that half steps between the second and third and between the fifth and sixth steps of a scale represent the minor mode in its natural or unaltered version.

83.

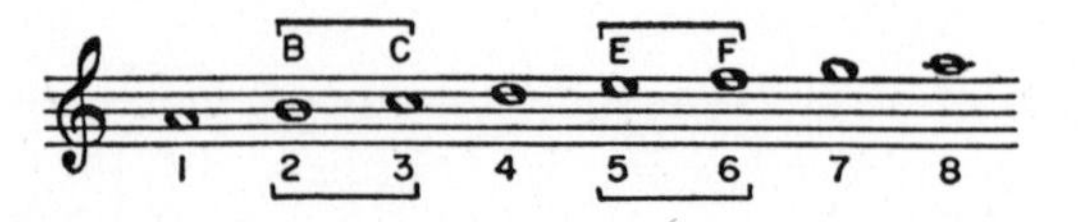

Starting a scale on C will produce the mode which has half steps between the third and fourth and between the seventh and eighth steps, i.e., our major mode.

84.

These two scales are called the "natural" minor and major scales because they use the natural half steps contained in our system of alphabetical names for notes. On our keyboards this man-made custom is exemplified by the fact that we can play the "natural" scales by using only white keys.

85.

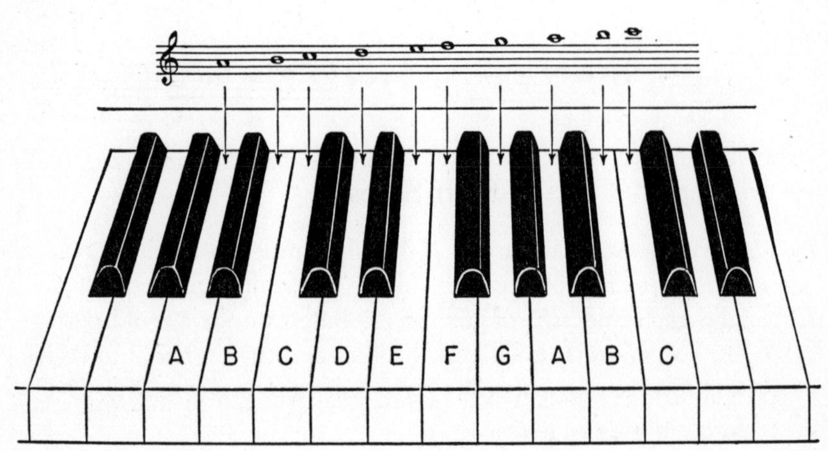

Unfortunately, though, the "natural" semitones are not discernible in our system of notation. For reasons of tradition and in order to save space

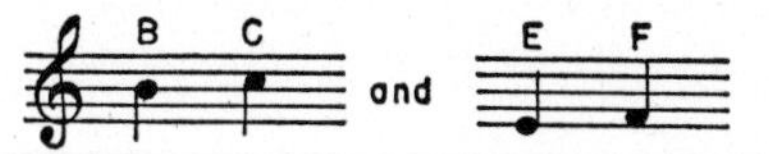

seem just the same distance apart as [D E] on our staff.

A true picture of their pitch relationship would, rather, have to look like this:

86.

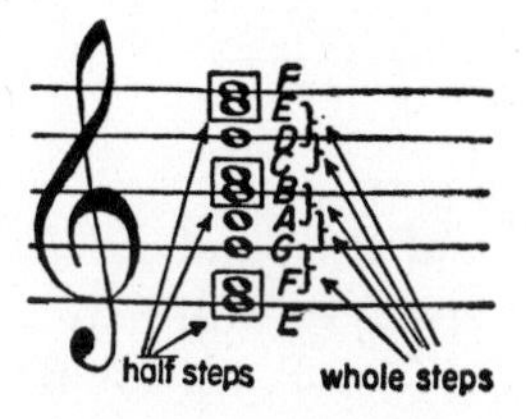

Sharps and Flats

While using only natural minor and major scales (i.e., playing only the white keys on the piano and music without any sharps or flats) would be paradise for those who are unwilling to learn to sing and play music, it would limit our available tone material to the bare rudiments. We can, of course, insert extra half steps between any whole-step limits, in other words, between any letter pair except B and C or E and F, and thus choose any of the twelve semitones of the octaves as central tone for our modes. The procedure would be as follows:

Problem 1: To erect a scale on G in the major mode (i.e., half steps between 3 and 4 and between 7 and 8).

87.

1. The half step B–C which falls between 3 and 4 in this scale conforms to the required pattern.

2. In order, however, to put 7 and 8 (F and G) closer together and 6 and 7 (E and F) farther apart, we will have to play and write the next higher half step which is derived from F, namely F-sharp (F♯).

88.

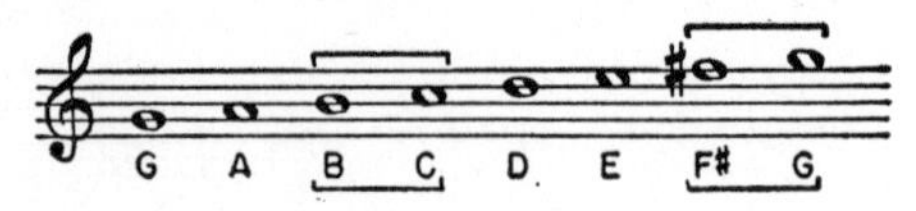

Problem 2: To erect a major scale on F.

89.

F G A B C D E F

F G A B C D E F
1 2 3 4 5 6 7 8
½

1. The halfstep E–F is correct.
2. In order to put A and B (3 and 4) closer together and B and C (4 and 5) farther apart, we will have to use the next lower half step which is derived from B, namely B-flat (B♭).

90.

F G A B♭ C D E F

It will immediately be asked why F-sharp and not G-flat is used, and why B-flat and not A-sharp. The answer is that even though [F♯] and [G♭] are played by the same key on the piano, "grammatically" they are not the same. A scale is supposed to move step by step (diatonically), which demands consecutive letter names for each degree or step and, visually, the moving from space to line to space, etc., on the staff. The following:

91.

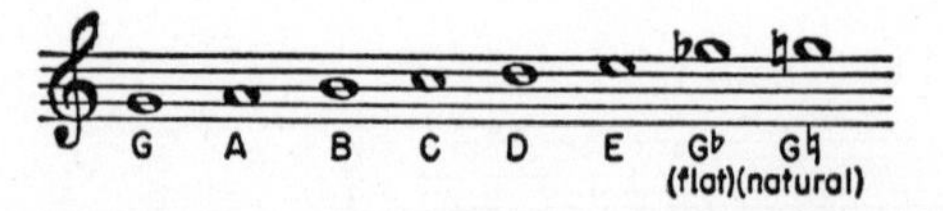

would read G–A–B–C–D–E–G(♭)–G(♮) and, furthermore, the highest three notes appear in the order space–space–space. It is, therefore, neither grammatically nor graphically a scale. To insist on the correct spelling of scales and melodies may at first seem like an unnecessary pedantry to the beginner. However, in order to avoid ambiguity in more complex contexts we will have to spell correctly in English as well as in music. Just as the words *dew* and *due* sound the same, but represent entirely different and unrelated meanings, so may G♭ and F♯ in a melody sound alike but fulfil different musical functions.

In another case, that of identical spelling but divergent meaning, the ambiguity may be dispelled only by the context of the phrase; think, for instance, of the two meanings of the word *saw*. In a similar fashion, in music the same tone or chord is sometimes intentionally repeated, but spelled differently (*enharmonic change*) in order to produce and indicate a modulation (see p. 162). Here the reader of music will be forewarned, while the listener may only gather from the context whether, e.g., G♭ or F♯ is meant by the composer.

Key Signatures

In order to save composers the labor of inserting three sharps, for example, in a piece in A major whenever the tones F, C, and G appear, the so-called *key signature* was invented. When at the beginning of every line three sharps occur the singer or player knows that the composer wants F-sharp, C-sharp, and G-sharp played whenever the note F, C, or G appears, regardless of its range.

92.

Whenever in a special instance an extra sharp or flat is inserted this will be valid only for the measure in which it occurs. For purposes of revoking a sharp or flat the "natural" sign (♮) is used (also valid only for the duration of the measure in which it stands). Nowadays, key signatures are written in a standard fashion, e.g., always not ; the sharps and flats appear in the order of their cumulative occurrence— not —and on the line or space which denotes the tone to which they belong. We will have to contend with the paradox that we say F-sharp but write "sharp F," that the accidental applies to the note which *follows*.

Tonic, Dominant, Subdominant

We had said that the first tone of a scale, our central tone, or *tonic*, as it is called in proper musical terminology, its higher or lower counterpart, the octave, and the intervals of the fifth and the fourth have always been considered important "beams" in music. Whether the reason for this lies in their simple frequency ratio (2 : 1, 3 : 2, 4 : 3) or in the construction of our ear, or both, it is a fact that the intervals of a fifth and a fourth above *and below* a central tone of a melody play a strategic role in most of the music which we know today. When a melody has established a certain central tone (tonic or key tone) the fifth tone of its scale commands the field. No one would dream of leaving a concert or applauding at the end of the following excerpt:

93. SYMPHONY NO. 94 IN G MAJOR (**"Surprise," Second movement**)

Joseph Haydn (1732–1809)

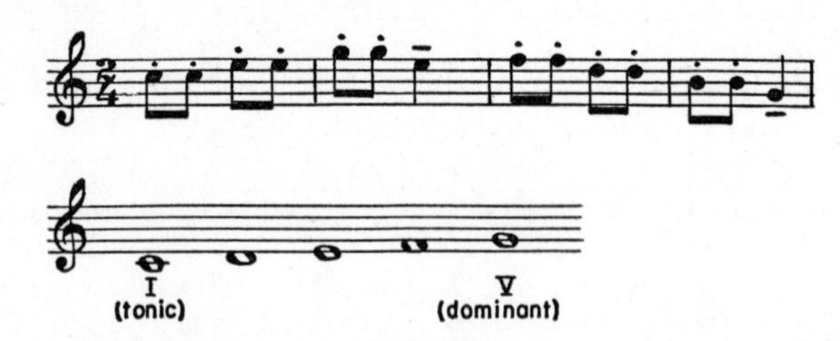

In these and similar cases we must know how the tune goes on and how it ends, whether the pull of the central tone wins out immediately or whether we go on to further excursions into the field of the scale before giving in to the final central tone. Most aptly, the important position of the fifth tone of a scale has been underlined by calling it the *dominant*. It does not matter whether this fifth scale tone (or *degree*, as it is also called) appears in its basic position, i.e., at the interval of a fifth above the tonic

or—transposed into a lower octave—at the interval of a fourth below the tonic,

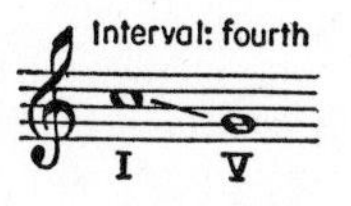

The letter names (here C and G) and the scale degrees (tonic and dominant) and their functions remain the same. Only the melodic interval changes through the octave transposition: from C up to G is the interval of a fifth, from C down to G is the interval of a fourth.

Here we see once more the necessity of establishing the tonic in one's mind when hearing or reading a piece of music: it is truly the central tone around which the other scale tones are grouped. Because in a melody the dominant may appear as a fifth above the tonic or as a fourth below it, it is not sufficient to measure the intervals of a tune; we must in addition establish the central tone and its scale, so as to find our "bearings."

The fourth scale degree, on the other hand, is called the *subdominant*, because it lies, when transposed into the lower octave, five steps below the tonic. (One might say that the subdominant "dominates from below," while the dominant dominates from above the tonic.)

94.

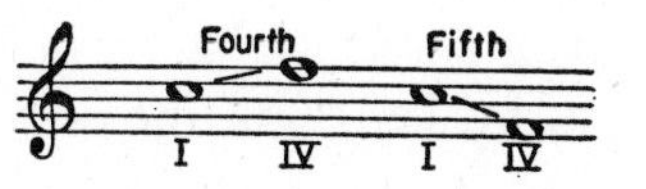

Here is an example of a tune (the end of "Good King Wenceslas") in which the subdominant plays an important role:

95. GOOD KING WENCESLAS

Our understanding of the structure of a melodic outline will be improved immeasurably if we conceive the center or key tone as flanked, kept in balance, and checked by the two companions who come next in importance, the dominant and the subdominant.

96.

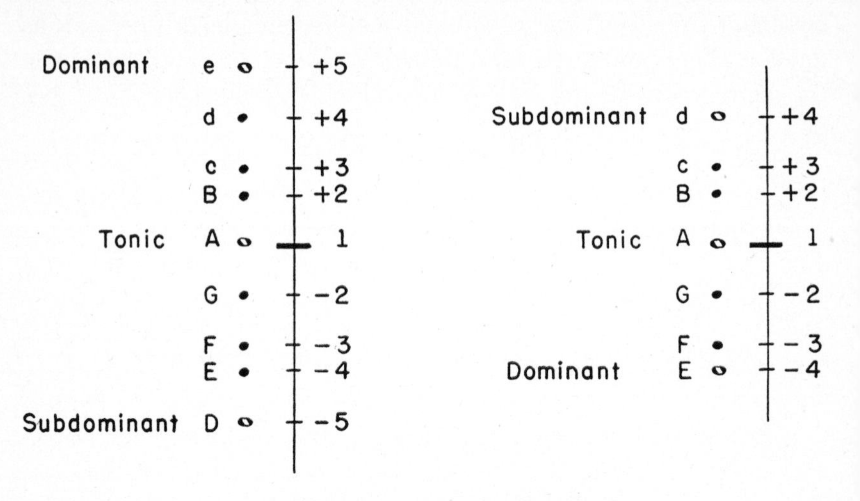

+5 = the interval of a fifth above A
−5 = the interval of a fifth below A

The close relationship between tonic, dominant, and subdominant may become even more evident if we substitute, for the letter-names of the various tones, numbers which correspond to their string-length relationships. Let us assume that our tone A is produced by a string which measures one foot. Its higher fifth, the dominant (E) would then necessitate a string length of only ⅔ of the basic one-foot string. Transposing the dominant an octave lower, we would have to employ a string twice as long as ⅔, i.e., 4/3 of the original one-foot string.

97.

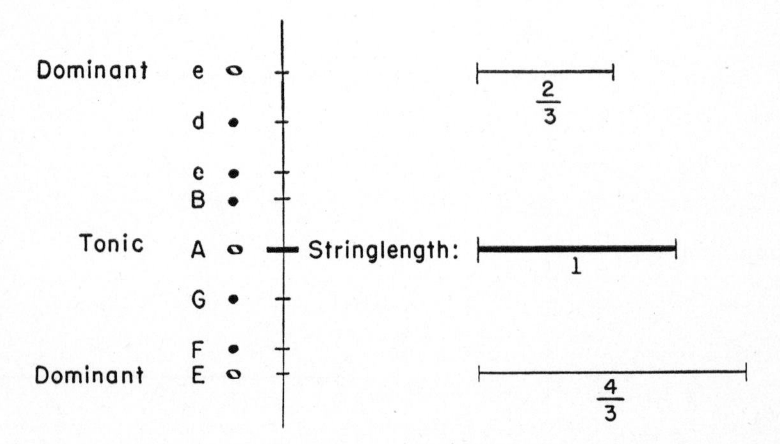

In an analogous procedure with the string length of the subdominant D above A, we would find that its string length is $\frac{3}{4}$ of the tonic A. Transposing the subdominant D an octave lower, we obtain the string length $\frac{3}{4} \times 2$, or $\frac{3}{2}$ for the D which lies below ("sub-") A.

98.

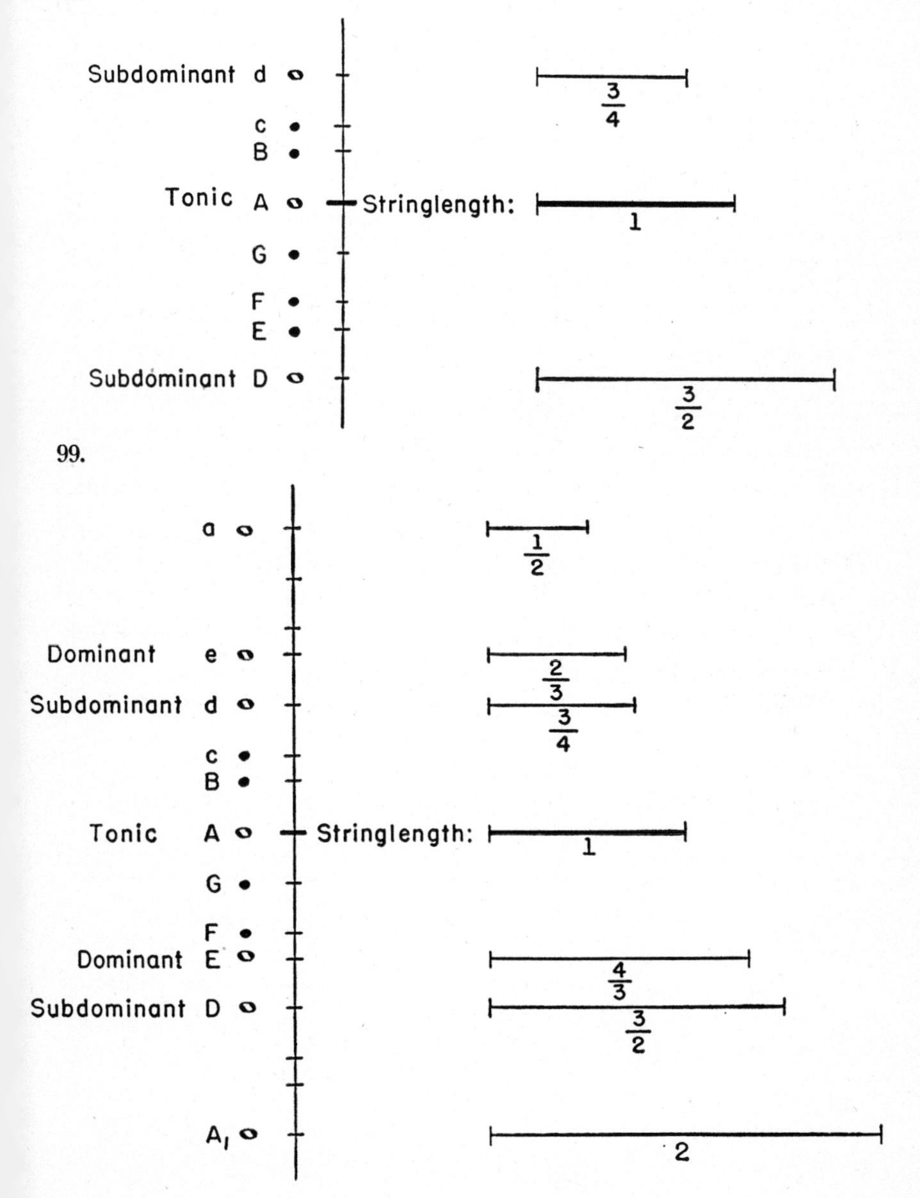

The complete diagram illustrating the string lengths of tonic, dominant, subdominant, and their lower octaves will show in numbers and fractions of string lengths the multiple relationships which exist among these structural forces of music. (See Fig. 99.)

Conclusions and Examples

We have found in different kinds of scales the raw material of melodies. Because melody is a very personal ingredient of the language of a composer, no rules or all-inclusive observations can be stated about what constitutes a "good" melody. Nor will it suffice to trust one's immediate reaction. Sometimes melodies will be built on the basis of unfamiliar modes, at other times the central tone will be difficult to detect, or the melodic intervals will be so wide as to upset our sense of continuity.

Nevertheless, even the modest and elementary musical tools with which we have become familiar so far should enable us to gather certain significant details which recur in the melodic procedure of various composers. By taking a melody apart and observing its behavior we will surely not arrive at the "swooning" or "snap judgment" kind of "evaluation," but we may instead become more keenly aware of the various essential steps, intervals, and outlines in a melody and the changing direction and intensity of its flow, and thus become more intimately acquainted with the music itself.

Melody is motion. If we sing or play a tone of constant pitch uninterruptedly we have no melody, nor, though time passes, rhythm. If we interrupt the tone and resume it on the same pitch we will have a rhythmic pattern, though still no melody. As soon, however, as we change the pitch level, i.e., move vertically in space, we will be able to observe: (1) the amount of change, (2) the direction of change, and (3) any formal design appearing in repeated or symmetrical patterns.

We have seen that, in our scales (the man-made systems of interval-measuring), certain pitch levels are structurally more important than others. The reason for this is believed to lie in their physical relationship to each other as it can be observed in nature. Thus we have called the central tone or tonic, the subdominant, and the dominant the structural beams of any melody, at least if it is constructed with the materials of our major and minor scales. All melodies can be roughly divided into those which move by leaps (skipping one or more steps of the scale) and those which move stepwise. The former are more frequent in instrumental music and the latter in vocal music. Yet there are countless instances where a composer uses voices instrumentally (Bach and Beethoven, for example) and where others make the instruments "sing" (think of Mozart and Schubert).

When a melody contains large leaps these are frequently nothing but broken chords, outlines of a harmony, or simply a statement of the structural beams.

100. BUGLE CALL

101. EINE KLEINE NACHTMUSIK (K. 525)

Wolfgang Amadeus Mozart (1756–1791)

Melodies which thus outline a harmony belong properly under the topic "harmony." These "harmonic" melodies convert a simultaneous sound (harmony) into a successive line (melody). They require from the listener not so much an awareness of a gradually bending line as rather a comprehension of a particular chord whose components are broken up into several successive tones—all widely spaced in respect to their large intervals as well as their delayed occurrence in time.

In melodies which move stepwise, an additional tone of the scale, the seventh or *leading tone*, will acquire a special significance, because it moves up so closely to the tonic that one anticipates with a certain impatience the appearance of the tonic. The result is a heightening of the melodic intensity:

102. O COME, ALL YE FAITHFUL

John Reading

103. THE COVENTRY CAROL

104. PIANO CONCERTO IN C MINOR (K. 491)

Wolfgang Amadeus Mozart (1756–1791)

In order to obtain similar effects or for reasons of embellishment or gradation of motion, *chromatic* (nonharmonic) steps are sometimes introduced into a melody.

105. MASS IN B MINOR (Crucifixus)

Johann Sebastian Bach (1685–1750)

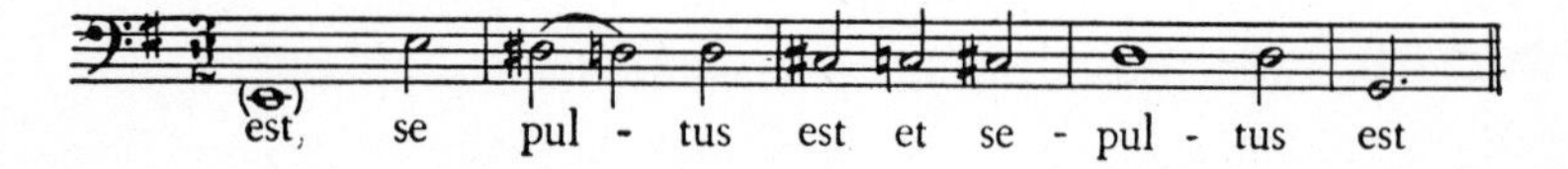

These create at times the illusion of a sort of melodic ritardando.[3]

106. TILL EULENSPIEGEL

Richard Strauss (1864–1949)

[3] Chromatic alterations which lead to modulation will be discussed later (p. 154).

We will notice that in many cases a composer uses both skips as well as steps in his melody, outlining a frame at first and then filling it out gradually.

107. VIOLIN CONCERTO IN E MAJOR

Johann Sebastian Bach (1685–1750)

108. STRING QUINTET IN G MINOR (K. 516)

Wolfgang Amadeus Mozart (1756–1791)

In the majority of cases, however, a melody will follow more or less the course of a scale; that is, its basic melodic structure may be reduced to a scale.

109. VIOLIN CONCERTO NO. 2 IN G MINOR

Serge Prokofieff (1891–   )

Frequently what appear as wide skips constitute, when compressed into the range of one octave, a stepwise progression. (See Fig. 110.)

110. VIOLIN CONCERTO IN D MAJOR, OP. 77

Johannes Brahms (1833–1897)

The direction of an unaccompanied melody and one which moves in steps rather than in skips can best be compared to the flow of a river, the level of which is at times artificially changed by man. If we imagine the tonic as the point of the final dissolution of the river into the sea, as the ultimate plain level, all fluctuations of a melody will acquire significant meanings. The upward motion will require an overcoming of the gravitational pull (of the tonic), certain strategic levels (the subdominant, the dominant) will serve as gathering reservoirs where strength is stored for additional climbs or rest is found before the final plunge to the ground level. Repeated up- and downward motion will increase the current. However, if the change of level occurs too frequently over short stretches of territory, the gravity pull is counteracted and the sense of direction is lost. This comparison may help us to understand the reasons for characteristics which many melodies have in common: (1) Almost all melodies fall toward the tonic after they have first reached a certain height of level in a more or less devious climb. (2) Whenever they reach the tonic stepwise from below they do so because they have plunged down too far ("overshooting the mark"), and the momentum they have gathered in their fall carries them up to the last stretch, back to the final resting place (observe in this instance the important role of the leading tone). (3) The highest and lowest points in the range of a melody are especially exposed. For this reason they will be reached only in critical or climactic moments. By the same token the highest tone of a melody is rarely the tonic, which is destined to bring calm and repose *after* a climax. (4) Frequent and quick changes of up- and downward motion in small intervals will obscure the central structure and may produce another set of structural beams (see Modulation, p. 146). (5) Consequently, the frequent and rapid changing of central tones will produce the sensation of restlessness and continuous flow, the "endless melody" which Wagner and his successors (including Schoenberg) desired and attained. Finally, the repeating of melodic segments on various pitch levels leads us into the realm of *form* in music.

111. STRING QUARTET IN F MAJOR, OP. 59 NO. 1 (First movement)

Ludwig van Beethoven (1770–1827)

These and other formal treatments of melodies, i.e., sequences, inversions, and augmentation and diminution, we will have occasion to discuss in later chapters.

In observing the elements and the behavior of melodies, we had occasion to speak of the howling of storms, the shouting and crying of children, the current of a river. Gravitation was mentioned and much play with "mysterious numbers." We may add that of the elements of music, melody is the only one which an amateur without any musical training may sometimes be able to create. However, many melodies which seem born of a momentary inspiration are in reality the result of extensive calculation and experimentation (cf. the sketch-books of Beethoven). In our listening we will do well to remember that besides mysterious and intuitive forces, modal and harmonic considerations have entered into the creation of melodies, according to the interests which prevailed during a given historical period.

In view of the history of music, we are justified in calling melodies, exclusive of harmony, *music*. Singing and playing single melodies is both the most primitive and the most natural way of making music, and it may have been, for all we know, the exclusive custom until about A.D. 850. Ever since that time Western civilization has been concerned with "harmonizing," combining several tones to be sounded at the same time. The experience in harmony thus gathered produced an ever-increasing number of harmonically conceived melodies—especially in instrumental music. Further harmonic intricacies (chromaticism) tended to complicate melodies and harmonies to such an extent, that the contemporary musical layman complains, really with a good deal of justification, about the complicated "modern music." Conversely, from the dark beginnings of music's history until about A.D. 850, the human race developed subtleties in constructing, shaping, and expressing a single melodic line, which largely escape our overfed ears today. The Asiatic people and folk singers of all countries have continued to cultivate the single (mostly unaccompanied) melodic line to this day. That explains why all of us are puzzled by authentic Chinese music and why those who are reared on Bach and Beethoven exclusively fail to perceive any value in contemporary folk singers. In order to combat somewhat this onesidedness, it is recommended that the reader find additional examples which are typical for the melodic categories as tabulated below.

A Suggested Procedure for the Study of Melodies

I. *General Survey*

Find from the most diverse musical sources possible:

A. *Melodies which move in steps*

among these find examples for:

1. A prominent leading tone.
2. Chromaticism.
3. Melodies which move essentially in scales.

B. *Melodies which move in skips*

among these find examples for:

1. An outlined harmony.
2. Skips which may be reduced to steps.

II. *Detailed Analysis*

1. Determine: (a) tonic, (b) dominant, (c) subdominant, (d) the leading tone.
2. Determine the mode.
3. Observe the highest and lowest points of a melody and draw a graph of its flux.

Suggestions for Listening

Bach	Mass in B Minor
	Violin Concerto in E Major
Ballads and folk songs	
Beethoven	String Quartet in F Major, Op. 59, No. 1
Haydn	Symphony No. 94 in G Major ("Surprise")
Mozart	Piano Concerto in C Minor, K. 491
Oriental music	
Prokofieff	Violin Concerto No. 2 in G Minor
Schubert	Symphony No. 8 in B Minor ("Unfinished")
Strauss, R.	*Till Eulenspiegel*

6

Harmony

Horizontal and Vertical Aspects

BECAUSE in musical notation successive tones (melodies) are indicated in a rising and falling horizontal line, we speak of the *horizontal* aspect of music when we observe melodies. Conversely, inasmuch as tones which are sounded at the same time are written above each other on our musical staff, we use the term *successive vertical* observation whenever we deal with harmony. The word *successive* indicates that any vertical consideration of harmony implies a horizontal element as well, or in other words that even in harmony time is of the essence. We have seen that melody cannot exist without rhythm. If we will now also grasp the fact that harmony cannot exist without melody, we shall have advanced an important step toward the better understanding of the role of harmony in music.

Playing two tones of different pitch at the same time we call playing a harmonic interval. When three or more tones of different pitch are played at the same time, we speak of a *chord.* Now, a single harmonic interval or a single chord constitutes harmony as little as a single tone or drumbeat represents a melody or a rhythm. There must be at least two chords present before we can speak of harmony.

We may gain a better insight into this vertical-horizontal interrelationship contained in the term *harmony* through a few typical examples. Let us assume that we sing a folk song without any accompaniment. In that case we produce a single horizontal (melodic) line, or in other words, *monophony*. (See Fig. 112.)

If we have drums and a guitar available, we may add a dynamic accent and a chord here and there to emphasize important points in the rhythm or melody of the song; the single horizontal line is supported by occasional vertical additions. (See Fig. 113.)

112. SIMPLE MELODY ("Londonderry Air")

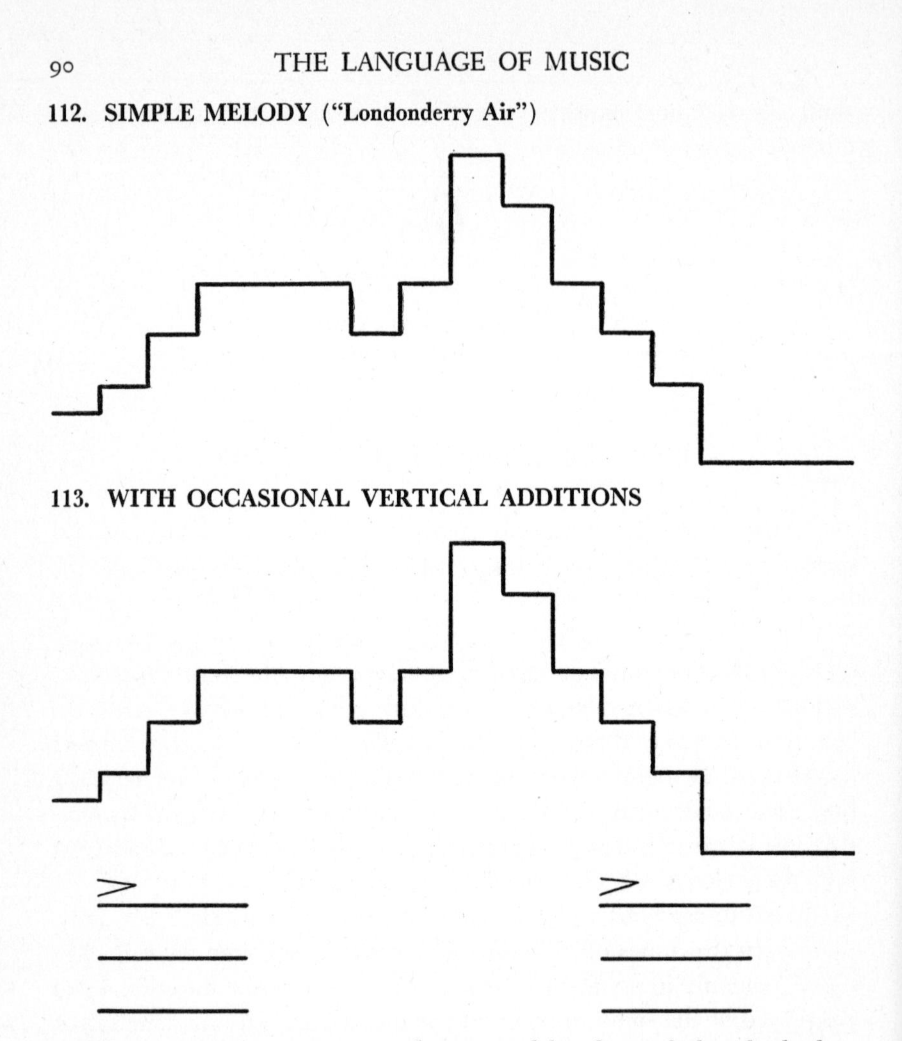

113. WITH OCCASIONAL VERTICAL ADDITIONS

These vertical supports are determined by the melody which they emphasize and which in turn defines their placement. This sort of harmonizing we may call incidental accompaniment, and while it has probably been used ever since man made drums and string instruments, it is not at all the earliest historically documented method of making harmony which has come to us. Perhaps this sort of accompaniment has always been improvised and nobody bothered with writing down "popular" music, especially as for centuries only churchmen knew how to write down music, anyway.

Another way of harmonizing a folk song is the popular adding of a second voice, an alto to a soprano part, or a florid descant above the tune proper. Graphically speaking, we combine in this case two horizontal lines which stand in a particular vertical relationship to each other at any given moment:

114. WITH AN ADDED ALTO PART

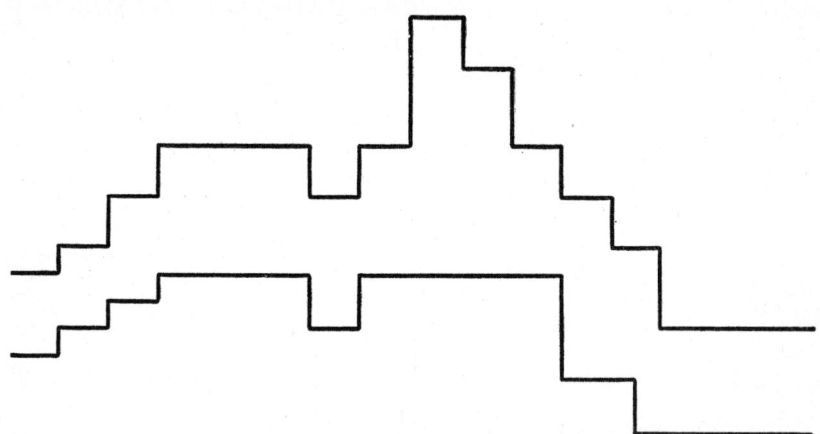

It is this conception of harmony, the combining of two (or more) melodic lines, which governed music between the ninth and sixteenth centuries. Let us remember that in that kind of music which combines several melodies and is therefore called *polyphony* (many-voiced), the horizontal aspect still prevails over the vertical; the original tune dictates the shape of the added melodies. The additions are conceived as lines and the resulting harmonies occur more or less accidentally.

A combination of the "incidental accompaniment" with the polyphonic principle may be achieved if several added voices combine into chords and thus accompany the main melodic line with a stream of continuous harmony. Our folk tune would appear thus when arranged for a four-part chorus, the melody placed in the soprano and the harmony in the other voices. In this case, the horizontal and vertical considerations become rather complicated; the principal melody governs the flow of its harmony, and the secondary voices contained in the accompaniment have to fulfil two functions: to be horizontal melodies which accompany and at the same time to combine into vertical chords. (See Fig. 115.)

This last type of harmonizing is called *homophony*, that is to say, all added voices "sound together in a similar fashion," they are made to serve one goal: namely, to strengthen the melodic trend of the principal line through harmony. Homophony came into use during the sixteenth century, and it developed, during the ensuing centuries, harmony to such an extent that polyphony was overshadowed at times and during certain periods even forgotten. The vertical aspect sometimes became so important that accompanying "melodies" occasionally were nothing but broken chords. At other times, the accompanying ("inner") voices became so lively, combined into such "interesting" harmonies that the principal melodic line became an integral part of harmony, and finally disappeared altogether. When that happened, around 1900 chiefly, all voices were made equal again, subdued and combined in "chord-streams" which move simultaneously, as in some music of Debussy, Ravel, and Stravinsky.

115. WITH SEVERAL VOICES ADDED TO THE PRINCIPAL MELODY

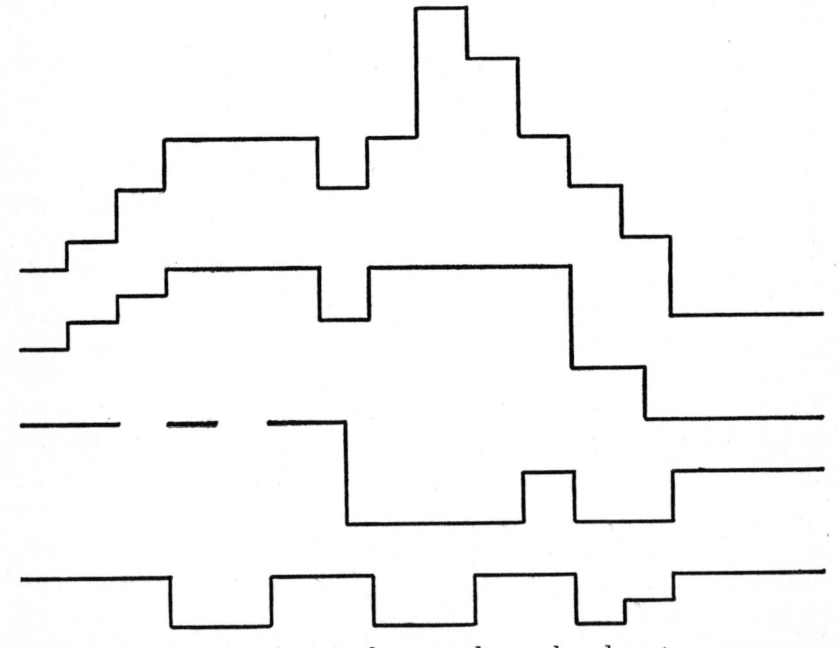

Both horizontal and vertical aspects have played an important part in music for a long time. However, the emphasis, especially in the nineteenth century, shifted on the whole from horizontal to vertical considerations. During more recent years the pendulum has begun to swing backward, among modern composers, toward a more pronounced preoccupation with "linear" polyphony (cf. the music of Paul Hindemith). However, because our commercial outlets for music emphasize to this day the "vertical" music of the romantic and postromantic era and imitations of it, we find among us a large degree of unresponsiveness to music from before 1600, which was mostly "horizontal." The widespread passive resistance which a number of our contemporary polyphonic composers encounter may likewise be explained by this situation.

Composers have always been influenced by the traditions and musical ideals of preceding generations which they either continued or opposed. In observing, then, the evolution of polyphony, we shall gain an insight into the changing use and evaluation of intervals and chords; we shall become better equipped to listen to music if we know "what to listen for"—where a tradition was continued and where it was broken. Only with the help of a historic perspective can we learn about the chief concern of composers in different eras of history.

If, therefore, we briefly discuss in the following pages a kind of music which seems "dead" at first, the fact needs stressing that we are dealing with procedures of composing which have been and are being used to this day. By gaining a better insight into a few of the ever-valid principles of creating music we can sharpen our ears and minds for a keener perception of modern as well as of ancient music.

The Evolution of Polyphony

Let us keep in mind the fact which was mentioned before—that, from the ninth to about the sixteenth century, harmonies were arrived at by the combination of several musical lines, and that they were produced by horizontal structural methods. Music was truly *composed* during that time, that is, "put together" by placing one note or melody (=*punctus*) against (i.e., above or below) another. This procedure was called the setting of *punctus contra punctum*, abbreviated *contrapunctus*, and translated into English, *counterpoint*. The combining of two and later even more melodic lines (polyphony or counterpoint), then, constitutes the beginning and early development of harmony in its original sense. The early forms of writing polyphonic or contrapuntal music were called *organum, discant*, and *fauxbourdon*. While all these methods developed and changed during the course of time, they have one thing in common; they use the horizontal manner of composing and add *counter* melodies to a *tenor* part (from *tenere*, to hold). In most cases the tenor sings a liturgical (Gregorian) *cantus firmus*, that is, a "firm" or fixed melody.

Parallel Organum

The problem of how to construct an additional melody to the *cantus firmus* was solved by the early polyphonists in a manner which sounds at first strange to our ears: for about two hundred years parallel moving voices were used: when the fixed chant went up one step so did the added voice, and vice versa.

116.

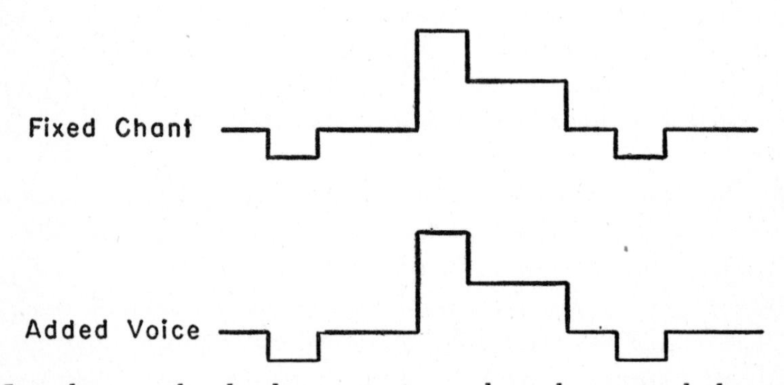

In other words, the harmonic interval used remained the same throughout the piece. What is even stranger to our ears than this reliance on one harmonic interval only is the fact that the first polyphonists used, instead of thirds and sixths—the stock in trade of our barbershop harmonies—octaves, fifths, and fourths as favored intervals.

Favored Intervals

More or less favored intervals have, since the Greeks, been called *consonances* and *dissonances*. The common belief that "pleasing and displeasing" sounds would be an adequate translation is unfounded. These are arbitrary terms which change with the historic and specific circumstances. No better proof for this can be had than the fact that fifths and fourths were called *perfect* consonances throughout the Middle Ages, and thirds and sixths, dissonances.[1]

Instead of judging a sound as pleasant or ugly, let us rather try to understand why these intervals were chosen as favored harmonic intervals during many centuries of music. If we remember that hori-

[1] To this day we have retained the term *perfect* for the intervals of the octave, the fifth, and the fourth, in spite of the fact that "parallel fifths or octaves" were strictly forbidden during the late polyphonic and the classic era.

zontal melodic considerations were foremost in the minds of the medieval polyphonists, we may also understand that the modes, the backbone of melodies, governed the construction of contrapuntal lines.

A glance at our modes (pp. 59–62) will show us that some of them are composed of two identical halves. In several cases, each four-tone group, or *tetrachord*, as the Greeks called it, has the same arrangement of whole and half steps (cf. the Dorian, Phrygian, and Major modes). Once it was decided that parallel motion of several voices would enhance the *cantus firmus* and its mode, the octave, fourth, and fifth were the most logical (perfect) harmonic intervals for this purpose, because they permitted, with very little adjustment, identical melodic (successive) intervals in both voices.

However, there are still other reasons why the octave, fifth, and fourth were favored. We have seen that already in monophonic music octaves, fifths, and fourths had a prominent position as a sort of "natural" framework for melodies because they were easiest to hear accurately and they could be mathematically arrived at in a simple and logical way. We may add that they are being used for the tuning of string instruments to this day, and that the average range of human voices is "tuned" similarly, i.e., bass, tenor, alto, soprano voices are each about a fifth distant from their neighbor. Still another advantage is that if we invert the harmonic interval of a fifth, transposing the lower tone into its higher octave, we obtain a fourth, and vice versa.

117.

Fifth Fourth   Fourth Fifth

This means that when you put tones 5 to 8 of a major mode above tones 1 to 4 you get the distance of a fifth between the two melody sections. And placing tones 5 to 8 *below* tones 1 to 4, you will have the distance of a fourth between the two melodic fragments.

118.

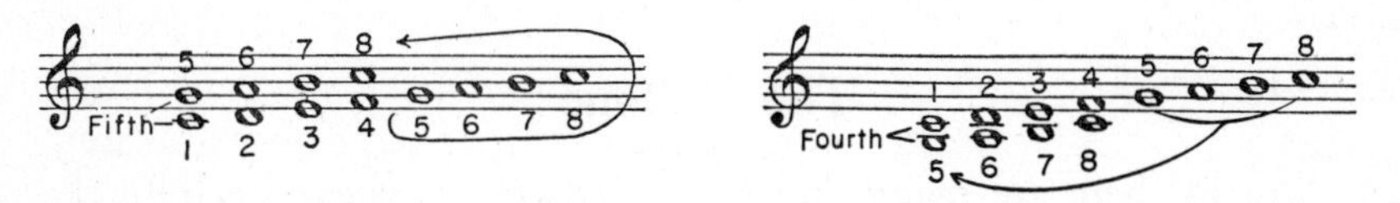

Should we add higher and lower octaves to any of these tones, we would obtain four different voices all related to each other through

the intervals of the octave, the fifth, and the fourth. This procedure is called *composite organum*:

119.

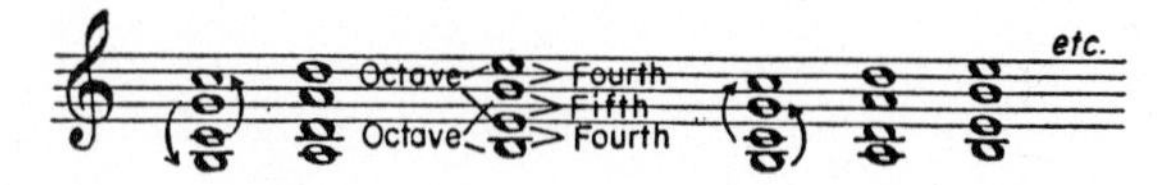

As usual, an actual experiencing of the sound of this earliest type of polyphonic music is immediately more impressive than the most detailed theoretical explanation. There are a few phonograph recordings available of the parallel (or strict, or pure) organum. These records may give an approximate idea of the sound with which monasteries and cathedrals were filled around the ninth and tenth centuries. A much simpler and more vivid way, however, toward a momentary re-creation of medieval sound is to have two or more persons sing a song or hymn (preferably one which moves stepwise and in a Gregorian mode), in two parts which move parallel and at the distance of a fourth or a fifth. Three or four different pitch ranges may be used if additional voices sing an octave above and below the original two parts, as shown in our example of composite organum.

Even for those among us who have little interest in history, the listening to and the singing of a few examples of parallel organum will prove to be advantageous in several respects:

1. It teaches us to hear two-part music.
2. It makes us thoroughly familiar with the sound of three different harmonic intervals, the octave, the fifth, and the fourth.

In order to become equally familiar with the sound of parallel thirds and sixths the reader is advised to listen to (and sing) barbershop ballads and in addition to provide himself—toward a better balance of his "musical diet"—with recordings of the following pieces: (1) Chopin, "Etude in Thirds," Op. 25, No. 6 (in G♯ Minor); (2) Paganini, "Caprice No. 13 for Violin"; (3) Chopin, "Etude in Sixths," Op. 25, No. 8 (in D♭ Major).

The Tritone

Just as there are major and minor seconds, so there are different kinds of fourths and fifths in our scales. When the distance of these intervals is measured more accurately, we see that all is not "perfect" when two voices a fifth or a fourth apart move in parallel direction. Counting the number of whole and half steps which our perfect intervals contain, we find that the perfect fifth consists of three whole steps and one half step, and the perfect fourth, of two whole steps and one half step.

120.

1 + 1 + ½ + 1 = 3½ steps. 1 + 1 + ½ = 2½ steps.

If we move the interval of the fifth step by step up the scale in parallel lines, we will arrive at a point where the lines are diverted from their parallel course, where the lower voice moves up a whole step and the upper voice only a half step.

121.

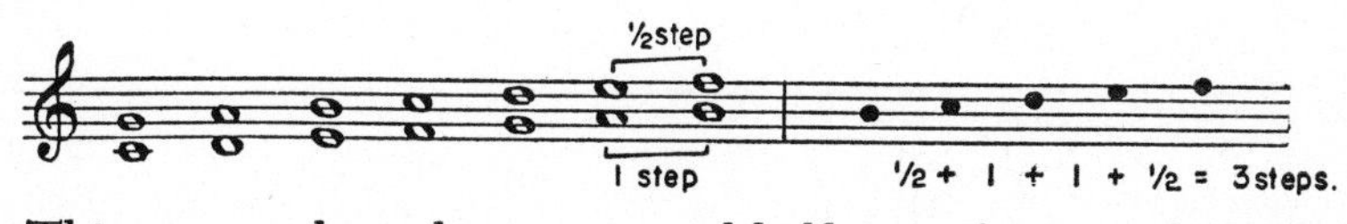

This occurs where the two natural half steps (see p. 74) B–C and E–F are both included in the fifth.

122.

C D E F G A B C D E F

Here the fifth consists only of *two* whole steps and two half steps, smaller than a perfect fifth by one half step. This interval is called a *diminished* fifth. At the corresponding point of two parallel lines of fourths the upper line moves one whole step and the lower line only a half step.

123.

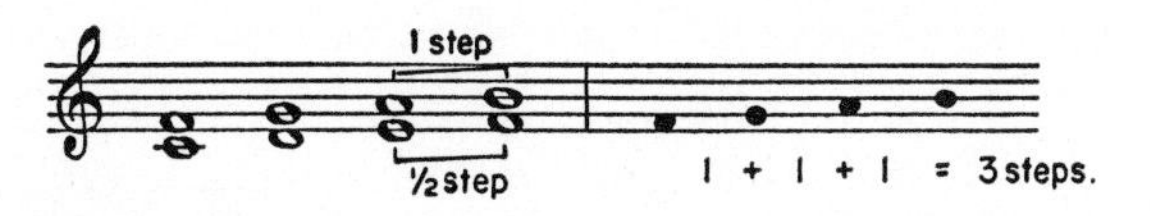

This interval consists of three whole steps instead of two and a half steps; it is larger than a perfect fourth and is called an *augmented* fourth.[2]

[2] The diminished fifth ($2 + \frac{2}{2}$ steps) and the augmented fourth (3 steps) consequently sound identical and can only be distinguished from the musical context or else from the score.

Let us observe in passing that a perfect interval when inverted remains a perfect interval, while an augmented interval when inverted becomes a diminished interval, and vice versa.

124.

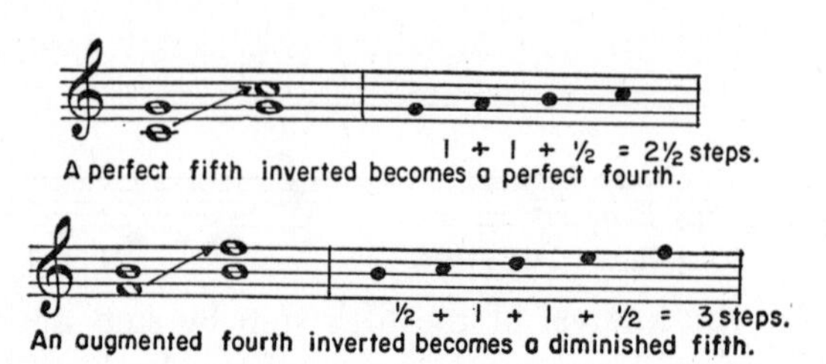

The interval of the augmented fourth, also called *tritone* because it consists of three (whole) tones, bears watching. It is this interval and its inversion which have created havoc throughout the history of music, from the time of the earliest Gregorian Chant to that of Hindemith.

If there is an interval which has been considered truly a dissonance, both horizontally as well as vertically, by all Western music, it is the tritone, which was called *"diabolus in musica"* during part of the Middle Ages. Enumerating some of the vetoes, rules, and devices which were brought forth by composers and theorists whenever they encountered an augmented fourth or its inversion (which was sometimes called the *"quinta falsa"*) may help us to obtain a better insight into the characteristics of dissonances in music.

First of all it is hard to sing. Try it!

125. SIEGFRIED (Second Act)

Richard Wagner (1813–1883)

(To be played an octave lower than written.)

126. PASSION ACCORDING TO ST. MATTHEW ("Let Him Be Crucified")

Johann Sebastian Bach (1685–1750)

Secondly, it interrupts the parallel flow of melodies. For this reason, the early polyphonists used two means to avoid it: (1) either the B was flattened or the F was sharpened (the only instance of the use of an accidental—♯ or ♭—in the Middle Ages).

Or (2) the parallel motion was converted into an "oblique" motion until the danger of a tritone had passed.

127.

c. 850

Source: Davison and Apel, *op. cit.*, I, 22.

In the preclassical and classical eras, the augmented fourth was not allowed to stand alone: it had to be imbedded in a chord consisting of additional intervals, and this chord had to *resolve* into another, *consonant* chord. The tritone, then, had to be avoided, camouflaged, resolved. Yet Bach and Wagner, as well as many other composers, used it deliberately! We shall return to this problem in a later chapter. Let us now continue with the history of polyphony.

Free Organum

The parallel organum of the ninth and tenth centuries was followed by the "free organum." Here the voices moved in contrary motion. The long development of polyphony toward the greatest independence of individual voices (or parts) had begun. All intervals came into use, but thirds and sixths were still considered dissonances until about 1350. Until that time the number of consonances was limited to the octave, the fifth, and the fourth. All other intervals, all dissonances, were used and "allowed" in passing only (they had to move on to other tones), or—what amounts to the same thing—only at unimportant points as far as the text and rhythm were concerned.

Melismatic Organum

Under *melisma* we understand the singing of several ornamental tones to one syllable of text. Gregorian Chant, for example, has sections which are *syllabic* (one tone to a syllable):

128.

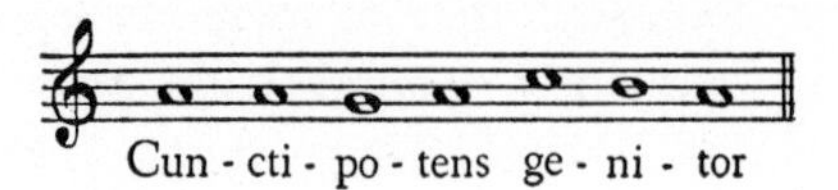

Source: Davison and Apel, *op. cit.*, I, 23.

and others which are melismatic:

129.

Source: Davison and Apel, *op. cit.*, I, 22.

In the *melismatic organum* of the twelfth century the original idea of "*punctus contra punctum*" was developed one step further, into a "melody against melody," rather than a "note against note," system. A free embellished melody was added, with many notes set against each single, long sustained tone of the cantus firmus.

130. SCHOOL OF COMPOSTELA (*c.* 1125)

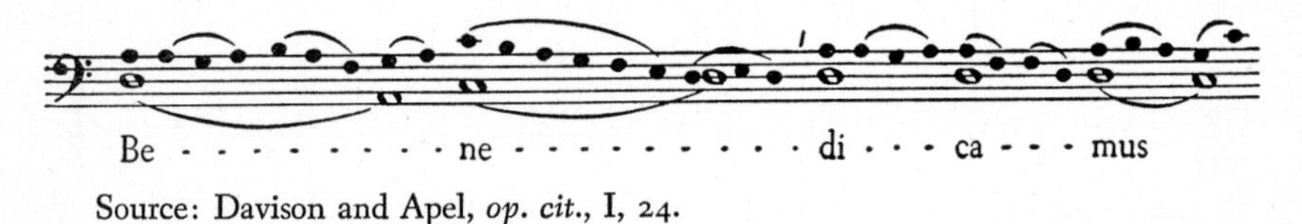

Source: Davison and Apel, *op. cit.*, I, 24.

Let us not forget that the Gregorian Chants which were thus embellished by long, drawn-out melodic lines were the common spiritual and musical property of all who heard and sang this type of music. We might, for a comparison, think of modern compositions which weave melodies and harmonies around a tune which everybody knows.[3] The familiar element holds the composition together for the listener and lets him anticipate "what comes next." It is to the credit of the composer if the familiar tune appears in a new light through his additions and the way he handles it. If the original cantus firmus is a sacred melody its inspired and meaningful character will be enhanced the more it is worked over by a devoted composer.

[3] Cf. *American Salute* ("When Johnny Comes Marching Home") by Morton Gould; "Under the Spreading Chestnut Tree" by Weinberger; Dvořák's Symphony No. 5, "From the New World"; Brahms' *Academic Festival Overture*, etc.

This attitude of the musical craftsman who labors over his musical material as another does over stone or metal or wood, "for the Glory of God only," and frequently anonymously, we may find in many later composers. The method of using religious melodies as basis for extended compositions is found in the music of J. S. Bach; he never ceased to invent new settings for his favored chorales, which he embellished and introduced in his "Chorale Preludes," and which he used frequently as a cantus firmus in his cantatas and oratorios (as an example, Bach's Cantata No. 4, "Christ Lay in Death's Bondage," which is entirely based on the tune of its final chorale).

The best way to approach these many old and new compositions which use a cantus firmus is first to become thoroughly familiar with the tune and the text of the chant, chorale, or song which provided the composer with his initial inspiration.

Discant Organum

Around 1200 the "rhythmic modes" (see p. 17) made each voice of an organum still more distinct and clearly shaped in the *discant* style of polyphony.

131. IN THE STYLE OF LEONINUS (*c.* 1175)

Source: Davison and Apel, *op. cit.*, I, 29.

The Thirteenth-Century Motet

A medieval method of composing for which we will hardly find a more recent counterpart was used in the *thirteenth century* (or *Paris*) *motet*. Above a melismatic section (comprising frequently only one syllable) of a Gregorian Chant, melodies were added which were sung to different words (*mot* = word). At times even secular French texts were added above the liturgical cantus firmus. Usually, however, the various combined texts were all in Latin and chosen so as to express a uniform basic thought.

132. DOMINATOR—ECCE—DOMINO (Motet)

School of Notre Dame (*c.* 1225)

Here is a free translation [4] of the three texts which are superimposed in the above example of a thirteenth-century motet:

Upper voice: O Lord God who, born of a Virgin Mother, was sacrificed for man, cleanse us from sin so that rejoicing with redoubled praise, we may bless Thee without end, O Lord.

[4] Excerpt and translation from Davison and Apel, *op. cit.*, I, 25.

Middle voice: Behold, the womb of a Virgin brings forth the ministry of Christ miraculously, like a ray of light. That birth removes the sin of the first man. Now without end we sing a hymn to the Lord.

Lower voice: (Benedicamus Domino): Let us praise the Lord. Thanks be to God.

Fauxbourdon

Finally, in the fourteenth century in England—and later in France—thirds and sixths were admitted as consonances in the so-called *faux-bourdon* style of polyphony. The discussion of chords in the succeeding chapter will explain why fauxbourdon is also sometimes called "sixth chord style" whenever it uses a chain of inverted triads (see Fig. 153).

133. GLORIA IN EXCELSIS (from a Mass)

School of Worcester (14th century)

Source: Davison and Apel, *op. cit.*, I, 62.

Summary and Suggestions for Ear-Training

Let us recapitulate a few points of our survey of early polyphony:

1. The horizontal aspect prevails.
2. Intervals, not chords, are the chief vertical concern, whatever there is of it.
3. Octaves, fifths, and fourths are considered consonances and only much later also thirds and sixths.
4. Dissonances have to pass on to consonant sounds.
5. The tendency points gradually toward more and more melodic and rhythmic independence among individual voices.

More specifically, in hearing music from between the ninth and the fourteenth centuries we may ask ourselves the following questions in order to make our listening more articulate:

1. Is it monophonic or polyphonic? (Include medieval dances and the songs of the troubadours and trouvères in your test.)
2. Is it Gregorian or secular?
3. Is it melismatic or syllabic?
4. Are rhythmic modes involved? (If so, tap them and name them.)

If the composition is polyphonic, is the method employed:

1. parallel, oblique, or free organum?
2. melismatic organum?
3. discant organum?
4. fauxbourdon?
5. thirteenth-century motet?

Now, a word of caution: we must not think that pointing out a few principles embodied in early polyphony, or reading or playing a few excerpts, will suffice to do justice to centuries of music. Only repeated hearing and singing will make us gradually familiar with the finely shaped melodic lines, the hidden rhythmic intricacies, and the carefully balanced vertical distances between individual strands of melodies of the music of the Middle Ages. If we remember that the last hundred years brought a rediscovery of the forgotten music of the Baroque (Monteverdi, Schütz, Vivaldi, Bach, Händel) and the Renaissance (Josquin des Prés, Lassus, Victoria), we may hope that our musicians and choral societies will in the near future follow the labors of the musicologists and unearth the treasures of medieval music in live performances.[5] A musical experience which is described so vividly in the quotation which follows should now be made available to the general public.

> Amédée Gastoué revived the difficult works of Perotinus (ca. 1180–1236) at the Sainte Chapelle in June 1914, during a Congress of the International Society of Music. They were at that time known only to a few students who spoke of them in the condescending manner which art critics a century ago adopted towards Romanesque sculpture and "primitive" pictures. But the music turned out to be surprisingly beautiful and aroused great historical interest. Thirteen years later, during the Beethoven Centenary commemorations . . . a performance of the works

[5] At the moment, this is done only by a few college choirs and by the Dessoff Choirs (Paul Boepple, director).

of Perotinus . . . was a revelation, a flash of beauty, like the windows of Chartres or of Bourges, suddenly illuminated by the sun, and famous composers were seen moved to tears by what was hitherto considered merely an object of historical curiosity.[6]

One had the feeling that the sleeping soul of the Gothic Cathedral—that fanciful setting of fairy tales—had come to life, animated by the ornate discant of Perotinus.[7]

Suggestions for Listening

Bach	Cantata No. 4, "Christ lag in Todesbanden"
	Chorale Preludes for organ
	Passion according to St. Matthew
Brahms	*Academic Festival Overture*, Op. 80
Chopin	Etudes, Op. 25: No. 6 in G♯ Minor and No. 8 in D♭ Major
Dvorak	Symphony No. 5 in E Minor, Op. 95 ("From the New World")

Examples of fauxbourdon

Examples of organum

Gould	*American Salute*
Hindemith	*Das Marienleben*
	Mathis der Maler

Music of the Troubadours and Trouvères

Paganini	Etude No. 13
Piston	Flute Sonata (1930)

Thirteenth century Motets

Wagner	*Siegfried*
Weinberger	"Under the Spreading Chestnut Tree"

[6] Prunières, *A New History of Music*, footnote, p. 53.
[7] *Ibid.*, p. ix (in the introduction by Romain Rolland).

7

Harmony
(*Continued*)

Chords

When the individual voices of polyphonic compositions became more and more flexible and independent of each other in the fourteenth, fifteenth, and sixteenth centuries, when the number of voices combined became four, five, and six divergent strands of melodies, two principles of unification set in: imitative devices which pulled the various voices together diagonally as in a round, and harmonic vertical "pillars" in the form of "triads." If we look at the beginning of the famous round "Sumer Is Icumen In," we notice that the three sections (A, B, C) of the melody occur in three ways, horizontally, diagonally, and vertically.

134. SUMER IS ICUMEN IN (*c.* 1310)

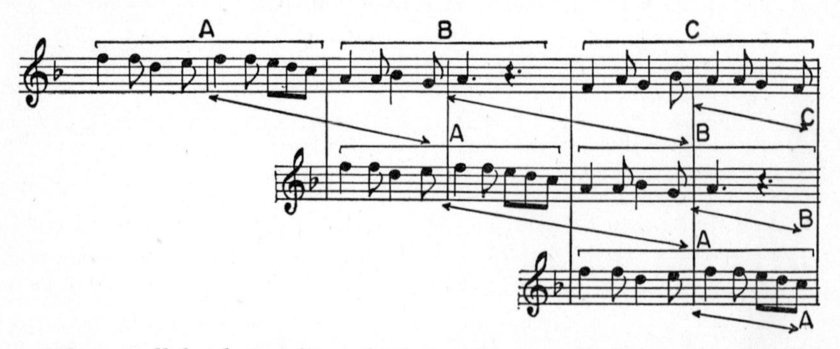

The parallel relationship which would exist if all voices started at the same time in octaves or fifths or fourths has been transformed into a diagonal relationship which adds up during the course of the piece to vertical harmony. While we are used to melodic and harmonic listening nowadays, diagonal structural principles, the backbone of the Golden Age of counterpoint (fifteenth and sixteenth centuries), are frequently unfamiliar to our ears. Even so, it should be clear at least graphically from our example that composing diagonally tends to make a musical structure more closely knit, more coherent. We shall leave, however, the further discussion of canons, rounds, and other polyphonic forms and imitative devices until later (p. 269) and proceed with the second point, the vertical pulling together of horizontal voices in chords.

135. O DOMINE

Giovanni da Palestrina (1525–1594)

To state that playing C together with the third above, E, and another third above, G, simultaneously, results in a pleasant-sounding chord or *triad* seems today a truism. For generations, ever since the piano became a household instrument, every child has found, played, and enjoyed the natural or C-major triad. It is for this very reason that it cannot be stated too emphatically that the triad in this form has only been used since about 1450. And until about 1600 it was considered the result of the concurrence of several independent voices; its incidence was planned as a steadying frame for horizontal lines, not as accompaniment. The fact that, for example, in Palestrina's music the vertical planning is equal to the horizontal lines of extraordinarily singable melodies accounts for his great popularity among persons who listen chiefly to harmonies. Yet whoever hears only harmonies in Palestrina misses half of the music—the individually expressive melodic lines. (See Fig. 135.)

Playing the above example on the piano will not even begin to do justice to the music, because the sound dies down as soon as the keys are struck. We must hear—or better still, participate in—a choral performance in order to become aware of the four equally important horizontal lines which flow together into a stream of harmony.

Major and Minor Triads

Although chords consisting of thirds, fourths, fifths, and sixths had appeared previously (cf. fauxbourdon, p. 103), the seemingly simple method of the piling up of thirds, and the recognizing of chords thus found as basic, occurred regularly only after the Renaissance. The reason for this is the relatively late appearance of the major and minor modes, which are better fitted for harmonies than the melodically conceived Greek and Gregorian modes. We can see this by a comparison between triads erected on each step of various scales. At a first superficial glance the design in the following diagram seems to be regular:

136.

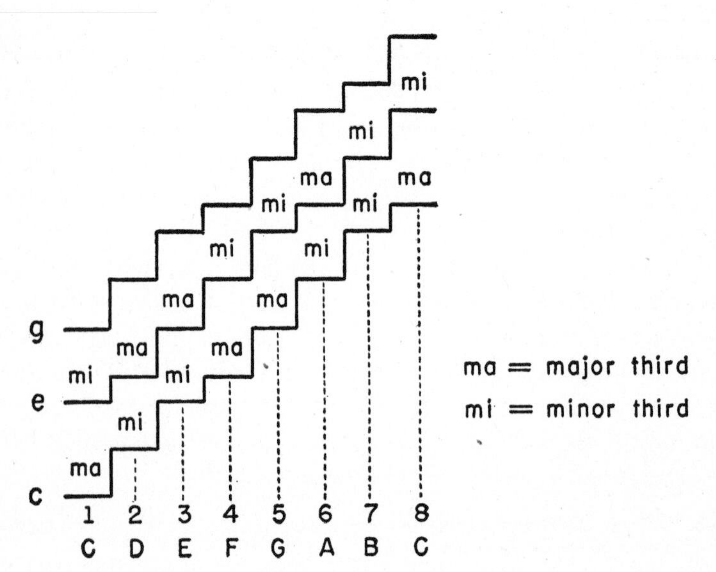

Similarly, a row of triads played on each successive tone of the C-major scale seems to the casual listener to consist of identically constructed sounds.

137.

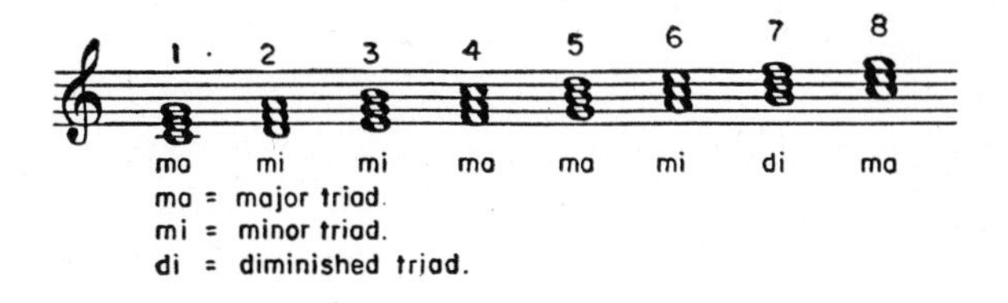

Closer observation, however, shows that the outer lines come together at the seventh step and that the middle line meanders sometimes closer to the upper (at 1, 4, 5, 7, 8) and at other times closer to the lower line (at 2, 3, 6). Turning to our triads, we find that number one, C–E–G (one always reads chords from the bottom up), consists of a perfect fifth which embraces two unequal thirds, one consisting of two steps and the other of only one and a half steps.

138.

1 + 1 = 2steps(major third) ½ + 1 = 1½steps(minor third)

The larger third is called major, and the smaller third, minor. If we continue this analysis upward, we find that with one exception each triad consists of one major and one minor third. Triads are named *major* or *minor triads* according to what kind of third comes first. According to this terminology we find major triads on 1, 4, 5, 8 (which is the same as 1), and minor triads on 2, 3, 6. The triad on the seventh degree of the major scale consists of a diminished fifth and contains, consequently, two minor thirds. Furthermore, because it contains a "dissonant" interval in an exposed position it has always been considered a dissonant triad.[1]

If we now erect triads on the scales which represent various modes, using only the tones which belong to each particular scale, we find that in most cases the tonic, subdominant, and dominant triads within any given mode are not uniform in their structure.

[1] The same holds true for the augmented triad, which contains an augmented fifth, and, consequently, two major thirds.

139.

Only in two cases are the chords on the first, fourth, and fifth steps of the scales alike: in the major and in the Aeolian modes.

When composers became increasingly aware of the harmonies resulting from the combining of three or more melodies and when they realized the clarifying and stabilizing effect of triads, they paid particular attention to the chords appearing at strategic points of the melody; the tonic, the subdominant, and the dominant. The very terms "major" and "minor" modes were substituted for "Ionian" and "Aeolian" when it was found that of all modes only two had three major and (respectively) three minor triads at the important places of their scales.

While the major mode has continued in this (Ionian) form to the present day, the minor mode has undergone adjustments which assimilated it in a way to the harmonic effect of the major mode. We have already seen during our discussion of modes that there exist modifications of the minor mode which produce at times its "melodic" or its "harmonic" versions. These alterations (e.g., of the basic Aeolian scale into what we call today melodic or harmonic minor versions) were not always indicated in writing, but frequently were only improvised during the performance. It cannot always, therefore, be determined with certainty in music before 1600 whether or not chromatic alterations of a given mode (i.e., "*musica ficta*") are intended by the composer. However, a general historical tendency toward the sharpening of the leading tone in minor melodies and harmonies may be observed. As a result, the dominant triad in the minor mode became more frequently a major than a minor chord. We might speculate that this procedure was also caused by the feeling that a major triad is more final, decisive, *dominant*, than a minor chord (cf. cadences, p. 135 and also the "Picardy third," p. 146).

Inversions

In a triad the lowest tone is called the *root* (1), the middle tone the *third* (3), and its highest tone the *fifth* (5). We see, then, that the two upper tones are named according to their interval relationship with the basic tone. It is a characteristic of the vertical consideration of music that a triad is called a C-major triad in *root position* whenever its lowest tone is C—regardless of the order or spacing in which the remaining tones appear:

140.

However, when the third or the fifth of a chord occurs in the bass, we speak of an *inverted* chord.

141.

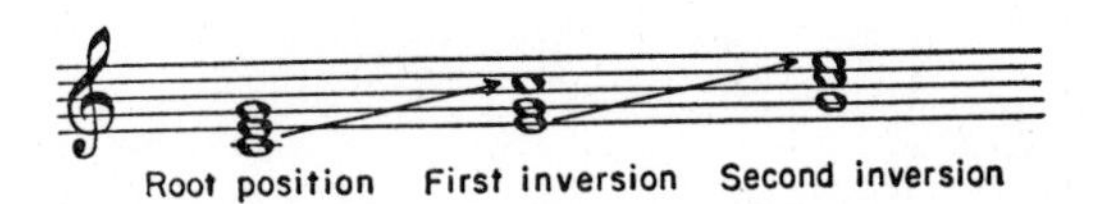

The first inversion of a chord in root position produces a minor third and a *minor sixth.* (Therefore it is called a *sixth chord.*) The second inversion yields a *perfect fourth* and a *major sixth.* (A *six-four chord* is the result.)

142.

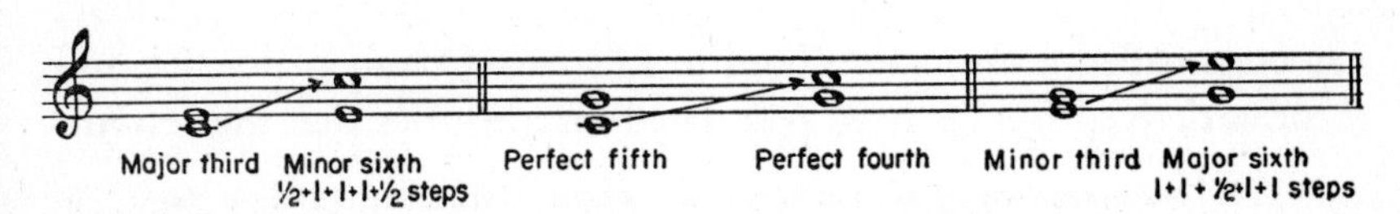

Let us note in passing that through inversion a major third becomes a minor sixth, and a minor third becomes a major sixth. We may safely deduce from this that a minor interval when inverted becomes a major interval and vice versa.

Comparing once more horizontal with vertical aspects, it seems noteworthy that in harmonic considerations it should be immaterial in which order the tones of a triad appear,[2] while in melodies the succession of tones is essential. The following examples are, of course, melodically entirely different; harmonically speaking, however, they are all broken C-major chords.

143.

Similarly, the number of tones "doubled" in a triad do not change its harmonic designation. Four-, five-, or six-part music can express a triad by duplicating the three essential tones in unison or in octaves.

144.

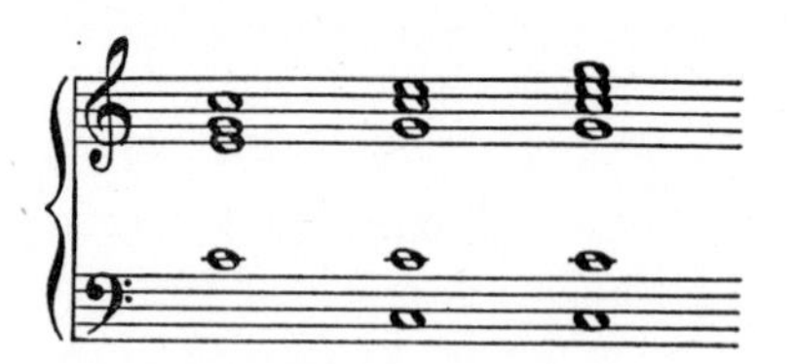

Seventh Chords

Starting about 1600, chords consisting of *three* thirds were considered as chord units as well. The *seventh chord,* so called because it contains the interval of a seventh between its root and its highest tone, has been called a *dissonant* chord to this day. Common practice and theories derived from it have postulated for centuries that the seventh

[2] This "harmonic" conception was first advocated by Rameau (1683–1764).

chord and its inversions should be "prepared" and resolved according to certain rules with which we may dispense in this context. We should, however, notice that these rules were followed in order to produce a *smooth* progression of chords. The first inversion of a seventh chord produces the following intervals:

145.

A seventh (C–B) inverted becomes a second (B–C).

We see that a *seventh,* when inverted, becomes a *second,* and we may add that these two intervals, in addition to the tritone, are the ones which have retained their connotation of harmonic "dissonances" to this day. We know already that there are minor and major seconds, consequently their inversions produce major and minor sevenths.

146.

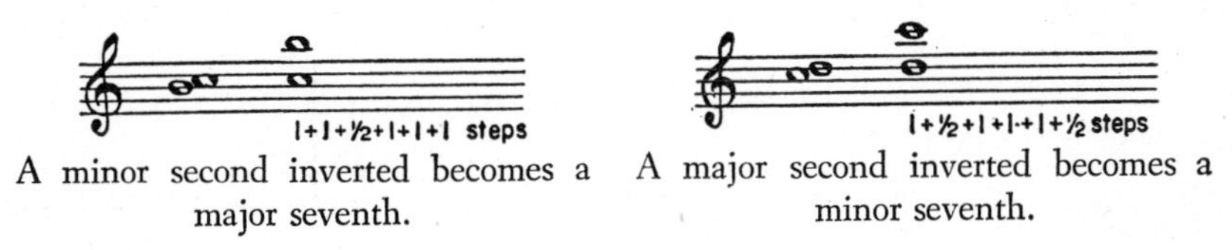

A minor second inverted becomes a major seventh.

A major second inverted becomes a minor seventh.

Additional Intervals

In finding names for the various intervals which occur between the tones of a major scale, we had occasion to use the terms "perfect," "augmented," "diminished," "major," and "minor." We may also expand or contract these "given" intervals by chromatic alterations, i.e., by raising or lowering tones through sharps or flats which do not belong to the original scale.

147.

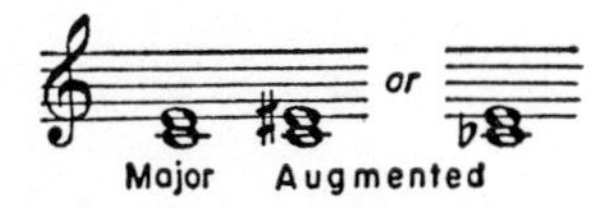

A major third expands to an augmented third.

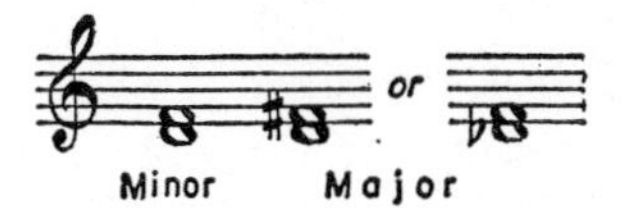

A minor third expands to a major third.

The occasion for these alterations arises whenever our melodic line becomes more flexible and our chords become more complicated or "unusual." The traditional nomenclature used for these changes is as follows: a minor interval, made smaller through the subtraction of a semitone, becomes a *diminished* interval.

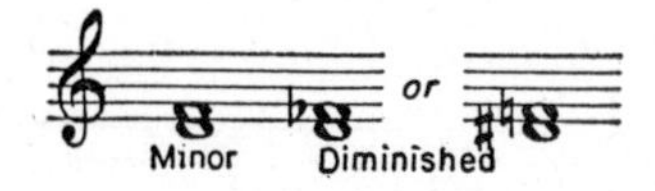

A major interval, made larger through the addition of a semitone, becomes an *augmented* interval. Perfect intervals, being neither major nor minor, contract to diminished and expand to augmented intervals only. The use of tones which are nondiatonic (not belonging to the scale) belongs to a comparatively late stage in the history of music, as the expression "flexible and complicated melodies and chords" would indicate.

148.

Table of Intervals

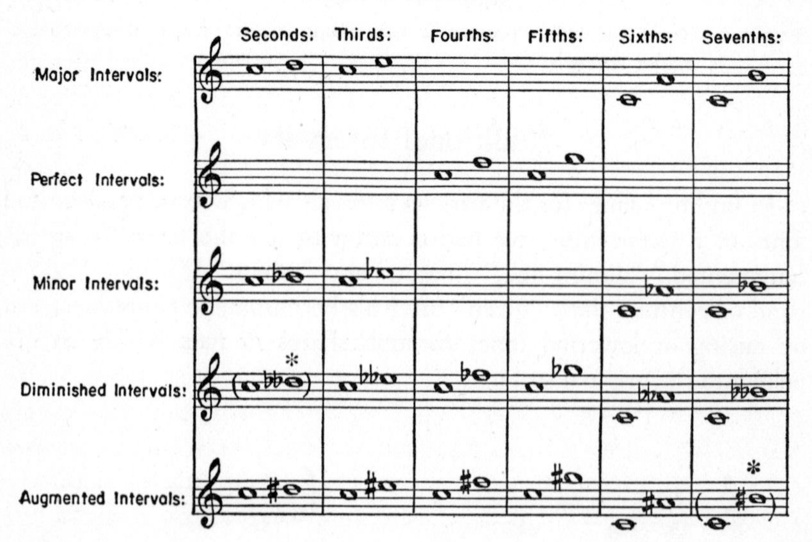

* Rarely used inasmuch as these intervals sound like a unison (prime) or octave, respectively.

Summary

Looking back from our present-day harmonic outlook, the beginnings of what is sometimes called "Tertian harmony" (i.e., concerned with *thirds,* and thus describing the period 1450–1900), seemed at first rather meager in promise. No wonder then that a century and a half before 1600 the emphasis fell on complicated counterpoint and that as a reaction after 1600 the single melodic line supported by harmonies was the chief new development. "Dissonances" in the polyphonic period (before 1600) occurred through the clash of independent voice leading, while after 1600 they were used for expressive and dramatic purposes. In a dispute over Monteverdi's use of dissonances in his madrigal "Cruda Amarilla," for example, the composer wants his critics to "be assured that, with regard to the consonances and dissonances, there is still another way of considering them, different from the established way, which, with satisfaction to the reason and to the senses, defends the modern method of composing."[3]

One of the characteristics of the Baroque Era (1600–1750) was that it was so concerned with a single, finely shaped melodic line which could serve to express poetic or dramatic feeling or instrumental virtuosity that harmony was used as a servant to melody. Because the contours of music, the upper and the lowest voices, became all-important, the middle voices shrank to a harmonic skeleton. During this era a *figured bass* line indicated the chords and intervals to be played above the bass in support of the melody. Only the top and bottom lines of compositions were written down; it was left to the skill and ingenuity of the conductor and harpsichordist to fill in the harmonies.

Through this kind of "service" harmony developed into an art of *progression,* underlining and punctuating melodic motion. The experience gained in using harmony in the homophonic compositions of the opera and in the rising instrumental music of the seventeenth century was finally applied in the late Baroque, by Bach especially, to a revised kind of polyphony. The vertical aspect had conquered the horizontal line to such an extent that melodies were conceived in terms of harmony, where formerly the melodic flow had governed the use of in-

[3] Claudio Monteverdi in the foreword to his *Fifth Book of Madrigals* (1605). Reprinted in Oliver Strunk, *Source Readings in Music History,* pp. 409 ff.

149. SONATA IN E MINOR FOR VIOLIN AND FIGURED BASS

Johann Sebastian Bach (1685–1750)

tervals and chords. The preoccupation with harmony beginning in the eighteenth century grew so rapidly that soon chord progressions determined the structure of melodies.

Exercises in the Reading and Hearing of Chords

The necessity for and the value of a reading knowledge of music as a help to our listening is never more obvious than when we try to comprehend the elements of harmony. While we may learn a melody by rote—if it is repeated a sufficient number of times—the sense of harmony can only be developed by "spelling" the various chords into which several horizontal lines may combine. Just as certain more complicated words have to be spelled, read, and written before they are understood and remembered, so a momentary visual approach to music will hasten its aural perception. The simplest harmonies may be grasped by a process of *mental* spelling. Most persons will, for example, hear the simple basic chord as a major triad without feeling the need of reading it. At first the intervals of this chord may be analyzed mentally by converting the simultaneous sound into a successive melody. This will clarify the fact that is a major third and a perfect fifth, even without necessarily singing or thinking the steps of the scale which were skipped:

150.

1 + 1 + ½ + 1 = 3½ steps = perfect fifth.
1 + 1 = 2 steps = major third.

If, however, the chord appears widely spread the mental condensation of the tones to the basic chord will become a subconscious habit only after a few "spelling exercises."

In the case of inversions this procedure will become even more necessary. Just as we had to learn to become and to remain aware of the central tone or tonic during the course of a melody, so we should now train ourselves to recognize the root of a chord. Whenever we read or hear we must—first in writing and reading, later mentally—"unscramble" the chord C–E–G, i.e. from E–G–C and thus learn to recognize instantly the first inversion of a triad.

It is recommended that the reader take a book of four-part songs or hymns and analyze the chords which are used in portions of several tunes. No attention should be paid at this point to the basic scale or "tonality," but you should simply determine in each case:

1. the root of the chord.
2. whether the chord is a seventh chord or a major, minor, or diminished triad.
3. in the case of an inversion whether it is the first or second, etc., inversion.

Here is an example of the recommended procedure:

151. THE OLD HUNDREDTH

Louis Bourgeois (written 1551)

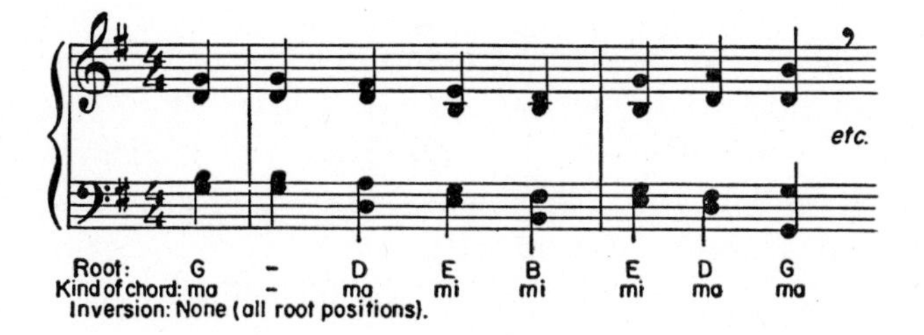

After a short while this sort of analysis may be extended to a few of the recitatives which occur in such abundant number in the cantatas, oratorios, and operas from the time of the Baroque to the romantic period.

152. ELIJAH ("The Angel," alto solo)

Felix Mendelssohn-Bartholdy (1809–1847)

Finally, when our sense of hearing and understanding chords has been improved sufficiently, we may approach the indescribable wealth of that kind of Renaissance music which embodies a balance of horizontal and vertical considerations, e.g., our Palestrina example (Fig. 135). To do this we must select from the music of the fifteenth and sixteenth centuries the many pieces which move in chords (in chordal or familiar style—see p. 333). Those compositions which are principally contrapuntal will become clearer to us after we have discussed the problems of "texture" (Chapter 16).

If before analyzing the chords in the following excerpts we read and sing each voice part separately, we will acquire very rapidly a sense for the equivalent values of horizontal and vertical aspects in this type of music.

153. MAGNIFICAT

Guillaume Dufay (*c.* 1400–1474)

Source: Dessoff Choirs Series, No. 29 (New York: Music Press, 1945). Copyright by Mercury Music Corp., New York. Used by permission.

154. TU PAUPERUM REFUGIUM (Motet [4])

Josquin des Prés (1450–1521)

Source: Davison and Apel, *op. cit.*, I, 92.

155. BON JOUR, MON COEUR (Chanson)

Orlando di Lasso (1532–1594)

Source: Davison and Apel, *op. cit.*, I, 159.

156. MY BONNY LASS (Ballett)

Thomas Morley (1557–1603)

Source: Davison and Apel, *op. cit.*, I, 180.

[4] The Renaissance motet has nothing but the name in common with the thirteenth-century motet.

157. WHAT IF I NEVER SPEED (Ayre)

John Dowland (1562–1626)

Source: Davison and Apel, *op. cit.*, I, 185.

158. THE SILVER SWAN (Madrigal)

Orlando Gibbons (1583–1625)

Source: Concord Series, No. 17, p. 242. Copyright, 1935, by E. C. Schirmer Music Co. Used by permission. Cf. *The A Capella Singer*, p. 68.

Suggestions for Listening

Examples of chordal style from the music of Palestrina, Dufay, Josquin, Lassus ("di Lasso"), Dowland, Gibbons, Marenzio, Morley

Mendelssohn	*Elijah*
Monteverdi	Madrigals and operas
Rameau	Pieces for harpsichord and opera excerpts

Sonatas for one instrument (violin, viola, gamba, cello, flute, oboe) and figured bass (also called continuo = harpsichord or piano, preferably with cello) by Bach, Corelli, Händel, Vivaldi, Purcell, etc.

"Sumer Is Icumen In"

8

Harmony
(*Concluded*)

Harmonics

A SINGLE major triad played in its root position has been considered a consonant chord ever since harmonies began to be used for the clarification, support, and punctuation of melodies.

This combination of sounds: root, major third, perfect fifth, strikes us to this day as clear, logical, perfect, beautiful, final. No other chord seems to deserve these attributes in our scale of aesthetic evaluations. Any minor or diminished chord, even the inversions of the major chord, sounds less final when played as a separate unit.

159.

A possible explanation for the aesthetic effect of this chord may be derived from the work of Helmholtz (1821–1894). He found that almost all musical tones are composed of a number of simple "pure" tones, which are called the "partials" of the composite tone. In most musical tones, the frequencies of these partials are simply related: the ratios of the partial frequencies one to another are 1 : 2 : 3 : 4 : 5, etc. In the case of a vibrating string, the corresponding string lengths would have the ratios $1 : \frac{1}{2} : \frac{1}{3} : \frac{1}{4} : \frac{1}{5}$, etc.

The partial with the lowest frequency is called the fundamental, and it is from this partial that the pitch of the composite tone is derived. The other partials are called "harmonics" when their frequencies are integral multiples of the fundamental frequency. For example, fixing the fundamental tone as C with 64 vibrations per second, we would attain the following series:

String length..........	1	1/2	1/3	1/4	1/5	1/6
Number of partial[1]....	1	2	3	4	5	6
Frequency	64	128	192	256	320	384

The analogous notation in musical symbols would be:

160.

etc.

1 2 3 4 5 6

Because the first six partials constitute the tones of a major triad, this combination of tones has sometimes been called the "chord of nature." Usually, the lower harmonics are stronger than the higher ones. One can experience this by way of a simple and popular experiment. Let us assume that we want to single out the harmonics of the tone C, i.e., two octaves below middle C on the piano. If we depress on a piano keyboard the key of the second partial (in this case the C which lies one octave below middle C) without playing the tone and, with the damper of that tone thus suspended, attack sharply and then release immediately the key of the fundamental C, we will hear the sound of the second partial. The undamped string, though not struck directly, responds to the second partial of the struck string, and continues to sound that pitch even after the struck string ceases to vibrate. The same experiment may be repeated with the other harmonics, but we will notice that they sound fainter the further we ascend in the series. In a sense, we are using the set of tuned piano strings as a sort of analyzer, to pick out the partials in the tones of the struck string.

In a similar way, the piano strings can be used to detect the partials in a sung tone. When you lift all the dampers of the piano strings (by lowering the right foot pedal) and sing a tone into the strings of the instrument, you will hear that tone and some of its

[1] It is customary to call the "fundamental" the first "partial" or "harmonic." To use the term *overtone* instead of partial or harmonic is inadvisable, inasmuch as the "first" overtone would be the "second" partial.

harmonics produced by the piano. Those piano strings which correspond to the fundamental of the sung tone and *its harmonics* are set into vibration by remote control, as it were.

Further illustrations for the existence of a "bundle of tones" within every single tone are the harmonics or natural tones of string and wind instruments. On a string instrument the various partials can be heard clearly separated from the fundamental if we touch the string lightly so that it vibrates in halves, thirds, fourths or fifths.

161.

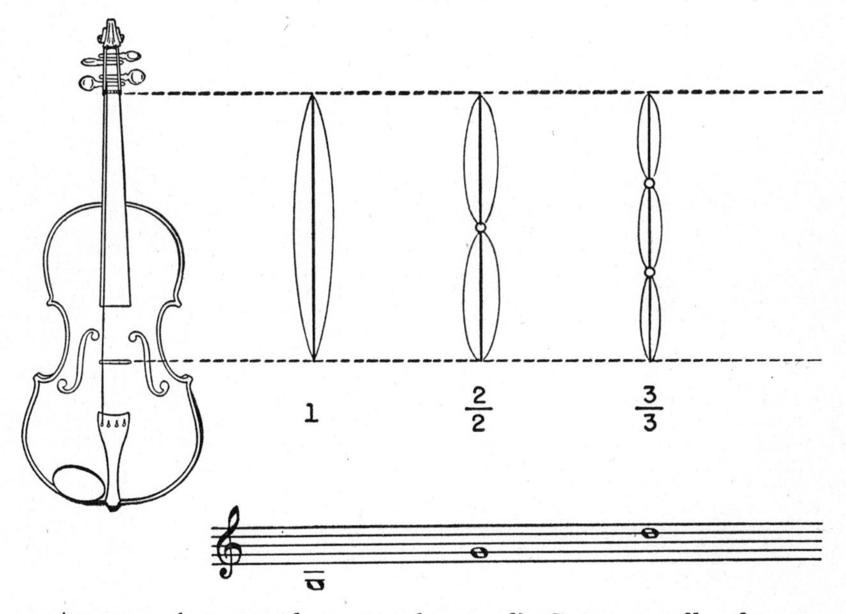

An open (unstopped, i.e., unshortened) G string will, when set into vibration by the bow, produce on a violin the tone G below middle C.

When lightly touched at its middle point by a finger of the left hand, the string will vibrate in two halves and produce the tone G above middle C.

By touching the string at a point either one third or two thirds distant from the bridge we may again induce the string to vibrate partially, i.e., in this case in three sections of equal length, and thus produce the tone D.

Similarly a bugle, trumpet, or French horn will produce "harmonics" or "natural tones" through changes in the "embouchure," i.e., the manner in which the lips produce the tone. In this case the length of the air column (instead of the string length) remains the same while the various partials are brought into the open through changes in tone production. We will return to these phenomena in a later chapter. For the present, let us keep in mind that the use of harmonics on string and wind instruments (and our experiment at the piano) shows that every single tone implies through its inherent six first partials a major triad.[2] In the row of partials the tones of a major triad occur widely spread, repeatedly, and, for example, in the order of C–C–G–C–E–G instead of C–E–G, but they nevertheless represent a chord in root position, according to the traditional conceptions of harmony (see p. 111). We are justified, then, in claiming that a triad C–E–G played in root position above or below a tone C which occurs in a melody does clarify, underline, point up this tone by bringing its partials into the open so to speak. Or, in other words, a single tone C is in reality a major triad C–E–G in root position. The reason now that the inversions of triads do not sound as final as the root position may be explained by the fact that, in a chord E–G–C, the two upper notes do not represent harmonics of the bass tone.

162.

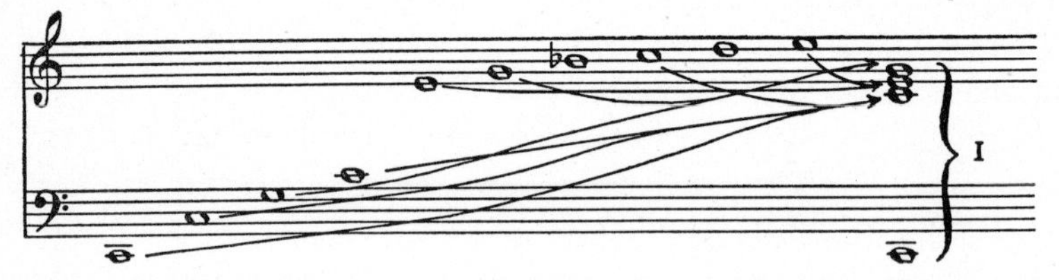

Harmonics of C Contained in the C–Major Triad in Root Position

Harmonics of E Contained in the First Inversion of the Same Triad

[2] It seems somewhat arbitrary to stop at the sixth partial and not to include the seventh harmonic in our "proof" of nature's approval of man-made harmonies. However, the seventh, eleventh, thirteenth, and fourteenth harmonics are the "black sheep" in the row of harmonics; they do not conform with our system of tuning (see p. 154) and notation, a fact which in itself indicates that our traditional harmony is based on a limited use of the resources available in nature.

Furthermore, although a chord E–G–C does contain harmonics of C, these do not appear in the order of intensity in which they would occur if C were the bass tone. For example, on the piano the first six partials of a low-pitched tone are more prominent than those of a high-pitched tone. Because now it is customary in harmonic settings to place the bass in a considerably lower range than the other voices of a chord, the prominent harmonics of the bass tone will tend to reinforce the bass tone *and its harmony*. Whenever we hear an inversion, as for example E–G–C, the harmonics of the bass tone E will tend to establish a chord E–G♯–B instead of reinforcing the basic harmony C–E–G. In the case of the second inversion a chord G–B–D will compete with the C-major chord. We perceive, then, a certain struggle of competing harmonics whenever we hear inverted chords, and conversely, a confirmation of the bass tone and its harmony whenever a chord appears in root position.

Consonances and Dissonances

The firm establishment of the physical existence of partials in musical tones led Helmholtz to a theory about consonances and dissonances which corroborated once more the findings of Pythagoras. As we have already seen, the only interval which has been conceived as consonant by all peoples throughout history is the octave. As a matter of fact, it has always been so obviously a consonance that two tones an octave apart are almost considered alike, not different at all, a "unison" sound rather than an interval (see p. 48).

Pythagoras saw as reason for this the fact that the ratio of the string length of two tones an octave apart consisted of the two smallest integral numbers possible (2 : 1), next to the true unison (1 : 1). More generally, he stated that intervals are the more consonant the smaller the numbers are which appear in their frequency ratio, i.e.:

Intervals Ordered According to Pythagoras

	1 Unison	2 Octave	3 Fifth	4 Fourth	5 Major Sixth	6 Major Third
Interval	c–c	c–c′	c–g	c–f	c–a	c–e
Frequency Ratio.	1:1	1:2	2:3	3:4	3:5	4:5

	7 Minor Third	8 Minor Sixth	9 Major Second	10 Major Seventh	11 Minor Seventh
Interval	c–e♭	c–a♭	c–d	c–b	c–b♭
Frequency Ratio.	5:6	5:8	8:9	8:15	9:16

Source: *Harvard Dictionary of Music*, p. 180.

Helmholtz through his theory of *Klangverwandtschaft* (relationship of sounds), arrived at almost the same order of intervals. He defined as consonant those intervals the harmonics of which have one or more tones in common (excluding the "uncertain" seventh, eleventh, etc., partials). (See p. 124.) On this basis he found octaves, fifths, fourths, major and minor thirds, and sixths to be consonant, and seconds and sevenths to be dissonant.

163.

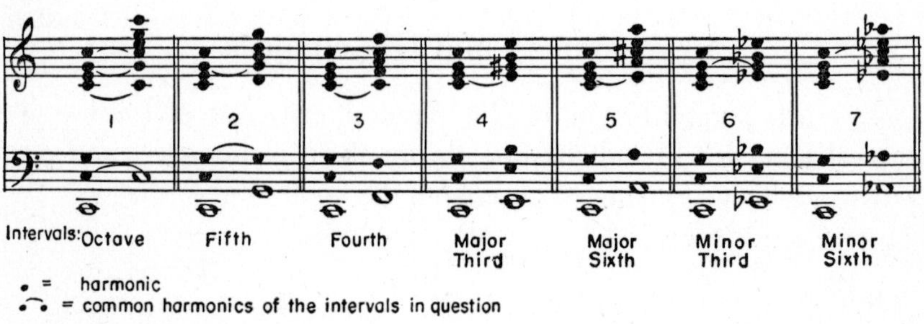

Source: *Ibid.*, p. 181.

A theory which goes further, stating that there is no absolute limit between consonances and dissonances, was established by C. Stumpf (1883) in his experiments concerning *Tonverschmelzung* (amalgamation of sound). In extensive psychological tests it was found that two pure tones an octave apart seemed to blend into a single tone for about 75 per cent of the "musically untrained" persons who were tested. The interval of a fifth seemed a single tone to about 50 per cent, the fourth to 33 per cent, the third to 25 per cent, the tritone to 20 per cent, and the second to 10 per cent!

If we remember that intervals came into use in the history of music (and were "permitted" by theorists)—in exactly this order, and that they occur similarly in the row of harmonics, we should be ready to abandon the concept of consonance and dissonance as absolute terms and rather substitute a sliding scale of consonant values. In passing we might note that this concept is anything but modern: it was already recognized among the Arabs in the tenth century.[3] With this in mind, let us list in arbitrary order the various epithets and "rules" used in connection with consonant and dissonant intervals and chords at one time or another. We thus may be able to extract a few fundamental concepts about consonances and dissonances which developed throughout the several centuries of Western music.

1. Octaves are perfect consonances, so perfect that to move in parallel octaves was forbidden in the late polyphonic era and afterward, as uninteresting and empty-sounding, i.e., reducing the number of voices employed through a "unison effect." Moving in octaves was, and is, considered the equivalent of constant consonance.
2. To a smaller degree the same holds for fifths and fourths.
3. Thirds and sixths came into use late, appearing first in popular music of England [4] and fauxbourdon of the fifteenth century.
4. The tritone was to be avoided, camouflaged, or resolved.
5. Seconds and sevenths had to be "prepared" and had to "resolve."
6. Chords containing in prominent position the intervals which were mentioned under (4) and (5) had to resolve.
7. Major triads in root position were considered stable and final. Minor chords and inversions were considered less so.

We may add that consonances, whatever they are at various periods, are popularly called "pleasant, calm, static, boring"; and dissonances "unpleasant, disturbing, dynamic, clashing, exciting." Finally, non-harmonic tones, i.e., dissonant tones which do not fit into a given harmony, have long been called "passing notes, suspensions, anticipations." In other words, terms which denote the passing of time have been used in explaining or excusing dissonances.

Looking over these admittedly simplified, generalizing, and subjective descriptions of consonant and dissonant elements in music, we come to the conclusion that *dissonances* come and go, that motion is involved in their existence—while *consonances*, on the other hand, stabilize, stand still, rest in themselves. The static nature of consonances might be explained by the fact that strong (low-numbered) and closely related (neighboring) partials reinforce the consonant intervals and chords. Dissonances, on the other hand, consist of competing melodic elements which do not amalgamate vertically but

[3] *Harvard Dictionary of Music*, pp. 45–46.

[4] Cf. The gymel style of early polyphony (*cantus gemellus* = twin song), an English form of organum which moves in thirds.

rather originate and resolve on a horizontal plane. Dissonances first came into music when several voices moved in contrary motion; they were caused by the motion of different melodies. When the melodic tendency of each individual voice is obvious, as in stepwise and/or contrary motion, when the dissonance occurs in passing, i.e., at unimportant places as far as the rhythm and the text are concerned, the dissonance will not be noticed, the horizontal aspect will prevail over vertical "disturbances." Whenever, on the other hand, a dissonance appears prominently, it demands a resolution. The composer is forced, so to speak, to lead on those voices which produce a dissonance in such a way that the combined melodies resolve into a consonance.

We can experience this fact—that dissonances consist of the combination of moving melodies—by "reconverting" the vertical sound into successive horizontal segments. Take for instance the following excerpt from the Brahms Violin Concerto: The sharp dissonance, coinciding with the metric accent of the second measure, is produced by the "inside bending" of the two melodic lines. Considered separately, the melodic fragments and may continue in many different ways. As soon, however, as they are combined, their course of continuation seems fixed. The way in which they combine in the dissonant interval seems to command a particular kind of "unbending" of the melodic lines, a certain "most obvious, satisfactory, natural" *resolution*. We may call this type of dissonance a critical moment in the leading of voices. If we plan and prolong dissonant sounds, if we arrest the motion of melodies at these critical moments, we store up the kinetic energy.

Another kind of dissonant sound is caused by passages in unresolved seconds:

164. VIOLIN SONATA NO. 2

Bela Bartok (1881–1945)

We may successfully approach these dissonances which occur frequently in contemporary music by a simple mental transformation: by converting the simultaneous sound into a wavering melodic line. If for example, for the above excerpt we substitute mentally the rapid alternation between two tones which are the interval of a second apart —i.e., a *trill*—for the prolonged simultaneous clash, the passage will sound perfectly harmless.

165.

Perhaps the composer intended by "freezing" such an imagined trill to create a condensed melodic line, concentrating musical events to a point of almost unbearable tension.

Similarly, dissonant passages which move more rapidly, or which consist of parallel sevenths, may be at first imagined as single tones which are preceded by *grace notes*:

166. VIOLIN SONATA NO. 2

Bela Bartok (1881–1945)

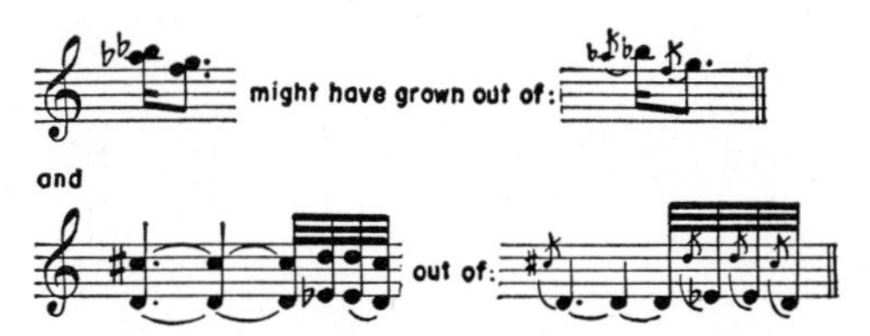

Conversely, an actual trill may be considered as a vertical dissonance. Its exciting, restless character, which heightens the expectation for the solution of a reiterated dissonance, puts this brilliant ornament half way between melody and harmony, makes it half consonant and half dissonant.

In the development of harmony since 1600, dissonances have been used more and more to build up tensions which then are resolved more or less gradually into consonances. The continuum of consonance and dissonance has served for more than 300 years as a propelling and retarding element in music; it produces harmonic tension and relaxation. Sudden dissonances seem to hasten the pace of music, regardless of the actual tempo, and the harsher they sound the more urgently do they seem to demand a solution. Moving from one strong dissonance to another, we will feel pushed forward violently; entering dissonances gradually, well prepared, and leaving them through expected and logical resolutions, we seem to go forward more calmly. Progressing in consonances only will put us safely—to sleep. Sometimes a dramatic situation in an opera or oratorio gives us an indication why a composer writes a sudden unconventional dissonance. In Bach's *Passion according to St. Matthew,* for example, Pilate asks the crowd whom it wants to let go free, Jesus or Barabbas, and the answer is a dissonant chord.

167. PASSION ACCORDING TO ST. MATTHEW

Johann Sebastian Bach (1685–1750)

Here the bass progresses a tritone upward into an unprepared dissonance which dissolves only when the story resumes. If Bach had proceeded in a musically "correct" fashion, if he had been afraid to "shock" his listeners with a prolonged dissonance, he would have been one of the crowd, not himself.

Not always will we have such a clear indication in words of what the composer wants to express in terms of harmonic tension or relaxation. In all "music without words," that is, any piece from the tremendous literature of instrumental music, we are left to our own devices: to listen to melodic and harmonic progressions and thus gradually to become familiar with the more common harmonic formulas. We must, however, always remember that the difference between consonances and dissonances is relative in two respects: (1) historically, that is to say, what seemed very dissonant to past generations sounds only mildly so to our ears; (2) in a piece of music which bristles with dissonances, imperfect consonances may serve as a resolution. In the two examples which follow, the dissonances are so prominent that even usually "unstable" chords, a seventh chord and an inverted triad, give the illusion of a harmonic resolution and of comparative peace.

168. TRISTAN UND ISOLDE (Erster Aufzug)
Richard Wagner (1813–1883)

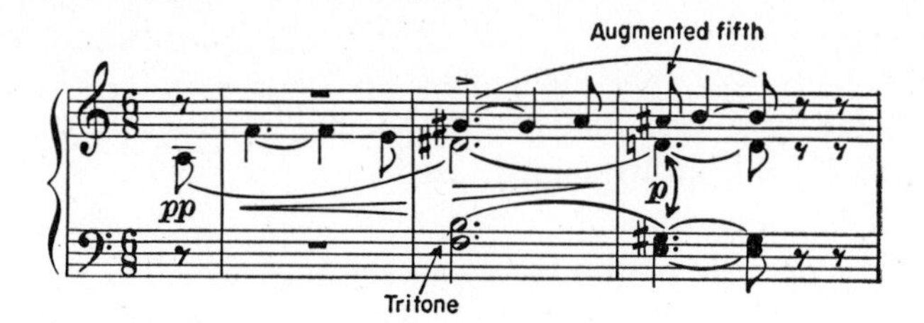

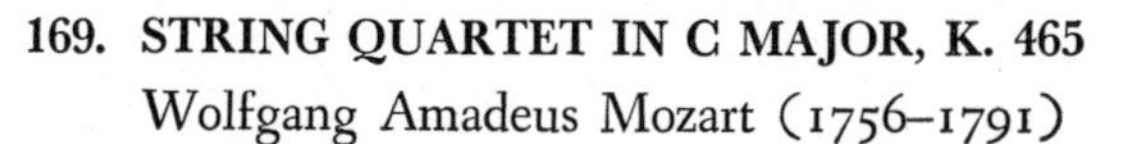
169. STRING QUARTET IN C MAJOR, K. 465
Wolfgang Amadeus Mozart (1756–1791)

Observe in both examples: (1) the chromatic line of the melodies; (2) the contrary motion in the two upper melodies; (3) the tritone between two voices; (4) the underlining of metric accents. In addition (Fig. 169): (5) the crescendo toward the resolution; (6) the imitation in the three upper voices. The resolutions in these examples seem satisfactory although they are in themselves unstable chords. We see, then, that the terms "consonance" and "dissonance" are not absolute, but relative. Just as in a blue sky the smallest white cloud will be noticeable, so the smallest bit of blue will assume significance in a gray, cloudy sky.

Chord-Progression

It should be clear from the foregoing that some of the important considerations for a composer are what harmonies to use for a given melody—or, how to arrange simultaneous melodies vertically. Further problems are: where to underline a point or section of a melody, where to plan harmonic tension and relaxation, in what manner and for what duration of time to prepare and dissolve dissonances. Furthermore, we have seen how composers, for reasons of characterization, imitation among voices, dramatic impact, and for other purposes which can be observed if not explained, used various dissonances. These are frequently obtained through "extra" tones which do not belong to the original key or scale of the piece, an instance which is indicated by the use of *accidentals* (sharps and flats occurring before individual notes).

Let us now, for simplicity's sake, try to "harmonize" a simple melodic fragment, using only chords which belong to its scale. An experiment of this kind may give us an inkling of the problems of "what chords to choose and where to put them."

170.

The key is D, and the mode, major. Placing triads under each tone of the melody would, because this particular tune descends stepwise, produce a row of triads on each degree of the D major scale. Because the melody may be root, third, or fifth in each chord, we have three sets of chords to select from in this kind of harmonization. We shall designate the chords by using Roman numerals according to the step of the scale on which they are erected.

171.

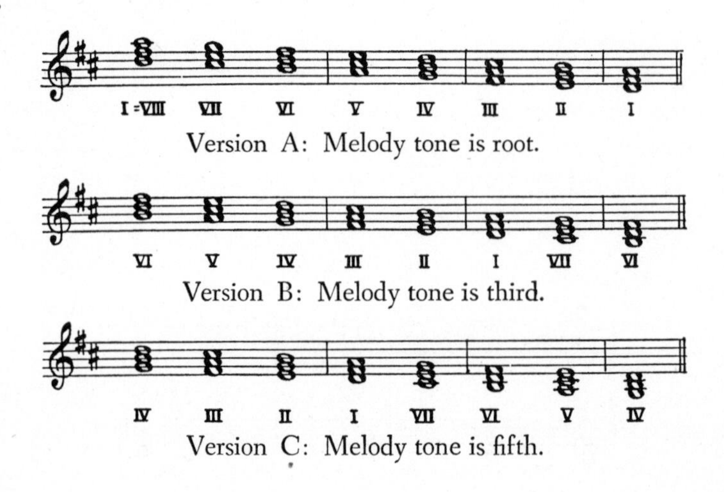

Versions B and C we can throw out immediately because they end on VI and IV instead of on the tonic chord (I), as should be required of a harmony for a tune in D major. Version A ends in the tonic triad, but has—like the other versions—all four voices going parallel, and, consequently, moving in consecutive fifths and octaves, which are to be avoided in good voice leading. Setting the accompanying voices in contrary motion to the melody will help somewhat. In order to do this throughout, however, we will have to use inversions of chords in several cases. This is especially disturbing in the final triad, which ought to be more stable.

172.

However, if we insist on having the root of the final chord in the bass, we will have to change the last chord and have thus again parallel octaves and fifths leading into it. Even if we let this go for a moment, the harmonies still seem unconvincing and anything but helpful to the melody. Here are some reasons: (1) There is a strong unresolved dissonance producing a harmonic accent on the second note of the tune, i.e., *between* metric accents. (2) There are two minor chords immediately before the final chord, which ought to be more convincingly introduced. Worst of all, (3) the melody, which is lively anyway, changes its chords with each tone. If we consult the melody and ask ourselves which places invite support, we might say: the beginning and end, the long note, and the metric accents. Following this suggestion and going (harmonically speaking) to the other extreme, to use as few kinds of chords as possible, we might write the following:

173.

We have in this case considered the melody as a single broken chord with a few inserted passing notes. The result is dull, because there is no harmony, only a single chord. We should at least strengthen the finality of the last tone by preceding it with the chord of the dominant.

174.

If we want to have a little more harmonic variety and lively help in getting away from the long note in the second measure, also in order to avoid bringing the tonic chord in root position before the end, we could insert a chord II in first and I in second inversion.

175.

Finally, distributing the tones better within the piano range, we might prefer to play our harmonization in the following manner:

176.

It will be noticed that even in such an elementary attempt of harmonization as we have just made, various factors had to be considered, such as frequency of harmonic changes, meter, melodic accents, voice leading, beginning and ending, etc. The interrelationship of vertical and horizontal aspects in harmony may be clearly recognized if we analyze our procedure in harmonizing: first, we have given a harmonic interpretation to certain groups of tones of our melody; and secondly, we have brought these chords into an effective and logical horizontal progression, into a pattern of harmony. The phases of this process are so intimately dependent upon each other that composers frequently have had to change harmonies for the sake of the melody, or vice versa. In addition, stylistic and idiomatic considerations will enter. Our harmonization would appear with added "frills," extra tones, broken chords, scale runs, dynamics, etc., according to the historical period and the personal handwriting of its composer. Furthermore, the same harmonies would be "set" differently according to the medium for which they were planned: piano, harpsichord, strings, wood winds, brass, voices. If all these considerations present problems even in a short fragment of a few measures, you can imagine how they are multiplied a thousand times in a symphony.

Cadences

The propelling and retarding effect of harmony which we had observed in progressions containing dissonances and consonances exists to a similar degree between various consonant chords. The harmonic closing formulas, called *cadences* (from *cadere* = to fall) offer a good example. Experience with harmony duing the last few centuries has shown that, to our tradition-bound ears at least, a piece or a section of it can best be ended by the chord on the first degree of its scale in root position. As we have just seen ourselves, in order to make this ending "stick," to heighten the effect of finality, the tonic chord is best preceded by the dominant chord. In this combination the gravity pull which the tonic exerts upon the dominant, as we observed even in unaccompanied melodies, is underlined, strengthened, by the "chords of nature," the triads of the respective steps of the fundamental scale.

1. This kind of cadence, known by sound if not by name to every human being, is called an *authentic* cadence.

177.

2. If we stop a melody on the dominant chord, we speak of a *half cadence*. As the term indicates, the effect is that of a half-finished, incomplete sentence, or that of a question which needs to be answered.

178.

3. Another, the *plagal cadence*, consists of the tonic triad preceded by the subdominant triad.

179.

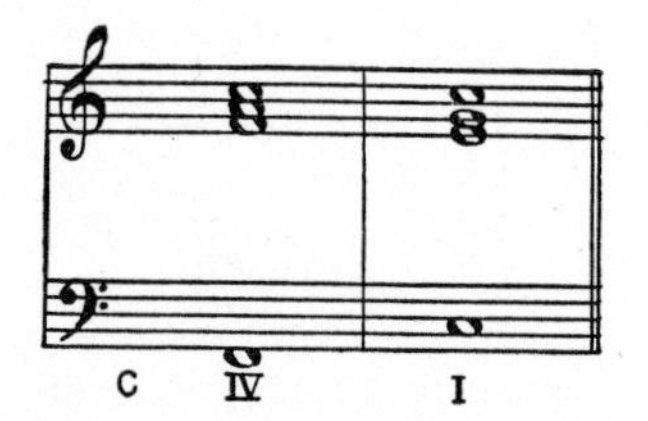

4. Frequently, both the subdominant and the dominant triads are used to indicate the ending of a section or piece.

180.

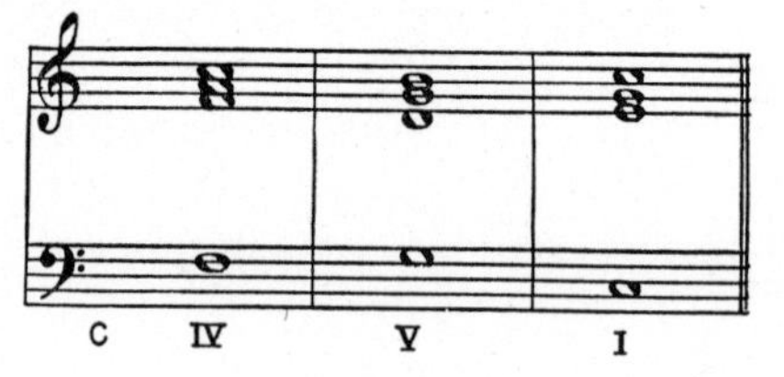

5. Or the dominant triad is expanded into the ubiquitous dominant seventh chord:

181.

6. A *deceptive cadence* "fools" the listener. Instead of the tonic chord which is expected after the dominant chord, the composer sets another chord which leads on rather than finishes the musical discourse.

182. SYMPHONY NO. 5 IN C MINOR, OP. 67 (End of third movement)

Ludwig van Beethoven (1770–1827)

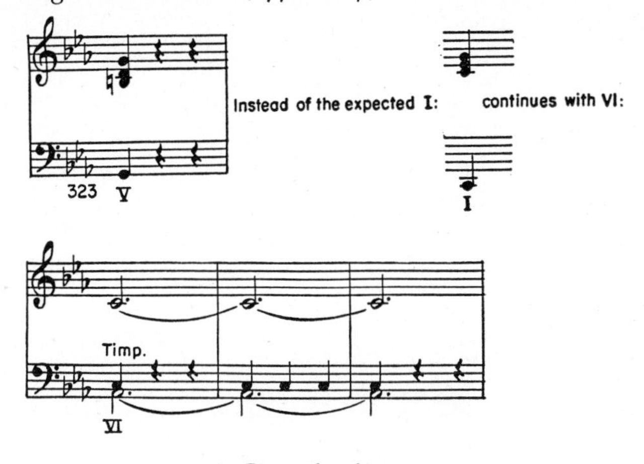

Conclusions

When an amateur pianist plays an accompaniment by ear, he will in most cases use no more than three chords: the tonic, subdominant, and the dominant triad or seventh chord. Whenever he improvises he will glide aimlessly from one chord to another. The listener will soon be bored and lose interest. A composer, on the other hand, will use each tiny fragment of his musical building material in a variety of well-calculated ways. The same idea will be presented in such profusion of artistic detail that the music expands in time and in depth, and the listener may be lost in the complexities of an extended composition. Let us mention three extreme cases: (1) A single tone is capable of different harmonic interpretations.

183. DON GIOVANNI (Act II, Scene 3)

Wolfgang Amadeus Mozart (1756–1791)

(2) A single chord may be subjected to endless melodic interpretations, as in the Prelude to Wagner's *Das Rheingold,* where the E♭-major chord prevails throughout the entire prelude. The static harmonic effect which this has is counteracted by melodic or decorative lines; the interest (i.e., motion) lies solely in the melodic aspect. There is, in this case, no harmony, no harmonic motion possible, inasmuch as only a single chord appears. Perhaps Wagner wanted to describe how the Rhine daughters circle the Rheingold constantly, without "getting anywhere."[5] (3) The piece may consist entirely of harmonic motion, as in the famous First Prelude of the *Well-tempered Clavier* by Bach.

184. THE WELL-TEMPERED CLAVIER, BOOK I (Prelude No. 1)

Johann Sebastian Bach (1685–1750)

The interest here lies entirely in the harmonic progression of broken chords. (This fact, that there is no "melody" present, has produced the "improved" version of Gounod, who added a melody, "Ave Maria" to it—a barbarism which may be compared to providing a hat for the "Venus of Milo.")

If we remember that in most music a combination of the three above-mentioned composing procedures will be found, it becomes clear that the listener must be able to switch from the horizontal preoccupation to a vertical one, and frequently to a combination of both. Especially in the case of dissonances he has to be aware of where they came from and where they tend to go. Because added voices give perspective to a single line, and because consonances and dissonances pull together and push forward musical events, we can conclude even at this point that these concentrating and expanding forces of harmony are some of the most important form-giving elements in music.

[5] Wagner's statement that he dreamed of his Rheingold triad hardly offers a conclusive explanation.

Exercises in the Recognition of Cadences

A good way to become better aware of chord progressions is to concentrate for a while on cadences. Because the various kinds of cadences play in music a role which might be compared to the importance of punctuation in literature and poetry, we will develop a keener sense for the structure and the meaning of music if we gradually learn to recognize cadences, even when they are embellished and seemingly hidden. It is advisable to select for this kind of study at first those sections of music which use the major mode and which are free of extra (chromatic) tones.

Next, excerpts in the minor mode may be chosen, as long as they include only those chromatic tones which convert an unaltered minor scale into its melodic or harmonic versions.

Our procedure might be as follows:

1. Choose a short excerpt from a four-part song or hymn, then one from a simple piano piece, and finally a section from a Schubert Lied ("Art-song").
2. Determine the tonic and the mode of the particular excerpt by analyzing its melody (p. 54).
3. Recognize cadences while listening, and mark them in the score.
4. Specify the kind of cadences used and the position (root position or inversions) in which the chords appear.

185. TRURO

Charles Burney (written 1789)

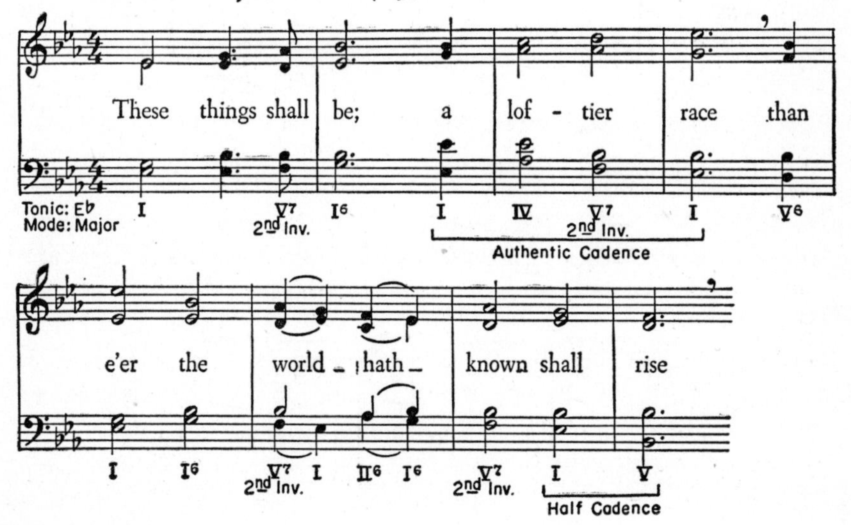

It is recommended that the reader analyze the excerpts which follow in the manner of the above example.

186. PIANO SONATA IN C MAJOR

Joseph Haydn (1732–1809)

187. SICILIENNE, OP. 68, NO. 11 (Middle section)

Robert Schumann (1810–1856)

188. CRADLE SONG, OP. 98, NO. 2

Franz Schubert (1797–1828)

Suggestions for Listening

Bach — *Passion according to St. Matthew*
Well-tempered Clavier, Book I, No. 1

Ballantine — *Variations on "Mary Had a Little Lamb"* (in the styles of famous composers)

Bartok — Violin Sonata No. 2

Beethoven — Symphony No. 5 in C Minor, Op. 67
Violin Concerto in D Major, Op. 61

Examples of Arabian music

Examples of Gymel

Mozart — *Don Giovanni*
String Quartet in C Major, K. 465

Piano pieces by Haydn, Mozart, and D. Scarlatti

Songs by Schumann and Schubert

Wagner — *Das Rheingold* (Prelude)
Tristan und Isolde, Act I

9

Tonality

Melodic and Harmonic Cadences

WE SAY that a melody is written *in the key of C* when it uses the tone C as central tone, or tonic, and consequently G as dominant and F as subdominant. We use the term *tonality* in order to express the importance which the tonic attains during the progress of a piece of music, and the gravitational pull which is exerted through the tonic on the dominant and subdominant. One could say that the two words *key* and *tonality* are synonymous for all practical purposes, were it not for the fact that the former is commonly used in a narrower sense than the latter. In saying that a piece is in the key of C, we usually imply no more than that it is built with the material of the C scale (major or minor). On the other hand, when we speak of the *tonality* of a piece, we stress the functions of the most important segments of its scale and especially the way they combine in harmony.

An unaccompanied melody, in order to give the impression of a particular tonality, needs to touch the tonic and dominant at least, and then will have to end on the tonic. As soon, however, as additional voices—chords—are added, the melody has only to agree with one of the three tones which constitute a tonic or dominant triad. If we think of our graphic picture, one or more melodies moving in space, one could say that in polyphony and especially in homophony a melody becomes less earthbound, is allowed to float freer in space inasmuch as the chords anchor it firmly to its tonality.

The fact that tonality can be better expressed, that is, more clearly and promptly, by harmony than by melody may be shown by comparing the results of the horizontal and the vertical approach to a cadence. We have said that a melody will suggest a certain key or tonality if it contains the tonic, the dominant, and again the tonic.

A still better way would be to include the subdominant,

or to let the melody rise an octave and then fall toward the tonic by way of the dominant.

It is true that all the last three examples may imply natural chords, i.e., major triads, based upon their melodic steps, especially if these melodic progressions are metrically and dynamically reinforced; yet they could also belong to entirely different chords, within the tonality which we assumed or even within other tonalities. In the key of C, the tone C, for example, could occur as a member (root, third, or fifth) of the triads I, IV, and VI; C could also be a part of several chords in the tonalities of G, F, B♭, etc. In order to express one tonality unmistakably in an unaccompanied melody, we would have to bring *all* tones of the scale, preferably in succession and up and down, or at least downward, inasmuch as that would emphasize the "fall" (cadence) toward the tonic:

Another way of expressing a tonality through melody is the use of broken chords which are ordered in a cadential progression.

189.

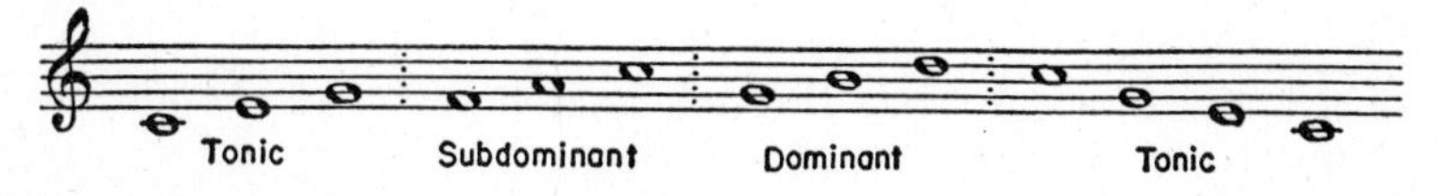

From these "melodic" cadences let us now return to harmonic procedures and, for reasons of comparison, let us attempt to express the entire tonal material of a scale in triads. We will then see that we need only three chords—three successive combined sounds—where our scale melody needed eight successive tones.

190.

If we combine the dominant seventh chord with the tonic triad, we represent the entire scale, with the exception of its sixth step, in two chords.

191.

No wonder, then, that music, melody as well as harmony, dared to employ "extra" chromatic tones and altered chords once it was found that the basic tonality could be expressed so promptly and clearly in the few chords of a cadence.

Modality and Tonality

We have seen that the Greek and ecclesiastical modes came into being through the cataloguing of certain melodic progressions, and that when harmony was invented, only two modes, our major and minor, remained in general use because they alone could be expressed in characteristic *harmonic* fashion. Even so, from the seventeenth century until about 1900, composers were so preoccupied with chord progressions, with experiments of tonality, that melodic progressions, "modal" thinking, retired still more into the background. The filling out of a broad musical space through bold harmonies, the observing and directing of the behavior of vertical masses of sound, superseded the former art of proceeding in space along finely chiseled and carefully interrelated melodic lines. Observing a few details should make this clear. In analyzing the triads erected above major and minor scales, we found that in the major mode, I, IV, V are major chords and II, III, VI are minor:

192.

In the unaltered minor mode, on the other hand, I, IV, V are minor chords and III, VI, VII are major. The "dissonant" diminished triad appears on the seventh degree in major and on the second step of the minor scale.

193.

I Minor — II Diminished — III Major — IV Minor — V Minor — VI Major — VII Major

In other words, the crucial difference between the major and minor modes occurs in the three strategic triads: the tonic, subdominant, and dominant chords. The other chords are minor in the major mode and major in the minor mode. The diminished chord is found one step below the tonic in the major, and one step above the tonic in the minor mode:

194.

Tonic (major) — Diminished — Tonic (minor) — Diminished

One might assume that music would have preserved these modal differences incorporated in the cadences I, IV, V, I of the natural major and minor keys. However, as we have seen (p. 63), even the difference between these two remaining modes diminished in time. The *harmonic* minor scale was introduced, "sharpening" the seventh tone of the minor scale

195.

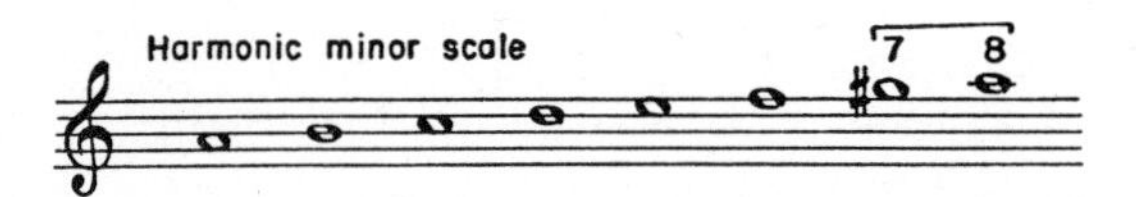

and thus making the dominant triad a *major* chord in both modes.

Dominant of A Minor *and* A Major

A further obscuring of the dividing line between major and minor occurs through the old tradition, which remained alive from the sixteenth to the eighteenth century, of finishing a piece in the minor mode with a major triad on the tonic, as happens frequently in the music of Purcell, Bach, and many later composers.[1] Finally, if we add that chromatic changes produce melodies which may be in part major, minor, Lydian, pentatonic, chromatic, etc., we may readily understand how modes lost their importance when harmony developed. This fact may serve as another explanation for our unfamiliarity with old music—which employs modes exclusively. It may also underline once more our previous statement that major or minor modes do not as such represent specific characteristic "moods."

Although many modes have disappeared, we should nevertheless remember that they also have been revived by composers from time to time (see p. 58). Frequently, these ancient modes are hidden; they occur within pieces called, for instance, F major or A minor in spite of the fact that, correctly labeled, they would be "in the Lydian mode and in the tonality of F," etc.

Modulation

Let us assume that a composer has exploited various modes and chord progressions and various chromatic melodic and harmonic alterations within one tonality. Would not the next step in an era concerned with harmony be a change of tonality within a given piece of music?

By such a procedure, a piece could be extended from a harmonic skeleton of, for example, six chords in A minor—I, V, III, VI, V, I—to: six chords in A minor, four in E major, and six more in A minor. When this takes place, we speak of a *modulation,* i.e., the piece *modulates* from A minor to E major and back to A minor. In doing this the composer changes the gravitational level or the perspective, if you will, from one tonic to another. To accomplish this, a basic tonality has to be established first, then a convincing transition to a new one has to be found, and finally a safe and clear return must be made to the initial key. We know already that the best way to establish a certain tonality is a cadence, a certain progression of chords. Next, in order to produce a smooth transition, a chord capable of an ambiguous harmonic inter-

[1] The major third in these cases is called the "Picardy third."

pretation is needed. The triad C–E–G, for example, may belong to the tonalities of C, F, or G major or to A, E, or F minor. We may use such a chord as a pivot, as a turning point at which one tonality changes into another. As shown in Figure 196, the C-major triad which is I in C major may be reassessed as V in F major, IV in G major, III in A minor, and so forth: [2]

196.

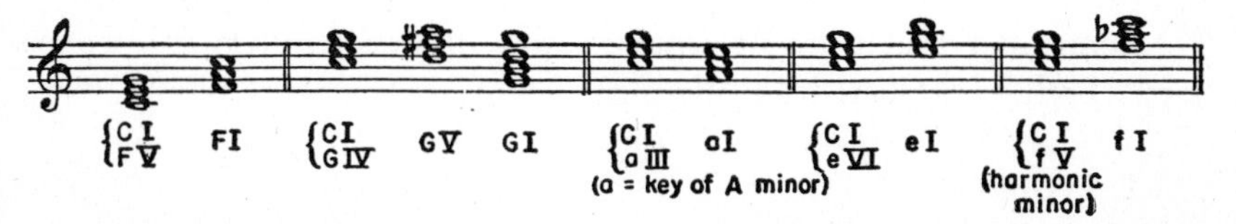

We may best study the endless possibilities inherent in a procedure of this kind by investigating the relationship of all tonalities available to us.

The Relationship of Tonalities

In starting the pattern of the major mode on tones other than C, we found it necessary to introduce "extra" half steps, indicated by sharps and flats and not belonging to the natural major scale (i.e., white keys on the piano keyboard). In erecting a major scale upon the tone G, for example, we were able to use tones 5 to 8 of the C-major scale as 1 to 4 in G major. To make the remaining tones, 5 to 8 of G major, agree with the pattern of "half steps between 7 and 8" we had to adjust the tones by playing and writing F-sharp instead of F-natural.

197.

Similarly, in order to construct a major scale on F, we found the first part of the C-major scale in order. Here, the first part of the F-major scale needed adjustment—we had to substitute B-flat for B-natural:

[2] The requirements of proper "voice leading" are here ignored for reasons of clarity.

198.

Remember that a major scale consists of two tetrachords (see p. 95), both constructed in identical patterns: namely, whole step, whole step, half step—and that these two tetrachords are separated by a whole step:

199.

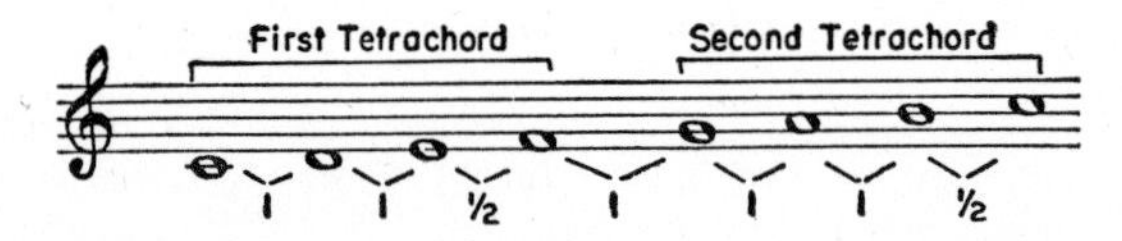

The G-major scale, then, uses as its own first tetrachord the tones which constitute the second tetrachord in C major. The scale of F major, starting five tones (i.e., a fifth) below C, uses as its own second tetrachord the tones which are the first tetrachord in C major:

200.

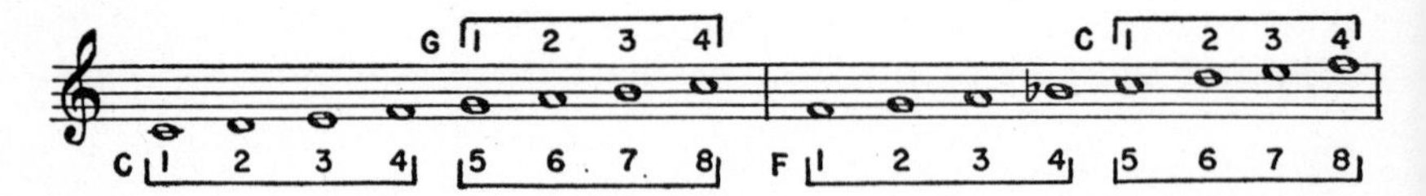

In other words, scales which are a *perfect* fifth apart have one tetrachord in common. Proceding upward in perfect fifths from C, we find that the leading tone of each consecutive scale needs adjustment—that another sharp has to be added for each new scale. Going downward from C, we find, on the contrary, that the leading tones are correct, but that, instead, the fourth degree of each scale needs adjustment through cumulative flats.

In progressing thus in fifths above and below the tone C for the purpose of constructing new scales we must adhere to two principles:

1. To proceed in the interval of a *perfect* fifth (e.g., F-*sharp* above B, and B-*flat* below F).

2. To retain all sharps or flats which have to be inserted while moving away from C (e.g., A major retains the F-sharp and C-sharp of the two preceding keys, G and D Major).

Tonality and Key Signatures

We could now decide at a glance, by memorizing the key signatures, which tonality a given piece has, were it not for the minor modes. We remember that the unaltered minor scale, that is, the minor scale without any sharps or flats, is based on A. Half steps between tones 2 and 3 and between 5 and 6 of a scale occur when we start on A, that is, let the natural half steps (B–C and E–F) come at the scale degrees demanded by the minor pattern.

We will find the same conditions fulfilled at a perfect fifth above and below A, only if we insert one sharp or one flat, respectively.

201.

The minor scales, then, progress likewise by fifths—accumulating one sharp or flat with each digression from A—exactly as the major scales do in moving away from C. Let us now order all major and minor scales according to the number of sharps or flats which occur in their key-signatures:

Signature	Major Scales	Minor Scales
6♭	G♭	E♭
5♭	D♭	B♭
4♭	A♭	F
3♭	E♭	C
2♭	B♭	G
1♭	F	D
No ♯ or ♭	C	A
1♯	G	E
2♯	D	B
3♯	A	F♯
4♯	E	C♯
5♯	B	G♯
6♯	F♯	D♯

We see that the tonality of A requires three sharps for the major mode but neither a sharp nor a flat for the minor mode. A simple rule by which to remember *relative* major and minor keys, i.e., keys with identical key signatures but (naturally) of varying tonalities, is: major and minor keys with the same key signature are a minor third apart. For example, in our table above, A minor occurs opposite C major, i.e., the interval of a minor third separates the key notes of those major and minor scales which have identical key signatures; the minor key column is a minor third distant from the major key column.

Co-ordinating identical tonalities we have:

202.

	2♭	1♭	No ♯ or ♭	1♯	2♯	3♯	4♯
Major:	B♭	F	**C**	G	D	A	E
Minor:	b♭	f	c	g	d	**a**	e
	5♭	4♭	3♭	2♭	1♭	No ♭ or ♯	1♯

Let us suppose now that we see three sharps in the key signature of a piece:

How are we to tell whether it is in A major or in F♯ minor?

203. MAZURKA, OP. 6, NO. 1

Frederic Chopin (1810–1849)

The easiest way to find the answer is to look for the final chord or interval which will always bring the tonic, as root, in the bass.

204.

Another way is to look for additional accidentals which the melodic and harmonic versions of the minor mode would require. In our natural A minor the following temporary changes are necessary to convert it into a melodic or harmonic minor scale.

205.

Harmonic A Minor Scale Melodic A Minor Scale

According to this pattern, the melodic version of F♯ minor would require, going up:

and going down:

and the harmonic minor scale on F♯ would necessitate one extra sharp besides the three indicated in the key signature:

It should be remembered that the accidentals required by melodic or harmonic versions occur as true accidentals from case to case, and not as part of the key signature. Should these extra accidentals, then, occur frequently in our piece, in addition to the key signature of three sharps, we may assume that the mode is minor and the tonality, F sharp.

In music for instruments, modulations were at first used sparingly by composers; they did not move too far away from the natural scales. Tonalities which require more than three sharps or flats occur rarely in the instrumental music of the seventeenth century. The reasons for this are not only the infancy of harmonic thinking but also difficulties in tuning keyboard instruments. Only when the system of *well-tempered* tuning came into general use did it become possible to move in and out of any tonality based on the twelve semitones of our modern chromatic scale.

Well-Tempered Tuning

When Pythagoras constructed a scale and determined mathematically the relationships of various tones, he took one single string, one tone, as the basis for his experiments. Similarly, when Helmholtz presented his theory of frequencies as apparent in the row of partials, one single tone, the fundamental, served as point of departure. The higher octave of the tone C (i.e., C′) has a frequency twice that of C; the frequency ratio is 2 : 1. The tone G, a perfect fifth above C, has the frequency ratio 3 : 2, or 1.5 times the frequency of C.

With a slight exaggeration, we may say that the *tonality* of C, as expressed in the harmonics above C, served as the point of reference in these calculations of pitch. As soon now as we change the "tonality," i.e., the fundamental, the relationships between tones will change also. When the same tone has to assume various functions, i.e., to be tonic, fifth, third, leading tone, its exact pitch varies with each function. In simple terms, we can tune a piano in exact octaves or in exact fifths—never so that both fifths and octaves are pure. Let us fix the frequency of a fundamental tone, C, as 1 and proceed upward in seven octave progressions:

Tone	C	C′	C″	C‴	C^4	C^5	C^6	C^7
Frequency	1	2	4	8	16	32	64	128
Number of Octave Steps	0	1	2	3	4	5	6	7

The seventh C, being seven octaves above the fundamental C, would then have a frequency of 128.

A similar tone (B♯) would be reached by 12 progressions in the interval of the perfect fifth.

Tone	C	G	D′	A′	E″	B″	F♯‴	C♯^{4}	G♯^{4}	D♯^{5}	A♯^{5}	E♯^{6}	B♯^{6}
Number of Steps in Perfect Fifths	0	1	2	3	4	5	6	7	8	9	10	11	12

Because the frequency ratio of a fifth is 3 : 2, the upper tone will have 1.5 times the frequency of the lower tone. Each step of a fifth, therefore, increases the frequency by a factor of 1.5. Inasmuch as there are twelve steps, the final B♯ has a frequency of $(1.5)^{12}$ or 129.75. Although we all know that B♯ and C have the same key on the piano, their pitch is not really the same if we follow Pythagoras. In one case the function of the tone (C) is the octave relationship to a lower fundamental C; in the other case (B♯) we have a 3 : 2 (third to second harmonic) relationship to a lower fundamental tone E♯. If we wanted to tune our instrument according to the system of Pythagoras, we would have to use one frequency whenever a tone is tonic, and another when it is the dominant.

The difference in actual pitch in our above example amounts to a little less than a quarter of a half step. This inaccuracy, when occurring repeatedly, seems unbearable to human ears. We must remember that, within the range of one octave, the major scale contains 4 fifths, 4 perfect fourths, 3 major thirds, 5 major seconds, and 2 minor seconds. If all these intervals were given their proper mathematical relationship, as indicated in the row of partials, we would need a piano keyboard about four times as long as the one we are used to. Instead of the twelve tones within one octave, we would need forty to fifty subdivisions.[3]

While this problem, aside from keyboard considerations, has vexed musicians and theorists since Pythagoras, and although several methods of solving were used, e.g., the "mean-tone system" of tuning—the

[3] Cf. *Harvard Dictionary of Music*, articles on Arcicembalo (p. 47) and Enharmonic (p. 244); also Sir James Hopwood Jeans, *Science and Music* (New York, 1937), p. 190.

situation became really impossible when harmony in the seventeenth century began to exploit various harmonic interpretations of single tones and the many-sided relationships of tonalities.

The solution, well-tempered tuning or *equal temperament,* came when musicians in the seventeenth century began to tune in pure octaves and compromised with regard to other intervals, dividing the difference among thirds, fourths, etc., and making every whole step consist of two equal halfsteps. Since then tonalities have been related in a workable man-made system as against the infinite variety contained in the laws of nature. (We shall discuss this problem further in Chapter 10.)

Exercises in the Perception and Analysis of Modulation

Because a modulation is commonly confirmed by a cadence in the new tonality, we will do well to concentrate once more on cadences. This time, however, we should choose excerpts which do employ chromatic tones (accidentals) and therefore indicate through their very notation that modulations occur. Our previous studies have taught us to recognize in reading and listening the chord progression V–I or similar cadences. If we now will learn to determine the changing tonalities which these cadences confirm, we will advance considerably toward a more sensitive awareness of modulations. Again it must be said that progress in this direction is almost impossible without a reading knowledge of music. As so often happens, the eye and brain will have to help our sense of hearing until we develop an aural imagination and perception which approximate those of the composer.

The 389 *Chorales* by J. S. Bach furnish excellent material for the study of modulations. The *fermata* 𝄐, (indicating a "hold"), which occurs regularly as a textual and musical punctuation mark in these chorales, always designates a cadence, and frequently a modulation. If we analyze each chord which carries a fermata and analyze and hear it as the final link of a cadence, we will be able to recognize the modulatory scheme of an entire chorale. It is hoped that the reader may add many excerpts of his own choosing to the example which follows (Fig. 206):

206. NUN DANKET ALLE GOTT (Chorale No. 257)

Johann Sebastian Bach (1685–1750) (after Johann Crüger)

Scheme of modulation in this piece: A Major—E major—B minor—A major

Suggestions for Listening

Bach	Concerto for 2 Violins in D Minor
	Any of the 389 *Chorales*
	Inventions
Brahms	Symphony No. 1 in C Minor, Op. 68
	Symphony No. 4 in E Minor, Op. 98
Chopin	Mazurkas: Op. 6, No. 1, and Op. 24, No. 2
Franck, C.	Symphony in D Minor
Händel	*Messiah*
Modal compositions:	
Berlioz	*Damnation of Faust,* "Invocation à la Nature" (Part 4, Scene XVI)
Debussy	*"La Damoiselle élue,"* "La Martyre de Saint-Sébastien"
Gounod	*Faust* (Final chorus)
Liszt	*Christus*
Moussorgsky	Boris Godunov, "Polacca" (Act III, Scene 2)
	"Chants et Danses de la Mort"
Wagner	"Funeral March" (Titurel's) in *Parsifal* (Act III)
Mozart	*The Marriage of Figaro*
Purcell	Sonatas for 2 Violins and Continuo
Ravel	Duo for Violin and Viola
Schubert	"The Linden Tree"
Schumann	Songs
Sibelius	Symphony No. 2 in D Major, Op. 43

10

Tonality
(*Continued*)

The Circle of Fifths

NO BETTER illustration for the significance of equal temperament in music can be found than the two mathematical figures of a spiral and a circle. We have seen that moving in perfect fifths upward and downward from C will give us with each step the number of sharps or flats needed in the key signatures of various major scales. Let us now indicate the progressions in form of a spiral. If we move too far away from C the names of tones, e.g., F𝄪 (F double-sharp, or two halfsteps above F) and B𝄫 (B double-flat), and the high number of sharps and flats needed in the key signatures give a good description of the endless complexities to be encountered in following the path of natural tones without knowing when to call a halt.

We mentioned earlier that the twelfth progression upward from C in distances of perfect fifths produces a tone, B-sharp, which is slightly higher than the C reached in seven octave progressions. Because this difference in frequencies bothered Pythagoras, it is called the *Pythagorean comma.* The same discrepancy occurs 12 fifths below C, at D double-flat.

What equal temperament did was to make each fifth slightly smaller (for the amount of $\frac{1}{12}$ the Pythagorean comma) so that after twelve steps away from C in "smaller" fifths, the comma disappeared. In other words, B♯ and D𝄫 obtained the same frequencies as the C seven octaves above and below the starting point, respectively. The spiral became a circle, indicating the coincidence of fifth and octave progressions whenever one complete cycle is completed.

207. THE SPIRAL OF NATURAL (UNTEMPERED) FIFTHS

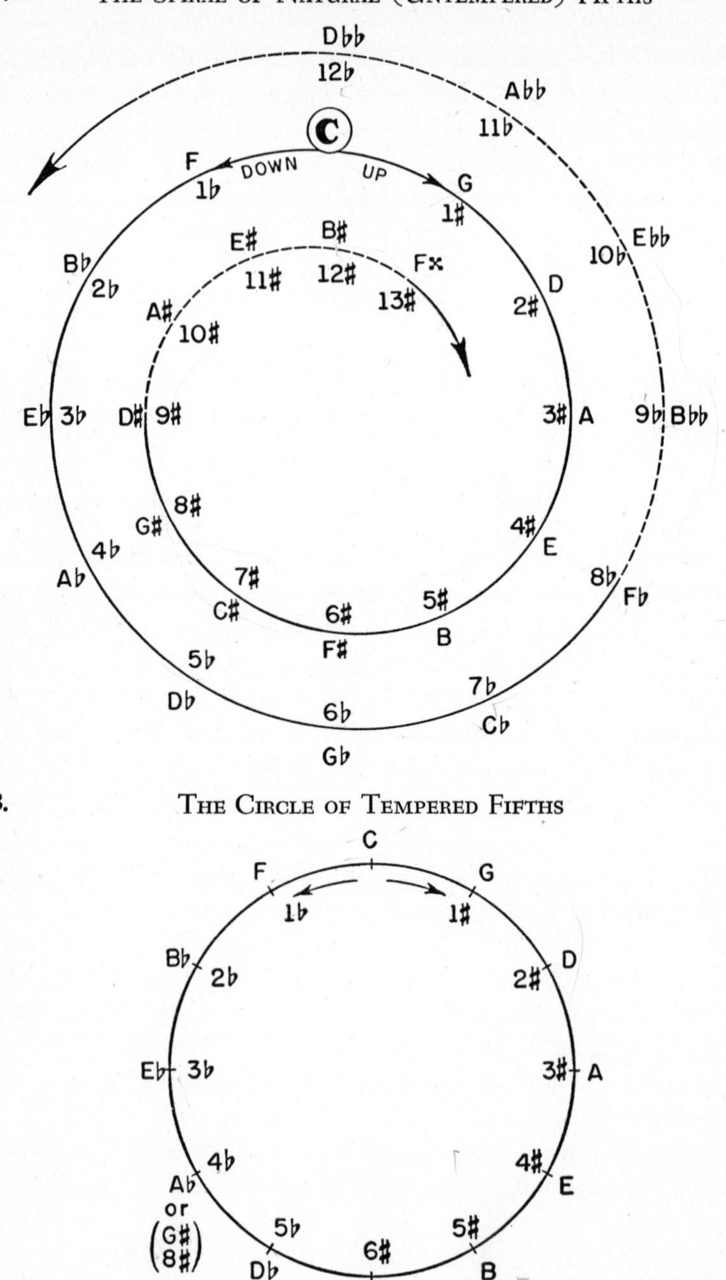

208. THE CIRCLE OF TEMPERED FIFTHS

C
F 1♭
G 1♯
B♭ 2♭
D 2♯
E♭ 3♭
3♯ A
4♭ A♭ or (G♯ 8♯)
4♯ E
5♭ D♭ or (C♯ 7♯)
5♯ B or (C♭ 7♭)
6♯ F♯ or (G♭ 6♭)

While each tone on the circle may receive two names (e.g., G♭ or F♯), while each major scale may be written in sharps or flats, simplicity and common sense recommend that no more than six or seven accidentals should appear in the "spelling" of a scale. As long as G♯ and A♭ sound alike on our keyboard instruments, we might as well substitute A♭ major with four flats for G♯ major with eight sharps (one of these being a double sharp).

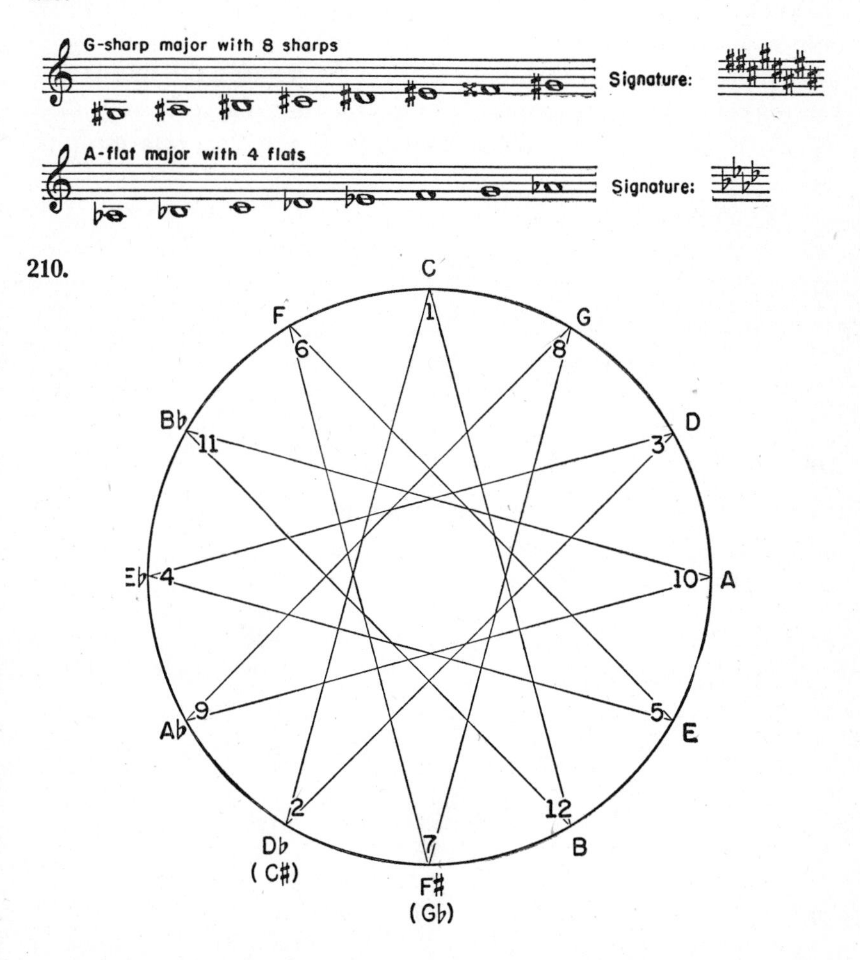

A closer observation of the circle of fifths discloses that all twelve chromatic tones of our scale are represented; connecting each tone with its chromatically higher neighbor produces a twelve-pronged star. In tracing the lines which connect the twelve points we follow the course of a sort of chromatic scale which is inflated, so to speak.

In moving clockwise from C to C♯ in our circle, we make seven equal steps. Continuing from C♯ to D, we continue another seven steps, and so forth. In other words, the semitones are equidistant. In order to understand that these relationships between tones of the circle of fifths are always stable, regardless of octave range, we need only to remember that the natural octave (2 : 1) remains unchanged in equal temperament. That is to say, each interval found on the circle can be compressed or expanded for as many octaves as desired without losing its basic proportional relationship. In terms of frequencies, this means that the multiplication of a frequency by powers of 2 (2, 4, 8, or $\frac{1}{2}$, $\frac{1}{4}$, $\frac{1}{8}$, etc.) transposes the tone of that frequency 1, 2, 3, etc., octaves up or down.

211.

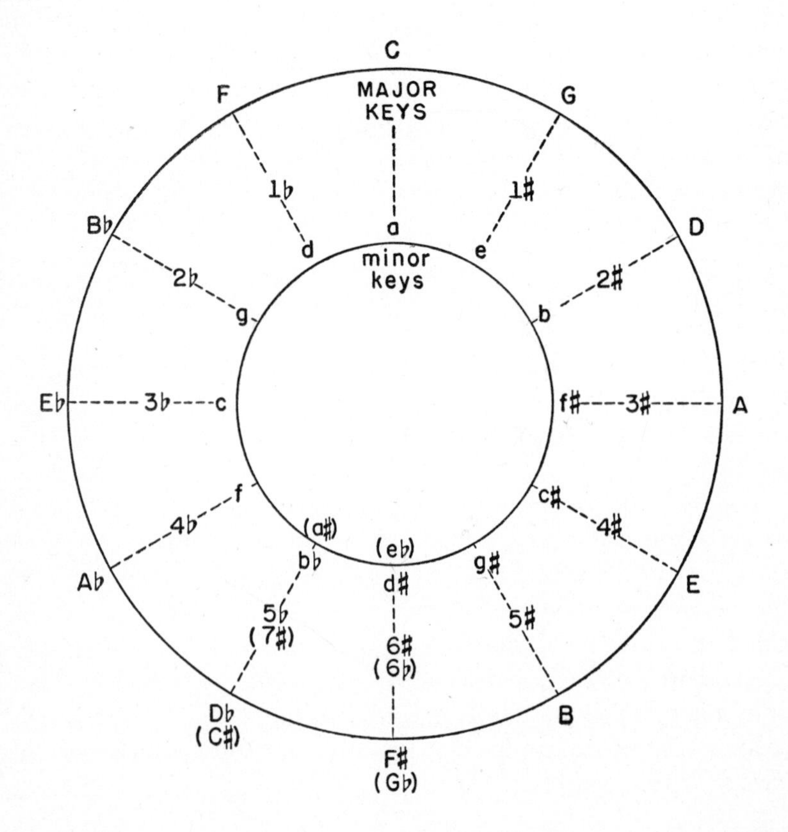

The circle of fifths also tells us the relative minor scales if we start on A instead of C as the zero or noon hour, i.e., the key tone of the natural minor scale without any sharps or flats. We see that major and minor modes of the same tonality are a quarter turn apart on the circle.

Combining major and minor scales in one diagram, we obtain two circles, the inner band carrying tones a minor third below the tones of the outer ring. Relative major and minor keys appear thus at the same "steps" of the circle. Here, major and minor modes are ordered according to identical key signatures. The tonalities of the two circles do not coincide. (See Fig. 211.)

The conception of equal temperament and the subsequent invention of the well-tempered tuning of keyboard instruments made it possible to compose music in all major and minor keys contained in the chromatically divided octave. While heretofore only a few major and minor scales had been in tune on organs, harpsichords, and clavichords, and the remaining scales had been out of tune, all tonalities now became equally inaccurate, and thus, equally playable. While previously only the upper half of each circle of fifths had been feasible for instruments of constant pitch, the compromise between true pitch and tonal material available now made it possible for composers to utilize the tonalities of the complete major and minor circles. The greatest monument to this ingenious solution of a problem posed by the nature of tones was erected by J. S. Bach in his *Well-tempered Clavier* (clavier = keyboard). In this work Bach wrote two preludes and fugues in every major and minor key of the circle of fifths, i.e., twenty-four major plus twenty-four minor preludes and fugues.

Let us now, with the help of the circle of fifths, consider once more the most important change which was brought to music through equal temperament: the freedom to modulate from any one to any other tonality.

The major keys nearest to C major, namely F major and G major, use scales each of which differs only in one tone from the C-major scale: F major has one flat, and G major, one sharp, in its key signature. These keys, then, each have six tones of their scales in common with C major—a pivot chord can easily be found. That neighboring tonalities are closely related is made further evident by the fact that C, for example, is dominant to F and subdominant to G.

That keys which are farther distant on the circle also have a few tones at least in common can be seen if we compare the "sectors" of the circle formed by the scale tones of two tonalities as, for instance, C and E: they overlap.

212.

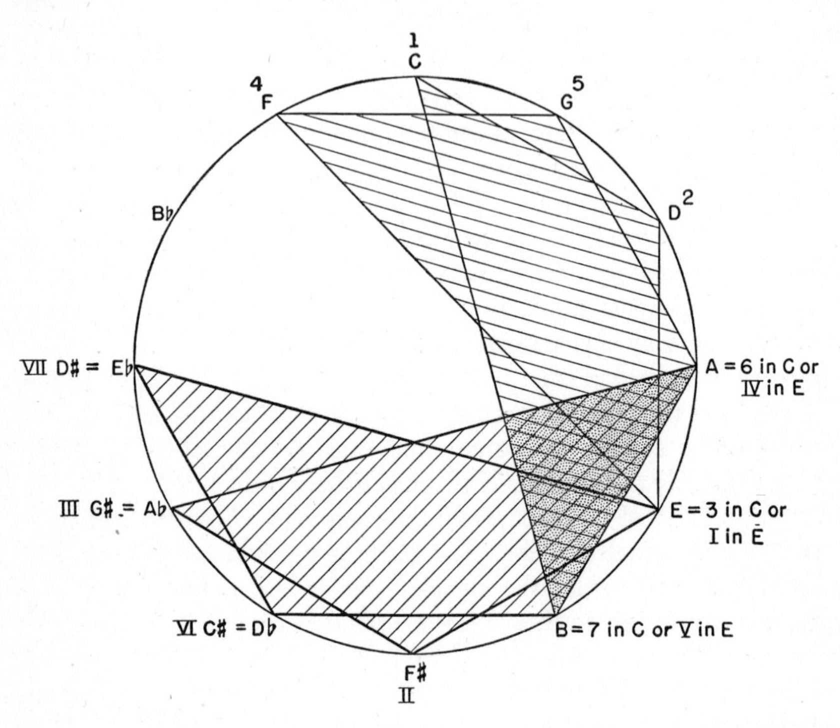

The scales of C and E major have three tones in common: A, E, and B.

1–7 = scale tones of C major

I–VII = scale tones of E major

If we add that minor keys have—in their harmonic version—major dominant triads, we may gather the endless possibilities available. A minor, for example, has all tones except G♯ in common with C major. The dominant triad of A minor, on the other hand, E–G♯–B, is the same as the tonic chord of E major, the subdominant of B major, the dominant of A major, and so forth. In other words, a composer who writes a piece in A minor will be strongly tempted to modulate during the course of the music to C major, E major, B major, A major, etc.

Enharmonic changes, that is, the considering of G♯ as A♭, etc., offer still more opportunities for modulation. The chord F♯–A♯–C♯, for example, may be considered G♭–B♭–D♭, and will thus be able to fulfil new tonal functions.

Finally, if we remember that melodies and harmonies may be altered, i.e., that sharps and flats which do not belong to the basic tonality may be inserted, we can understand the fact that with the development of chromatics any tone or chord may belong to any tonality—in other words, that tonality may become meaningless, as happened in the late nineteenth and early twentieth centuries.

Pitch and Tonality

Before we conclude our discussion of the elements of music, let us investigate for a moment the role which pitch plays in connection with mode, tonality, and modulation.

We may, of course, sing or play the scale of every mode within any pitch range. The choice of pitch will be governed by practical considerations, i.e., comfortable range of human voices and instruments, or by aesthetic purposes, as, for example, the desire to express high-pitched excitement, eeriness, piercing shrillness, low-pitched rumblings from far away, calmness, or bigness. While these descriptions of different meanings of pitch are crude, they are nevertheless fundamentally true. Composers as well as amateurs will use low-pitched sounds for giants and high tones for dwarfs. However, most music is concerned with more subtle impressions than those made by freaks or animals. The aesthetic reasons why composers choose a certain pitch remain, therefore, in most cases a mystery.

When it comes to tonality, similar conditions prevail. The melody may be above, within, or below the range of the accompaniment; the accompanying or contrapuntal voices may wander over the entire keyboard—the tonality chosen may be expressed in any pitch which is practical and which fulfils the musical intentions of the composer.

Even modulation and pitch are largely independent. That is to say, when a composer wants to modulate, for example, from C major to G major, his melody and harmony may go *up or down* in pitch or it may stay in the same range. In the circle of fifths, tones were, for convenience sake, ordered in ascending and descending fifths. However, we could just as well reverse the direction and go up and down from C in fourths.

213. THE CIRCLE OF FOURTHS

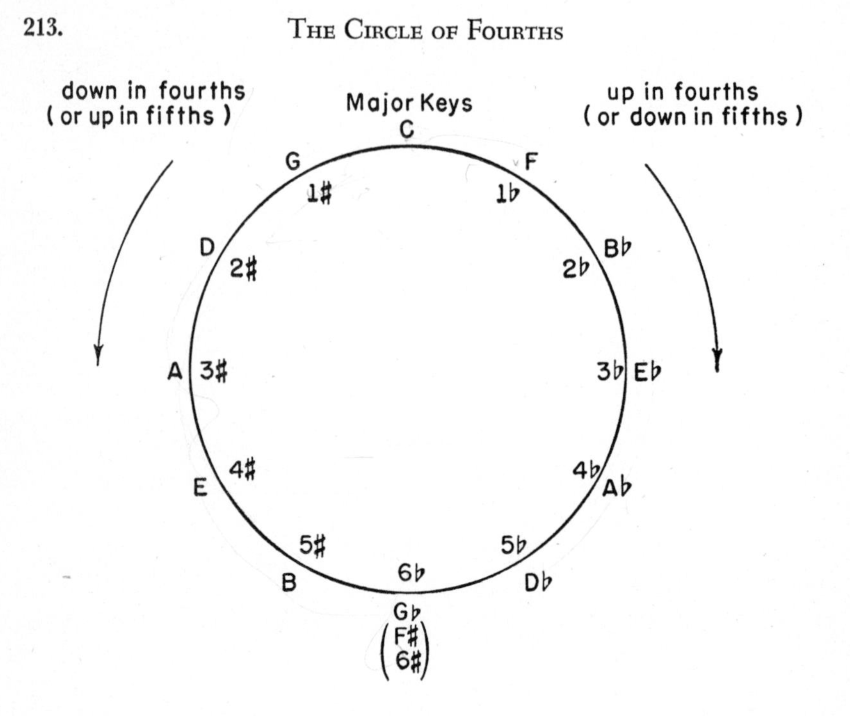

Or we might compress all the tones contained in the (seven-octave) circle into a single octave, i.e., write a chromatic scale. All this means that a melody with the range of may modulate *within this range* from C major to G major:

Or it may move *up* in pitch:

Or *down:*

The same is true with harmonies. Three persons playing all possible C-major chords on the seven-octave piano keyboard may modulate to other keys without changing the over-all pitch range. (The small pitch change in the lowest bass voice becomes immaterial whenever many doublings of the bass tone are used.)

The characteristics of modulation, then, are not a change of pitch level but the change of the center of gravity. Let us compare the changing from one tonality to another with moving from one house to another which has a different ground level. We may reach the new house by moving upward:

214.

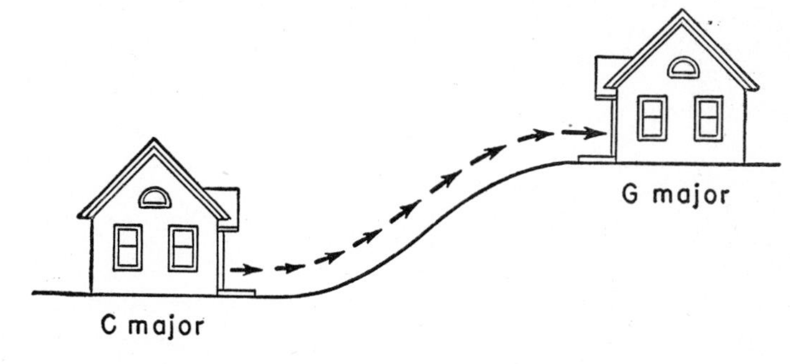

By going down hill:

215.

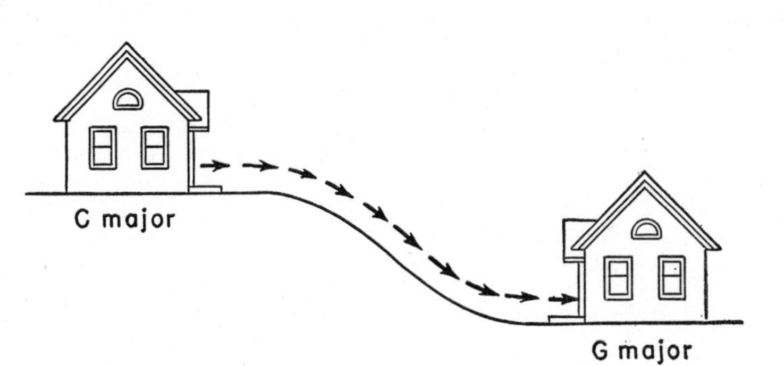

Or by staying on the same level, entering the house on the second floor as it were:

216.

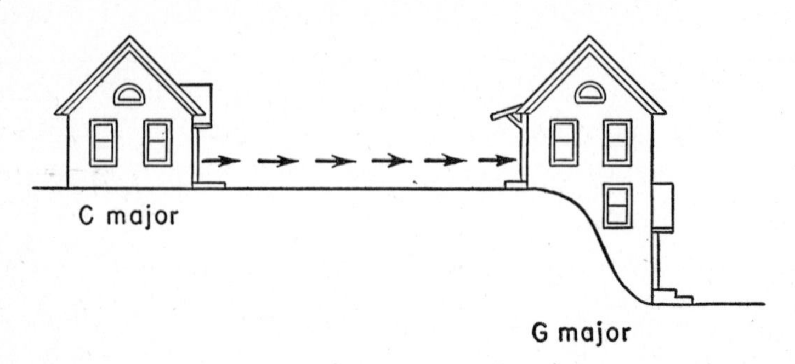

In the latter case, we walk straight over (keeping the pitch) to a house which hugs a hill; the gravity center lies lower than that of our first house. The opposite case can be illustrated if you reverse the trip and return from G major to C major; the pitch remains the same but the center of gravity has risen. And it is exactly this change of the gravity center which gives one, with gradually increasing experience in listening to music, the illusion of "moving in space" whenever modulations occur.

We may hasten the occurrence of such a sensation if we now extend our investigation of modulations to an entire Schubert song and to a movement from a symphony by Haydn or Mozart. Proceeding in the manner which was described in connection with our Bach Chorale, we will find that this process will be rather time-consuming when applied to a more extended excerpt of music. However, a few attempts at discovering the modulatory scheme of a piece of music by ourselves will reward us with a finer sensitivity toward modulations in all music which we hear subsequently.

Summary

While separating the elements of music for close inspection, we had found that rhythm may exist without melody and harmony. This possibility has not been fully explored yet by Western civilization. The endless rhythmic variety of the music of Bali and Java, for example, and the best specimens of African and American jazz are therefore still unknown to most concertgoers, in spite of the impression they made on Debussy, Ravel, Milhaud, Varèse, Stravinsky, Gershwin, Copland, and others.[1]

We also noticed that rhythm developed from quantitative to qualitative (metric) preferences when language changed from the quantitative to the accentual stress. Although the music which we know best uses both approaches simultaneously (because its sources are the word as well as the dance), qualitative stress is more common nowadays. Accentuation has, since Beethoven, interspersed melodic lines with a certain percussiveness in music and, similarly, the piano has changed from an instrument for accompanied melodies to one for percussive chord streams.

Melody, as we have seen, cannot be separated from rhythm, nor can harmony exist without melody or rhythm. The road of unaccompanied melody was all but abandoned by Western civilization approximately in the ninth century; the finely wrought single melodies of Gregorian chant and other Oriental music and the new and old authentic folk tunes of various countries have become, therefore, a "foreign" language to many, as we mentioned. The finest independent shades of pitch and expression as they exist in the tones of nature have been forced into a network of complexly interrelated polyphony. The resulting harmony took over as supreme ruler of music. In the operatic homophony of the seventeenth century, harmony was used to underline, even to *interpret melodies* for reasons of dramatic expressiveness. The instrumental music of the Baroque, on the other hand, used instruments *polyphonically* in order to fill out or represent a harmonic space. When the material of single or several closely related tonalities seemed exhausted, well-tempered tuning was invented and all tonalities became feasible and "exchangeable."

As against the shortcomings of equal temperament, which are, for example, the fact that the melodic line becomes standardized and that no interval except the octave remains "pure," stands the great advantage of the expansion of tonal material. Music expanded to such an extent that a single piece would traverse several tonalities, while formerly, in the early phases of harmony, chords of *one* scale or tonality presented the complete harmonic skeleton of a piece. In the nineteenth century a single movement of a symphony might well include large sections of the circle of fifths.

[1] See pp. 225–29 ff. for a few titles of pieces of music which are predominantly rhythmical.

The sounding of two or more tonalities at the same time, *bitonality* and *polytonality*, does in terms of tonalities what individual voices did in regard to dissonances: successive tonalities or harmonies are converted into simultaneous dissonant clashes. With a slight exaggeration the point could be made that Beethoven was the first [2] to embark on such a dangerous adventure. In the *Eroica* the second horn sounds the principal theme based on the tonic chord of E♭ major while the strings imply the dominant seventh chord on B♭:

217. SYMPHONY NO. 3 IN E♭ MAJOR, OP. 55 (First movement)

Ludwig van Beethoven (1770–1827)

When the *Eroica* was first rehearsed and performed, musicians and critics complained that either the horn player did not know how to come in right, or else Beethoven did not know how to write music (a criticism which is frequently voiced about contemporary music). By now, however, we have come to the point where we praise Beethoven for this "stroke of genius." The effect of the musical drama seems today heightened by this device of reintroducing the theme in a startling, exciting manner; musical events appear highly concentrated by the overlapping of two sections—in this case, the "development" and the "recapitulation" (see p. 302).

The counteracting of tonality, the so-called *atonality* of the early 1900's, was an outcome of the chromaticism of Wagner and the iridescent impressionism of Debussy, which avoided cadences and moved largely "in between" tonalities. It could well be that the possibilities of harmony became exhausted in the early twentieth century. Electronic instruments of the future may perhaps introduce perfect tuning in music and do away with harmony and equal temperament. In the meantime, however, inasmuch as we are here concerned with the music of the present and the past, let us investigate next the role which traditional instruments have played in the evolution of rhythm, melody, and harmony.

[2] Contrapuntal polytonality may be found in music of the thirteenth, fourteenth, and fifteenth centuries. Cf. *Harvard Dictionary of Music*, article on Partial Signature.

Suggestions for Listening

Bach	Brandenburg Concerti
	Well-tempered Clavier, Book I
Beethoven	Symphony No. 3 in E♭ Major, Op. 55 ("Eroica")
Berg	*Wozzeck*
Debussy	*The Children's Corner*
Gershwin	Piano Concerto
Gregorian Chant	
Haydn	Symphony No. 94 in G Major ("Surprise")
Milhaud	*La Création du Monde*
	L'Orestie d'Eschyle
Music of Bali	
Peri	*Euridice*
Prokofieff	*Peter and the Wolf*
Ravel	Piano Concerto
Schoenberg	*Five Pieces for Orchestra*, Op. 16
Stravinsky	*Petrouchka*
Varèse	*Ionization*
Wagner	*Tristan und Isolde*

11

Tone Color and Instruments: String Instruments

Living in an age of mechanical amplification and reproduction of tone, we are apt to forget that composers usually have a certain tone color in mind when they compose music. It is true that much of the Renaissance and Baroque music was written for voices and/or instruments, and that composers frequently indicated an option "for winds or strings, or both." This however, does not refute the fact that whenever these same composers did specify particular instruments, they were very much aware of certain distinct tone colors. Monteverdi, for example, prescribed for his opera *Orfeo* thirty-six specific instruments. And Bach wrote decidedly in a different idiom according to whether his compositions were meant for the organ, the violin, or the harpsichord. Whoever thinks that tone color was of no importance in the Baroque era has paid little attention to the way the flutes, oboes, and trumpets are used in the music of the time of Purcell, Händel, and Bach. It is sufficient to listen to the recitativo "O Golgatha" of the *St. Matthew Passion* (No. 69 in the score) to remember ever after that Bach was a master in the use of tone color.

Let us remember then that the notion of Hollywood and Broadway that a piece of music has to be dressed up by another man, a professional orchestrator who specializes in clothing another's musical ideas, is of recent origin. The tone ideal varies among countries, eras, and composers. Determining factors are the function which music is called upon to fulfil, the progress of instrument builders, and aesthetic preferences. Whenever we ignore these factors, we pervert the meaning of music. This happens, for example, when we bring a brass band to the living room and a piece of intimate chamber music to a stadium. (Cf. "An ensemble of 76 [sic] organs and 18 harps is expected to play

Debussy's 'Clair de Lune' at Soldier's Field, Chicago, today . . ." New York *Times*, August 20, 1950.)

The word *progress* in music as everywhere else expresses two simultaneous phenomena: going forward into new territory and leaving stretches of land behind; acquiring new values and losing old ones. The fact that ancient Greek temples are built without steel and concrete does not diminish their beauty and perfection. Yet, because the ancient architecture grew out of functions and structural materials which were indigenous to Greece and Rome, its forming factors cannot be transplanted totally into our own age. To build Greek temples today for banks, insurance buildings, colleges, is as senseless as to expect skyscrapers among the ruins of ancient Greece and Rome.

When applied to music, this means that performing Bach by employing a post-Bach orchestration *à la* Tchaikovsky or Wagner is missing the point made by all three composers. Each composed for the orchestra of his time; the essential tonal characteristics of their eras are inseparably built into their music. There is no doubt that Bach, if he were alive today, would make ample use of the opportunities of the huge modern orchestra and the perfected piano instead of his chamber orchestra and the harpsichord and clavichord.[1] Obviously, though, he would also write today an entirely different kind of music from what he did write. Dressing up a composer of the past is like coloring a black-and-white etching by Rembrandt—not an improvement.

As to the different aesthetic tone ideals, we may understand their existence by observing the fact that the guttural tone production used in Hebrew chants and by Asiatic peoples is far different from the sound produced by opera singers of the West. On the other hand, within the Western Hemisphere, a contemporary ballad-singer projects his voice differently from an Italian opera tenor. Not always are shiny surfaces desired in painting or in music; dull finishes, iridescent glows, semitints, and pastels are used as well as bold splashes and geometrical figures and lines formed by colors.

Tone colors in music will be determined by the environment and by the imagination of the composer. While composers are influenced by the status of music, its social aspect, the kind of instruments avail-

[1] "He [Bach] had praised the tone of [the Silbermann piano], indeed admired it, but had objected that it was too weak in the upper part, and that it was much too hard to play." Agricola, quoted in Albert Schweitzer, *J. S. Bach*, translated by Ernest Newman, I, 202.

able, and the skill of musicians, they in turn have sometimes inspired new methods of using old instruments and the invention of entirely new ones, e.g., the "Wagner tubas." When a violinist complained to Beethoven about the difficulties of one of his quartets, declaring his part "unplayable," Beethoven burst out, "Don't assume that I think only of your miserable violin when the spirit moves me."[2] The Brahms Violin Concerto was at first thought so difficult that someone quipped, "This is a concerto against, not for, the violin"; yet today its technical intricacies are mastered by any advanced conservatory student, as are Beethoven's quartets. Similarly, demands which seemed unreasonable at the time were made of instrumentalists and singers by Bach, Weber, Berlioz, Liszt, Wagner, Richard Strauss, Stravinsky, and other composers whose music remains difficult but not impossible to perform.

We may conclude from this that it is practically impossible ever to characterize, circumscribe, or predict the possibilities of single and combined instruments in mere words. The same holds for the "literary" description of tone colors; they miss their goal, which is to clarify and to intensify our reaction to the music. Every concertgoer or radio listener is familiar with commentaries on music along the following lines: "The silvery chains, executed in elflike triplet runs by the flute, are interrupted by the fateful syncopated rumblings of the trombones."

Such paraphrasing of music, which originated in the Romantic Era, interferes with the direct impact of music; it leads away from the matter which it purports to "explain" by inserting images which are highly individualistic and therefore timebound, and frequently of questionable taste. Even as great a composer as Berlioz defeats his purpose when he attempts to describe the impression made on him by clarinets:

> The character of the clarinet is epic rather than idyllic—like that of the horns, trumpets and trombones. Its voice is that of heroic love; and if the mass of brass instruments in grand military symphonies suggests the idea of warriors covered with glittering armor, marching to glory or to death, so do numerous clarinets playing in unison seem to represent loving women who, with proud glances and deep affection, exalted by the sound of arms, sing during the battle, crowning the victors or dying with the vanquished.[3]

[2] Romain Rolland, *Ludwig van Beethoven*, p. 136.

[3] H. Berlioz, R. Strauss, *Treatise on Instrumentation* (translated by Theodore Front; New York: Edwin F. Kalmus, 1948), p. 209.

To this, Richard Strauss appended, apparently in all seriousness, the remark "Compare Brünhilde's exit in the second act of 'Walküre.'"

The danger of this kind of description is that, if taken seriously, the sound of clarinets may be connected forever after with the thought of loving women, a procedure which is of doubtful value as far as music is concerned.

Even when commentators' descriptions refrain from interpreting imagined actions of musical instruments, and confine themselves to the verbal description of the *timbre*, i.e., the "color" of an instrument and the emotions which it may evoke, they help us little—and frequently they are contradicted by later developments in the history of music. For example, in 1844, a few years after the saxophone was invented, Berlioz wrote as follows:

> Saxophones can be used in any kind of music; but they are particularly suited to slow and tender compositions . . . their low tones, however, have a sublime and, as it were, priestly calm. . . . Ingenious composers are going to achieve wonderful, still unpredictable effects by joining the saxophones with the clarinet family or by means of other combinations.[4]

During the more than one hundred intervening years, saxophones have indeed been used in a few instances by Meyerbeer, Bizet, R. Strauss, Stravinsky, Milhaud, Honegger, Virgil Thomson, and a few other contemporary composers. However, they appear by far most frequently in popular dance music and, as we all know, rarely in the mood of a "priestly calm." In order, then, to avoid the many pitfalls of literary interpretation, we should avoid descriptive adjectives wherever possible and rather train ourselves to recognize various instruments when we hear them. In short, let us, by investigating their mechanism and actual sound, become more directly aware of the basic properties of musical instruments.

The Causes of Tone Color

We may become more sensitive to music once our minds have understood what causes tone colors in terms of elementary physics. Let us start by considering what happens when we produce tones of different pitch and tone color on string instruments.

[4] *Ibid.*, p. 399.

218.

Diverse Strings Producing Middle C

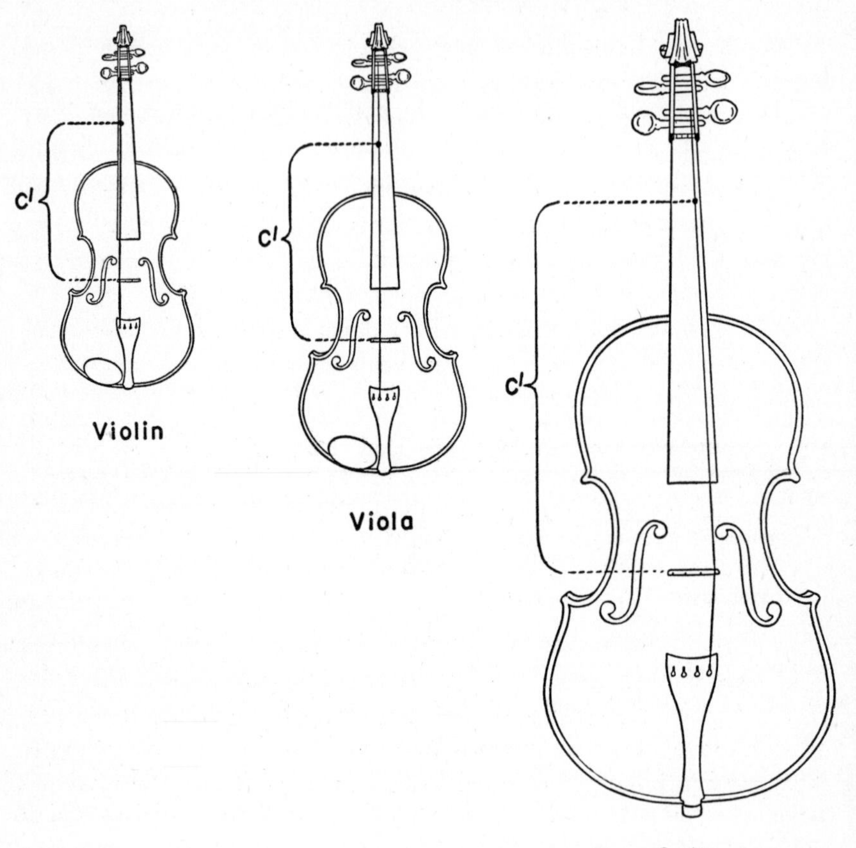

Three factors determine the pitch of strings: their length, weight, and tension. The shorter, lighter, and tenser a string, the higher the tone it produces, and vice versa. The bow moving across a string produces vibrations which are conveyed through the bridge to the body of the instrument, which serves as a sound box. The tone color is affected by the speed with which the bow moves, its pressure, and the spot where it attacks the string. In addition, the size and construction of the sound box, or "body," will influence the timbre and so again will the length, weight, and tension of the string, and the construction of the bridge. We know that two tones of identical pitch sound entirely different when produced by a low soprano voice and when sung by a high tenor. Similarly, for example, the tone middle C appears in different tone colors when played successively by a violin, a viola, and a cello. The divergence in the length, tenseness, and thickness of the string and in the size of the sound box will make us expect to hear tones of different tone colors.

Even on a single instrument, tones of identical pitch but varying tone colors may be produced on different strings by shortening the sounding portion of the strings with the fingers of the left hand. The tone E  , for example, may be played on the E, A, D, or G string of the violin. In each case—although the pitch level remains the same—the length, thickness, and tension of the string segment will cause a variety of tone colors. (See Fig. 219.)

If we add that the manner of moving the bow and its weight may vary the tone color considerably, we should have an idea of the endless possibilities to be achieved on a single string instrument. Obviously, the combination of several instruments will yield a still richer variety of tone color.

In physical terms, differences in steady-state tone color correspond to differences in harmonic structure. With the help of *harmonic analysis*[5] Helmholtz found that in a single tone the relative intensities of the *harmonics* or *partials* determine the tone color of a steady tone.

The typical flute tone, for example, contains few harmonics, while the oboe and the English horn are rich in harmonics. The trumpet tone has a great many high and relatively strong harmonics, a fact which accounts for its "metallic" sound. Generally speaking, even-numbered partials add brilliance, and odd-numbered ones certain characteristics which we call nasal, throaty, hornlike, etc. (Cf. the clarinet, which in its low range, has weak even-numbered harmonics).

The fact that the presence and intensity of different harmonics determine the tone color has been used in the building of pipe organs for centuries, and it is being explored again in the construction of synthetic electronic "organs." The "mixtures" in an organ, that is, the registers or stops which produce particular tone qualities, are combinations of pipes which sound particular partials together with a funda-

[5] In the above sense, the term *harmonic analysis* is used to denote the physical and mathematical analysis of sound waves into their component parts. By musicians, however, the same term is also used in describing the structure and progression of chords within a piece of music.

219.

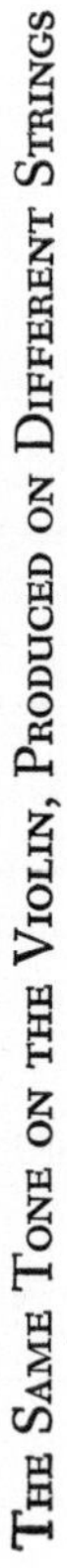

THE SAME TONE ON THE VIOLIN, PRODUCED ON DIFFERENT STRINGS

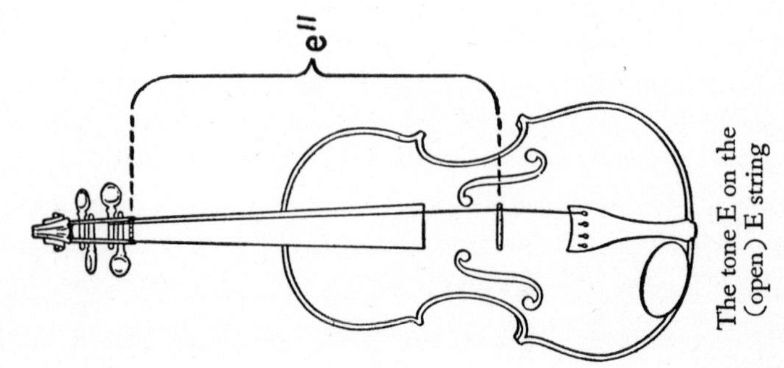

The tone E on the (open) E string

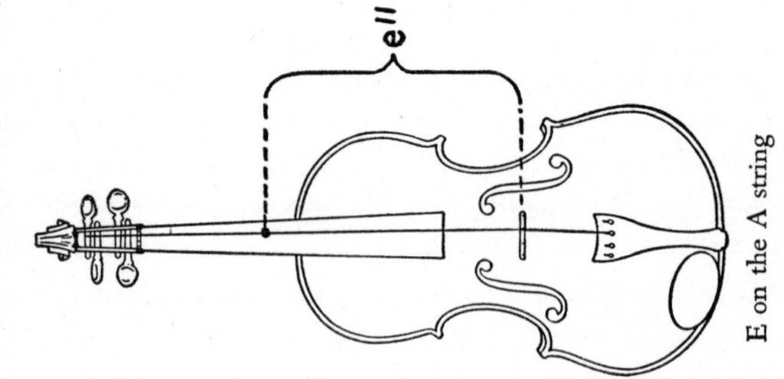

E on the A string

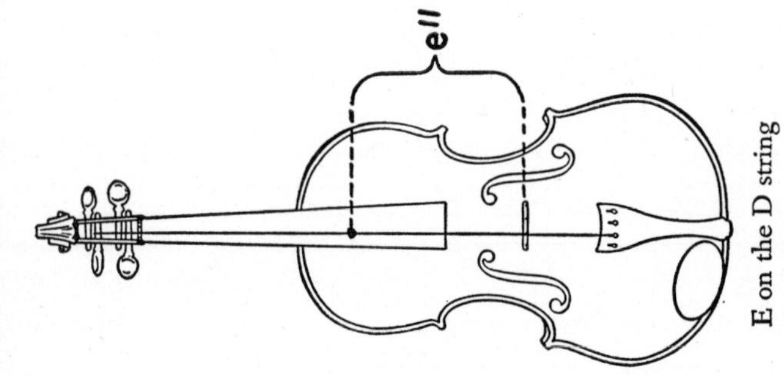

E on the D string

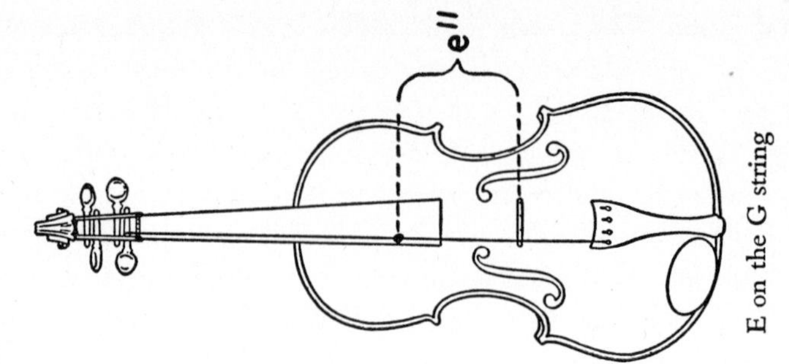

E on the G string

mental tone. Thus, when a single key is depressed, mixture or mutation stops add selected harmonics, to be sounded simultaneously with the fundamental, and thereby imitating the tone quality of strings, reeds, or brasses.[6] These color-producing, added harmonics cannot be individually distinguished, but are blended, or "mixed," so as to produce the illusion of a single tone of a particular quality.

A high tone on the cello sometimes sounds similar to a low tone on the violin, really *almost* more like a violin than a cello. This is caused by the fact that each instrument emphasizes those partials which lie within certain characteristic frequency bands. The material of which an instrument is made, its size and shape, favor harmonics of certain pitches. Everyone has experienced the strange sensation that in a church or a hall with wooden floor and benches the wood may start to vibrate when a tone of a particular pitch is sounded. The soundbox of a violin has a great many *resonances* of this sort which are very important in coloring the tone. These resonances are particularly strong within a certain range of frequencies. This range is called the "formant" of an instrument. In the violin, for example, the range of the formant is approximately the octave from 3,000 to 6,000 vibrations per second. Hence, all tones which contain strong harmonics of frequencies between 3,000 and 6,000 vibrations per second sound typically violin-like. A high tone on a cello which has strong partials within this range of frequencies may thus sound as if it were coming from a violin. Whenever partials in this range are weak or missing, even the violin will sound more like another instrument. The difference between violin, viola, and cello tone color, which was exemplified previously (Figure 218), may thus become magnified or minimized on account of the specific formant of each instrument: the violin may sound like a viola, the viola like a violin, and the cello like a viola, according to the pitch range and the string lengths which are chosen.

Composers sometimes indicate that they want a special tone color, different from the one characteristic of the instrument. The marking *flautato* (flutelike) in a violin part instructs the player to draw the bow at some distance from the bridge, above the fingerboard, thus eliminating the high partials. Without these partials the violin sounds somewhat like a flute. Conversely, drawing the bow across the string close to the bridge produces a nasal, sharp, oboe-like tone color, because of

[6] Conversely, octave doublings of flute, oboe, bassoon, in an orchestra piece sound "organlike."

the prominence of the higher harmonics in the tone. Finally, the glassy, unearthly, shattering sound produced by *sul ponticello* (on the bridge) playing is caused by the fact that only very high and shrill partials are apparent.

In *playing* "harmonics" (Figure 161) the player singles out and emphasizes a particular partial of the string, thus producing again a flutelike sound, a pure, neutral tone quality relatively weak in all harmonics except the one which is played. The *mute* or *sordino*, when clamped on the bridge, also alters the normal distribution of partials and changes the tone color. Plucking the strings (*pizzicato*) produces a harplike effect, and throwing the bow in short, elastic strokes upon the string (playing *spiccato*) results in a harpsichord-like effect.

The fact that pizzicato and spiccato change the tone quality in an essential way leads us to assume that the distribution of harmonics is not the sole determining factor as far as tone quality is concerned. If the same tone on the same instrument changes its tone color considerably according to the method of attack and release, we may deduce that harmonic analysis tells only a part of the story. Harmonic analysis deals only with a steady tone, ignoring the manner in which the tone comes into being and the manner in which it dies away. The "attack" and "decay" of the tone will strongly influence the tone quality perceived by the listener.

It is rare in music that a tone lasts long enough to be considered in terms of its "steady-state" tone quality. At every moment of its being its components are changing so that its inner structure is changing rapidly. The order and rapidity with which these changes occur is of great importance for the tone color which we perceive. The recorded sound of a piano played backward, for example, loses the typical piano quality almost entirely. The sound of a cymbal heard backward is almost identical with that of a snare-drum. It is to be expected that through further research we will know more about the causes of tone color than we do now.

The bewildering variety of tone color on single and combined instruments especially preoccupied the minds of composers of the Romantic Era. The mixing of colors in the music of the nineteenth and twentieth centuries stands in contrast to the plain colors of the Baroque. When Bach chooses a violin for one part, he contrasts it by giving additional parts to the flute, oboe, or trumpet. The melodic material used for all the instruments is the same; variety results from the intertwining of similar strands of melodies each presented by instruments of different tone color which combine, yet conserve a certain distance in color from each other. Even in the Baroque music for combined instruments of one family, e.g., for string orchestra, the over-all homogeneous sound and the unity of melodic material consist of divergent elements; when celli state a theme which was first presented by violins, they retain their own identity; in other words, celli sound like celli and violins like violins throughout.

This should give us a hint about what music to listen to if we want to become more sensitive to the tone colors of individual instruments. In order to appreciate the complicated mixtures of tone colors in orchestra compositions of fairly recent vintage, we must at first observe various instruments in small combinations. Furthermore, in order to follow the music of a romantic or modern composer, who demands the violin, for instance, to sound in turn like a viola, cello, oboe, flute, bagpipe, and harp, we should first be thoroughly familiar with the straight, plain, idiomatic sound of the individual instruments. Because the strings, the oboe, and the trumpet reached a high state of perfection as early as the Baroque Era, music of that era will be a particularly happy choice for the study and enjoyment of clear-cut tone colors.

Acoustics of String Instruments

In the case of low-pitched tones on a string instrument, the actual motion of the string can be observed with the naked eye. For this reason, the string instrument is a natural starting point for the discussion of the physical means by which harmonics are produced.

We have seen that a string set into vibration gives forth a fundamental tone of a certain frequency. We found further that a string also vibrates in parts, at higher frequencies (harmonics or partials). Finally, we said that these partials can be "singled out" by touching the string lightly at one-half, one-third, etc., of its length.

The C string on the cello, for example, sounds the fundamental C with the frequency of 64 vibrations per second.[7] We can observe the

[7] For reasons of convenience, it is customary to use for calculations the old standard pitch of a′ = 431 vibrations per second instead of the concert pitch of a′ = 440 vibrations per second which is the present international standard. Throughout history the "standard pitch" for a′ has fluctuated between a low of 374 and a high of 563. In performances during the classic era, for example, the music of Haydn, Mozart, and Beethoven sounded a semitone lower than it does today (cf. *Harvard Dictionary of Music*, "Pitch," pp. 584–85).

string vibrating in the following pattern as soon as we draw the bow across the string:

220.

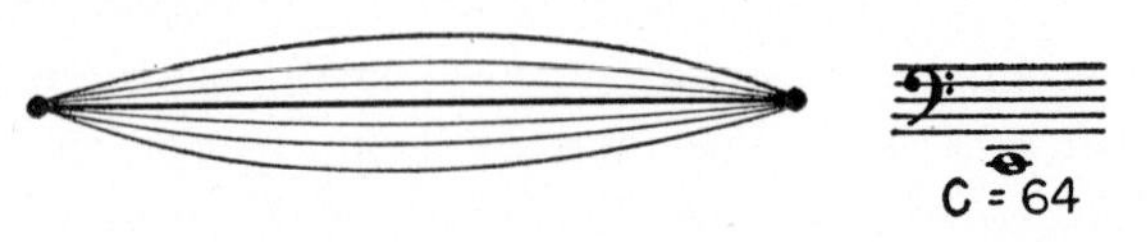

By touching the string lightly at half of its length, the fundamental is suppressed. The second harmonic may then be observed as the string vibrates in two equal parts. This harmonic will sound at twice the frequency of the fundamental. The pitch perceived and the pattern of waves will be as follows:

221.

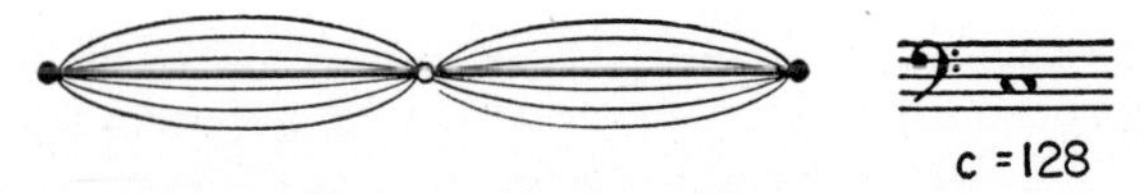

By touching the string lightly at the middle point, we have simply encouraged the natural tendency of the string to vibrate in two parts. Both parts of the string vibrate equally strongly, i.e., with the same "amplitude." The hills and valleys, the highest and lowest points of vibration, are called *loops* and *nodes*. The greatest amplitude of motion of the string occurs at the loops, and the least near the nodes of the string.[8]

We may likewise single out the third harmonic by touching the string at a point one third of the way to the bridge.

222.

The string then vibrates in three equal parts, thus producing a tone (g) of $3 \times 64 = 192$ vibrations per second. Touching the string at a point one fourth of the way from the nut to the bridge will produce the fourth harmonic (c′) with the frequency of $4 \times 64 = 256$ vibrations per second; separating the fifth partial will yield the fifth harmonic (e′) with the frequency of $5 \times 64 = 320$ vibrations per second. These first five harmonics of an open (unstopped) string are easy

[8] The term *node* (*nodus* = knot) thus describes very aptly the point where motion is restricted.

to produce on any string instrument.[9] We must only guard *not* to press the finger down firmly, not to shorten or "stop" the string, but to touch it lightly at the exact spot so that its *total* length may vibrate in 1, 2, 3 or more equal parts, depending on which partial we desire.

We may approximate the behavior of a string in slow motion if we fasten a clothesline at one end and set it into motion through movements of our hand. By doubling, tripling, etc., the speed of our swinging hand, the line will describe the wave patterns of our diagrams for harmonics; it will swing in one, then two, then three segments, according to our method of setting it into vibration.

In a musical instrument, many such vibration patterns occur simultaneously whenever a single tone is produced. The wave pattern of a single rich tone consists of a number of interwoven waves of the sort pictured above.

Before we continue, let us stop for a moment and analyze how the string is set into vibration by the bow. When a stretched string is set into motion, the tiny hooks of the horse hair of the bow (aided by the sticky resin) pull the string sideways for a certain distance. Eventually the tension of the string counteracts the pull of the bow, and the string jumps back—overshooting the position of equilibrium. Then the bow catches it again, and the process is repeated.

In discussing string instruments, inevitably the question is raised, What was the "secret" of Stradivarius (1644–1737)? The answer is: There is no "secret" as such: the excellence of his instruments is derived solely from the incredible skill, craftsmanship, and artistry of a great master. Stradivarius was as unique among instrument makers as Rembrandt was among painters. Both were the product and immediate cause of a peak of craftsmanship and art. Generations of patient skill and devotion produced in both cases excellent craftsmen and, once in a while a genius, among Dutch painters and Italian violin makers. After Stradivarius, the tradition of string instrument building was continued sporadically in Italy, Germany, France, England, and America for a little while only. While there are a handful of excellent string instrument makers alive today, the tradition created by uninterrupted generations devoted to violin making has vanished. Men who would at other times have had the patience and sense of security to embark on a long apprenticeship, craftsmen who would unceasingly

[9] The higher harmonics are barely visible except on the low cello or double bass string.

improve their skill and search for the highest perfection in instrument making, are today designing bridges, planes, power dams.

We expect of a good string instrument that its tone "carries," that the tone is uniform throughout its entire range, and that it "speaks" easily when the bow is drawn across the strings. In other words, we demand that the instrument follow exactly the intentions of the player in regards to sonority, dynamics, tone quality, at every instant. In order to fulfil these requirements, an instrument should ideally have a smooth "response curve," as it is called in acoustics, so that no single tone stands out one way or another in tone quality.

Inasmuch as the form and construction of a violin have changed little since the time of Stradivarius, the differences in violins must lie in the curvature of the front of the instrument, the position of the bridge, the age and thickness of the wood, the varnish, etc. So many factors are involved that even violins by the same maker never sound entirely alike. The part taken by the player in bringing out the merits and in compensating for the weakness of an instrument is often an important one, but it can be measured only by the player himself. This explains why, in demonstrations of valuable and cheap violins before an audience, a Stradivarius is often misjudged: the skill of a great player succeeds, through endless minute adjustments, in making up for the raggedness of a poor instrument. While an audience, even of "experts," may sometimes be fooled by the artist, the player himself will always be aware, even when blindfolded, on what kind of instrument he plays.

Players of string instruments are rapidly becoming as rare as instrument builders. The fact that dance and marching bands are more popular with children than string quartets and orchestras is one reason. Then there is the misconception that the violin is principally a solo instrument and as such obviously difficult to master and preferably listened to only when played by a few great artists. The literature of the strings seems to many persons to consist largely of arrangements, lullabies, or show-off pieces; consequently the best part, the concerti for string orchestras, quartets, trios, sonatas, etc., are unknown to many young people who might otherwise be tempted to take up a string instrument for the sake of co-operative, concerted music, written especially for the idiom of strings. In reality, the matter-of-factness and restraint of the original music of the seventeenth and eighteenth centuries, and its motoric playfulness, are more to the taste of the young

223A. STRING INSTRUMENTS

The scale of size used in the above illustration is fifty per cent larger than that used in Fig. 223B.

The "Earl of Plymouth" Stradivarius violin (dated 1711). This instrument was discovered about 1939 in an old trunk in a country house in England, where it had lain for over a hundred years. Courtesy of Rembert Wurlitzer, New York.

Viola d'amore by Hofman Woelfersdorf (dated 1727). Courtesy of the Isham Collection, Harvard University.

The "Paganini" Stradivarius viola (dated 1731). Paganini became so enamoured of this instrument that he asked Berlioz to compose a piece for viola and orchestra. This work is "Harold in Italy." Courtesy of Rembert Wurlitzer, New York.

Viola da gamba by Barak Norman, London (dated 1717). Courtesy of the Isham Collection, Harvard University.

The "Castelbarco" Stradivarius cello (dated 1697), now in the Library of Congress. Courtesy of Rembert Wurlitzer, New York.

Double Bass by Paolo Testore (*ca.* 1730). Courtesy of Rembert Wurlitzer, New York.

people of today (whenever they have an opportunity to hear it) then the sentimental emotionalism and bombast of virtuoso-arrangements of the last century.

The "Air on the G String" and Schubert's "Ave Maria" are both truly great pieces of music; however, Bach did not intend his Air for the G String, nor Schubert his song for the violin. If we muster a remnant of the true pioneer spirit and patiently search, we can find dozens of comparable treasures in the authentic literature of string instruments.

In the following section of this chapter the reader will find an annotated list of string instruments and an enumeration of many compositions which exemplify instances of the prominent use of strings in all kinds of combinations. To follow all the suggestions for listening which are contained in the list of compositions would take a long time. Even so, it should be remembered that this list is far from complete and that it is meant rather as an initial checklist which should lead on to further, individual search for unknown treasures of string music.

An Annotated List of String Instruments and a Few Suggestions for Listening

I. Bowed String Instruments.

A. The Violin.

Sonatas and partitas for violin alone by Bach.[10]

Sonatas with piano by Corelli, Händel, Bach, Mozart, Beethoven, Brahms, César Franck, Debussy, Ravel, Hindemith, Bartok.

Concerti[11] by Vivaldi, Bach, Mozart, Beethoven, Mendelssohn, Tchaikovsky, Brahms, Prokofieff, Sibelius, Stravinsky.

Bach, Concerto for Two Violins and String Orchestra in D Minor.

B. The Viola Family.

1. The Viola.

Reger, three suites for viola alone.

Stravinsky, *Elegie* (Prelude and Fugue) *for Viola Solo.*

Sonatas by Bax, Bloch, Hindemith, Loeffler, Milhaud.

Concerti by Bartok, Hindemith, Milhaud, Walton, Vaughan Williams.

[10] "Sonatas" for wind or string instruments always include a keyboard instrument unless stated otherwise.

[11] Concerti are always for one or more solo instruments plus orchestra. The only exception is the *Italian Concerto* by Bach, which is for harpsichord solo.

Duos for violin and viola by Mozart.

Mozart, Symphonie Concertante for Violin and Viola (with orchestra).

Hindemith, *Music of Mourning* (for viola solo and strings).

Orchestra solos in *Harold in Italy* by Berlioz and in *Don Quixote* by R. Strauss.

2. The Viola d'amore.

This instrument was popular in the eighteenth century; it had fourteen strings, seven of which were sounded by the bow and seven additional ones below the fingerboard, sounded through sympathetic vibration. Note: the music written for viola and viola d'amore employs the *alto* or *viola clef*; i.e., a C clef (denoting middle C) appears on the third line of the staff.

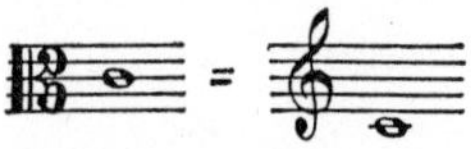

Sonatas by Ariosti, Loeillet, Hindemith.

Concerti by Vivaldi and Hindemith.

Arias with viola d'amore obbligato in Cantata No. 132 and in the *St. John Passion* by Bach.

Orchestra solos in the *Sinfonia Domestica* by R. Strauss and in the operas *Louise* by Charpentier, *Les Huguenots* by Meyerbeer, and *Madame Butterfly* by Puccini.

C. The Cello Family.

1. The Cello (originally called violoncello).

Bach, Suites for cello solo.

Sonatas by Beethoven, Boccherini, Brahms, Chopin, Debussy, Grieg, Mendelssohn, R. Strauss.

Concerti by Barber, Boccherini, Dvorak, Elgar, Haydn, Hindemith, Saint-Saëns, Schumann.

Duos for violin and cello by Kodaly, Martinu, Ravel, Toch.

Beethoven, Triple Concerto for Violin, Cello, and Piano (with orchestra).

Brahms, Double Concerto for Violin and Cello (with orchestra).

2. The Viola da Gamba (predecessor of the cello). Note: The music written for cello and viola da gamba employs—among other clefs—the *tenor* clef; i.e., a C clef (denoting middle C) appears on the fourth line of the staff:

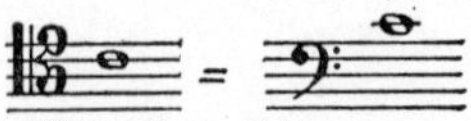

Sonatas by Bach, Händel, Hervelois, Marais.

Tartini, Concerto.

Arias with viola da gamba obbligato in the *St. Matthew Passion* and the *St. John Passion* by Bach.

D. The Double Bass.

(Also called string bass, bass viol, contrabass). It sounds one octave lower than written. In the classical era this instrument frequently "doubled" the part of the celli in the lower octave. The beginning of the Recitative in the last movement of Beethoven's Ninth Symphony is a famous example. However, with the invention of lower wind instruments (bass clarinet, contrabassoon, tuba, etc.), its individual tone color was stressed more and more by composers like Weber, Berlioz, Wagner, Verdi, R. Strauss.

Hindemith, Sonata for Double Bass and Piano.

Concerti for double bass by Dittersdorf, D'Albert, Koussevitzky.

Chamber music works which employ the double bass: Beethoven, Septet, Op. 20; Piston, Divertimento; Schubert, "Trout" Quintet; Stravinsky, *Histoire du Soldat.*

Orchestral solos in: R. Strauss, *Also sprach Zarathustra*; Verdi, *Othello,* Act IV; Wagner, *Tristan und Isolde,* Act III.

II. Plucked String Instruments.

A. The Lute had in the musical world of the Sixteenth century the place which the piano had in the Nineteenth century. Some of the charming and fascinating dances, songs, transcribed motets, and fantasies are gradually being revived. Cf. music by the great Spanish composer, Luis Milan (*c.* 1500–1561) and the English madrigalists, John Dowland, Morley, and Pilkington. Bach wrote two sonatas for lute and used the lute in his *St. John Passion.* Wagner employs the lute in Beckmesser's serenade in *Die Meistersinger.*

B. The Guitar, another very ancient and internationally popular instrument, is well known today through its greatest living exponent, Andres Segovia. Weber, Paganini, and Verdi were all accomplished guitar players. The guitar is used in Verdi's *Falstaff,* in Berlioz's *Benvenuto Cellini,* and in Rossini's *Barber of Seville.* See also pieces of De Falla, Virgil Thomson, etc. (Note: guitar music sounds an octave lower than it is written.)

C. The Mandolin has been prescribed in Händel's oratorio *Alexander Balus* and Mozart's *Don Giovanni,* also in Mahler's Eighth Symphony, and in Verdi's *Othello,* where it is combined with guitar and bagpipe. Beethoven wrote a sonatina and adagio for mandolin and harpsichord.

D. The Harp, which often takes the part of the lute, guitar, or mandolin when no player is available, is too well known visually as well as aurally to need any emphasis. However, we should include in our listening eventually these works:

Debussy, Sonata for Flute, Viola, and Harp.

Ravel, Introduction and Allegro for String Quartet, Flute, Harp, and Clarinet.

Mozart, Concerto for Flute and Harp (with orchestra).

E. The Harpsichord, as well as its simplified forms, the virginal and the spinet, was the forerunner of the piano. It was used during the Baroque era for opera and oratorio recitatives, for chamber music, and as solo and orchestral instrument. Composers and conductors (in most cases a synonym at that time) used to lead performances from the harpsichord. Wanda Landowska has done more than any other artist to revive the instrument in the present time. Here are main characteristics:

1. The strings are plucked by crow quills or leather pieces.
2. To each tone belong several strings, tuned in unison with, and an octave above and an octave below, the fundamental tone.
3. Two manuals may create different tone colors through the use of different plectra. Furthermore, by adding or subtracting octave combinations, variations in volume as well as in tone color may be produced.

The results of this construction are:

1. Polyphonic music sounds clearer than on the piano through the differentiation possible between individual melodic strands (by playing, e.g., two parts on different manuals).
2. The tone sounds plucked, percussive, metallic, glittering, at best.
3. Dynamic and tone-color changes occur in stepwise, terrace fashion, never on a sliding scale.
4. Tones and chords may appear fuller in actual sound than on paper, if octave stops are used.
5. Sudden emphasis and dynamic accents are impossible; instead trills, turns, grace notes, so frequently occurring in harpsichord music, serve as a substitute.

The literature for the harpsichord defies description. It is further expanded or restricted according to the ever-changing opinions and findings of music lovers, musicians, and musicologists. Which music was meant for the clavichord, the piano, or for the harpsichord during the eighteenth and early nineteenth centuries will never be, and probably never was, clear. Haydn and Mozart both had clavichords and harpsichords in their possession, but also grand pianos. It seems safe to assume that both composers wrote their solo keyboard music for the piano even if Haydn conducted oratorios from the harpsichord and Mozart composed his *Magic Flute* and *Requiem* partly at the clavichord.[12]

III. Struck String Instruments.

A. The Clavichord, another still older forerunner of the piano, is the intimate, flexible and sensitive counterpart of its younger sister, the harpsichord. It is really nothing else but several monochords (single strings) combined and struck by keys (claves). The bridge which

[12] Cf. Geiringer, *Musical Instruments* (New York: Oxford University Press, 1945), p. 160.

divides the string into shorter segments is at the same time the tone producer. A metal tangent at the end of each key determines the pitch and in doing so creates a very soft but controllable, flexible sound. The resulting tender, singing sound lends itself to romantic musical dreams. How much the instrument was used besides for practice purposes, for individual intimate music making, remains uncertain because of its very nature. The pieces of *Das Wohltemperierte Klavier* by J. S. Bach were certainly not all meant for the clavichord, but many if not most of them were designed for the harpsichord.[13] K. P. E. Bach was one of the most ardent advocates of the clavichord. In listening to the radio and to phonograph reproductions one should guard against having the soft tone volume "blown up" to untrue dynamic dimensions.

B. The Piano needs no description and its tremendous literature defies any attempt of a selective listing of compositions. Suffice it to remember the advantages which it holds over its predecessors:

1. The tone is round, full, and flexible in endless shades.
2. Tones can be rapidly repeated; the technique of tone production is superior.
3. Through the use of pedals the tone color may be enriched by producing sympathetic vibrations when the dampers are lifted; or the tone color may be dulled, by using the left pedal and thus having the hammers strike only one instead of two or three strings of identical pitch.
4. The tone dies out gradually; you sometimes do not know whether you actually still hear it or whether your memory imagines it—a decidedly romantic asset.
5. A single tone may be sustained throughout changing harmonies through the use of the middle pedal.

As against these advantages stand the following shortcomings:

1. The rigid well-tempered tuning forces other instruments to play equally "out of tune."
2. Each tone makes a diminuendo; the tone colors are therefore unsteady, mixed, never plain.
3. Under the hands of the careless player it may become more mechanical and brutal-sounding than most other instruments.
4. Harmonies may run into each other through a faulty pedal technique.

Let us remember, then, that the piano is not only the most popular and versatile instrument, but also one of the most difficult and exacting ones.

[13] Cf. Bodky, *Der Vortrag alter Klaviermusik* (Berlin: Max Hesse, 1932).

12

Brass Instruments

The Acoustics of Wind Instruments

LET US now compare a wind instrument with a string instrument. A vibrating column of air behaves in a fashion analogous to a vibrating string, and the vibration may include partials in addition to the fundamental. In other words, each tone consists again of a group of harmonics which stands in a fixed relation to the fundamental. Not only do the number of partials present and their intensity determine the tone color, but they may be singled out on a wind instrument as well as on a string instrument. Furthermore, the sound pressure at various points along the air column corresponds directly to the motion at various points along a string.

The number of harmonics, or *natural tones,* as they are called in this connection, which can be played on a wind instrument depends on various factors, as, for instance: (1) the length and diameter of the air column; (2) the material of which the instrument is made; (3) the shape of the bore (conical or cylindrical); (4) the manner in which the air column is set into motion (mouthpiece or reed); (5) the air pressure; and (6) the formation of the player's lips. These factors will also determine the tone color of the instrument.

The behavior of a wind instrument will also depend upon the kind of tube which encloses the air column: is it open at both ends, or only at one? When we blow over a piece of open pipe, a tone is sounded. We can produce another tone, an octave lower, as soon as we close the lower end of the pipe, i.e., convert the open pipe into a closed or *stopped*[1] pipe, as it is called in musical terminology. The fact that a

[1] Unfortunately, the word *stopped* is used in three different ways in music: in connection with the strings, organ pipes, and horns.

stopped pipe sounds an octave lower than an open pipe of the same length is used in many organs where space considerations prevent the installation of large pipes. Let us see now what goes on inside a stopped pipe.

We said that in a vibrating air column the molecules of air form a pattern similar to the one executed by a vibrating string. One or several arcs of vibration are formed, with pressure *nodes* at the points of least sound pressure (or greatest motion) and *loops* (or "antinodes") at the points of greatest condensation of air, where the sound pressure is greatest and the particle motion is least. At the open end of a pipe, there is no restriction on the motion of the air, while at the closed end the sound meets a rigid barrier: for this reason, a loop of sound pressure cannot be developed at the open end of a pipe, nor a node at the closed end. Hence, in the stopped pipe the fundamental pattern is the one with a pressure node at the open end and a loop at the stopped end.

224.

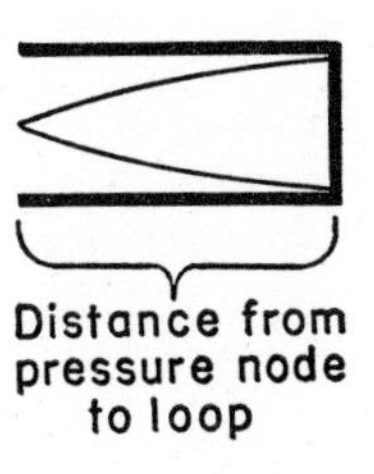

As soon as we convert the stopped pipe into an open one of the same length, the wave pattern will have to shift. The motion of the air particles at the right hand end of the pipe is no longer restricted by the solid plug which forced a loop to occur at the stopped end in the above example. Therefore, both open ends become pressure nodes, and the loop will move to the center of the pipe length.

225.

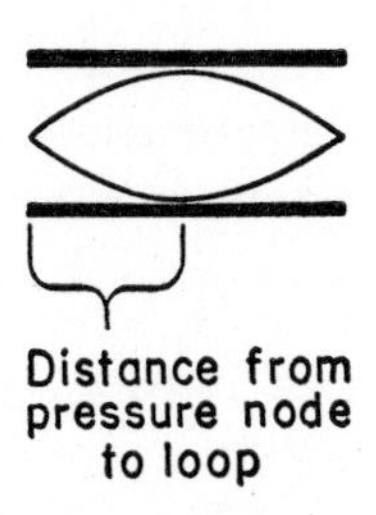

The distance from node to loop in Figure 224 is twice as great as the distance from node to loop in Figure 225. Hence it may be deduced that the frequency of the fundamental for the stopped pipe is half (one octave below) that of an open pipe of equal length.

By inserting graphically in various pipes the waves produced by the second, third, and fourth partials, we arrive at a very important conclusion: because the stopped end of a pipe can never be a pressure node, nor the open end a loop, stopped pipes are deficient in the second, fourth, and other even-numbered harmonics. The best way to see this is to start with our diagrams of the harmonics of a string and to superimpose, as it were, the limitations effected by open and stopped pipes whose air columns vibrate as we had said in a similar manner, i.e., totally and in $\frac{1}{2}$, $\frac{1}{3}$, $\frac{1}{4}$ of their effective length.

226.

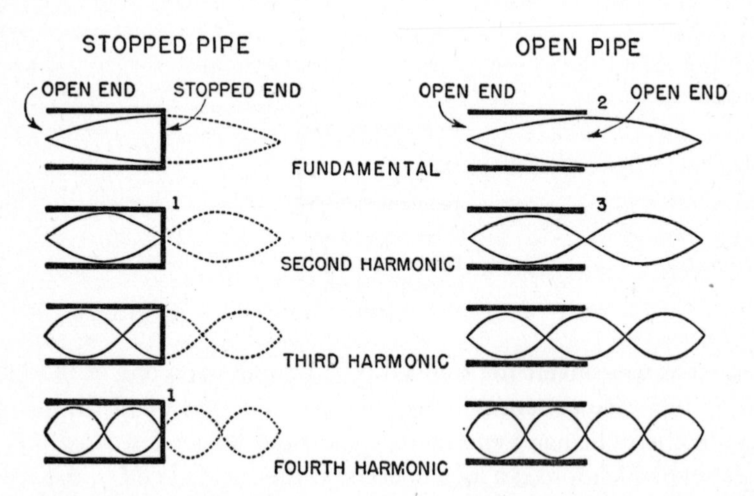

1. Note: The second and fourth harmonics cannot be produced on a stopped pipe because they would require pressure nodes at the stopped end.
2. Note: Almost impossible to produce and unsatisfactory as to tone quality on horns, trumpets, and trombones.
3. Note: The second harmonic is the ideal "fundamental" tone in open pipes.

We can now make several observations about wind instruments which employ a vibrating column of air:

1. In some instruments, e.g., the trumpet, the true fundamental or *pedal tone* (of the open pipe) is exceedingly difficult, in some cases impossible, to produce.

2. For analogous reasons, stopped pipes cannot normally produce the even-numbered harmonics because these would require a pressure node to occur at both ends of the pipe simultaneously.
3. The lack of harmonics in stopped pipes of the organ is responsible for the mild, neutral tone quality of those pipes which are stopped (*gedackt*).
4. The shape (conical or cylindrical or a combination of both) and the diameter of the bore affect the number and kind of waves possible in a wind instrument, i.e., the harmonics which are present in a tone, and those which can be "singled out" by human lung power and lip formations.

Because wind instruments are in reality more complicated than open or stopped pipes, they will sometimes behave in an unexpected manner. One instrument, for example, which reacts at times like a stopped pipe in spite of its being "open" is the clarinet. The reason for this is its mouthpiece which, through the reed, converts the instrument temporarily into a stopped pipe.[2] The resulting weakness of the even harmonics causes the mellow, hollow sound of the clarinet in its lower range. In the middle and especially in the higher range, on the other hand, the tones of the clarinet contain a number of strong harmonics, both even and odd, which produce a shrill trumpetlike effect which stands in marked contrast to the tone color of the low range.

"It seems, then, that the clarinet tube acts as a closed pipe only to a limited extent, and more so in the low register than in the other two."[3] Again, we may hope that future research will give us a clearer picture of the acoustical behavior of various wind instruments and of the roles which, for example, mouthpieces and reeds, lip pressure, air pressure, and pitch play in connection with tone color.

Brass Instruments

The divergent considerations of physical laws, convenience in handling, desired tone color, and pitch range have throughout history created a residue of tradition, preferences (or prejudices), and limitations in instrument building, and composing instrumental music, which are still with us today. It was, for example, found centuries ago

[2] Cf. C. S. McGinnis and C. Gallagher, "The Mode of Vibration of a Clarinet Reed," *Journal of the Acoustical Society of America*, Vol. XII, 529 (1941). Also: C. S. McGinnis, H. Hawkins and N. Sher, *ibid.*, Vol. XIV, 228 (1943).

[3] Cf. S. E. Parker, "Analyses of the Tone of Wooden and Metal Clarinets," *ibid.*, Vol. XIX, 417 (1947).

that on a conical metal tube, wound up in a circular form for convenience sake, a great number of natural tones could be produced. The lowest possible tone which could be produced depends on the length and bore of the tube. On such an instrument, the natural horn or Waldhorn, the predecessor of our French horn, a skilled player can, by blowing through a funnel-shaped mouthpiece and by varying his lip formation and air pressure, produce the following harmonics:

227.

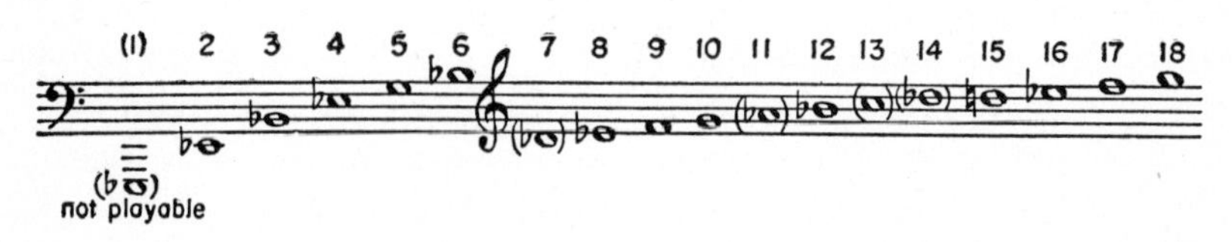

We notice that the first playable interval, a perfect fifth, corresponds to the second and third harmonics, that the first harmonic, the pedal tone one octave below E♭, cannot be satisfactorily produced on the horn; that, however, seventeen harmonics are playable as compared to five on the cello string, and that the only complete major scale possible on a horn tuned to E♭ as fundamental is the scale in E♭ major. For this reason, a horn of this particular build is called a horn in E♭. This instrument has two basic faults: (1) the tones in parentheses in Figure 227 do not fit in with equal temperament; and (2) while they may be adjusted and additional tones can be obtained through "stopping," i.e., inserting the hand into the bell, these tones sound so different in tone color from the natural tones that they seem to issue from an entirely different tone source. In order to remedy this deficiency in equality of tone color and in order to make other keys besides E♭ major available, the metal tube was made longer by various extensions which were attached according to the scale desired. Whenever, for example, the piece to be played stood in C or D or B♭, the E♭ horn became a C or D or B♭ horn through the attachment of the appropriate lengths of tubing (so-called "crooks"). At this stage of the history of the horn, which lasted until well into the first half of the nineteenth century—the instrument was only slightly improved by 1754 through the "invention horn"—the poor horn player had to take off the mouthpiece, insert a crook, and replace the mouthpiece, whenever the key of a piece changed: reason enough for composers to use horns sparingly, to modulate rarely, and to simplify the notation for the horn. Let us assume, for instance, that the horn part contains the following two phrases in quick succession:

228.

In that case the player has to change his instrument rapidly during the three measures rest from an E♭ to a D horn and he will have to find the correct tones on the changed instrument in a hurry. The harmonics required are in both cases the eighth, tenth, and twelfth (see Figure 227), in other words, the wind pressure and lip position are to be set and changed in an identical manner in both phrases. To stress this relationship, in our case the identity, of phrases on differently sounding horns in their notation, one uses to this day the expedient of writing all horn parts in C. The above example (Figure 228), for instance, would appear thus:

229.

The composer proceeds as if all music for horns were written in the tonality of C, and it is left to the instrument to transpose the music automatically into the appropriate key. For this reason, the French horn and its predecessor, the natural horn, belong to the so-called *transposing* instruments.

Whenever we read in a score, e.g., Corno (= horn) in E♭ we have to reason in the following manner: Corno in E♭ means that written C sounds actually E♭ in notation, therefore

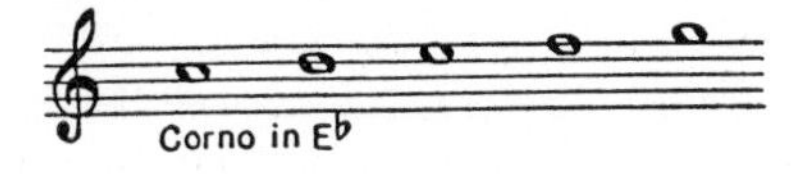

sounds:

Consequently,

230. SEPTET IN E♭ MAJOR, OP. 20 (Menuetto)

Ludwig van Beethoven (1770–1827)

sounds:

231.

The natural horn was improved in the early nineteenth century through the invention of the valve mechanism. This ingenious device, which has since been applied also to the trumpet and tuba, attached three extensions to the metal tube in such a way that through the pressing of a valve or piston the air column of the instrument could be extended instantly.

232.

Piston and Rotary Valve, Both in Rest and Action

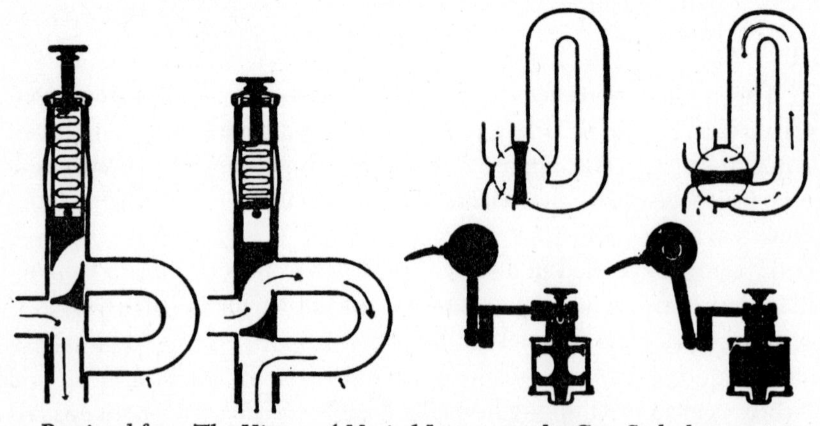

Reprinted from *The History of Musical Instruments* by Curt Sachs by permission of W. W. Norton & Co., Inc. Copyright 1940 by W. W. Norton & Co., Inc.

In the above illustration the air passes through the instrument without any detour when the piston or valve is in its resting position. As soon, however, as the piston or valve is depressed it opens the extension supplied by the extra tubing and thus lengthens the vibrating air column and lowers the pitch.

The valves lower the pitch by 1, 2, and 3 halfsteps respectively. Combination of valves yields additional tubings so that all chromatic tones within the compass of about three and a half octaves can be played as "natural tones."

A glance at Figure 227 will show us that the widest gap between tones in a series of harmonics playable on horns occurs between the second and third harmonics. This interval of a perfect fifth is bridged on most valve instruments[4] in the following manner:

233.

Valves which are depressed:

written O O O No.2 No.1 No.3 (or 1+2) 2+3 1+3 1+2+3 O

sound

O = playable without use of valves.

Valve Number	Number of Steps by Which Pitch is Lowered	Interval Produced
2	1/2	Minor second
1	1	Major second
3	1 1/2	Minor third
2 and 3.........	2	Major third
1 and 3.........	2 1/2	Perfect fourth
1, 2, and 3......	3	Tritone

If we remember that upon each newly won "fundamental" a series of harmonics can be obtained, we may understand the tremendous enrichment in tonal material which was brought about during the nineteenth century through the application of the valve mechanism. Once we have understood that several tones of widely different pitch have to be produced even on a modern French horn solely by changing the wind pressure and lip formation, we will cease to be surprised at a wrong tone played here and there by the horn section. The instrument requires such superb musicianship, sense of pitch, and lip and breath control that in orchestras its range is divided: high-pitched melodies are played by the first and third horn players and the lower parts by the second and fourth horns.

Even more astonishing than the present-day skill demanded from a horn player must have been the art of playing the trumpet in the

[4] The tuba and the contrabass tuba have a fourth valve which facilitates a more complete range in the lower compass of these instruments than is possible on the three-valve horns and trumpets.

eighteenth century. The music of Bach and Handel, for example, abounds in rapid trumpet passages in the highest regions of the "natural" trumpet, the predecessor of our modern valve trumpet. At that time players specialized either in the high or low range of the trumpet, using the same kind of instrument but different mouthpieces. Playing the highest trumpet part was called playing *clarino*.[5] Since the early nineteenth century only the B♭ (valve) trumpet has survived from the time when natural (valveless) trumpets in A, B, C, D, etc., were common.

Thus tradition has decreed that the trumpet should be another transposing instrument: the tone C in the B♭ trumpet part sounds B♭, and so on.

234. LEONORE OVERTURE NO. 3

Ludwig van Beethoven (1770–1827)

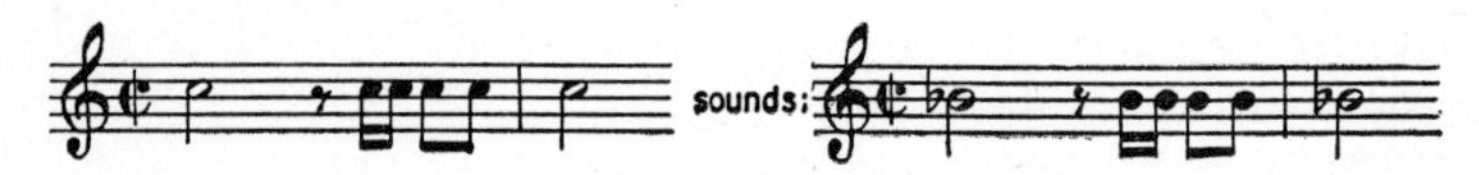

The trombones and the tuba and contrabass tuba are nontransposing instruments. That is to say, they sound the same pitch as the written notes indicate. The tubas are valve instruments operating as the horns and trumpets do. The trombones, on the other hand, use a simpler device for the changing of the length of the air column: through a sliding extra piece of tubing the air column is lengthened or shortened according to the pitch which is desired.

Tone Production in Brass Instruments

The air column in brass instruments is set into vibration with the help of mouthpieces. The shape of the mouthpiece (funnel-shaped or cuplike) influences the kind of waves of condensation and rarefaction which are formed inside the tube. The lips of the player create through the rapid interruption of an airstream the pulsating "stop and go" of puffs of air which cause the air column to vibrate. It is the tongue which articulates and accentuates tones in a multitude of ways. In the so-called double and triple tonguing, for example, the tongue accen-

[5] Subsequently, on account of the similarity between the sharply blown high clarinet tones and the high clarino tones of the trumpet, the name clarinet was chosen for the wood-wind newcomer.

tuates tones by dividing the air stream into a quick succession of explosive attacks. (If you pronounce in a sharp hissing whisper the letters *t-k* and then *t-k-t* in quick succession you have an idea of double and triple tonguing.)

An Annotated List of Brass Instruments and a Few Instances of Their Prominent Use

I. The Horns (Corno, Natural, Valve, Wald, French Horn).

Of the many different keys in which the horns were built before the invention of the valve mechanism, the horns in F and B♭ are most widely used today. The so-called *double-horn* has a mechanism which changes a single instrument instantly from an F into a B♭ horn. It is this instrument which is most frequently used in modern orchestras. With the help of the valves, horn players may change their B♭ horn to an A, A♭, G, etc., horn, and their F horn into an E, E♭, D, etc., horn.

Because of its mellow tone when played softly, the French horn blends well with the wood winds (below which it occurs in the score). On the other hand, when played loudly, bell turned up, its brassy sound makes it appear as belonging to the trumpets in tone quality. Stopped tones (indicated by a cross +) have an echolike, ghostly, faraway sound. No wonder then that the French horns are most versatile and that they are the instrument par excellence for the Romantic composers: Weber, Berlioz, Wagner, and Brahms.

Sonatas by Beethoven, Hindemith, Kauder, Quincy Porter.

Concerti by Haydn, Hindemith, Mozart, R. Strauss.

Concertino by Weber.

Schumann, *Konzertstück for Four Horns and Orchestra,* Op. 86.

Additional chamber music:

- Bach, Brandenburg Concerto No. 1.
- Brahms, Horn Trio, Op. 40.
- Britten, Serenade for Tenor, Horn, and Strings, Op. 31.
- Beethoven, Quintet, Op. 16; Sextets, Op. 71 and Op. 81b; Septet, Op. 20; Octet, Op. 103.
- Haydn, Octet for 2 Horns, 2 English Horns, 2 Violins, and 2 Bassoons.
- Hindemith, *Kleine Kammermusik,* Op. 24, No. 2; Septet (1948).
- Mozart, Horn Quintet in E♭ Major, K. 407;[6] Quintet for Piano, Oboe, Clarinet, Horn, Bassoon in E♭, K. 452; *Ein musikalischer Spass* (A Musical Joke), K. 522.
- Schubert, Octet, Op. 166.
- Schumann, Adagio and Allegro for Horn and Piano, Op. 70.

[6] In connection with Mozart's works, "K. 407," etc., refers to the chronological list of Mozart's compositions which was first established by L. von Köchel in 1862.

II. THE TRUMPET (TROMBA).

Now usually in B♭ (sounds a whole tone lower than written) or A (sounds a minor third lower). Trumpets in D, E♭, E, F, sound one, one and a half tones, etc., *higher* than written.

Hindemith, Sonata for Trumpet and Piano.
Haydn, Concerto for Trumpet and Orchestra.
Bach, Brandenburg Concerto No. 2.
Bach, Suites (Overtures) for Orchestra Nos. 3 and 4.

Additional chamber music:

D'Indy, *Suite in Old Style*, Op. 24 (for trumpet, two flutes, and string quartet).

Glazounov, *Quartet in Modo Religioso* (for trumpet, horn, and two trombones).

Saint-Saëns, Septet, Op. 65 (for trumpet, strings, and piano).

A. The Cornet, a poor relation of the trumpet, has a conical bore as compared with the cylindrical bore of the trumpet. It is, therefore, more mellow and agile. Although chiefly used in band compositions, it occurs also in works for orchestra by Berlioz, Bizet, Franck, Meyerbeer, and Rossini. Hindemith uses a cornet in his Violin Concerto, and Stravinsky in his *Histoire du Soldat*.

B. Bass trumpets. These occur in works by Wagner, Schoenberg, Stravinsky, and R. Strauss.

III. THE TROMBONE.

For a number of years now the glissando (sliding) trick and various mutes for trumpets and trombones have been used to such excessive degrees in the jazz music of our sarcastic age that a reminder is needed that trombones used to accompany softly the voices singing in church and that, later, Mozart, Beethoven, Weber, Schubert, Berlioz, Liszt, Wagner, Bruckner, and Mahler used them for deeply moving and dignified, majestic purposes.

Beethoven—Three Equales for Four Trombones.

Hindemith—Sonata.

IV. THE TUBA.

This instrument and its band versions, the Sousaphone, helicon, and euphonium (see Stravinsky's *Petrouchka*), sound as written. The tuba and the still larger contrabass tuba can best be observed in all of Wagner's operas (cf. *Faust Overture, Rheingold, Walküre, Siegfried, Götterdämmerung, Tannhäuser*). In Mendelssohn's *Midsummer Night's Dream* overture, in his *Elijah,* and in Berlioz's *Requiem,* the tuba nowadays takes the place of the defunct ophicleide.

235A. BRASS INSTRUMENTS

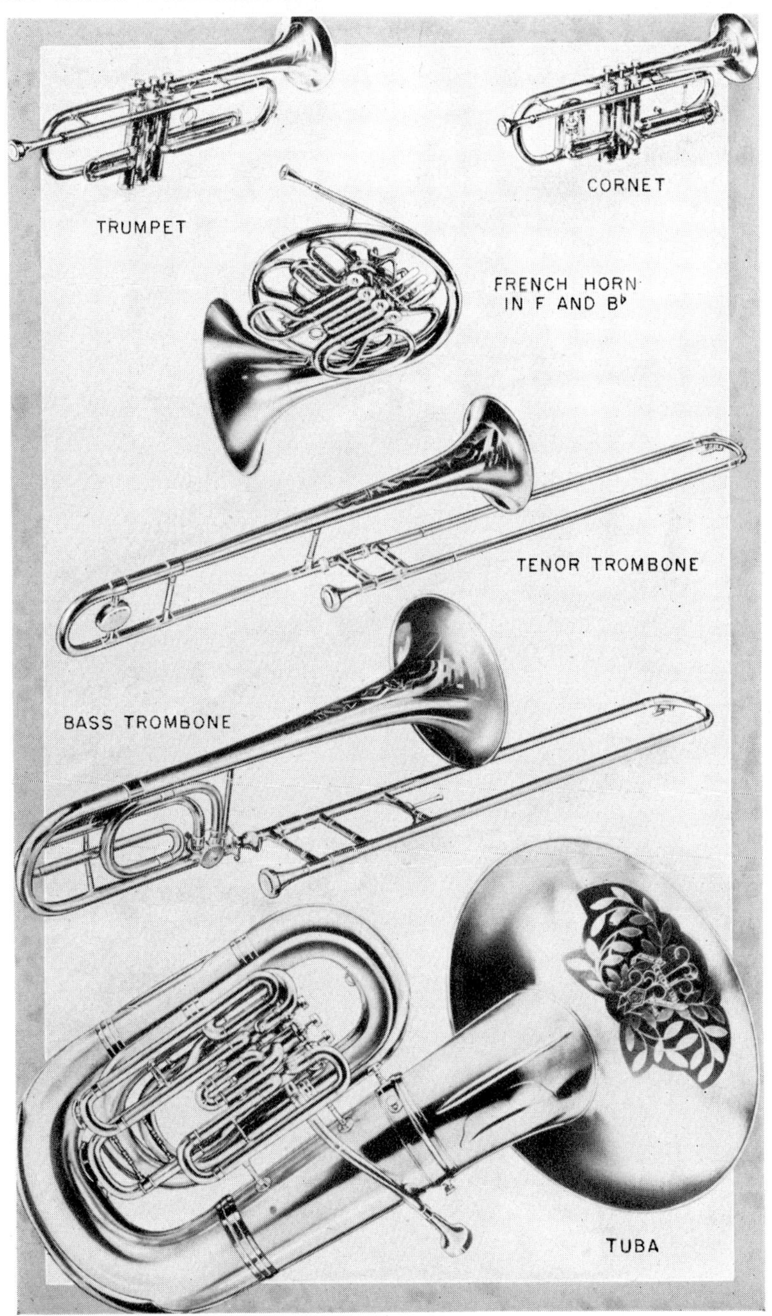

Courtesy of Conn Band Instruments, Elkhart, Ind.

235B. MOUTH PIECES OF BRASS INSTRUMENTS

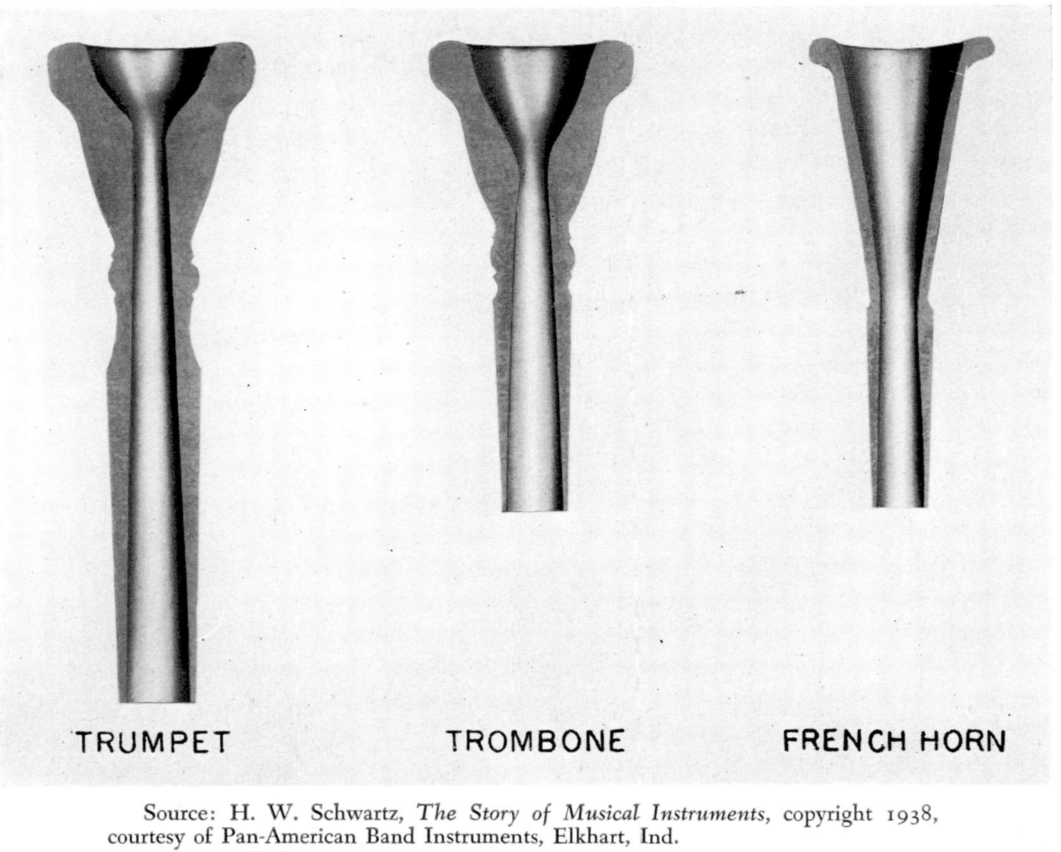

Source: H. W. Schwartz, *The Story of Musical Instruments*, copyright 1938, courtesy of Pan-American Band Instruments, Elkhart, Ind.

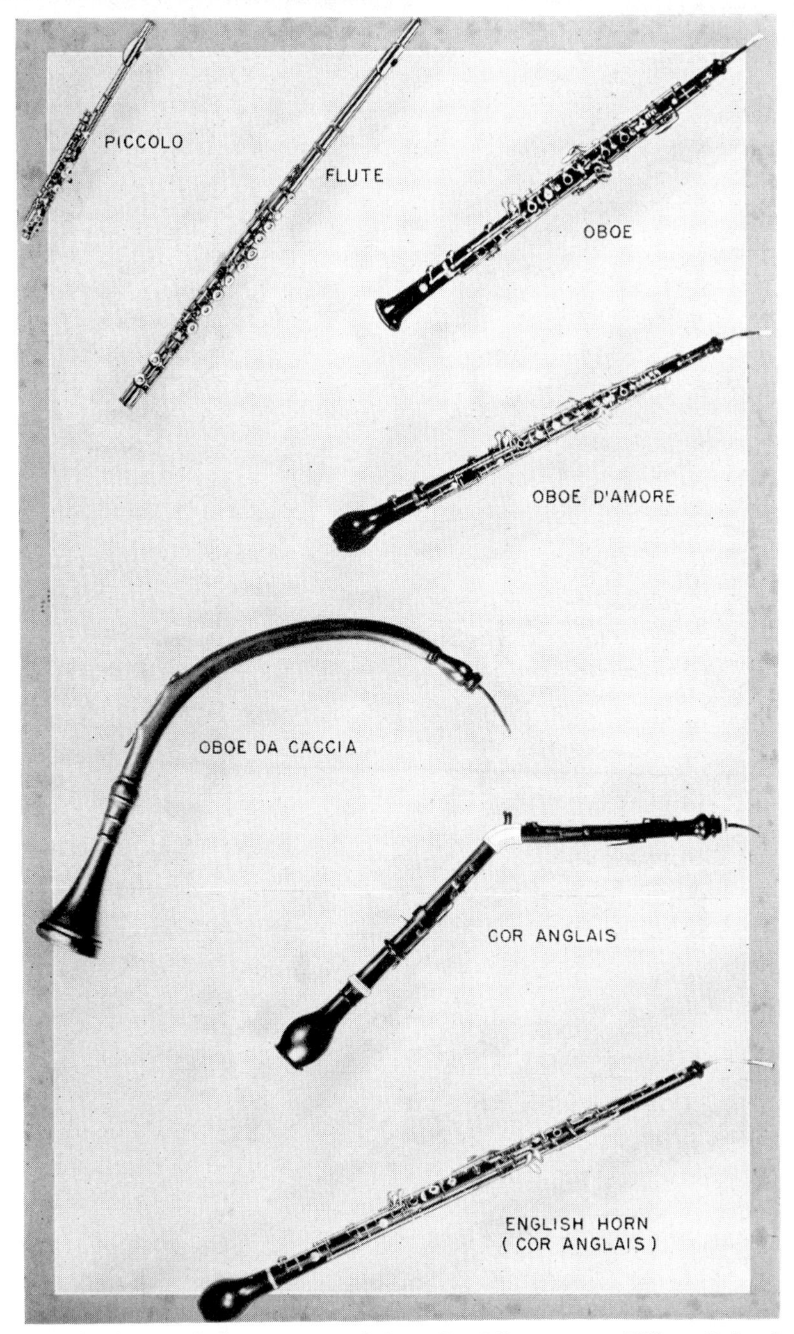

Piccolo, flute, and oboe, courtesy of Conn Band Instruments, Elkhart, Ind.; oboe d'amore, courtesy of Daniel P. Norman, Ipswich, Mass.; oboe da caccia and cor anglais, courtesy of Museum of Fine Arts, Boston; English horn, courtesy of Louis Speyer.

Contra-bassoon, courtesy of Wilhelm Heckel, Biebrich am Rhein, Wiesbaden; other instruments, courtesy of Conn Band Instruments, Elkhart, Ind.

13

Wood-Wind Instruments

In the genus wood-wind instruments we include the flutes, which used to be made of wood but are now made of silver, and the saxophones, which are made of brass but belong in one respect to the clarinets and in another to the oboes. We may even include "bone flutes" of prehistoric times, if for no other reason than to exemplify the difference between wood winds and brasses. While in the brasses the length, mouthpiece, and diameter favor the playing of many harmonics, a process which is called *overblowing,* the wood winds, because of their construction, material, and "mouthpiece," are able to produce only the second, third, and sometimes the fourth harmonic.[1] Furthermore, while the brass instruments extend their range downward by lengthening the air column, the wood winds increase their tonal sources upward by shortening the column of air. This is done by drilling holes into the instruments. When all the holes are closed the fundamental tone is heard, and the successive lifting of fingers raises the pitch by shortening the vibrating air column. Now, even within a single octave there are twelve half steps, and yet we have only ten fingers available for the closing and opening of holes and for the holding of the instrument. Furthermore, the laws of acoustics will frequently require a fingerhole in a place and of a size not convenient for human fingers. The early wind instruments, therefore, were deficient inasmuch as certain scales, modulations, or melodic phrases were awkward or impossible to play in tune. Only when Theobald Böhm (1794–1881) invented in 1832 a system of ring-keys, padded covers, and levers, did first the flute and later the oboe, clarinet, and bassoon, etc., become more flexible instruments. Böhm and his many successors in France and Germany changed the construction and fingering of

[1] The tone of these instruments may contain many partials or harmonics, but only a few can be singled out and utilized in this way.

wood-wind instruments by searching not for what was most convenient and simple but for what was scientifically correct. They found the acoustically perfect places and diameters for fingerholes and worried only later about how to manipulate the many distant holes by "remote control."

237. RING KEY

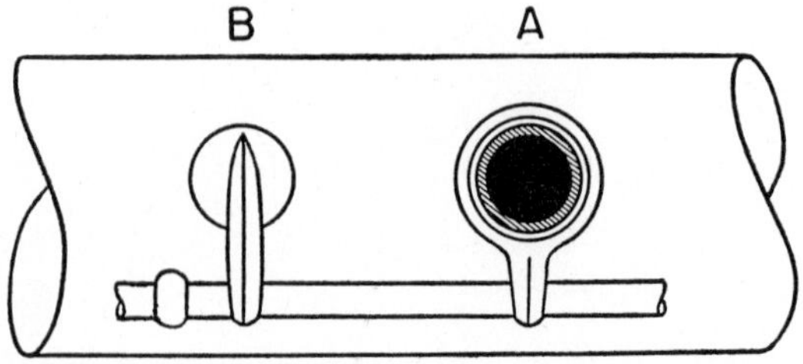

Ring key *A* and pad key *B* are mounted on the same axle and are sprung open. When hole *A* is closed with the finger, the ring is also pushed down. As the axle turns, pad key *B* also closes hole *B*. In this way two or more holes can be closed with one finger.

Source: H. W. Schwartz, *The Story of Musical Instruments*, copyright 1938, courtesy of Pan-American Band Instruments, Elkhart. Ind.

The result, which cannot be described here in detail, may be appreciated through observing illustrations and still better through the handling of one of these marvels of mechanical perfection.

Tone Production in Wood-Wind Instruments

The *flutes* have, instead of a mouthpiece, a side hole for the mouth cut near one end, which is called *embouchure*.[2] The air column of the flute is set into vibration in a manner similar to that which is used when one blows over the top of a bottle. The windstream is divided by a sharp edge, periodic "eddies" of air form on both sides, pushing to and fro in pulsating vibrations, and this "organized turbulence" is passed on to the air column of the flute. The flue pipes of the organ and the recorder are built on the same principle, the only difference being that the air stream is guided toward the edge not by human lips but by a narrow fluepipe.

[2] This term is sometimes also used for a brass mouthpiece and the players' adjustment to it. (See p. 123.)

238. A Flue Organ-Pipe

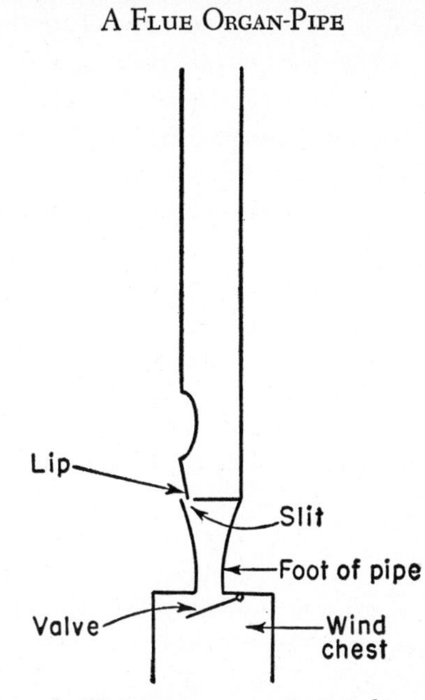

Air escaping through Slit impinges on Lip and produces an edge tone, thus setting the column of air inside the pipe into vibration.

Source: Sir James Jeans, *Science and Music,* p. 131. By permission of the Cambridge University Press.

239.

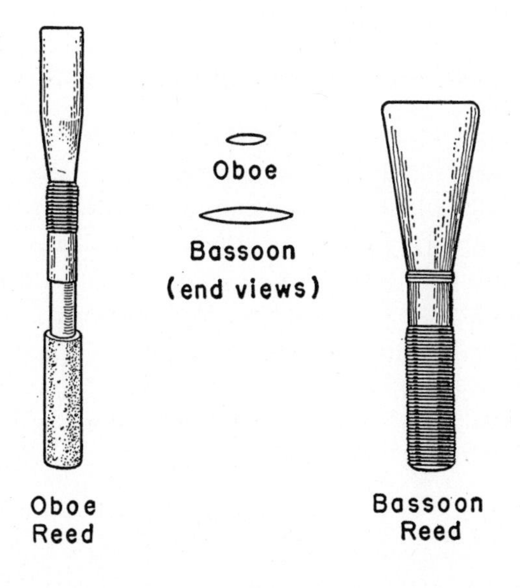

In the double reed family (*oboe, bassoon,* etc.) the role which the lips fulfil in playing brass instruments (see p. 196) is taken over by two pieces of cane reed which are bound together. The resulting tiny slit opens and closes through its own resiliency under the impact of a steady air stream. The vibrations of the double reed are passed on to the air column and converted into tones of definite pitch and tone color, determined by the length and the material and bore of the tube.

The single reed of a *clarinet* is fastened against a "table" and its knifelike thin edge forms, together with the extreme end of the mouthpiece or "beak," an aperture which is closed and opened under air pressure similar to that of the double reed or the lips.

240.

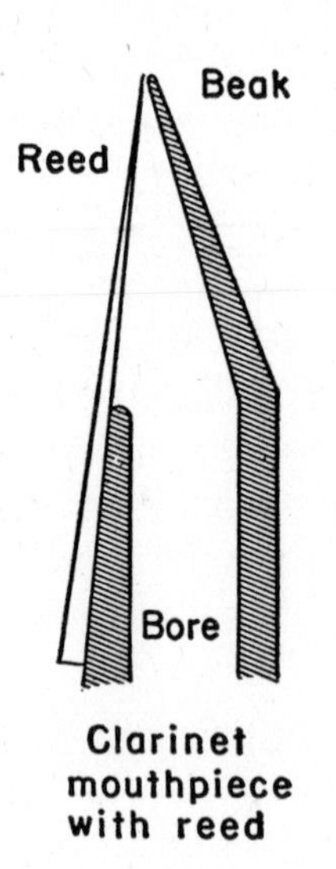

Clarinet mouthpiece with reed

We mentioned that the clarinet behaves similarly to a stopped pipe. This has several interesting results: (1) The clarinet goes much lower in pitch than the oboe, which is approximately of the same length. (2) Because the low even-numbered harmonics are missing or very weak, the clarinet overblows to the interval of a twelfth (= octave plus fifth), that is to say, the next tone which can be produced after the fundamental through tighter lips and stronger air pressure is the third harmonic. This increases the range upward but complicates the fingering, inasmuch as a greater number of tones have to be fingered than in all the other instruments which overblow to the octave, i.e., play two octaves with identical fingerings solely by changing the air pressure.[3] (3) In order to overcome these complications, older clarinets were originally built in C, E♭, B♭, A, etc., and composers and players selected the instrument which was most convenient for the piece in question. The clarinet, then, is another transposing instrument, and although its mechanism and the player's skill have improved, clarinet parts to this day are mostly written for B♭ clarinets and sometimes for A clarinets.

Summary on Transposing Instruments

Transposing instruments, of which a far greater number are in existence than have been mentioned so far, are used and occur in scores for three reasons: (1) They are a convenience for the composer and the player. (2) They have been retained as a leftover from the time when musical instruments were limited to incomplete scales and to a limited range. (3) They are selected by composers for reasons of tone color. Although these reasons overlap (especially the last and the first), and in spite of the fact that transposing instruments inevitably confuse and enrage the layman, we should attempt to see their *raison d'être* and perhaps even gain an insight into the use of instruments by composers and musicians.

In considering the first reason, it can readily be seen that the part for a piccolo is more conveniently noted an octave lower rather than with its actual sound, which would require a great number of leger lines above the staff.

241. VARIATIONS ON A THEME BY HAYDN, OP. 56A

Johannes Brahms (1833–1897)

Piccolo Presto non troppo
pp sempre
actual sound:
pp sempre

The same holds true for the double bass and contrabassoon, which sound an octave lower than written; to notate their actual sound would require a great number of leger lines below the staff.

[3] It is this fact which distinguishes the saxophones, in spite of their having a single reed, from the clarinets; the saxophones overblow to the octave as do the oboes, flutes, etc.

242. OTELLO

Giuseppe Verdi (1813–1901)

In these cases the octave transposition does what the viola clef accomplishes for the viola—it keeps the written parts legible. This is no doubt of profit for the composer as well as for the player.

The next instance of convenience (we are still considering the first reason above) is designed for the player only. Whenever there is a lower instrument of one family group to be played, e.g., an alto flute or an oboe d'amore, the flutist and oboist prefer to have their instrument do the transposing rather than to have themselves risk getting mixed up in two or more sets of fingerings. Consequently, the fingering which produces C on flutes and oboes proper sounds other (lower) tones on an alto flute and the oboe d'amore. Whenever an oboist fingers while playing an oboe part it will sound as written: however, on an oboe d'amore the same fingering will sound a minor third lower, i.e., A . While the oboe is tuned to C (as are the strings, flute, bassoon, etc.) the oboe d'amore is tuned in A, which is a minor third lower than C. An oboe d'amore part, therefore, sounds a minor third lower than it reads.

243. MAGNIFICAT (Quia respexit)

Johann Sebastian Bach (1685–1750)

The second reason for the existence of transposing instruments is purely traditional and derives from the problems which we discussed in connection with the natural horn. Because the various instruments were deficient until the invention of the valve mechanism for brasses (1813) and the Böhm system for wood winds (*c.* 1832), differently tuned wind instruments had to be used according to the key in which the composition stood. If we keep in mind that it was not until 1835 (Beethoven lived from 1770 to 1827!) that parts for the valve horn and valve trumpets appeared in a score (in Halevy's opera, *La Juive*), we may grasp the fact that Mozart and Beethoven were handicapped in using horns, trumpets, clarinets, flutes, and in the tonalities and modulations which they could prescribe for these instruments. Today, the mechanism of instruments and the experience and skill of professional musicians is so advanced that, for example, on a double horn all tones are possible, where formerly a change was required to E, E♭, D, C horns, etc. Nevertheless, the old notation has been retained, perhaps out of respect for the composers who wrote for transposing instruments, or perhaps out of conservatism, or for the convenience of conductors and score readers with professional ambition—a possibility which we shall explain in a moment.

The third reason for the retaining of transposing instruments is a serious matter which is frequently ignored by musicians. We had seen that a high tone on a low-pitched instrument and a low tone on a high-pitched instrument sound similar, yet not alike in tone color. Now, when a composer wants a shrill high-tuned clarinet or in another case a lower mellow one, he has a certain tone quality in mind, not just the convenience of the player or the limitation dictated by the deficiency of the instrument. Supposing that in some cases a clarinetist may play all the tones required by a high E♭ or low A clarinet part on his B♭ clarinet, and granting that a "warmed-up" instrument reacts or "speaks" more easily than a cold one, yet when Richard Strauss prescribed an E♭ clarinet, and Brahms an A clarinet, they knew what they wanted in regard to tone color, and the composer's wish should always supersede considerations of convenience. In short, an instrument in a certain key has often been chosen (for more than a hundred years) not for technical reasons, but rather for aesthetic ones. In doing so, composers have inevitably reverted to the method of writing parts in the manner which is traditional for transposing instruments: on B♭ instruments C sounds as B♭, D sounds as C, and so forth.

As if all this were not enough confusion, further complications arise: transposing brasses are notated without key signatures while transposing wood winds *have* key signatures. That is to say, that in a piece in G major, for example, the horn in F has an accidental inserted before C in its part whenever the actual sound of F♯ is required. And in addition, the F of the horn part becomes F♯ in order to produce the actual sound of B natural.

244. DIE MEISTERSINGER (Act III)

Richard Wagner (1813–1883)

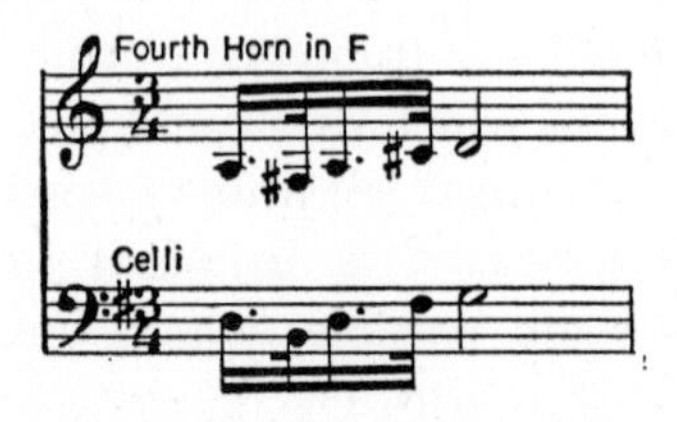

Fourth Horn and Celli Sound Identical in This Case

The B♭ clarinet, however, and other transposing wood-wind instruments indicate their *relative change* of tonality by signatures: e.g., in a piece in G major the B♭ instruments carry in their part an *A major* key signature. Because C major will sound B♭ major on a B♭ instrument, i.e., a whole tone lower than written, we will have to play and write A major in order to sound G major on a B♭ clarinet. A piece in G major then will have one sharp in the key signature for the violin, viola, cello, bass, flute, oboe, and bassoon parts, but will have an A-major signature for B♭ clarinets and a D-major signature for the English horn (which stands in F and sounds therefore a fifth lower than written.) It is this difference in key signatures which helps the experienced score reader distinguish among the many different instruments of a large score. Whenever he sees in a piece in G major the staff lines with the key signatures of A major or D major, he will notice at once that the particular staves belong to the B♭ clarinet and the English horn respectively. Likewise, the lack of a key signature, where the violins, e.g., have one, will in most cases indicate in a score the notation of transposing treble-clef brass instruments (French horns and trumpets).

There is some consolation for the layman contained in these complicated matters: only a few professional musicians can really follow an involved score and hear its sound when they read it. Whoever has reached that stage hears as well without the score as with it; he has learned to discern a complete sound through constant reading exercises.[4] There is, then, an endless task of improving both his reading and listening for the beginner, and while the goal seems far distant, each step discloses more secrets and new aspects in the art of music. It should be clear at this stage, for example, that the choice of the tonalities of a piece may be strongly influenced by the composer's imagining a certain tone color. Suppose that he intends to use French horns in their highest possible range in a prominent melody: he will then be limited or inspired in the choice of the key by his intimate knowledge of the possibilities and characteristics of a certain instrument, and in some cases he will even demand the construction of new instruments, in order to convert his musical ideas into sounds.[5] In a similar way, many violin concerti are written in the keys of the strings of the violin—in G, D, A, or E major or minor. The open (unstopped) resonant strings serve as excellent basic (tonic) tones and their neighbors a fifth apart constitute the natural invitation to modulate to the keys of the dominant and the subdominant.

Again, the repeated reading and hearing of less complex scores should precede preoccupation with large, complicated orchestra compositions. In the list of suggestions which follows, this principle has been adhered to as much as possible; however, there are exceptions, inasmuch as the occurrence of many wind instruments is limited to orchestral music.

Music for Wood Winds

I. The Flute Family.

In the Baroque Age "flute" meant what is called today "recorder" or "Blockflöte." Whenever Bach and Händel wanted our present-day flute (minus the Böhm mechanism, of course), they called for a "flauto traverso."

A. The Recorder.

Recent years have seen a revival of the building and playing of recorders and the subsequent publication of the music of the Renaissance and the Baroque for groups of soprano, alto, tenor, and bass recorders. Much of the music of Purcell, Händel, and Bach should, if one wants to follow the wishes of these composers, be performed on recorders.

[4] See Chapter 16, p. 253, for a further discussion of score reading.

[5] Cf. the Wagner tubas, which are low-pitched French horns; the Aïda trumpets, which are elongated "ceremonial" trumpets; and the Heckelphone (used in Strauss' *Salome* and *Electra*), which is an enlarged English horn.

The most famous instance is the Fourth Brandenburg Concerto by Bach, which is meant for two recorders and strings.

B. The Flute.

The sound and the visual appearance of the flute are too well known to need detailed description. However, the following chamber-music works are suggested for playing and listening.

Debussy, *Syrinx* (for flute solo).

Sonatas by Bach, Händel, Hindemith, Milhaud, Piston.

Schubert, *Introduction and Variations*, Op. 160.

Weber, *Romanza Siciliana*, Op. 45.

Concerti by Bach (Triple Concerto in A Minor and Brandenburg Concerto No. 5), Boccherini, Gluck, Haydn, Mozart, Vivaldi.

Additional chamber music: Bach, Suite in B Minor for Flute and Strings; Beethoven, Serenade, Op. 25; two quartets for flute and strings by Mozart.

C. The Piccolo.

This instrument sounds an octave higher than written. It is still badly in need of technical improvement and it belongs in the open air or large opera and concert halls. Beethoven used it in his Fifth, Sixth, and Ninth Symphonies. Wagner used two piccolos in the Smithy scene of his opera *Siegfried* and three in the Storm in *The Flying Dutchman*.

D. The Alto Flute (in Low G).

C sounds G, i.e., this instrument sounds a fourth lower than written. Orchestra solos: Pfitzner, *Palestrina*; Ravel, *Daphnis and Chloe*; Stravinsky, *Sacre du Printemps*; Gustav Holst, *The Planets*.

II. THE DOUBLE REED FAMILY.

A. The Oboe.

Sonatas by Händel, Hindemith, Saint-Saëns, Telemann.

Schumann, Three Romances, Op. 94.

Concerti by Foss, Haydn, Marcello, Telemann.

Additional chamber music:

Beethoven, Trio for Two Oboes and English Horn, Op. 87; trio sonatas by Händel; Mozart, Quartet for Oboe and Strings, K. 370.

B. The English Horn.

A transposing instrument, sounding a fifth lower than written (C sounds F, etc.). It has been justly said that the English horn is neither a horn nor English. It used to be called oboe da caccia and cor anglais. The older forms of this lower-sounding relative of the oboe used to be built in the form of a sichel, or bent in an angle. It is said that the French expression for a "horn built in an angle" (cor anglé) was misunderstood and misspelled cor anglais and thus translated English horn.

If this is not a true story (and nobody seems to know whether it is or not) it is at least a cleverly invented explanation and we should let it go at that. In many of Bach's cantatas there are arias for a solo voice, one or more obbligato instruments, and harpsichord or organ with strings. (The Wedding and Birthday Cantatas employ several flutes in this way.) The oboe da caccia is used in this capacity in Cantatas Nos. 1, 6, 48, 101, and 167.

Sonatas by Hindemith, Kauder.

Honegger, Concerto da Camera for Flute, English Horn, and Strings.

Additional chamber music:

Beethoven, Trio, Op. 87; Mozart, Adagio for English Horn, Two Violins, and Violoncello, K. suppl. 94.

Copland, *Quiet City* (for trumpet, English horn, and strings).

C. The Oboe d'Amore.

This instrument sounds a minor third lower than written. It is used as obbligato instrument in Bach's B Minor Mass, the *St. John* and *St. Matthew* Passions, the *Christmas Oratorio,* and in many of his cantatas. An orchestra solo occurs in R. Strauss's *Sinfonia Domestica.*

D. The Bassoon (Fagotto, Fagott).

It is unfortunate that the bassoon is so frequently considered a "grotesque" instrument, ever since Wagner used it in the third act of his *Meistersinger* to poke fun at Beckmesser. In order to understand that the bassoon may be tragic, deeply moving, as well, listening especially to the way Mozart uses it is recommended.

Sonatas by Hindemith, Mozart, Saint-Saëns.

Elgar, *Romance,* Op. 62.

Weber, *Andante and Rondo Ungarese,* Op. 35.

Concerto by Mozart.

Mozart, Sinfonia Concertante for Oboe, Clarinet, Horn, Bassoon, and Orchestra, K. 297b.

Additional chamber music:

Beethoven, Octet in E♭, Op. 103 (for two oboes, two clarinets, two French horns, and two bassoons).

Schubert, Octet.

Stravinsky, Octet.

E. The Contra or Double Bassoon (Contrafagott).

This instrument sounds an octave lower than written (except in *Parsifal* where it sounds as written). Here are a few works in which the double bassoon occurs more or less prominently:

Beethoven, *Fidelio*; Symphony No. 5 (Finale); Symphony No. 9 (Finale).

Brahms, Symphony No. 4; *Variations on a Theme by Haydn.*
Dukas, *The Sorcerer's Apprentice.*
Händel, *L'Allegro; Coronation Anthem.*
Haydn, *The Creation.*
Ravel, *Mother Goose Suite* ("Beauty and the Beast").
Schubert, *Eine kleine Trauermusik* (for two clarinets, two bassoons, double bassoon, two horns, and two trombones).
R. Strauss, *Elektra; Salome.*

III. THE SINGLE REED FAMILY.

A. The Clarinet.

Most frequently used today are the clarinets in B♭ and in A.

Sonatas by Brahms, Honegger (sonatina), Reger, Saint-Saëns.

Beethoven, Three Duos for Clarinet and Bassoon, Op. 147.

Berg, Four Pieces, Op. 5.

Schumann, Fantasias, Op. 73.

Weber, Grand Duo Concertante, Op. 48.

Concerti by Copland, Mozart, Weber.

Concertinos by Busoni, Weber.

Debussy, *Rhapsody for Clarinet and Orchestra.*
Gurlitt, *Concert Piece,* Op. 70.
Jomelli, Aria for Clarinet and Strings.
R. Strauss, Duet Concertino for Clarinet, Bassoon, Strings, and Harp.
Additional chamber music:

Beethoven, Trio, Op. 11.
Brahms, Clarinet Trio in A Minor, Op. 114; Clarinet Quintet in B Minor, Op. 115.
Glinka, *Trio Pathétique* (for clarinet, bassoon, and piano).
Mendelssohn, *Two Concert Pieces for Basset Horn, Clarinet, and Piano,* Op. 113, Op. 114.
Mozart, Clarinet Trio in E♭, K. 498; Clarinet Quintet for Clarinet and Strings in A Major, K. 581.
Reger, Clarinet Quintet, Op. 146.
Schumann, *Märchenerzählungen for Clarinet, Viola, and Piano,* Op. 132.
Weber, Quintet for Clarinet and Strings in E♭, Op. 34.

Other than the B♭ and A clarinets are used, for example, in the following compositions.

(High) E♭ clarinet (sounding a minor third higher than written):
Berlioz, *Symphonie Fantastique*; Strauss, *Ein Heldenleben;* Stravinsky, *Sacre du Printemps;* Ravel, *Daphnis and Chloe.*

D clarinet (sounding a tone higher than written):
Liszt, *Mazeppa*; R. Strauss, *Till Eulenspiegel*; Stravinsky, *Sacre du Printemps.*

C clarinet (sounds as written):

Beethoven, Fifth Symphony (Finale); R. Strauss, *Rosenkavalier.*

A quartet of clarinets (2 in B♭, 1 in A, 1 bass in B♭) occurs in Berg's Violin Concerto.

B. The Basset-Horn.

Sounding a fifth lower than written, this is an obsolete form of an alto clarinet. It is mentioned here for the reason that Mozart had a great liking for it; he used it in several of his operas and in his *Requiem,* and in the following chamber-music works:

Mozart, Adagio for Two Basset-Horns and Bassoon, K. 410; Adagio for Two Clarinets and Three Basset-Horns, K. 411; Serenade for Thirteen Winds, K. 361.

Mendelssohn wrote two concert pieces (Op. 113 and Op. 114) for basset-horn, clarinet, and piano.

Orchestra parts occur in Roger Sessions' Violin Concerto; and R. Strauss's *Elektra* and *Salome.*

C. The Bass Clarinet in B♭.

The bass clarinet sounds an octave plus one tone lower than written. It is used in:

Meyerbeer, *Huguenots* (Act V); Wagner, *Tristan* (Act II, Scene 3, and Act III); and in many modern compositions.

D. The Saxophone.

The soprano in E♭ sounds a minor third higher than written.
The soprano in B♭ sounds one tone lower than written.
The alto in E♭ sounds a sixth lower than written.
The tenor in B♭ sounds a ninth lower than written.
The baritone in E♭ sounds an octave and a sixth lower than written.
The bass in B♭ sounds two octaves and a whole tone lower than written.

Soprano and tenor saxophones occur in Ravel's *Bolero,* an alto in Bizet's *L'Arlesienne Suite* and in Milhaud's *La Création du Monde,* and baritone and bass saxophones in Strauss's *Sinfonia Domestica.*

The Organ

The somewhat mechanized combination of string, wood wind, and brass tone color which the organ presents lends itself to the rather impersonal, objective tendency of Baroque and modern contrapuntal composers. The well-tempered tuning and the gradually increased technical perfection of the playing mechanism made possible the use of unlimited modulations, and the use of the organ in connection with orchestras. However, the very character of the organ demands that it either accompany (as continuo instrument, i.e., taking the place of the harpsichord in cantatas and oratorios), or dominate as a solo instrument. The attempt of the nineteenth century to make the organ follow the romantic trend of emotional dynamics and operatic grandeur failed because it destroyed the inherent characteristics of the instrument—the austere autonomy of the "king among all instruments." To sob and shout, to be tender or passionate, is unbecoming for an instrument which is deliberate, noble, complex, and traditional in its basic construction. If we add the complications brought about by various nonmusical demands made by churches—and movie houses—we may well understand that organ playing and organ music have been overshadowed by chamber music, orchestras, soloists, and opera during the last hundred years. The best proof that this is the case is the arrangements of Bach's organ works first for piano and then for orchestra: if Bach will not sound like Liszt and Wagner even on modern organs, let us change Bach's "orchestration" and make his music sound "modern." Fortunately a reaction has set in to this mixing of incompatible values: better organs are designed and built again and recitals of organ music are beginning again to be given—and attended. The reader may therefore gradually become better acquainted with organ compositions by Bach, Brahms, Buxtehude, Cabezon, C. Franck, Frescobaldi, Händel, Hassler, Hindemith, Kaminsky, Lübeck, Mendelssohn, Pachelbel, Reger, Scheidt, Sweelinck, and Weckmann.

14

Percussion Instruments

WE CALL percussion all those instruments which produce a sound when shaken, scraped, or beaten. These instruments have been the stepchildren in the European music of the modern era. And yet they are the strongest link with the prehistoric magic rituals which are the origin of music. Only in our reactions to percussion sounds may we nowadays sense a remnant of the attitude of primitive man toward music. In descriptions of European musical instruments the section on percussion is often notoriously meager. On the other hand, were we to give an account of music among primitive tribes, and of the highly developed instrumental music of Java, Bali, and India, we would have to describe "percussion instruments" almost exclusively. In our customary conception of music the use of percussion is usually confined to the "rhythm section" of a band or orchestra. In the "gamelans" (percussion orchestras) of Bali, on the other hand, percussion instruments produce remarkable sonorities; they create melodies as well as harmonies in addition to rhythm. The use of percussion, then, among primitives and the highly complicated conceptions of sounding materials in the Far East bear watching as an important link to the past and perhaps also as a hint in the direction toward which a music of the future might develop.

Possibly the character of European music will change in the future; the accent may fall on percussion and pure sound again rather than on artful melodic lines and formal design. The indications for such a turn of events are here already. Just as the painters of the twentieth century became fascinated with the conception and craftsmanship and the taste to be found in "primitive art," so have the composers Debussy, Ravel, Varèse, Milhaud, Stravinsky, Bartok, and Cowell, and others, studied and incorporated in their works Eastern and "primitive" ritual and ceremonial rhythms and percussion sounds. The studies of anthropologists and music historians, recordings of authentic Eastern folk music, and the appearance of Balinese and Indian dancers and musicians in various world exhibitions and concert tours in the last forty years have brought about a certain meeting of East and West in music. The vogue of jazz and its various fluctuating styles were influenced by and contributed greatly in turn to this course of events. And so did the fact that through psychoanalysis we have lost some of our fears of primitive, atavistic tendencies, and have, as a matter of fact, become very interested in them. Let us therefore postpone until later a discussion of the currently used percussion instruments (which are simple enough by themselves), and rather consider for a few moments the sometimes complicated concepts and the use of percussion sound among primitives, Orientals, and Europeans.

Primitive Concepts of Percussion Sound

By observing rituals among modern primitives we may reconstruct ceremonies among prehistoric peoples of comparative strata of human development, and the use to which musical instruments were put during the dawn of mankind.

We hear, for instance, of rattles which emphasize the movement of the body, transposing dance into sound, as it were. The use of a rattle in primitive religious rites was described most vividly seventy years ago by Stephen Powers, who had attended a secret meeting of the Maidu Indians in California.

> There was a silence of some minutes in the impenetrable darkness, then the sacred rattle began a low, ominous quivering close to the ground, in which there was sufficient suggestion of a rattlesnake to make one feel chilly about the scalp. Presently one of the four performers, apparently lying on his belly and holding his mouth close to the ground, began to give forth a series of blubbering gurgling sounds and nasal whining, with frequent intermissions, growing shorter all the while as the tone of his voice rose. At the same time the rattle rose up slowly, gaining a little in force, until finally it shot up all at once, and seemed to dart about the top of the room with amazing rapidity, giving forth terrific rattles and low, buzzing quavers . . .
>
> . . . When they have sung for about half or three quarters of an hour without cessation the rattle grows fast and furious, the great performer's fist goes tunk, tunk, tunk on the post with great violence, . . . the singers' voices sink into a long-drawn, dying wail; . . . The rattle drops to the ground and seems to hover close over it, darting in every

245A. PERCUSSION INSTRUMENTS

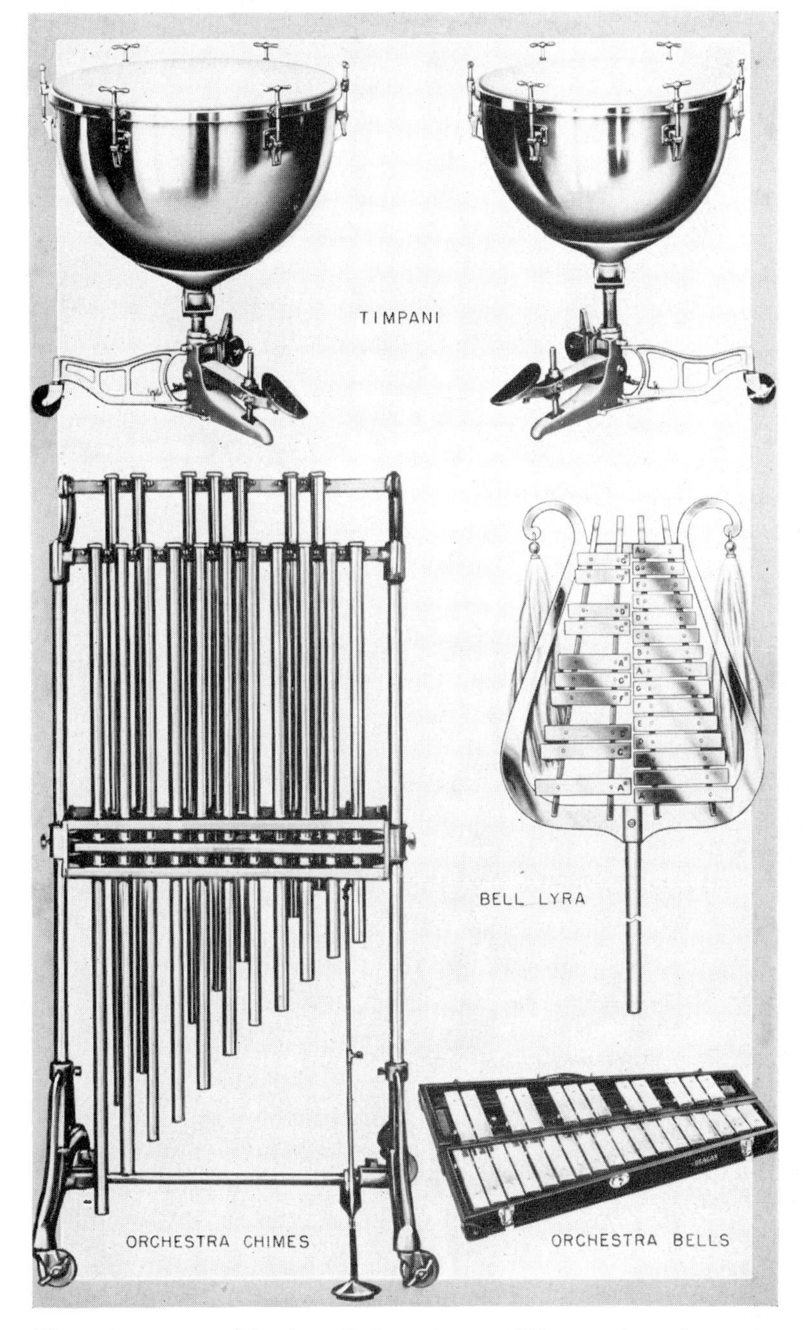

Timpani, courtesy of Leedy & Ludwig Drums, Elkhart, Ind.; orchestra chimes and orchestra bells, courtesy of J. C. Deagan, Inc., Chicago; bell lyra, courtesy of Slingerland Drum Co., Chicago.

245B. PERCUSSION INSTRUMENTS (*Continued*)

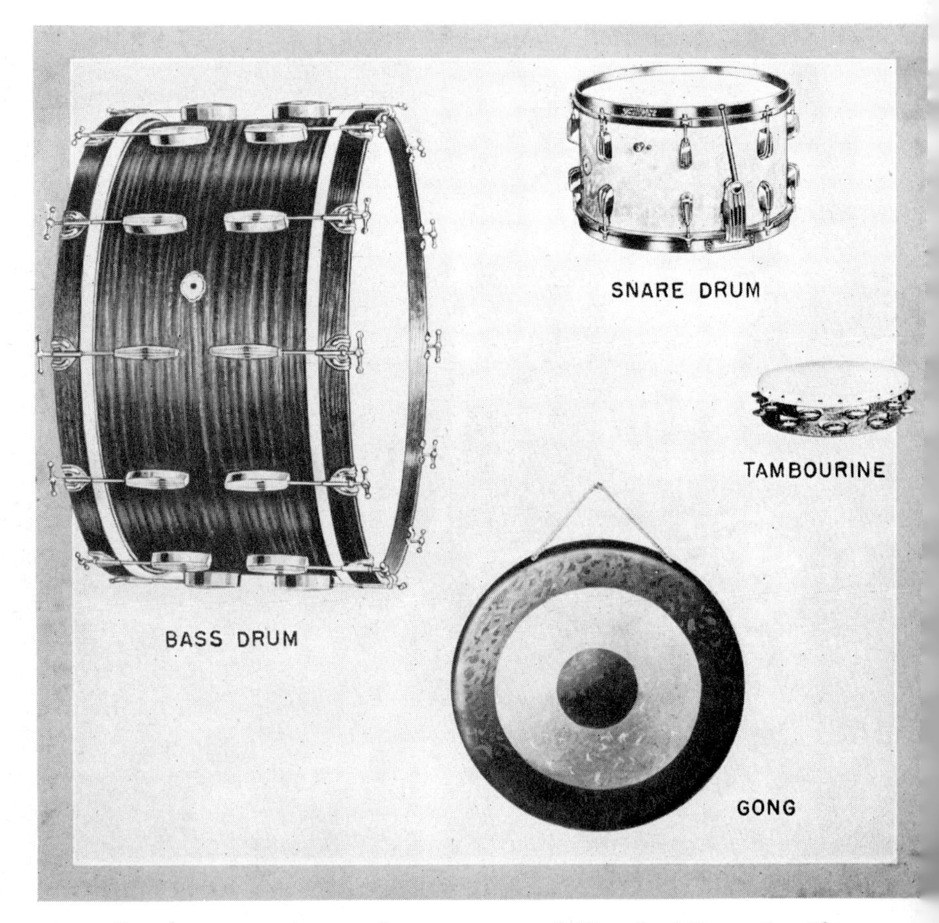

Bass drum, snare drum, and gong, courtesy of Slingerland Drum Co., Chicago; tambourine, courtesy of Leedy & Ludwig Drums, Elkhart, Ind.

> direction, and only two of the performers are heard, groveling on the ground and muttering petitions and responses, until finally the rattle dies slowly out . . . and all is over.[1]

Other primitive "percussion" instruments are the bull-roarer, a wooden "fish" on a string whirled in the air, representing the voice of an ancestor; and "sounding amulets," bells which are attached to the heads of animals in order to protect them from evil spirits. Primitive xylophones—slabs of stones, metal, or wood which sound when beaten—occur also in primitive times, and so do drums of many different shapes and sizes.

These and many other instruments (e.g., flutes, reeds, "megaphones") are used to this day among primitive tribes for funerals and fertility rites. Throughout the history of man, death and rebirth, mourning and mirth, stillness and noisy frenzied spring, love, and fertility rites, are always combined. We have only to remember, for example, the death dances of the Middle Ages, the wild epidemic dancing in cemeteries which spread through Europe between the eleventh and fourteenth centuries,[2] the Witches' Sabbath, and the funeral feasts of more recent dates. Even today the laughter in movie houses when someone cracks a joke in the midst of a gruesome, frightening situation may prove to us that the combination of mourning and mirth (the "The King is dead, long live the King" attitude) is eternally human. Similarly, the drums of today, when they are used muffled for funeral processions or loud for military marches, stir in us memories of the primitive past, way beyond reasoning: death and victory over death are both connected in a single instrument for us.

Returning to our authentic primitives, we should not be surprised, then, to find that the instruments used in the celebration of death and rebirth, the "voices" which are supposed to influence evil spirits and produce new sources of life, are held sacred. Drums, for example, are hidden, protected, painted with blood or red paint; and offerings of milk and animals are made to them.[3]

> Sometimes the guardian of the drums stated to the Mugabe [the chief of the tribe] that they required meat, whereupon the Mugabe ordered a cow to be brought from the herd of the drums. It was kept for

[1] Stephen Powers, "Tribes of California," Department of the Interior, *North American Ethnology*, Vol. III, 1877, pp. 306–7. Also quoted in part in Sachs, *The History of Musical Instruments*, pp. 27–28.

[2] Nettl, *The Story of Dance Music*, p. 47.

[3] Sachs, *op. cit.*, p. 35.

> one night near the house of the drums with other cows, and in the morning it was taken before the drums where the guardian presented it to them, saying, "This is the cow which the Mugabe consents to your having. Now let him live in peace with his neighbors, drive illness away from him and make him powerful!" The cow was then killed, the blood being caught and kept for smearing the drums.[4]

To the primitive man it is also of utmost importance who the player is of the various instruments. The playing of instruments is restricted as far as sex is concerned.[5] Only men may use drumsticks in playing drums. Certain instruments must not even be seen by women, under penalty of death.[6]

Oriental Concepts of Percussion

The concept that certain instruments are appropriate to be played by men and others by women only, and solely for special occasions, has also been found for centuries in the Far East. Small cymbals which are held and played like castanets are used by professional female entertainers to accentuate their songs and dances. And a huge bell in Peking, which was cast in the fifteenth century A.D. was to be struck only when the emperor prayed for rain.[7] This idea that sound may produce physical results is common to the primitive as well as to the Oriental mind—and to us, to a certain extent, as we shall see. For primitive man the sound of the rattle, for example, actually produces fertility and drives away physically present evil spirits; the bull-roarer is the actual voice of the ancestor, and so on. Mind and matter, "ideas" and their physical manifestation, are one in primitive and Oriental concepts.

On this basis the ancient Chinese, even before the Greeks, erected a system of definitions and uses of sound which is of the utmost importance for the understanding of Oriental music, and of certain recent European and American attempts to employ new sonorities by using percussion instruments. In the Oriental conception, sound itself is considered as something almost concrete, inseparably connected with the material which produces it; matter and sound are compared to body and soul.

[4] John Roscoe, *The Banyankole*, p. 48.
[5] Sachs, *op. cit.*, p. 35.
[6] *Ibid.*, p. 36. (Could it be that those conductors in America who still refuse to employ women in their orchestras are reverting to an age-old primitive custom?)
[7] *Ibid.*, p. 170.

A tone in Far Eastern conception does not need any definite length or rhythm; it should not be cut off or superseded by other sounds; the longer it lasts, and the more it is isolated, the more a listener perceives the life of the substance that has produced it.[8]

It follows that sound is "matter come to life." According to the ancient Chinese, music is the manifestation of the laws of the universe and there exists a close correlation between the seasons, the elements, the material of which an instrument is made, and the cardinal points. Consequently, in order not to destroy the balance of the universal laws, certain instruments may be used during particular seasons and for special occasions only.[9]

Conversely, to play the "proper" music may bring people into better "sympathy" with the laws of the cosmos, which in turn is embodied as mikrokosmos in the state. Music, then, may educate people toward becoming better citizens, as Confucius and later the Greek philosophers concluded.

European Concepts of Percussion

Let us now recall some instances of the use and the effects of percussion sound in the European history. During the times of the Crusades drums were introduced from the Orient as a soldier's instrument. In the Renaissance kettledrums became (together with trumpets) the symbol of aristocracy. To a disciplined churchman of the sixteenth century, drums appeared "satanic," and profoundly disturbing. Their noise kept awake peaceful citizens, as the radio and jukebox do today.

These [kettledrums] are enormous rumbling barrels. They trouble honest old people, the ill and the sick, the devotees in monasteries who study, read and pray, and I think and believe that the devil has invented and made them . . .[10]

In the eighteenth century we hear of the spectacular behavior of drummers who use "affected figures and fantastic contortions"[11] (think of our contemporary jazz drummers!). The Baroque Era used timpani (kettledrums) for festive marches and for the expression of joy and power in dramatic sections of operas and oratorios (cf. the

[8] *Ibid.*, p. 164.
[9] *Ibid.*, p. 163 ff.
[10] *Ibid.*, p. 329, quoted from Virdung, *Musica getutscht* (1511).
[11] *Ibid.*, p. 330.

works of Händel and Bach). Finally, in the classic era it became the fashion to imitate "Turkish music." The outcome of this is the use of the bass drum, cymbals, and triangle in Haydn's Military Symphony, in Mozart's *Abduction from the Seraglio,* and in Beethoven's Ninth Symphony. Ever since that time percussion instruments have been used in European festive music of a military, religious, or Oriental character. The Romantic Era used percussion also in order to add "mysterious sounds," and the modern era introduced "realism" especially through additions to the percussion section.

We could say then that in modern Western music, just as in Eastern and primitive music, certain musical instruments have always been associated with certain ceremonial exercises. However, there is a difference, depending on whether these associations are primary or secondary. For example, a flute or English horn is frequently used in connection with shepherd music, a French horn in connection with hunting, and trumpets with military occasions. Few of us have heard or played these instruments while herding sheep, hunting, or while going into battle; the sound association comes to us symbolically only, i.e., indirectly. Cowboy calls, on the other hand, the sound of galloping horses, airplane motors, sirens, telephone bells, will evoke in us a vivid picture and a direct physical as well as a mental reaction.

Similarly, the sound of a rattle or a Chinese gong will sound "typically" South American or Oriental to us, while it will recall to the primitive man fertility rites, and to the Chinese, religious ceremonies —with which both were intimately familiar from early childhood.

For us today an analogous reaction is exerted by a few instruments only. Drums and church bells affect us physically as well as mentally in a direct impact. The ominous disturbance of the air through drumming and the vibrations of huge bells seem to envelop us physically and simultaneously they stir up mental pictures of the supernatural and the eternal. It is in these rare and unexplainable moments that we approach the attitude of the primitive and of the Oriental man toward sound, that sound acts physically. Furthermore, the idea of sound governing matter, viz., the walls of Jericho crumbling under the trumpet blast of Joshua, is not too strange any more to a generation which has found that intense sound waves can be used to homogenize milk, and to perform many industrial functions. Even the ancient belief of the power of music to move body and soul is familiar to the European mind, although percussion is less used in that connection than was and is customary among primitives and Orientals. To sing hymns in churches and schools, to sing lullabies and to play the drums for parades is, of course, nothing but a continuation of the ancient idea of having "a song or dance for every occasion." To use music for the prevention of youthful delinquency, for the soothing of strained nerves in factories and restaurants, is an analogous idea. If we add that attempts to influence the sick in body and mind through appropriate musical activities and tones have persevered throughout history to this day, we may understand that our use of instruments is partly directed by age-old beliefs and customs, which were in use especially in connection with percussion instruments. The invention and employment of new percussive devices, directly connected with present-day ritual associations and the Orient-inspired use of percussion as absolute sonorities (sound per se) in modern music should prove less frightening the more we enlarge our historic and geographical horizon.

Contemporary Percussion Instruments

Percussion instruments are frequently classified into two groups: those which produce a sound of "definite pitch," such as the timpani or the celesta, and those which produce a sound of "indefinite pitch," such as the bass drum or the triangle. In one sense, this is a true distinction: instruments of the first group are often used as melodic or harmonic elements in the musical fabric, while instruments of the second group are used primarily for rhythmic punctuation and tone color or "sound effects." In the score of a piece of music, the exact pitch of the timpani is indicated, while only rhythm and dynamics are prescribed for the bass drum part.

In another sense, however, the distinction is far less obvious and we might do well to think of "definite" and "indefinite" pitch in relative terms. Just as in the case of consonances and dissonances, a sliding scale of values is in order.

On one extreme of this scale we find the pure sound of the tuning fork which emits one clear fundamental tone with practically no partials. Next come the many musical instruments in which a fundamental is reinforced or colored in various degrees by harmonic partials. In this case, the pitch corresponds to the frequency of the fundamental. Even if the fundamental is not physically present, the ear (or the mind) assigns this pitch to the composite tone.

An instance in which two distinct tones combine to produce a third tone was discovered in the eighteenth century in the existence of the so-called *difference tone*. Practical use of this phenomenon has been made for centuries in the construction of so-called acoustic basses in organs. Because a very low tone, let us say the C with a frequency of 16 cycles per second (one octave below the lowest C on our piano keyboard) would require a costly and cumbersome organ pipe approximately thirty-two feet in length, two shorter pipes are substituted and tuned to the second and third harmonics of the desired fundamental note. The resulting pitch corresponds to the difference tone (with the frequency of 16 cps.) between the second and third harmonics (32 and 48 cps., i.e., twice and three times 16).

An extreme case, where we perceive a definite pitch although *neither* a fundamental *nor* a series of harmonic partials is present, occurs in the church bell. The partials of which the tone of a bell is composed are not harmonically related, that is, they occur at frequencies which are not simple integral multiples of the lowest partial. As a result, the tone quality of a bell has a dissonant character. Even so, our ears detect one definite pitch, the so-called *strike tone* of the bell. Because the frequency of the strike tone cannot be found among the partials into which the tone of the bell can be dissected by physicists, it has been explained as the difference tone between two upper partials. It would lead us too far astray to go further into this particular topic, but the problem of bells provides a useful example. It illustrates one way in which the ear assigns a real and definite pitch to a sound which does not have harmonic partials.

It is characteristic of the sound of percussion instruments said to have "indefinite" pitch, that a number of inharmonic partials are present, but the ear can still assign a "pitch" to such a sound. The best proof for the fact that our distinction between definite and indefinite pitch is arbitrary is obtained when we hear a bass drum or triangle first alone and then within the "tonal frame of reference" of an orchestra. In the first case we might describe the sound as an indefinite boom, or ringing, in the latter case our ear infers a pitch which conforms to the harmonic environment of the moment. The same happens when we hear and compare two bass drums or two triangles, of different sizes: the larger instruments are definitely lower in pitch than the smaller ones within each species. Even knocking at various pieces of furniture will gradually train us to distinguish different shapes and materials solely by the pitch which we assign to them.

Actually, many of the percussion instruments with so-called "definite" pitch are very similar to others which are said to have "indefinite" pitch. Both the triangle and the celesta consist of vibrating metal bars, with inharmonic partials. But the celesta has, associated with each bar, a tuned resonator which modifies the sound of each metal bar and so emphasizes and sustains a single partial as to cause the ear to say—*that* is the pitch. The kettledrum and the bass drum are also very similar, except for the resonant cauldron of the kettledrum which again helps the ear to single out a definite pitch.

The discussion of the "definite" or "indefinite" pitch of percussion instruments, however false and arbitrary a distinction this may be, is particularly valuable for the light it sheds on modern musical developments in a more general sense. The majority of familiar musical sounds are made up of composite tones with harmonically related partials, and almost all our basic harmonies may be traced to this simple relationship. Yet we must realize, as modern composers have already realized to a varying degree, that such sounds are a very small group of the many sounds available for use in music.

If we are willing to accept as aesthetically valid in music certain combinations of sounds less simply constructed, the new musical horizons expand almost without limit. Such sounds may legitimately be described as "noise" by conservative listeners, since "noise" is officially defined as "any undesired sound."[12] To the modern composer, however, who is looking for new shades of color, such sounds are not *noise,* but *music* in the truest sense of the word. They are essential components of a structure which utilizes and selects from all sounds which are available in nature, rather than from the very limited family of tones with harmonic partials.

It will depend, then, upon the skill and vision of the composer and the status of concentration and experience of the listener whether the final verdict will be "chaos" or "a work of art." If we remember in addition that music expresses the impressions of the world made upon a composer, and the resulting fears, warnings, despair, as well as his hopes and idealistic dreams, we should be well prepared to expect

[12] *American Standard Acoustical Terminology,* American Standards Association, Inc., 1951, p. 7.

clashes, agonies, hopelessness, in the language of music and not only and always idyllic harmonies and happy endings.

In summarizing the present-day use of percussion instruments, one could say that they may fulfil one or more of the following functions: they may (1) underline a meter; (2) present a rhythm; (3) accentuate a rhythmic, melodic, or harmonic climax; (4) add tone color; (5) present a single tone or a melody; (6) combine in harmony. In fulfilling one or more of these functions, percussion sound may at times create associations, e.g., evoke the mental picture of military, religious, Oriental, or narrative occasions.

It is recommended that the reader study at this point, for a period of time, the use of percussion instruments in the music which he hears. The function of percussion sound at any one moment might be analyzed according to the above functional categories. The list of compositions at the end of this chapter should provide ample material for such investigations.

The Role of the Percussion Player

It is obvious from these many aspects of percussion in music that the percussion player must possess the same skill and musicianship which is demanded of a good string or wind instrument player: namely, a sense of rhythm, tone color, pitch, harmony, and an over-all picture of his ever-changing part within the total sound. All this is imperative for a timpanist as well as for his colleagues in the percussion section. In order to gain an insight into the physical skill necessary, let us consider Stravinsky's directions to the percussion player in the score of his *Histoire du Soldat.*[13]

> Percussion instruments (to be played by one player only): 2 side-drums without snare, of different size, drum without snare, drum with snare, bassdrum, cymbals, tambourine, triangle. . . .
>
> The bass drum is on the player's left and the 2 side-drums directly in front of the performer, very close to each other. These instruments to be struck with a stick with fibre head, held in the player's left hand. In his right hand he holds a thin stick with sponge head, to be held in readiness for no. 34. . . .

[13] Igor Stravinsky, *Histoire du Soldat* (Vienna: Wiener Philharmonischer Verlag). By kind permission of the composer.

General direction for the percussion in the Tango: The performer holds the stick for the bass drum in his left hand, and a cane stick with fibre head in his right. The notes with upward stems to be played by the right hand (i.e. the fibre stick), those with downward stems by the left (i.e. the bass drum stick). The cymbal (attached to the bass drum) to be struck lightly at the rim, and with the cane handle of the fibre stick only. . . .

All these percussion instruments are lightly struck with the triangle beater. The triangle is held by the performer's left hand; at his right, very close at hand and facing each other side-drum and tambourine (conveniently placed in an upright position); at his left the bass drum.

Special Sound Effects

Besides the "legitimate" instruments there are many unusual instruments which have been and are being used for special effects, e.g., the 18 anvils in Wagner's *Rheingold*; the rattle and the wind machine in R. Strauss's *Till Eulenspiegel* and *Don Quixote,* respectively, and the thunder machine in his *Alpine Symphony*. Cuban maracas (gourds filled with dry seeds or pebbles) and other primitive noise-making instruments occur in scores by Prokofieff, Stravinsky, Shostakovitch, Messiaen, and others. The machine age has been imitated through typewriters, automobile horns, airplane motors, sirens, machine guns, sheets of steel, etc., etc. The age of electricity produced vibraphones (used in Alban Berg's *Lulu Suite*) and radio tube instruments: the *Theremin* and the *Ondes-Martenot,* both of which emit tones through a loud-speaker (which is in reality an instrument in its own right).

The use of extramusical contraptions in a piece of music should not prove too shocking to conservative listeners if they remember that bird calls, battles, and thunder and lightning have been imitated in music for centuries. While conventional instruments were used as media throughout the classic and early romantic age, *realism* introduced the "real" (recorded) bird call (Respighi, *Pines of Rome*), the actual cannon (Tchaikovsky, *Overture 1812*), the airplane motor (Weill, *Lindbergh Flight*), the radio beam signal (Barber in the original version of his Second Symphony), etc. Once a composer is granted the artistic right to imitate nature, he is justified in choosing the most practical means for doing so. What counts in terms of music is whether he introduces and elaborates on such a device in a musically convincing manner. The trumpet call in Beethoven's *Leonore*

Overture No. 3, for example, is a signal, not a tune; it is the old-fashioned equivalent of a telephone call or a telegram, bringing—in this case—liberation in a moment of greatest agony. The deeply moving effect is caused by Beethoven's music before and after the call signal—it matters little whether a modern composer, in a similar situation, uses a different device for the signal, provided that he can express the unseen drama of the mind and soul as movingly and convincingly as Beethoven did (cf. the use of a ringing telephone in the last scene of Menotti's *Consul*).

Mechanical Instruments

Before concluding our discussion of instruments, a word must be said of mechanical instruments. Compositions for mechanical carillons, clocks, pianos, organs, are not new. Should it become the rule for composers to design music directly on sound films, constructing rhythms, melodies, harmonies, and tone colors, different from all now existing musical patterns and instruments, we still should not despair and bemoan the "decline of the art of music." There may be a question of necessity and taste involved; however, the precedent to compose music expressively for a device which reproduces the intended sound mechanically has been set by many great composers. Beethoven's *Battle of Vittoria* was originally written for Maelzel's Panharmonicon (a predecessor of the jukebox); Mozart wrote music for a mechanical organ, and Haydn for a mechanical "flute-clock."

In the nineteenth century the "pianola" and Welte-Mignon piano rolls not only made it possible to preserve and duplicate on a real piano the playing of great pianists but also to compose music for the piano which was not limited to the two hands of a human pianist. This procedure may indicate the direction in which a modern composer may progress if he thinks similarly to the forward-looking Berlioz. Combining Berlioz's dreams of an orchestra of 465 instrumentalists and 360 singers with economic considerations and the possibilities of electronics, we may yet see and hear "push-button" music which creates its own sounds and laws of construction and which is not a mere mechanical imitation of "hand-made music." As always, new means of expression will be found as soon as there is something to be conveyed in the language of music which cannot be said in old-fashioned words and grammar.

A List of Percussion Instruments and a Few Instances of Their Prominent Use

I. Percussion Instruments of "Definite Pitch."

A. Timpani (Kettledrums, *Pauken*).

These instruments usually occur in pairs tuned to the tonic and dominant—at least throughout the classic era. (In Beethoven's Eighth and Ninth Symphonies, however, the timpani are at times tuned to the interval of an octave.) Later, larger numbers were employed (cf. the eight pairs of timpani in Berlioz's *Requiem*). In 1872 a mechanism was invented which facilitated the instant changing of the pitch of kettledrums through pedals. Since then rapid changes in the tuning of timpani during a piece have become frequent.

Barber, *A Stopwatch and an Ordnance Map* (for male chorus and three kettledrums).
Bartok, Sonata for Two Pianos and Percussion.
Hindemith, Concerto for Piano and Percussion.
R. Strauss, *Burleske for Piano and Orchestra.*

Bach, *Christmas Oratorio*; Overtures (Suites) No. 3 and No. 4; *Easter Cantata*; and many other joyful, religiously militant cantatas.
Mozart, *Serenata Notturna in D Major for Two Orchestras,* K. 239.
Stravinsky, *Les Noces* (for voices and all-percussion orchestra, including four pianos).

Almost every symphony or opera contains important timpani parts. Here are a few works among hundreds in which at times the timpani are particularly in evidence:

Beethoven, *Fidelio,* Finale of Act I and Introduction to Act II; Symphonies Nos. 4, 5, and 9 especially.
Bruckner, Seventh Symphony.
Elgar, *Enigma Variations* (Variation VII—solo).
Mahler, Symphonies Nos. 2 and 7.
Mozart, *Magic Flute,* Finale of Act I (here the timpani are muted); Act II (March).
R. Strauss, *Salome.*
Stravinsky, *Sacre du Printemps.*
Tchaikovsky, Symphony No. 4.
Verdi, *Ballo in Maschera.*
Wagner, *Gotterdämmerung; Die Walküre.*

B. The Bells (Orchestra Chimes).

In concert halls and operas, tubular steel bars are used instead of actual church bells.

Berlioz, *Fantastic Symphony,* Op. 14, Fifth movement (Witches' Sabbath).
Debussy, *Iberia.*

Mahler, Symphony No. 2, Fifth movement.
Puccini, *Tosca* (Acts I and III).
Sibelius, Symphony No. 4, Fourth movement.
Tchaikovsky, *1812 Overture.*
Wagner, *Parsifal* (Acts I and II).

C. The Glockenspiel.

This instrument appears in three versions:

1. The *orchestra bells.* Small steel plates of varying size (and therefore pitch), struck with hammers.
2. The *bell lyra.* In military bands the steel plates are arranged vertically within a steel frame which has the form of the ancient lyra, and in addition a handle by which the instrument is carried during parades.
3. The *keyboard glockenspiel.* Today this instrument is rare. The most famous part written for it, in Mozart's *Magic Flute,* is usually played by the celesta nowadays.

Delibes, *Lakmé* (Bell Song).
Dukas, *The Sorcerer's Apprentice.*
Ravel, *Daphnis and Chloe* (Suite No. 2).
Rimsky-Korsakov, *Russian Easter Overture.*
Mahler, Symphony No. 8, Second part.
Puccini, *La Bohème.*
Saint-Saens, *Samson and Delilah* (Act III, Scene 3).
R. Strauss, *Sinfonia Domestica; Don Juan; Also Sprach Zarathustra.*
Tchaikovsky, *Nutcracker Suite* (Chinese Dance).

The glockenspiel sounds two octaves higher than written—except in the works of Wagner and Mozart, where it sounds one octave higher than notated.

D. The Glass Harmonica.

Although strictly speaking not a percussion instrument, this instrument might be mentioned here on account of its distant relationship in sound to the celesta. The glass harmonica was invented by Benjamin Franklin in 1763. It consists of glass bells of different size which are made to rotate on a spindle which is turned through a treadle. The glass bells are kept moist by traversing a water basin and the tones are produced by touching the edge of the bells lightly with the fingers.

Mozart, *Adagio in C Major,* K. 356; Quintet for Harmonica, Flute, Oboe, Viola and Cello, K. 617.

E. The Celesta.

This is a keyboard glockenspiel in which the tone is magnified and made mellow by wooden resonators. Dampers are provided and may be lifted by a pedal, just as in the piano. The resulting tone quality is similar to a mixture of the tone colors of the glockenspiel, the glass harmonica, and the harp. (The celesta sounds one octave higher than written, except for the *Nutcracker Suite* by Tchaikovsky, in which it sounds as written).

Bartok, Music for String Instruments, Percussion, and Celesta.
R. Strauss, *Der Rosenkavalier* (Act II).
Tchaikovsky, *Nutcracker Suite* (Fée Dragée).

F. The Xylophone.

Bartok, Music for String Instruments, Percussion, and Celesta.
Humperdinck, *Hänsel und Gretel* (Act. III, Scene 3).
Mahler, Symphony No. 6, Second movement.
Saint-Saëns, *Danse Macabre*.
Shostakovitch, Symphony No. 5; Ballet Suite, *The Golden Age* (Introduction to No. 1, and Polka, No. 3).

The xylophone is written according to its actual sound. Only in the *Danse Macabre* by Saint-Saëns is it meant to be played an octave higher than written.

II. PERCUSSION INSTRUMENTS OF "INDEFINITE PITCH."

A. The Bass Drum (*Gran Cassa* or *Tamburo Grande*).

Beethoven, Symphony No. 9, Finale.
Berlioz, *Requiem* (Dies Irae and Rex Tremendae).
Haydn, "Military" Symphony.
Liszt, *Alpine Symphony*.
Mahler, Symphony No. 2.
Mozart, *The Abduction from the Seraglio* (Act I, No. 5—here the bass drum is beaten with a birch rod).
Prokofieff, Violin Concerto No. 2 in G Minor.
Stravinsky, *Sacre du Printemps*.

B. The Tenor Drum (*Caisse Roulante, Rührtrommel, Cassa Rullante*)

This instrument has a wooden shell which is deeper than the metal shell of the snare drum.

Copland, Symphony No. 3.
Gluck, *Iphigenie* (Act I).
Wagner, *Rienzi* Overture; "Ride of the Valkyries."

C. The Snare Drum (*Petite Caisse, Kleine Trommel, Tamburo Militare*).

A bundle of tight strings, the snares, are stretched across the lower drum parchment (or head), producing a rattling noise when the membranes are set into motion through the strokes of the drumsticks. The loosening or dampening of the snares through an injected piece of leather or cloth produces a muffled sound, appropriate for funeral marches.

Auber, *Fra Diavolo*, Overture.
Debussy, *Iberia*.
Mahler, Symphony No. 2.
Ravel, "Bolero."

Rossini, *The Thieving Magpie*, Overture.
Stravinsky, *Histoire du Soldat* (here the drums are most frequently used without snares).

D. The Tambourine.

Berlioz, *Le Carnaval Romain.*
Stravinsky, *Petrouchka.*
Tchaikovsky, *Capriccio Italien; Nutcracker Suite,* ("Arab Dance").

E. The Cymbals (*Piatti* or *Cinelli, Becken*).

Debussy, *La Mer.*
Gluck, *Iphigenie* (Act I).
Liszt, *Mazeppa.*
Tchaikovsky, Symphony No. 4.
Wagner, *Rheingold* (first scene—here a "roll" executed with timpani beaters on one freely suspended cymbal symbolizes the Rheingold).

Ancient tiny cymbals, smaller than the palm of the hand, are called for in the scores of Berlioz's *Romeo and Juliet* (scherzo), and originally also in Debussy's *L'Après-midi d'un Faune*; the glockenspiel is usually substituted. Debussy himself substituted the glockenspiel for the small cymbals in performances of his score.

F. The Gong or Tam-Tam.

Debussy, *La Mer.*
Meyerbeer, *Robert le Diable* (Resurrection scene).
Puccini, *Madame Butterfly* (Act I).
Ravel, *Mother Goose,* Third movement.
Tchaikovsky, Symphony No. 6 ("Pathétique"), Fourth movement.

G. The Triangle.

Beethoven, Symphony No. 9 (Finale).
Berlioz, *Le Carnaval Romain.*
Brahms, Symphony No. 4, Third movement.
Haydn, "Military" Symphony.
Liszt, Piano Concerto in E♭ Major.
Mozart, *The Abduction from the Seraglio,* Overture.
Tchaikovsky, *Capriccio Italien.*
Wagner, *Siegfried* (end of Act II).
Weber, *Preciosa* (Overture and Three Gypsy Marches).

H. Wind Machine.

Ravel, *Daphnis and Chloe Suite No. 1.*
R. Strauss, *Don Quixote.*

I. Castanets.

Bizet, *Carmen.*
Debussy, *Iberia.*
Saint-Saëns, *Samson and Delilah* (Act III, Scene 2).

K. Slapstick.

Moussorgsky, *Pictures at an Exhibition.*
Ravel, Piano Concerto.

L. Wood Block.

Gershwin, Piano Concerto in F.
Ravel, Piano Concerto.

A fascinating example of the use of percussion instruments is *Ionization* by Varèse, in which thirteen percussion players play the following instruments:

1. Crash cymbals, bass drum (very deep).
2. Gong, 2 tam-tams (high and low).
3. 2 Bongos (West Indian twin drums with parchment heads), side drum, 2 bass drums.
4. Tambour militaire, side drum.
5. Siren (high), string drum (friction drum).
6. Siren (low), slapstick, guiro (a serrated Cuban gourd to be scraped with a stick).
7. Chinese blocks (high, middle, and low), claves (Cuban sticks of hard wood), triangle.
8. Snare drum, maracas (high and low).
9. Tarole (a flat snare drum), snare drum, suspended cymbal.
10. Cymbals, sleigh bells, tubular chimes.
11. Guiro, castanets, celesta.
12. Tambourine, anvils (high and low), grand tam-tam.
13. Slapstick, triangle, sleighbells, piano.

15

Expression in Music

THE QUESTION of what a certain piece of music expresses and how it proceeds in doing so is one of the most complex and controversial problems. In a choral work or a song the words will give us a fair indication of the "content" of the music. In that case, either the expressive force of an action or a sentiment, or else a collective or individual reflection, will be intensified and underlined by music and we will have an indication of the direction into which the imagination of our minds and souls is being steered. In this connection, associative universal musical formulas have been used in music for centuries. In the madrigals of the Renaissance, mountains and the heavens were accompanied by a rising melody, earth and hell by a fall in pitch; peace and silence were expressed by long-held tones or by rests, and garlands of laughter and joy by rollicking coloraturas. Since the Baroque, a descending chromatic bass line has become the symbol for grief.

246. MASS IN B MINOR (Crucifixus)

Johann Sebastian Bach (1685–1750)

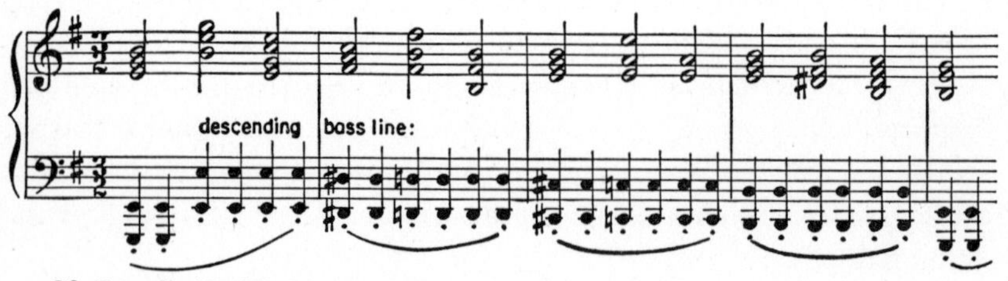

Cf. Purcell, "Dido's Lament," Fig. 323.

Albert Schweitzer has shown how Bach uses definite rhythms and melodic patterns in connection with words like *ascension, fall, waves, angels, cross, snake, walking,* etc. A careful analysis of operas by

Haydn, Mozart, Beethoven, Gluck, Weber, and Wagner, and of the songs of Schumann, Schubert, and Brahms, will reveal similar uses of melodic, harmonic, or rhythmical formulas for certain physical or psychological situations. One could conceive of dictionaries for the musical language that is used by various composers, as they exist already for Bach and Wagner. However, little would be won by such an approach except a few more labels. Music is a language which uses ever-changing "words" according to various occasions and different eras. To catalogue the many different meanings of tone combinations would freeze their impelling power of expression. Let us assume that a composer uses repeatedly the same motive for the expression of joy—would it not remain to be explained in each particular case what kind of joy was meant and why, how it originates and how it continues? We might also wonder whether a composer like Brahms, when he reused the musical figure of his "Rain Song" in his G-Major Violin Sonata, thought of rain, a melancholic atmosphere, or just of an appropriate last movement rondo?

Beethoven in his *Eroica* used the theme of Mozart's *Bastien and Bastienne* Overture:

247.

How can we decide whether Mozart divined a future "heroic theme" for his shepherd Singspiel which he wrote when he was twelve years of age or whether Beethoven started his hero in the countryside like Jeanne d'Arc? It is in this particular instance that we see clearly that a theme is not so much a static thing by itself, but rather derives its characteristic expressive force from the *musical* setting and development.

Let it be said then that music usually cannot be pigeonholed. The exceptions are few: just as there are certain universal simple general symbols in the history of art and the theater—gestures of compassion, prayer, grief, exaltation—so have we a few commonly understood symbols left in music: dance rhythms, marches, shepherd tunes, military bugle calls, lullabies, etc. In other words, only the most elementary common messages in music, a few basic formulas, have remained understandable and translatable. The rest is—music, a message and an impact of tones which are the more compelling *because* they cannot be "nailed down" as far as the "intentions" of the composer are concerned, an art, then, which has its own reasoning and logic, acting on a plane which is incompatible with words.

It is a well-known fact that the judgment of artists and writers in regard to their own works is of little value. The same goes even more for the explanations, especially of the Romantic composers, about how they felt or what they thought when composing. We do not admire great composers for the sake of their diaries, but because of that portion of their music which defies verbal translation even by the composer himself. It is only natural that the lives and loves of great composers are human interest stories to us—however, as guides to the content of their music or even as aesthetic evaluation of their work, they are less conclusive than is usually thought.

Perhaps we could compare a musical composition to a living being. The better we know a person the more difficult it becomes to describe his character in general terms. No person has constantly the same effect on others. We ourselves react differently toward the same person according to endless and variable circumstances. This seems to be the most charitable explanation for the incredible nonsense which has been and is being voiced about the meaning and the mood of certain pieces of music. Should it, for instance, happen that someone wants to "read up" on Brahms' F-Minor Piano Quintet before hearing it, he would have to choose between the following diametrically opposed "poetic interpretations" of two venerable and expert biographers: (See tabulated comparison on p. 233.) [1]

Again, it must be said that in this, as in all other cases, it seems more worth while to study the music itself, to read the score and listen to the music undistracted by prejudices, preconceived notions, second-hand daydreaming, but instead with keen ears and a mind made sensitive by a study of the real workshop of a composer, which is the place where and time when he writes music, not letters or literary footnotes.

Sometimes an amateur choral group or orchestra is told by their conductor, "Now let us sing or play this piece once more, but this

[1] Quoted in Henry S. Drinker, Jr., *The Chamber Music of Johannes Brahms*, p. 26.

NIEMANN

The finale . . . in spite of the minor key . . . is *thoroughly contented and jovial,* inclined to *all sorts of amusing little rhythmical tricks;* and *altogether sportively disposed.*

The coda . . . goes *laughing by* till it is finally concentrated still more drastically by means of syncopations. Yet all this does not succeed in checking its joyful mood, and, in the concluding lines, it takes its leave by breaking off abruptly as though *with bright ringing laughter.*

The end of the piano quintet is as *spacious and serene* as its opening is grave and full of pathos.

SPECHT

The introduction to the finale . . . leads to a rondo which takes its ease and yet *seems to find no comfort.* The curiously songless, exclamatory second subject, with its jerking up-beat, *brings no ray of light into the movement.*

The extensive coda . . . *dashes toward the dark unknown. The composer's heart must have been desolate indeed when he wrote this study in black.*

"Painfully born of the composer's soul" with its *"atmosphere of exalted joylessness."*

time with expression." In reality, expression cannot be separated from the "content" (the actual tones) of a piece any more than one can practice a piece in E major "first without the sharps" or a $\frac{3}{4}$ meter "first in $\frac{4}{4}$."

Music *is* expression and as such it consists of various interrelated factors. While the resulting product as a whole remains better unexplained, the various components may be observed successively in theory so that the mind and the senses may be better prepared to perceive them clearly when thy occur simultaneously in practice whenever music is performed.

Components of Expression

In order to focus our attention on those expressive factors which may be clearly separated and defined for reasons of a theoretical clarification, let us take a simple case for an analogy.

If we were to attend a graduation exercise of a high school in which we were all emotionally involved as graduates or parents, we would all be in a similar mood and filled with similar expectations; in other words, we would be an ideal audience (a condition which is rarely fulfilled at concerts or at opera performances). At a graduation the atmosphere is charged with emotional sensitivity in spite of the fact that everyone expects the same old graduation speech: the inevitable joke or quotation from the papers comes as an introduction or an attention-catching fanfare, next the occasion and the problems at hand are presented, then the failures of the older generation are developed, and finally the recapitulation ends with an "it is up to you" and a "good luck and good speed on your voyage."

Immediately our reactions will pronounce judgment on the expressive effectiveness of the speaker in terms like the following: effective, clear, convincing, forceful, fascinating, stimulating, etc.; or, pompous, confused, controversial, boring, sententious, self-centered, etc. Now, let us go one step further and assume (for reasons of analytical clarity) that the identical address could appear solely by a difference in delivery, as either effective, etc., or pompous, etc. What are the expressive factors which could make one and the same speech either successful as far as our reactions are concerned, or a failure? As usual, the criticized, faulty speaker is easier to describe than the perfect specimen: his voice is unpleasant and inflexible, its pitch is annoying, he shouts, there is no variety in volume, his tempo is unbearably slow and unyielding, his articulation is muddy, the structure of his speech is not clearly brought out (three times the final punch seems to have arrived, so that the real end peters out), he has a false tremolo in his voice and uses commonplace gestures which look awkward and seem insincere. Translated into musical terms, the delivery of the same speech (or piece of music) may be decidedly influenced by these factors: tone quality (tone color), melody, pitch, dynamics, tempo, rhythm, phrasing, revelation of formal structure, vibrato, ornamentation, and mental attitude. The last-mentioned factor is perhaps the most important one: all the separate deficiencies spring probably from a faulty attitude toward the task at hand—the speaker takes his task too lightly, talks down to his audience, bluffs, etc.

Let us now assume the ideal situation in the case of a piece of music: a composer whose mental attitude is beyond reproach, and who indicates in musical symbols as exactly as possible his intentions; furthermore, a performance which is faithful to the letter as well as to the spirit. The expressiveness of the music in such a case is caused by countless small musical details which are employed and ordered according to the musical vision of the composer. Whenever these details are observed accurately by performer and listener, the total expressive force of a composition assumes a life of its own without benefit of verbal commentaries. A great conductor will in rehearsals and performances insist on exactness of articulation, rhythm, tempo, dynamics, tone color, etc., rather than rely on speeches and program notes in order to convey an unadulterated version of what the composer has to say.

In the same fashion the listener may be led more directly to the gist of a composition through the minute analysis of the various expressive factors which are indicated in scores and brought to life in actual performances.

Through this kind of study and experience we may gradually become more sensitive to the over-all expressive impact which music exerts on our minds and on our emotions.

Elements of Expression and Articulation in Music

A well-known trick which is sometimes used in mental aptitude tests is reciting or reading what appears at first as a nonsense rhyme or sentence and letting the victim apply his power of reasoning and ordering perception so that a properly employed punctuation and emphasis may convey a definite meaning.

In music we have a great variety of factors which may obscure or reveal the articulation and thus the specific characteristics of musical "sentences."

1. Tempo. The most obvious means of changing the character of a piece is to sing or play a very slow piece in a very fast tempo or vice versa. (Try it!) If we remember that (inconclusive) tempo designations came into use only in the seventeenth century and that the metronome was invented as late as 1816, we will understand that a great deal of historical knowledge, familiarity with tradition, and the technical limitation of old instruments, and, above all, perceptive imagination are required of the performer in order to choose a tempo which brings the expressive elements of a certain piece of music into sharp relief. Not only may a tempo which is too fast hamper the clear articulation, and a tempo which is too slow obscure the musical lines by dragging and thus creating boredom, but the very character of the piece may change from a triumphal march into a funeral march according to the tempo which is chosen. Deviations from a steady tempo or the ignoring of proscribed tempo modifications, on the other hand, may also obscure the desired expressive effect.

2. Tone Color. That the choice of tone color, i.e., an instrument or a mixture of instruments, essentially influences the expressive character of a piece should be clear at this point. However, the way instruments are used, when they enter, and when they pause are important additional factors in the perception of the composer's intentions. Let us assume that a piece starts with a single melodic line played by one instrument (or several playing in unison). Whenever a new instrument enters it may either (1) add another melody, or (2) strengthen the first melodic line through added volume or (3) do so through a change of tone color. Obviously an added voice in the sense of (1), i.e., an independent polyphonic second voice, will also result in added volume and a change of tone color. To recognize the primary reason for the added voice in performing and listening means a step in the direction of *understanding* the intentions of the composer.

The use of instruments by a composer, his *orchestration,* may also give us a hint about the intended proper articulation, in the literal meaning of the word. Sometimes it appears doubtful where one musical sentence or *phrase* ends and where another begins. We might, for example, find ourselves at a loss where to put or perceive a musical period or comma, a breathing point (*Luftpause*). Frequently the infinitesimal stop, or drop in intensity which marks the end of a phrase, is not indicated at all by the composer. Two or more musical sentences may be so closely knit that there may be several possibilities of where to put a "punctuation mark." Let us assume that in the following diagram representing two successive strands of melody we are in doubt where Melody *A* ends and where Melody *B* begins.

248.

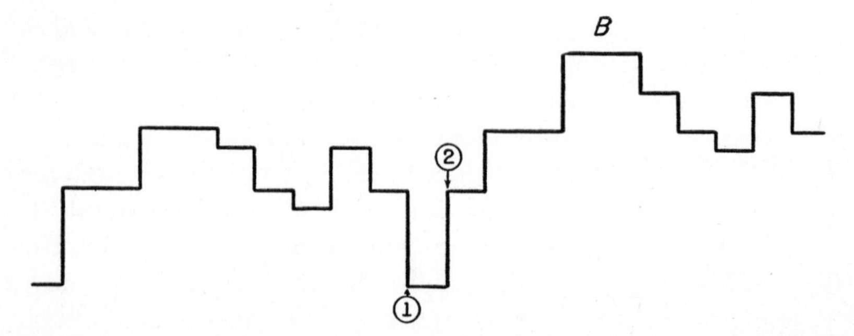

Points 1 and 2 are both possible as places where a caesura (punctuation) should occur.

The problem may be solved by observing the way in which the composer uses additional instruments: if a flute, for instance, is added at Point 2 we will know that the second phrase or melody begins with the entrance of the flute.

3. HARMONY. Harmony can play a similarly important role as an expressive and articulating force. Dissonant intervals may be brought out into the open or smoothed over by using slight modifications of the tempo, the rhythm, or the dynamics. And that harmonic progressions are some of the most important punctuation devices in music we saw in our discussion of cadences (p. 135). Performers as well as listeners might perceive an authentic cadence in the middle of a piece as final and thus be thrown off the track when the piece continues unexpectedly. In that case the structure or form of the piece is misunderstood. (There are, however, cases where Haydn and Beethoven especially produce this surprise intentionally, seemingly ending a piece and then unexpectedly taking off in another direction once more.)

4. RHYTHM. In articulating a given rhythm endless varieties of expressive means are possible beyond the tempo and dynamic indications usually given by the composer. The following rhythm of nine notes, for example, may be perceived in many different ways as far as its "nuclear structure" is concerned.

249.

DIFFERENT INTERPRETATIONS OF A RHYTHM

(1 and 2)

(2 and 3)

(2 and 3 and 4)

(1 and 2 and 3 and 4)

Depending on how you understand the inner structure of this rhythm, its expressive power or "meaning" will be changed markedly.

In addition, a rhythm may become lighter or heavier, marked or flighty, without a change of tempo or dynamics, by its *articulation*. When several tones follow each other it has to be determined how smoothly or detachedly the succession of tones should proceed. The smoothest way of connection is called *legato* and indicated by a curve (or *slur*) above or below the notes which are to be affected.

250. PIANO CONCERTO IN D MAJOR, K. 537

Wolfgang Amadeus Mozart (1756–1791)

Singers and wind players produce legato notes by singing or blowing several tones in one breath without interruption. String players use a single bow stroke for all tones which are combined within a legato sign. Pianists endeavor to approximate these techniques of singers and of other instrumentalists.

The opposite of legato is *staccato* (detached).[2] Here there are tiny rests between notes, and a more or less sharp attack in singing, blowing, or bowing produces tones which are more or less "hammered" and separated from each other. Unfortunately, there are insufficient signs for the endless variety of staccato or nonlegato singing and playing, and only since the late eighteenth and nineteenth centuries have composers bothered to use them.

A dot above or below the notes indicates a short staccato, i.e., a devaluation of the written time value; a dash, a sustained time value; and a dash plus a dot, an in-between procedure. Additional signs (e.g., ∧ or >) indicate an especially sharp attack and separation.

251. SUITE ARLESIENNE NO. 1

Georges Bizet (1838–1875)

[2] In addition, "staccato" means in string playing a certain brilliant kind of bowing: several rapid short notes played with a single bow-arm motion (cf. *Hora Staccato* by Dinicu-Heifetz).

Our rhythm (Fig. 249), then, could appear in additional ways, according to its articulation.

Even the time proportions in a dotted rhythm may be changed. In certain pieces of the Baroque Era, in the *French overtures,* such as the Overture to The *Messiah,* for example, the shorter note of the dotted rhythm was frequently shortened from a (written) sixteenth to a (played) thirty-second note, thus exaggerating the short-long polarity.

played:

(in French overtures, for instance)

On the other hand, when a dotted rhythm coincided with triplets in other parts, the $\frac{3}{4} : \frac{1}{4}$ relationship of the dotted rhythm was changed to a $\frac{2}{3} : \frac{1}{3}$ ratio.

in combination with triplets: played:

5. Melody and Phrasing. A given melody may be shaped in entirely different ways by various expressive means. The term *phrasing* is customarily used for the combining and separating of the various constituents of a melody. Inasmuch as this would involve rhythm, breathing, legato, staccato, and other factors as well, the terms *phrasing* and *articulation* overlap almost to the extent of synonymity. However, phrasing in the literal musical sense means usually the combination of successive and related musical thoughts. Because frequently there exist in music several layers of coherence within a single melody, the question of the "nuclear rhythmical and melodic structure" becomes complicated at times. An over-all phrase may consist of several subdivisions.

252. VIOLIN SONATA IN G MAJOR, OP. 78

Johannes Brahms (1833–1897)

In order to indicate the smallest segments as well as the over-all arch of a phrase in homophonic or polyphonic textures, an avalanche of phrasing slurs has sometimes been used by composers and editors, a procedure which is apt to confuse the layman.

253. PIANO SONATA IN E MAJOR, OP. 109 (Last movement)

Ludwig van Beethoven (1770–1827)

In the above example the phrasing slurs indicate three degrees of coherence: the smallest, and the intermediate units, as well as the extent of the total phrase. In the following example the overlapping phrases of three independent voices are outlined by the pattern of overlapping slurs.

254. THE WELL-TEMPERED CLAVIER, BOOK II (Fugue No. 17)

Johann Sebastian Bach (1685–1750)

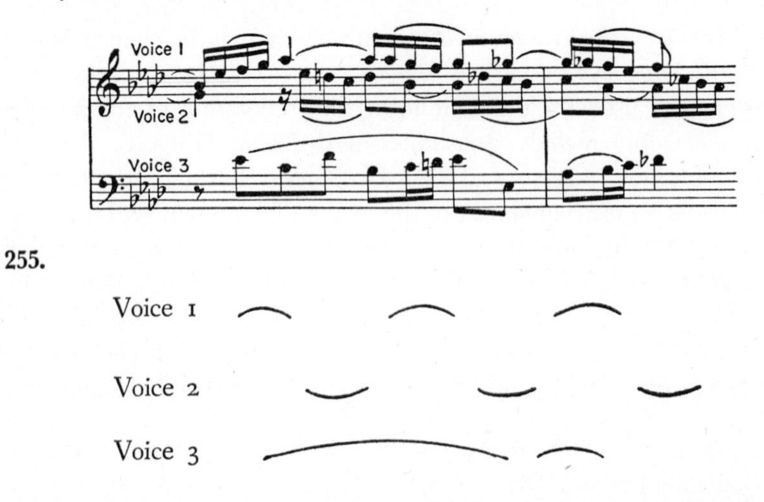

If we add that sometimes several short notes are combined in a group, an indication that they are to be sung or played *portato* (i.e., in between staccato and legato)—some of the reasons for the prevailing confusion and disagreements in interpretation should become evident.

256. SLAVONIC DANCE NO. 2

Antonin Dvořák (1841–1904)-Kreisler (1875–)

6. Pitch. Other expressive means in the interpretative shaping and in the perception of a melody are variations of pitch beyond the degree indicated by the composer.

There are several instances when the pitch of a melody is modulated during a performance. The first instance is the slight deviation from well-tempered tuning which is usually instinctively brought about in singing and in playing string or wind instruments. We saw during our discussion of well-tempered tuning (p. 153) that, for example, the two tones C♯ and D♭ are tuned to the same pitch. The fact that good musicians occasionally use a different pitch for the various tones which are "simplified" on the keyboard in regard to their relationship to each other is frequently explained in a manner which leaves out the main point of pure, or let us rather say functional, intonation. That C♯ sounds different in pitch from D♭ in accurate tuning is not as essential as the fact that *any* single tone changes its pitch constantly, depending on whether it is major third, dominant, leading tone, etc., to a given tonic. A good singer and player will therefore instinctively "sharpen" a C♯ when it is the leading tone in a D major melody, "flatten" it when it represents a minor third in A♯ minor, and so forth. If we remember that on our keyboard no intervals are exactly in tune except the octaves,[3] we can well imagine that a good chorus, string quartet, and orchestra may produce a perfect triad, i.e., pitch combinations which do not exactly coincide with the rigid well-tempered tuning. Conversely, instrumentalists and singers have to modify their intonation somewhat when a piano takes part in the performance. The resulting deficiency in perfect accurateness of pitch and the muffling of reso-

[3] Even the octaves are not all pure on our modern piano. It is customary to "stretch" octaves in the lower and upper ranges in order to satisfy our ears. Cf. W. T. Bartholomew, *Acoustics of Music*, Prentice-Hall, Inc., 1942, pp. 21 and 193.

nance is more than compensated for by the versatility of the piano, its percussive as well as dreamingly romantic possibilities, and its magnificent literature.

The vibrato is another deviation of pitch used more or less instinctively and—rather indiscriminately. Because the human voice trembles slightly in moments of excitement, singers and instrumentalists have endeavored (one does not know since when) to imitate this slight wavering in pitch. The result is at best an inherently personal, human touch which makes a melody come to life and adds infinitesimal shades of color and intensity. At worst an exaggerated vibrato sounds superimposed, "put on," whining, and spineless. Commonly, the term *tremolo* is substituted for *vibrato* when one speaks of human voices. This is an unfortunate substitution because *tremolo* means, in regard to instruments, the rapid repetition of tones of identical pitch—or, in the case of the piano, an octave apart. To make matters worse, a tremolo approach, i.e., the rapid interruption of a single tone or chord, is used as a vibrato device in electrical "organs." The childhood game of rapidly closing and opening one's ears with the hands while music is being played gives a good approximation of the dizzying effect of this sort of artificial "vibrato."

A third way of producing a vibrato effect is used in the "vox humana" stop in pipe organs. Here, two pipes of slightly different pitch are sounded simultaneously and produce a waxing and waning of intensity, called *beats*. This wavering of intensity does indeed approximate the trembling of a human voice.

The vibrato proper, a periodic wavering of pitch, and its substitutes become unbearable when used in excess and without discretion. The continuous unsteadying of pitch creates the effect of wailing and hardens the listener against taking any true musical emotional crisis seriously. This disturbed Mozart's father, who wrote in 1756: "[Performers] there are who tremble consistently on each note as if they had the palsy."[4]

The great artists use vibrato sparingly and in varying degrees, digressing in pitch widely or adhering to it closely, vibrating slowly or rapidly, as the occasion may demand. Never will the vibrato of a good musician be noticeable by itself (seemingly floating through the

[4] Leopold Mozart, *A Treatise on the Fundamental Principles of Violin Playing* (Editha Knocker, translator), p. 203. Date of original German publication, 1756.

air divorced from its basic pitch), nor will it ever approach the dimensions of a trill.

Unfortunately, it can be said that probably no other musical device has scared away children from the realms of music as much as the excessive, false, emotionally pretentious vibrato of many string players and singers. The fact that composers hardly ever indicate the amount of vibrato desired in their scores is a handicap in its reasonable application. The rare indications, "molto vibrato" or "without expression" (which latter amounts practically to a "without vibrato") describe the two extremes of greatest obvious excitement and the preservation of an outward calm. Let us remember that there are infinite degrees lying between these opposites and that an outward calm may be more telling in moments of importance than hysterical shrieks or wild gestures.

Another variation in pitch which acts as an expressive means in music is the slide from one tone to another. Sometimes composers revert to the sliding pitch relations of primitive man (see p. 45) and demand the bridging of a large interval by rapidly crossing the distance in sliding fashion rather than by walking or running "stepwise." This is indicated by the term *glissando,* or by a diagonal line connecting the starting pitch with the goal. A popular variation of the slide is the connecting of two tones of a melody in singing or in playing string instruments. This "carrying over" of one tone to the next is likewise called glissando or, more properly, *portamento* (carrying). Unfortunately, the portamento is rarely indicated by a composer and therefore is frequently used indiscriminately by singers and string players.

257. DER ROSENKAVALIER

Richard Strauss (1864–1949)

Die Auftakte stets mit dem Wiener süsslichen Glissando. (The upbeats always to be played with the sweetish glissando of Vienna.)

To apply the "sweetish Viennese glissando" (portamento) which R. Strauss demands in his *Rosenkavalier* to the following Beethoven theme would obscure and pervert the characteristic outline: the initial jump of a dramatic interval (the seventh), which is afterward reduced through a descending scale to a major third.

258. QUARTET IN D MAJOR, OP. 18, NO. 3

Ludwig van Beethoven (1770–1827)

A slide here would act as a compromise between the two characteristic tones of the dominant seventh chord; it would besmudge its outlines and anticipate the scale motion which follows: the intention of the composer would be reversed by this uncalled-for portamento.

Finally, the variations in pitch which make a melody expressive and articulate may take the form of ornamentation, consisting of trills, grace notes, turns, etc. To "break up" a given melody into many extra in-between runs and to embellish it with trills became the custom when in the seventeenth century the opera and violin virtuosos began to "interpret" the music at hand. Originally, the improvised ornaments were intended to intensify expression and to dramatize action in music; however, frequently (to this day) they have degenerated into a showing off of the virtuoso qualities of the performer. Because the harpsichord cannot accentuate individual tones, ornaments were used which played *around* the pitch of a certain tone in order to emphasize its importance. The Age of Reason finally brought order into the excessive overgrowth of ornamentation which the Baroque had produced and catalogued an endless number of musical embellishments according to their notation, execution, and their fashionable and effective use as far as the character of a piece was concerned. Ornaments were called *agréments* (pleasantries) in France, and *Manieren* (manners) in Germany. Frequently they were indicated by signs only (~ ⁓ ~w, etc.). During the Classic Era, however, it became more and more the custom to write out "longhand" the embellishments or connecting runs, turns, etc., which the composer had in mind. Karl Philip Emmanuel Bach, the famous son of Johann Sebastian, had this to say about the value of ornaments, in 1753: [5] "They connect and enliven tones and impart

[5] K. P. E. Bach, *Essay on the True Art of Playing Keyboard Instruments*, W. J. Mitchell, translator and editor, p. 79. Dates of original publication: Part I in 1753; Part II in 1762.

stress and accent; they make music pleasing and awaken our close attention. Expression is heightened by them; let a piece be sad, joyful, or otherwise, and they will lend a fitting assistance."

Dynamics

To our modern ears, *dynamics*, the variation of loud and soft and the infinite number of degrees possible through sudden or gradual changes, seem to be one of the most powerful means of expression. In a score of Beethoven the dynamic indications, loud (forte), soft (piano), suddenly accentuated (*sf.* = sforzato), the mezzo or double piano or forte (*mp, pp, mf, ff*), the gradual increase (crescendo) or decrease (decrescendo or diminuendo), and many other terms of intensity, seem to be essential for the musical context.

In J. S. Bach's music and that of all his predecessors, on the other hand, we *hardly ever* find a dynamic indication except in a few instances where an echo effect is indicated—or when a solo voice or instrument should not be "covered" by the orchestra.[6]

This does not mean that Bach had fewer emotions than Beethoven or Tchaikovsky—were it so, a dramatically gesticulating speaker would always have a more meaningful and heartfelt message to deliver than a calm, deliberate speaker who does not appeal to the eye. It simply means that in Bach's music, dynamics play a different expressive role from that which they assume in the Classic and Romantic Eras. Throughout the Baroque Era dynamics were used in the sense of black and white. In the concerto grosso, for example, an entire string group (the "tutti") was opposed to one or more solo instruments (the "concertino"). Changes in dynamics were brought about by the gradual addition or elimination of voices in true polyphonic manner. The resulting change is a terracelike profile.

Terrace-like Dynamics

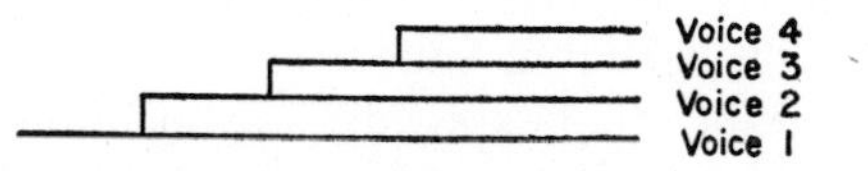

[6] It should be borne in mind that music publishers have only fairly recently begun to honor the text of a composer to the letter. "Practical editions" which do not indicate what Beethoven or Bach wrote, and where countless well-meaning editors have inserted their own "interpretations," are still the rule.

The custom of the Classic Era, where a whole orchestra would begin softly as a group and gradually increase its volume solely by everyone playing louder, produces a wedge:

WEDGELIKE DYNAMICS

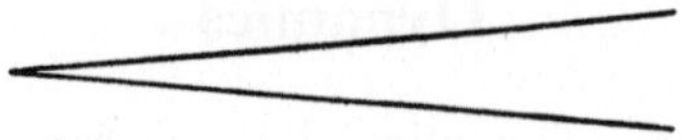

Let us remember that in the Baroque orchestra every player remains on the same dynamic level; the changes occur through the addition of voices while each single voice retains its initial volume. The continuity of each individual voice is retained because its own tone color does not change in itself. In the Classic orchestra, quite the opposite occurs: each instrument changes its individual tone color (the number and intensity of the partials present) while gradually increasing or decreasing its own intensity of sound. This difference in dynamic approach means that in a Baroque orchestra a violin sounds like a violin throughout, while in a Classic or Romantic piece the violin may sound successively like an oboe, trumpet, clarinet, flute, French horn, etc. (see p. 178). The invention of a gradual instrumental crescendo and decrescendo (indicated by the signs < and >) was perfected by the predecessors of the Classic orchestra, the *Mannheim School* of the Stamitz family.[7] The sensational effect on the audience is described by an eighteenth century witness in these words: "The listeners slowly rose to their feet during the *crescendo,* and during the *diminuendo* realised that they had been holding their breath and began to breathe again." [8]

In these matters of dynamics we do well to guard against two prejudices: that increased excitement can only be produced by increased loudness, and that emotion can only be expressed by dynamic waves. A decrease in intensity may produce an effect of breathless tension, or of an exciting echo or memory which we strain to grasp before it escapes us. The absence, on the other hand, of violent dynamics in the music of Bach and his predecessors and the fact that dynamic changes on a sliding scale were unknown to them should direct us to seek out the other expressive factors in their music: rhythm,

[7] In vocal music and operas gliding dynamics had been in use before the Classic Era. See Lang, *Music in Western Civilization*, p. 603.

[8] Quoted from Reichardt, *Briefe eines aufmerksamen Reisenden,* I, 11, in Abert, *W. A. Mozart* (Leipzig: Breitkopf & Härtel, 1923), I, 564.

polyphony, melody, harmony, pure tone color, articulation, phrasing, and ornaments.

Conversely, an arranger who "interprets" a Bach fugue by dressing the theme in a huge crescendo and with the glitter of several changing tone colors instead of using a simple line of constant ("sun-fast") color for it, distorts the intention of the composer.

Mental Attitude

In hearing music a great deal of sensitive imagination is demanded of the performers as well as of the audience if the task at hand is to be accomplished: to let the composer speak. None of the fragile factors of expression which we have discussed can even begin to work unless our mental attitude and the atmosphere in which we hear music become sympathetic to the soil out of which a work of art grows. It is usually granted that a football game or tennis match cannot be played while spectators walk across the field or the court. Yet disturbing noises in concerts are the rule, although complete silence is the prerequisite for any music, just as a clear ball field is for a game.

The disturbing factors in our mental attitude cannot be seen or heard but are just as real and plentiful as noisy concertgoers or air-conditioning machines. Take the man who wants to be entertained and dislikes *Tristan* because he has enough problems at home, or the one who wants his humor straight and dislikes Chaplin because he makes him feel sad. Others criticize a requiem for being too theatrical, thus implying that nothing tragic or genuinely important can ever happen on the stage.[9] Hardly anyone ever laughs when reading the "funnies" in the subway or when hearing one of the many jokes in Haydn's symphonies—the natural reaction is suppressed. The mental blocks which we frequently insert between the music and ourselves not only operate in sweeping criticisms but also in well-defined prejudices: Three-four time must always be a waltz, four-four a march, major is always gay, Tchaikovsky always sad (regardless of major or minor), Beethoven always angry, Mozart innocently gay, Debussy decadent, and so on.

Performers are not without similarly narrow attitudes: a mass or an oratorio will, of course, come out distorted in every musical detail if

[9] Before J. S. Bach came to Leipzig, the mayor of Leipzig expressed the hope that Bach would avoid everything "theatrical" in his music (Terry, p. 169).

the chorus is rehearsed in the rah-rah spirit of "now let's tackle this one and show them how tough we can get." A performer who considers every allegro a provocation to show his bravura and every adagio an occasion to air his own little personal tragedy will be useless as far as the majority of the musical literature is concerned.

It should be obvious that in the extreme case where performers are involved in their own glory instead of in something higher than any individual, every smallest expressive detail of the composition will come out distorted. Every tempo, rhythm, polyphony, harmony, melodic articulation, vibrato, ornament, will sound as false and as far removed from the intentions of the composer as the mental attitude of the performers is different from that of the composer. Similarly, a listener who hears an excellent performance of an oratorio expecting to hear entertainment and barbershop harmonies will misunderstand every single tone of the performance. All this will seem more self-evident on the surface than it really is. For one thing, no one, not even the greatest musician, was ever called upon to hear and "digest" and evaluate as much music of all kinds as our generation.[10] Secondly, never were there so many opposing viewpoints on "how to appreciate music" published as in the present century. We are better acquainted with quantity than with quality. The remedy is obvious: if we open our minds and hearts to the actual stuff of which music is made, from the smallest details to the over-all impact, and if we acquire a particle of the humility before the universe and the great ideas and beliefs which the great composers inevitably possessed, we cannot possibly miss the expressive content for which the music of the world provides the setting.

Suggestions for Listening

Bach	Cantata No. 104, *"Du Hirte Israel, höre"*
	"Crucifixus" from Mass in B Minor
	Well-tempered Clavier, Book II, Fugue No. 17
Beethoven	Piano Sonata in E Major, Op. 109 (Final movement)
	String Quartet in D Major, Op. 18, No. 3
	Symphony No. 3 in E♭ Major, Op. 55 ("Eroica")
	Symphony No. 5 in C Minor, Op. 67 (Third and fourth movements)
Bizet	*L'Arlesienne Suite No. 1*

[10] Cf. the popular advertisements for LP record changers: "Now you may have 18 hours [sic] of uninterrupted music."

Brahms	Piano Quintet in F Minor, Op. 34
	"Regenlied," Op. 59, No. 3
	Sonata for Violin and Piano in G Major, Op. 78 ("Rain Sonata")
Dinicu-Heifetz	*Hora Staccato*
Dvorak-Kreisler	*Slavonic Dance No. 2*
Händel	*Messiah* (Overture)
Harpsichord pieces by Couperin and Rameau	
Monteverdi	Madrigals
Mozart	Piano Concerto in D Major, K. 537
	Bastien et Bastienne (Overture)

16

Texture

THE MANNER in which a piece of fabric is woven offers several valuable points of comparison with the way in which a piece of music is constructed. If we trace the various voices of a vocal or instrumental score, the result will be a network of lines which diverge and converge or cross at certain points and which are from time to time held in place by vertical supports. Depending on the composition, the texture will appear closely or loosely knit. Some "threads" will be outstanding in "thickness" and "color" and others will appear intermittently only, in fragmentary fashion (See Figs. 259–268).

If the piece of material contains a certain definite design, a "theme," for example, or a "rhythm," or a certain color combination, these may recur in a repetitive pattern either on the horizontal plane or in a diagonal or vertical arrangement. Sometimes these patterns will seemingly change their shape according to the order in which we perceive them. In looking at certain Persian rugs, for example, we will find that the same design may change its contours according to whether we look at it vertically, horizontally, or diagonally.

The material and the thickness of a single thread, its color and length, and the way it is interconnected with other threads will also determine the durability and the ultimate all-around dimensions, that is to say, the "form," of a piece of material. Once we have understood the diverse relatedness of the component parts of a piece of material or music, i.e., as long as we remember that the parts of a composition are coordinated in *every* direction, we may, for the sake of clarity, narrow our field of observation momentarily to a single horizontal, diagonal, or vertical direction.

Thus we shall limit the use of the term *texture* in music to the meaning of the vertical and/or diagonal interrelationship of voices and instruments. In enumerating and analyzing some of the vertical devices used by composers in various kinds of texture, we will include horizontal aspects only as far as is necessary, i.e., because rhythm, melody, and harmony all need time in order to unfold, we will isolate whole chunks of music, a few measures at least, from the fabric, in order to inspect the vertical structure. Within these excerpts let us consider the vertical interrelatedness of rhythms, melodies, harmonies, which come into being through the imitation, opposition, accentuation, etc., among strands of voices. To consider each musical texture as a bundle of several "voices" becomes imperative in this sort of analysis. A chord played on the piano, for example, by five fingers or in an orchestra by five different instruments must become in our thinking the equivalent of five "voices" singing or playing together and progressing to other sounds of five or more or less voices. Let us remember that the subtraction or addition of voices (or instruments) during the course of a piece does not necessarily change its texture. It is the way in which voices are used, not their number, which determines the texture in music. We have already seen (p. 89) that *several* singers or instrumentalists may combine and produce any one of the three basic textures; i.e., either *monophony*, or *polyphony*, or *homophony*. It is therefore, not at all necessary that a symphony played by many instruments produces polyphony—most likely it will change its texture frequently, juxtaposing monophonic, homophonic, and polyphonic sections and even transforming horizontal elements into a vertical order. This latter happens whenever a melody played first by a flute, let us say, is during the course of a piece repeated in a "cut-up version," and presented partially by violins, cellos, clarinets—each group stating successively small sections of the total flute melody.

It should be obvious from this one example alone that perceiving vertical relations, i.e., the texture of a piece of music, at any one moment will bring us immeasurably closer to the intentions of a composer. Following the melodic thread—the story-line as the motion-picture makers would say—through the web of cooperating instruments will keep our attention focused. However, what happens besides, simultaneously with the "red thread" of a melodic line, should never be neglected. The "accompaniment" may bring a new harmonic interpretation or prepare a modulation; a new or derived rhythm or countermelody may occur, and so forth.

Because of the dazzling variety possible for the connecting of the elements of music vertically or diagonally, as it accumulated throughout the history of music and through the skill of great composers, the task of the modern listener in unraveling the texture of the music which surrounds him is truly formidable. His position in listening to music may be compared to the child who is in his room upstairs while a party goes on downstairs; he perceives a constant din of inarticulate noise interrupted here and there by laughter, calm interludes, the rattling of dishes and glasses, etc. Only rarely does he recognize the voice (not the words) of a friend of his family and seldom does his imagination succeed in reconstructing correctly the actual simultaneous and successive happenings of a world which is removed from him in space and time. Not before the child has become a member of the party and only after he is grown up will the strange doings and thinkings of the grown-up world make sense to him; he will develop out of his own experience and thinking a measure of accuracy in judging the "meaning and the mood" of what people say and do.

In our present problem, to develop a keener perception of the simultaneous and "diagonal," i.e., the reasonably consecutive sounds of a musical "texture," the two avenues of approach which we have mentioned from the start will serve us again exceedingly well: active participation in reproducing music, and the study of musical scores. Not all who sing or play music are good "teammates"; however, if and when a singer or player becomes aware of more than his own individual part, when he truly considers himself as contributing to and assisted and enriched by a sounding texture at every moment of musical action, he has developed the attitude of a sensible and sensitive musician—and listener. It is unfortunate that we usually surround ourselves with an atmosphere which is much too artificial, snobbish, esoteric, and pseudo-aesthetic to admit that the road to the inner workings of a fugue by Bach leads far more directly by way of the singing of rounds and madrigals (for one's own fun and experience, not necessarily for performance) than by way of a superrefined and critical comparison of various versions of the same piece played by contemporary performers in recitals or on records. The man who has worked hard and for weeks on end over one of the two flute parts of Beethoven's First Symphony, let us say, has come much nearer to the heart of the music and will therefore be better qualified to appreciate a professional performance than the record-fan who asks himself incessantly which version he likes best among three or four "perfect interpretations" which he judges without raising as much as a finger (thanks to the long-playing records).

For those, however, who refuse to learn to play an instrument (sometimes this is only postponed until retirement age) and for those who cannot "carry a tune" (rarely a tenable excuse) there remains active mental occupation with scores.

The Reading of Scores

To study the "blueprints" of music will provide the visual component of an audio-visual education in music. The habit of reading a score while listening to music used to be a fad among musical "connoisseurs" in Europe and is now spreading among well-meaning musical aspirants in this country. In connection with phonograph records, the custom of "reading along in the score" provides an exercise in reading and listening which is of definite value, especially if one repeats short excerpts frequently. In the concert hall, however, score-reading loses its value. The dimmed light, the disturbing noise made while turning pages, the obvious confusion among score-readers when they lose their place or when the performers ignore repeats which the score indicates—all this by itself should indicate that much of a live and unique performance gets lost for those who are preoccupied with reading while listening. Worst of all, however, is the sad fact that you do not have to read while listening if you know how to read a score, and that score-reading during a performance does not help your listening if you are not able to hear all simultaneous and successive sounds anyway. In other words, the expert listener sees the general outline of the score in his mind when he hears the music, and the expert score-reader hears the sound of the written music in his imagination while reading. To reach that stage is obviously possible for a few accomplished musicians only. We may grasp this degree of expertness and the resulting attitude by comparing it with something with which we are thoroughly familiar ourselves. To read the Gettysburg Address while it is being recited is useless for two reasons: we know it well, having heard and read it repeatedly beforehand, and only a slow individual rereading at home at our own tempo and with pauses for our individual reflection and associative thoughts may reveal new facets. Similarly, whenever musicians study a score, they take a long time for a single page—much longer than the actual performance of that page would take when played at the proper tempo. We have, then, the paradox that the amateur takes the score to a concert because he does not really know how to read it and that the musicians (most of them at least) leave it at home because they have learned to listen by reading music slowly and carefully before and after a performance, and because they know that it takes longer to read a score thoroughly than to hear a piece of music. This should not, however, discourage anyone from attempting to study a score. Just as when we see a play, the reading of it before and after the performance will enhance our insight and perception—without ever making a stage director or an actor of us that way—so will time spent over a musical score before and after a concert assist us immeasurably in the preparation for and the retention of music. And while the first steps in score-reading seem bewildering and seem to offer no help or progress at first, actually we learn better how to listen to music with every hour which we devote to a score. As so often, the "bliss of ignorance" gives way gradually to hard work, desperate confusion, and soon after to genuine admiration and a close and permanent attachment to the art of music.

An excellent and simple way to begin the study of score-reading is the tracing of individual instruments and voices through a piece of transparent paper which we have superimposed on a page of a score. Analyzing the resulting graphs, we can discern immediately a few of the vertical structural devices used by various composers.

In Figures 259 and 260, harmonies are held out by one part of the orchestra while melodies occur above and below, respectively. In Figure 261, a *motive* (the fragment of a melody) wanders down the string section twice and is consequently "echoed" by the wood winds. In Figure 262, a melody occurs above repetitive bass lines. In Figure 263, a third voice is added intermittently only. In Figure 264, melodies are gradually reinforced by additional groups of instruments. In Figure 265, we find a "twin" melody above a meandering bass line; in Figure 266, a melodic motive appears successively above and below a sustained interval; Figure 267 represents a thick bundle of parallel voices; and finally in Figure 268, we have a rapidly changing texture of heavy, sudden reinforcements and an interchange of gradually appearing and disappearing single lines. Comparing our patterns with the actual score, we will have to make a few reservations:

1. The lines do not represent exact rhythmical or melodic proportions. A half note, for example, does not always occupy twice the space of a quarter note in the score picture, and half steps and whole steps are visually not distinguishable (see p. 75).

259. SYMPHONY NO. 4 IN E♭ MAJOR (First movement)

Anton Bruckner (1824–1896)

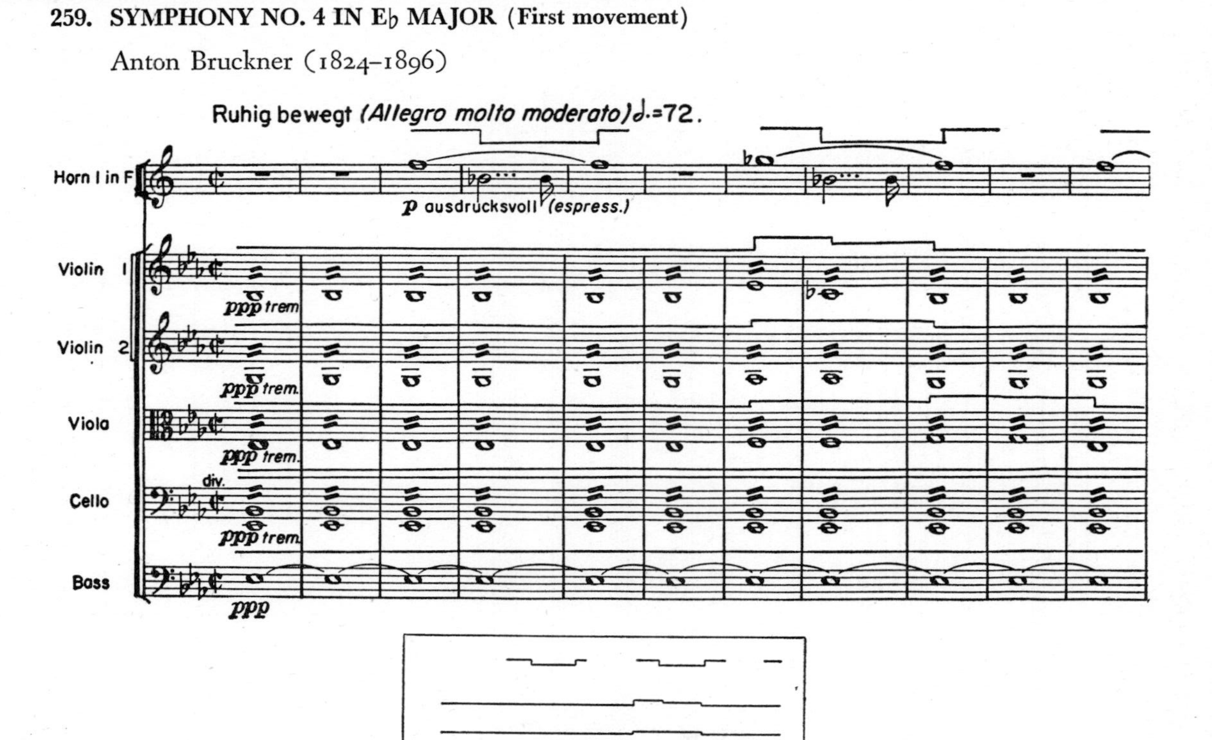

260. SYMPHONY NO. 7 IN A MAJOR, OP. 92 (Last movement)

Ludwig van Beethoven (1770–1827)

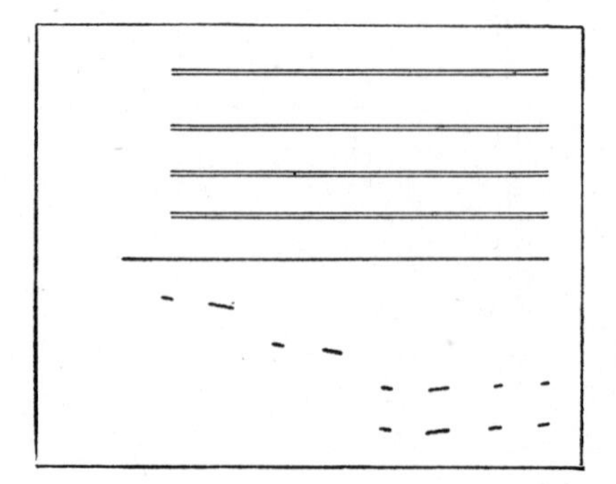

Flutes 1/2
Oboes 1/2
A-Clarinets 1/2
Bassoons 1/2
Timpani
Violin 1
Violin 2
Viola
Cello
Bass
cresc.

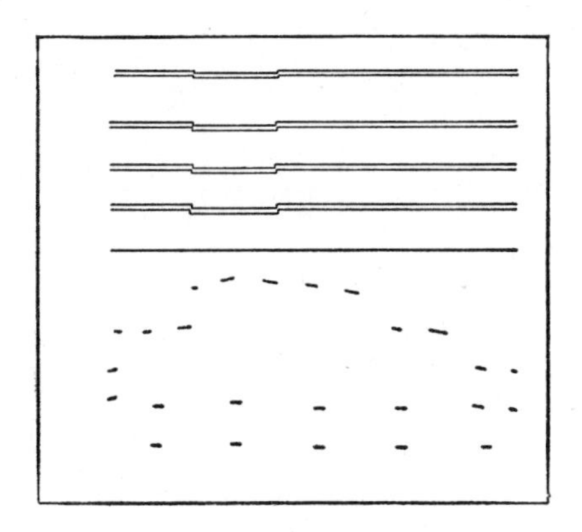

261. SYMPHONY NO. 5 IN C MINOR, OP. 67 (First movement)

Ludwig van Beethoven (1770–1827)

262. NUTCRACKER SUITE, OP. 71A (Danse Chinoise)

Peter Ilyitch Tchaikovsky (1840–1893)

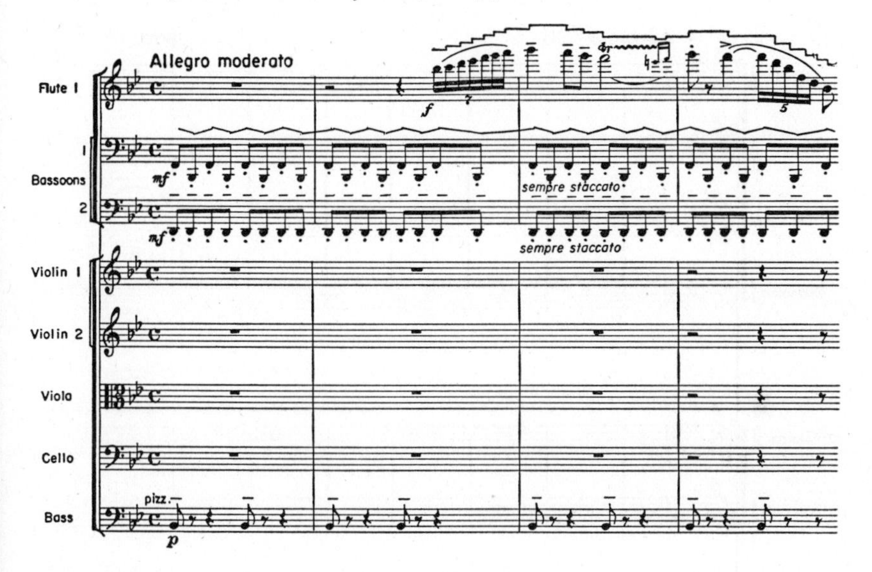

263. PIANO SONATA NO. 2 IN G MAJOR, K. 283

Wolfgang Amadeus Mozart (1756–1791)

264. SYMPHONY NO. 5 IN C MINOR, OP. 67 (Third movement)

Ludwig van Beethoven (1770–1827)

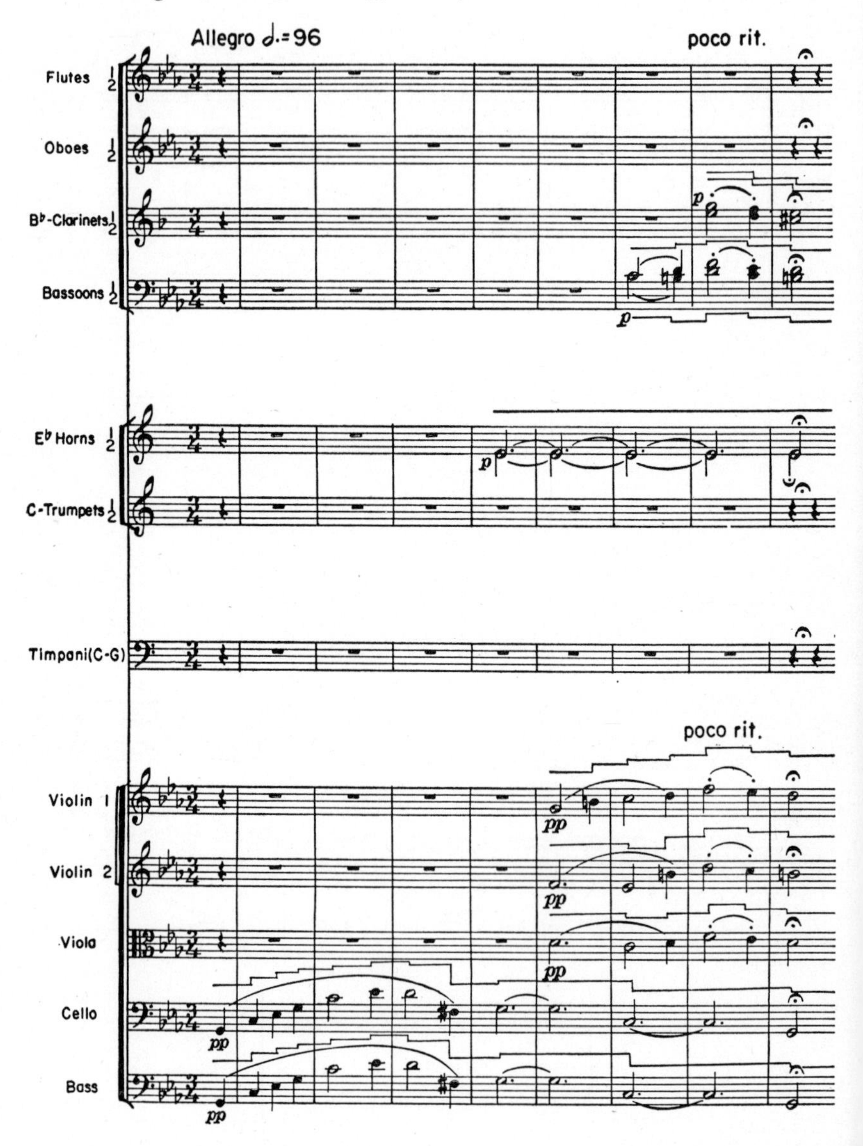

265. NOCTURNE IN B♭ MINOR, OP. 9, NO. 1

Frederic Chopin (1810–1849)

← Texture of Fig. 264.

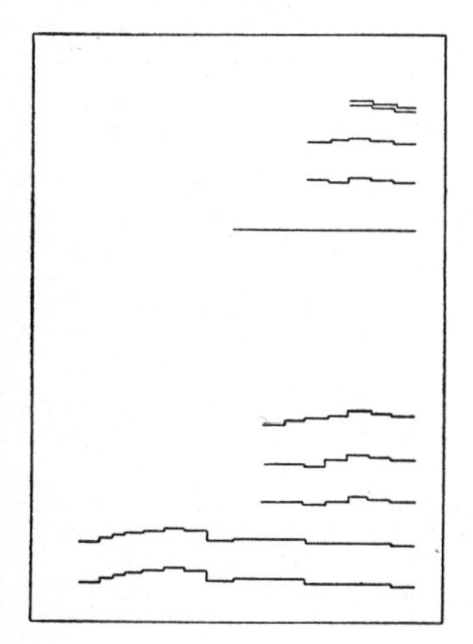

266. SYMPHONY NO. 5 IN B♭ MAJOR (First movement)

Franz Schubert (1797–1828)

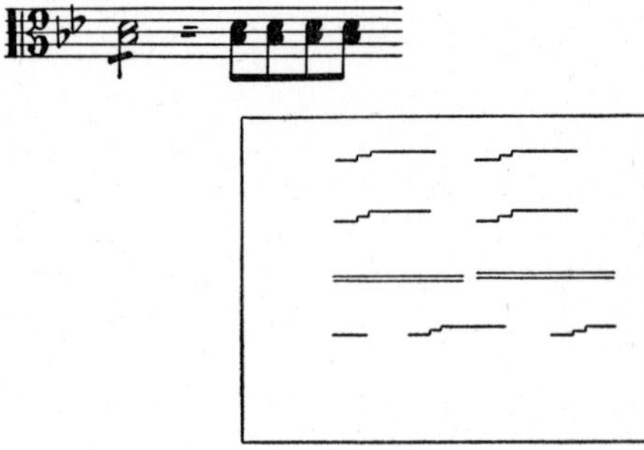

267. ALSO SPRACH ZARATHUSTRA, OP. 30

Richard Strauss (1864–1949)

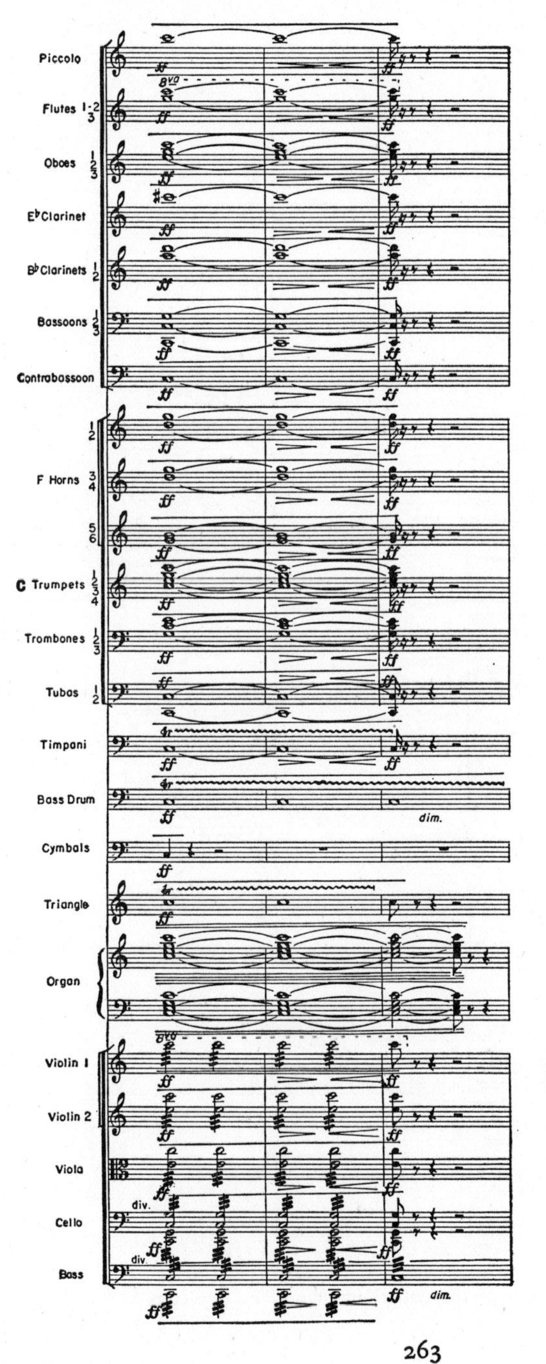

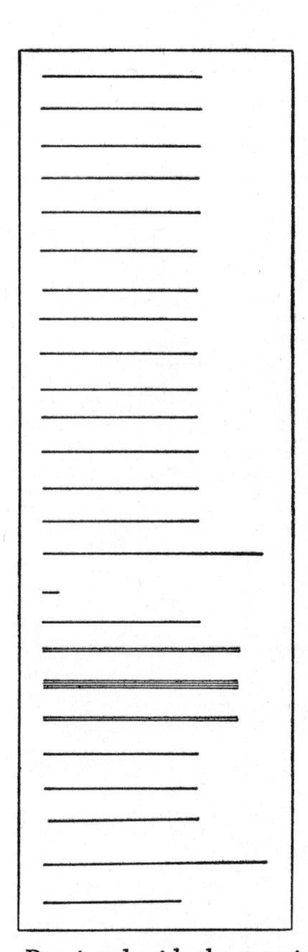

268. ALSO SPRACH ZARATHUSTRA, OP. 30

Richard Strauss (1864–1949)

← Texture of Fig. 268.

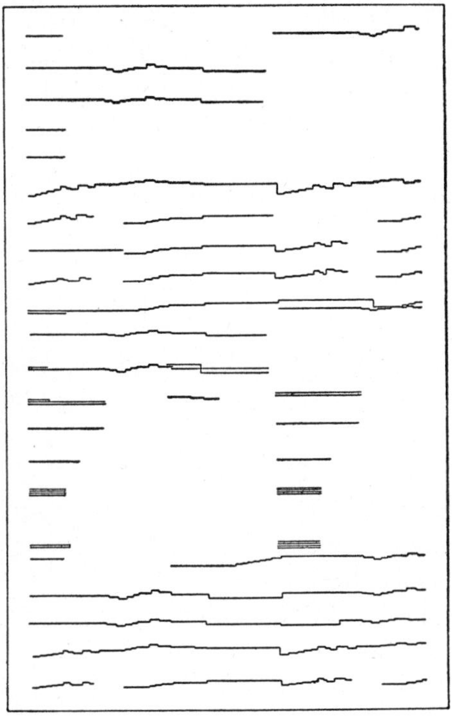

2. The pitch relationship of the lines is deceiving. While the upper line in a full orchestral score regularly represents the high-pitched flute (or piccolo) and the lowest line the low-pitched double bass, the middle of a score will contain a high-pitched French horn *below* the bassoon, etc. A good way to avoid confusion is to remember that each division of the orchestra, the wood winds, the brass, and the strings, may be subdivided into instruments with soprano, alto, tenor, and bass range. In this way we will obtain the following categories:

	Soprano	Alto	Tenor	Bass
Wood Winds....	Flute	Oboe	Clarinet	Bassoon
Brass	Trumpet	French horn	Trombone	Tuba
Strings	Violin	Viola	Cello	Double bass

It is customary to arrange a score in such a manner that the instruments read from top to bottom in this order: (1) wood winds; (2) brass; (3) percussion; (4) strings. Keeping this in mind, we will find that Figure 268, for instance, does not represent a "top-heavy" sound but rather two well-balanced streams of sound by the wood-wind and by the string *choirs* and two temporary reinforcements by the brass *choir*.

3. Because each instrument is presented by an individual line, unison sounds will appear as parallels.

4. Harmonic relations and progressions cannot be illustrated by our graphs. Inasmuch as chords contain rarely more than three or four different tones, an orchestra piece for sixteen or more instruments is hardly ever harmonically more complicated than a string quartet. However, to decipher the harmonic skeleton from a full orchestra is, because of the many parts to be considered and the necessary transposing of B♭ and other instruments, a very time-consuming procedure. If we do this, however, leisurely and patiently, we will be constantly surprised by the unexpected results. Figure 267, for instance, is simple indeed for the ears and complicated only on paper: three tones only are sounded (in various octave ranges) by approximately ninety-five instruments! All the composer intended here was dynamic force and a full mixture of tone colors (motivated in this case by his "program" of Zarathustra).

Our graphic lines, then, are helpful in the beginning only; they are most useful as the first prerequisite for score-reading. The next step must take the actual score and its sound into consideration. To help us in this phase let us discuss a few of the common vertical devices which have been and are being used within the three commonly heard textures: monophony, polyphony, homophony.

Monophonic Devices

It seems like a paradox to attach any vertical significance to monophony, i.e., the texture of a single melodic line. However, we have already seen that a melody may sometimes indicate the outline, the essence, the meaning, or the shape, whatever you prefer to call it, of a chord. A melody, then, may present by implication a harmony. In thus converting a horizontal line into a vertical conception, two factors may be of assistance: first, the fact that successive tones continue to sound faintly, as in the undampened piano tones which are obtained by the use of the sustaining pedal, and secondly, the imagination and the musical memory of the listener. Once we have learned to combine many successive single tones mentally into a single chord, our musical perception will improve in clarity and quickness of response.

269. PARTITA IN B MINOR FOR SOLO VIOLIN

Johann Sebastian Bach (1685–1750)

In the above example Bach converts into a single melodic line a melody and harmonies which were presented previously through chords. The resulting monophonic texture therefore contains both melodic and harmonic elements.

At other times a single melodic line may touch rapidly and repeatedly specific regions in its tonal range so as to give the illusion of polyphony. In Figure 270, for instance, two voices may be discerned, one ascending and the other descending chromatically: the eye and the ear perceive two voices which move in contrary motion.

270. FUGUE IN E MINOR FOR ORGAN

Johann Sebastian Bach (1685–1750)

The melodic profile of the above example would appear as a confusing zigzag line:

unless we recognize the "hidden polyphony" which consists in this case of two diverging melodic lines:

In Figure 271, on the other hand, the constantly recurring tone gives the illusion of a sustained pedal point (see p. 275); the monophonic line separates here into two imaginary voices which proceed in oblique motion.

271. PARTITA IN E MAJOR FOR SOLO VIOLIN

Johann Sebastian Bach (1685–1750)

Similarly, a single instrument may sound like two instruments of different tone range if the lowest tones of a melody are stressed and thus seemingly supply a separate bass line to a treble voice—all within a monophonic texture.

272. SONATA IN G MAJOR FOR VIOLIN AND PIANO, K. 379

Wolfgang Amadeus Mozart (1756–1791)

A melody which provides its own bass line

And later, two melodies in one

Finally, let us think of the case where a single melody carries its own harmonization or accompaniment—by implication.

273. VIOLIN CONCERTO IN D MAJOR, OP. 77 (First movement)

Johannes Brahms (1833–1897)

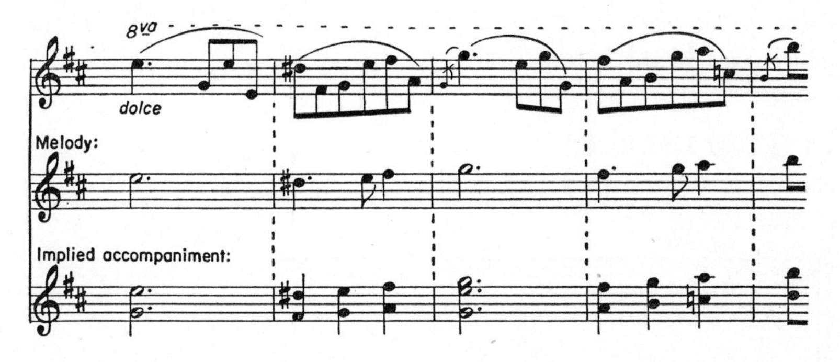

It will add to the pleasure and "understanding" of a piece of music if the listener becomes able, through experience, mental preparation, and close attention to the music, to complete in his mind the suggestive, sketchy lines which are implied by the composer's creation. "Single" lines which make use of these "vertical" devices will appear richer in texture and fuller in sound than they really are, through this kind of implied depth and perspective. And consequently, whenever several monophonic lines which imply polyphony are combined into real polyphony, as for example in many fugues by Bach, the result will seem "confusing, mechanical, without feeling, devoid of light and shade," etc., at first. Later, however, after repeated study, this first superficial impression will give way to the perception of most concentrated and complex happenings within the texture of a piece of music —the fugue begins to acquire a life and a glow of its own, generating motion and an inner speed (without changing the tempo) and arriving at its destination as if according to inevitable and inexplicable laws of its own.

Polyphonic Devices

By defining polyphony as consisting of two or more independent (horizontal) voices, we mean to say that each voice represents a melody (and frequently a rhythm) by itself, that no part of the texture is more dominating than another, and none merely an auxiliary voice.

Independence, however, does not preclude relatedness, and the vertical relation between polyphonic strands becomes clear when we realize that in all polyphonic devices the clue for the behavior of a single voice is given by one of its neighbors.

In the *imitation* device, for example, one voice follows in the "footsteps" of another at a certain distance, repeating a melodic profile which was heard before, while the first voice goes on to something else.

274. ECCO L'AURORA

Andrea Gabrieli (c. 1510–1586)

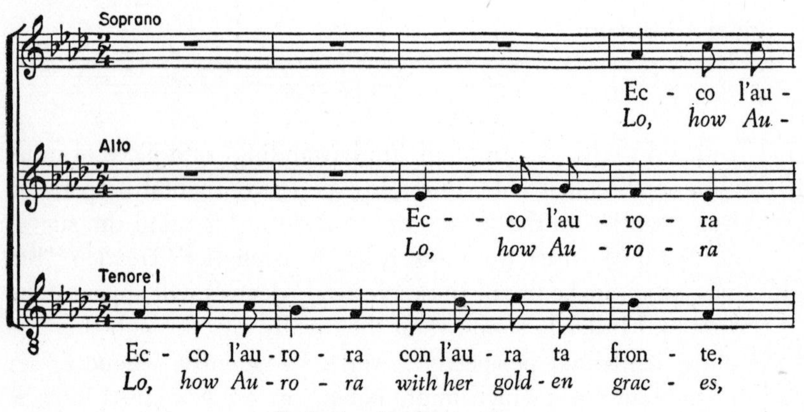

Imitation in three voices

Source: Alfred Einstein (ed.), *The Golden Age of the Madrigal*, p. 32.

Whenever the imitation takes place literally, i.e., at a fixed distance of measures and all the way through to the end, we have a *canon* or *round*. The difference between the two terms is that in a canon the second voice may start either with the same tone as the first voice, or a third, fourth, fifth, etc., above it, while a round starts always with the same tone as the leader (i.e., in "unison"). In addition, the round repeats each voice over and over and thus becomes a "perpetual canon in unison"—until someone calls a halt at a convenient moment.

Other polyphonic devices are *augmentation* and *diminution*. Here, an imitation takes place which is not literal as far as time is concerned, although exact in regards to the melodic intervals, and usually exact in rhythm. Quarter notes of a melody become half notes in the augmented version; the original quarter notes become eighths in the diminished version, and so forth.

275. PIANO SONATA IN A♭ MAJOR, OP. 110 (Fuga)

Ludwig van Beethoven (1770–1827)

Fugue theme:

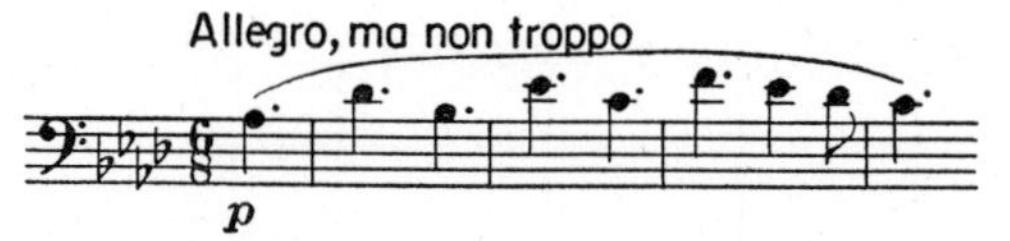

Fugue theme in augmentation:

Augmentation produces the illusion of a slower tempo in the respective voice because the time values of each tone are augmented. In reality, the tempo of the piece remains, of course, the same—else there would be no point in using the device of augmentation, that is to say, of *seemingly* slowing down *one* voice while the others proceed regularly.[1]

Diminution does the opposite, halving the time values of a melody so that the affected voice seems to rush ahead individually while the others keep the same pace as before.

276. FIVE MELODIES FOR VIOLIN AND PIANO, OP. 35B (No. 3)

Serge Prokofieff (1891-)

[1] This is one reason why arbitrary ("romantic") changes of tempo are uncalled for in polyphonic music.

277. THE ART OF THE FUGUE

Johann Sebastian Bach (1685–1750)

We obtain imitation in the negative, so to speak, when we use the device of *melodic inversion*.[2] Here black becomes white and vice versa: when the original tune goes up a step, down goes its inversion, and so forth. The device of inversion has been brought to its most incredible perfection by Bach in the Mirror Fugues of his *Art of the Fugue*. Three- and four-part fugues are so constructed that they may be played either straight ("*rectus*") or with every part inverted ("*inversus*").

[2] As distinguished from "harmonic" inversion (see p. 111).

← Texture of Fig. 277.

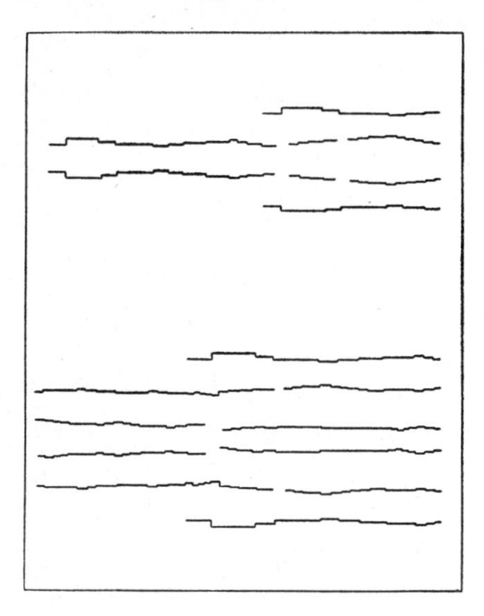

278. SONATA NO. 4 IN A MAJOR FOR VIOLIN AND PIANO

Joseph Haydn (1732–1809)

Observing closely every line in Figure 277 (preferably by turning the book sideways), we will detect that each line moves in the direction opposite its corresponding "alter ego."

The polyphonic device of inversion must not be confused with the so-called *retrograde* version of a canon melody or a fugue subject. In the *crab-canon* (*cancrizans*) each voice is first played forward and subsequently backward (the way a crab moves!). In Bach's *Musical Offering*, two examples occur of this device which—though seemingly contrived—may, if artfully used, produce great music. Haydn in a violin sonata, Mozart in his "Jupiter" Symphony, Beethoven in the finale of his *Hammerklavier Sonata*, Op. 106, and many other composers have used the same device. (See Figure 278.)

The meaning of counterpoint we defined as countermelody. A *double counterpoint* we call that polyphonic device which uses one countermelody first below another melody and later above the same melody (the counterpoint is made to do "double" duty, we might say, unless we frown upon mnemotechnical help.) The last two polyphonic devices which we shall mention, the *stretto* and the *organ point* (or pedal point) are mostly used in fugues and therefore also called fugal devices.

279. THE WELL-TEMPERED CLAVIER, BOOK II (Fugue No. 5)

Johann Sebastian Bach (1685–1750)

The subject:

The stretto (seven measures before the end):

In a stretto a melody or theme or *subject* (as it is called in a fugue) is stated in several voices in rapid succession. The voices start to imitate before the neighbor has finished his sentence, all stating *almost* at the same time what previously had been brought forward by one voice at a time. The result is an illusion of concentration of musical matter and a sort of accelerating clash of musical events.[3]

The organ point or pedal point is one of the oldest polyphonic devices. It is nothing but the drone of the bagpipe and the dance fiddles or the American five-string banjo utilized within the constructed texture of "art music." A single tone, usually the dominant or tonic, is sustained throughout several measures while conflicting voices and harmonies above it let it appear more or less stubbornly dissonant, until finally all resolves into a consonant calm. Usually the pedal point occurs in the bass (i.e., played on the *pedal* keyboard of the organ), and at the end of a piece (cf. the end of the third movement of Brahms' *Requiem*). On the other hand, sometimes a pedal tone is sustained in a high range (cf. Hindemith, *Mathis der Maler*; Smetana, *Aus meinem Leben*) or in the beginning or middle of a piece (cf. the opening of the *St. Matthew Passion*). We should, however, guard against considering every tone which is sustained for any length of time as an organ-point device. Frequently a single tone is given a varying harmonic evaluation (see Fig. 183); in that case the sustained tone participates as an integral part in the (vertical) combination of voices. The pedal point proper, on the other hand, presents in its stubborn perseverance and (horizontal) anticipation of an ultimate resolution an opposing force set against the rest of the fabric in a ruggedly individual fashion.

Homophonic Devices

In a pure homophonic texture, i.e., a single melodic line with accompanying chords below, above, or around it, the vertical devices to be used are few and of subsidiary importance only. If we remember that melodies are essentially horizontal and that harmonies, while consisting of vertical pillars of chords, progress horizontally also, this simplicity of texture in homophony should not surprise us. Nevertheless, the accompaniment will be important, as was mentioned before, because it may fulfil one or more of the following functions: It may

[3] It is important not to confuse the polyphonic "form" of a canon with the device of the stretto. In a canon the imitation is continuous, preserving a fair distance between voices, while in a stretto it is momentary and "accelerated," i.e., occurring in rapid succession.

(1) set the stage; (2) serve as background; (3) interpret the melody harmonically; (4) underline dynamics or rhythm; (5) provide contrast in dynamics and rhythm.

Repeated listening to and reading the scores of purely homophonic pieces and art-songs (*Lieder*) will train us to recognize these devices—will help us, in other words, to grasp a little more clearly what the composer wants to say.

This task will become immensely more difficult if we have to deal with one of the "mixed textures" which are usually included in the term *homophony*, although they contain elements of polyphony as well. As an example, let us consider the Baroque sonata for violin and basso continuo. Here the composer created: (1) a solo violin part; and (2) a bass line designed to support the solo part, to be imitative at times and independent at other times, and to support harmonies which bridge the gap between the treble voice and the bass.

This "continuous" bass support was called basso continuo or through bass (sometimes spelled "thorough" bass) and it was executed by a cello or viola da gamba and a harpsichord which played improvised or prescribed chords in addition to the bass line. Whenever the chords were not written out by the composer and whenever he did not want to trust the player's skill in improvising, a sort of musical shorthand was used, the so-called *figured bass*, which was mentioned above (p. 115). Figures below or above the basso continuo would indicate what kind of chord or inversion to play above a particular bass note (sometimes in the popular music of today we find the same kind of musical shorthand indicating in figures the chords to be played, or, in symbols, which string to use.)

280.

A FIGURED BASS AND ITS REALIZATION

Note: $\not{4}$ and $\not{6}$ mean to raise (sharpen) the fourth and sixth, respectively, above the bass tone.

Source: J. S. Bach, *Rules and Principles for the Four Part Playing of General Bass or Accompaniment* (1783). Reprinted in Spitta, *J. S. Bach*, III, 315–347 (American edition), Dover Publications, Inc., New York.

Another case of a mixed texture occurs sometimes when, as described above (p. 251), a single melodic line is divided up among several instruments or voices.

281. STRING QUARTET IN E MINOR, OP. 59, NO. 2 (Finale)

Ludwig van Beethoven (1770–1827)

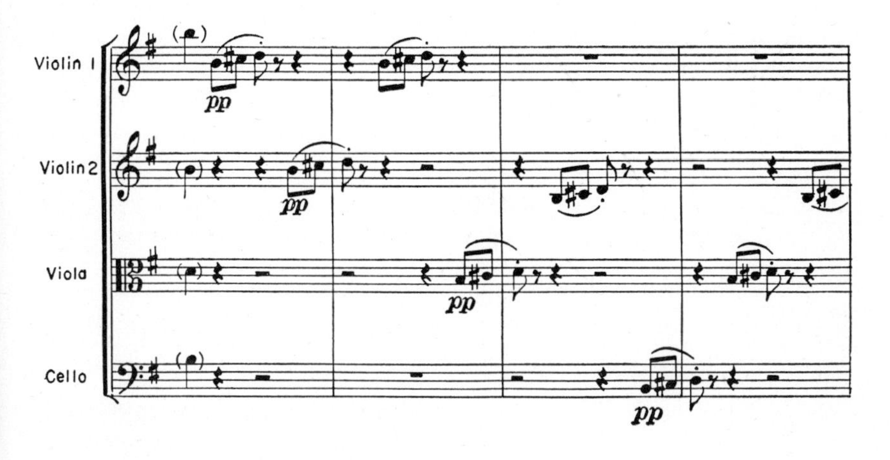

We have here monophony (a single melodic line) as well as polyphony (several voices are essentially involved and use the polyphonic device of imitation). This portioning out of melodic fragments among different instruments or singers is an old trick dating back to the medieval polyphonic period. Because of the odd spectacle of singers opening their mouths for a single tone only at a time, as if they were stuttering or gasping for air, this device was called *hocketing,* which meant possibly the same as having the hiccups.

282. JE CUIDOIE—SE J'AI—SOLEM (Motet)

Anonymous—13th century

Hocket Technique

Source: Davison and Apel, *op. cit.*, I, 38.

When this custom became too popular, serving as a means of showing off the teamwork and virtuosity of choristers, John XXII (Pope, 1316–1328) criticized it sharply:

> Certain disciples of the new school . . . [prefer] to devise methods of their own rather than to continue singing in the old way . . . they truncate the melodies with hoquets, they deprave them with discants, sometimes even they stuff them with upper parts . . . made out of secular songs. . . . Their voices are incessantly running to and fro, intoxicating the ear, not soothing it, while the men themselves endeavor to convey by their gestures the sentiment of the music which they utter. As a consequence of all this, devotion, the true end of worship, is little thought of, and wantonness, which ought to be eschewed, increases. . . .[4]

We may recognize the cooperative idea of the hocket device, which is called *stile brisé* or *Durchbrochene Arbeit* (lacy work) when used by the classic composers—also in the English tradition of the Bell Ringers.

Mixed textures which show a prevalence of *harmonic* thinking rather than a melodic emphasis are likewise frequently used by composers. The adding of extra voices (*Freistimmigkeit*) to a homophonic structure may produce a temporary counterpoint, or it may reinforce dynamics, add color, expand the range, etc. At other times a chorus or orchestra will produce a kind of pseudo polyphony—that is to say, a clearly harmonic texture is made more lively through short snatches

[4] H. E. Wooldridge, "The Polyphonic Period, Part I," *The Oxford History of Music*, I, p. 294–95.

of "imitation," countermelodies, counterrhythms, and similar devices. The most primitive example of this is Barbershop—"polyphony" where a few voices simply hold their tones until the other "imitative" voices have caught up with them. Here, then, the "polyphonic" treatment is of secondary importance; it *serves* the harmonic progression, while in true polyphony, on the contrary, the *harmonic* result is secondary, and the independence of each individual voice is of prime importance.

Conclusions

What goes on successively in music is on the whole easier to follow than what happens simultanously. Yet the course of a piece is largely dependent upon its internal (vertical) structure, which we here have called texture. The interplay of vertical and horizontal forces in a piece of music produces its ultimate form. The fact that all textures which are used in the music which we hear nowadays have been developed throughout centuries of experimentation and tradition, and through the skill of master craftsmen, makes our music a complex art of constantly changing devices and symbols of the musical language. Consequently, our attention must rapidly grasp the point, the line, or the harmonies which are of prime importance at every instant in a piece of music. To hear all the notes which are sounded is not enough. The intelligent listener will have to select, separate, and combine sounds if he wants to approximate receptively the composer's intentions. He will have to comprehend combined sounds as chords sometimes and as converging lines at another time. Augmentation, diminution, inversion will have to be grasped as related to an original version—otherwise the richness of texture and the art of the composer are lost on the listener.

Frequently, the "romantic" notion prevails that music which is devised, constructed, thought out, is of no value because "it does not come from the heart of the composer." If that were true, not a single piece of music would be worth while, because all music is constructed and uses its own logic, grammar, and vocabulary according to carefully thought out and applied principles. Were it otherwise, we should have to deny to the Gothic cathedrals of Europe any artistic value or emotional appeal—as being "engineered" and "constructed" so as to last through centuries instead of being a momentary, impetuous flurry of excitement without rhyme or reason, as our "romantics" would have them.

Similarly, it is often said that to know how a piece of music is constructed spoils the spontaneous pleasure in hearing it. This attitude may be compared to the one advocated by some "nature friends" who say, "Let us live like dumb animals and enjoy life without education, ethics, idealism, mental or physical achievements." The trouble here is that the composers choose another road: to perfect to the utmost the language, the logic, and the impact of what they have to say with all their heart and all their ability has been their goal through centuries. In approaching it they have employed every means: tradition, skill, innovation, passionate search, their overflowing hearts, and—their brains. The listener who approximates at least in his intentions the labors of the composer will be rewarded for his modest attempts. The wonders of great music unfold only at close and repeated inspection.

Suggestions for Listening

Bach	*The Art of the Fugue*
	Brandenburg Concerto No. 3
	Fugue in E Minor for Organ
	A Musical Offering
	Partita for Violin Solo in B Minor
	Partita for Violin Solo in E Major
	Passion according to St. Matthew
	Well-tempered Clavier, Book II, Fugue No. 5
Beethoven	"Bagatelle," Op. 33, No. 3
	Hammerklavier Sonata, Op. 106
	Piano Sonata in A♭ Major, Op. 110
	String Quartet in E Minor, Op. 59, No. 2
	Symphony No. 1 in C Major, Op. 21
	Symphony No. 5 in C Minor, Op. 67
	Symphony No. 7 in A Major, Op. 92
Brahms	Violin Concerto in D Major, Op. 77
	A German Requiem, Op. 45
Bruckner	Symphony No. 4 in E♭ Major
Chopin	Nocturne in B♭ Minor, Op. 9, No. 1
Examples of "Hocketing"	
Gabrieli, A.	"Ecco l'aurora" (Madrigal)
Haydn	Sonata No. 4 for Violin and Piano in A Major
Hindemith	*Mathis der Maler*
Locke	*Consorts of Four Parts* (Suites for Strings)
Mendelssohn	*Songs without Words*

Mozart	Piano Sonata in G Major, K. 283
	Sonata for Violin and Piano in G Major, K. 379
	Symphony No. 41 in C Major ("Jupiter"), K. 551
Prokofieff	*Five Melodies for Violin and Piano*
Schubert	Lieder (Art-Songs)
	Symphony No. 5 in B♭ Major
Smetana	String Quartet in E Minor ("From My Life")

Sonatas for violin or flute and figured bass by Bach, Corelli, Händel

Strauss, R.	*Also sprach Zarathustra,* Op. 30
Tchaikovsky	"Danse Chinoise" from *Nutcracker Suite,* Op. 71a

17

Form

FORM IN music means the shape, the dimensions—horizontal as well as vertical—of a piece of music, and its inner structure. In other words, all the elements of music are integrated so as to produce a form which is characteristic and functional as far as the purpose of the piece or the intentions of the composer are concerned. If we grant that the content, the idea, the essence, of a piece of music do not come into existence until they are clearly and convincingly formulated, we must admit that content and form are inseparable—one should really say, identical. It is of no importance in this connection whether the idea or the form comes first to the mind of the composer. In the first case he will have to find a suitable form for his musical ideas, and in the latter instance he will have to hunt for appropriate material to fit the over-all dimensions which he has in mind. In the process of doing so the form and the content will change many times until they take on their final inseparable shape. This is the reason why great composers have to make numerous sketches in notebooks or else mental notes of their musical raw material, which they change and work out until its possibilities are realized and clearly stated—in the final form of their composition.

Each piece of music, then, has its own individual form, and while there are certain similarities in the over-all proportions of many different pieces of music, the significance of a composition lies in its inside workings, not on the outside. Whenever form has been treated as a rigid immovable shell or a definite mold into which musical raw material is to be forced, we find the result unconvincing. We then speak of unoriginal imitators or of a musical content which is either "padded" to fit an oversize form or else is so ample as to split the seams of an undersized mold.

In comparing several symphonies written by the same composer, we will, of course, detect similarities in their form—but also many dissimilarities. Whenever we want to state what all symphonies have in common, we are forced to make meaningless statements comparable to describing a human being by saying that he has two arms and two legs. As soon as we dare to generalize at length about symphonies we have to append to each sentence, "But there are also many exceptions to this."

An attempt to define the fugue as far as its form is concerned encounters similar difficulties. It is debatable whether one should speak of the fugue as the "most representative and highest of Baroque forms" (Lang), or "a question of texture rather than of design" (Tovey), or rather a procedure of composing; however, no one will dispute that good fugues are well constructed, and especially those of J. S. Bach. Yet the venerable Ebenezer Prout tells that in his conservatory days the students in counterpoint were forbidden to consult or quote Bach's fugues because they contained too many "exceptions" to the book rules of music theorists.[1]

In trying to define musical forms, we are apt to vacillate between the two extremes which are combined in every good piece of music: unity and variety. Our approach becomes either too simplified or too complex. Form analysis has been further prevented from tackling effectively the problems of form in music by two interrelated idiosyncrasies of the nineteenth century: that the entire history of music had no other purpose than to prepare and make possible Beethoven's *Eroica* and Wagner's music-dramas; and that therefore melody and harmonic progression, i.e., horizontal factors, are all that count in the forms of music.

Thus, the scheme of musical forms is often indicated by "*A–B–A*," etc. This is meant to indicate that the piece in question has three sections and that the third section is identical with the first. This scheme is used for the description of the following widely varying forms: sonata allegro movement (wrongly so, as we shall see), minuet, scherzo, French overture, Italian overture, da capo aria, song, etc. Even when qualified by a statement that *B* is entirely different from *A*, or else is an elaboration, or that the second *A* is a literal repetition of the first, or is slightly modified—these descriptions seem of little help to the listener. Suppose he does hear that a motive or theme or section is repeated, do not just the "episodes, transitions, modulations, counterrhythms, and countermelodies, etc.," which intervene or were added

[1] Lang, *Music in Western Civilization*, p. 443.

make the "repetition" significant? The many "landmarks" in a piece of music—that is to say, new and old rhythms, melodies, harmonies, tonalities, tone colors, dynamics, textures—are without value to the listener unless he is aware of how the composer arrives at them, why he puts them where they appear, and how he continues. This is, of course, another way of saying that in listening we have to hear all there is to hear, and re-create, as it were, the composer's process of finding a form for his particular piece.

In addition, however, just as we found it necessary to select, combine, and evaluate outstanding factors in a texture (which is in itself an integral part of every form), so we must distinguish between the various formative devices according to their importance within a given era and even during the course of an individual composition. In order, then, to acquire the rudiments of what we call form in music, we might inquire into some basic principles of organization and enumerate specific formative devices which are used in fulfilling the general intentions of composers.

Principles of Organization

Whenever a piece of music has a well-defined function, the composer is not entirely free in the way in which he organizes his musical material.

A march and a dance will each require a specific meter, tempo, and sometimes also a specific rhythm. A lullaby and a fanfare will each impose their own appropriate character, which in these cases means particular instruments and dynamics. If the music is to be sung, the character of the poem, the message of the liturgical or secular text, the action of the musical drama or comedy, will have to be translated into music by the composer. He will have to find expressive means for the prayers, hymns, allelujahs, and for the love songs, passionate conflicts, and involved confusions in the spirit and in the order which his text prescribes. If he chooses a program, that is, a story, a painting, an extramusical impression or idea, he will have to distil his own perceptions into a musical substance which contains the essence, the consistency, and the shape of his program. In the latter case, the composer will select his musical material and its organization so as to intensify and elaborate a visual, emotional, or mental image.

In the case of *absolute music,* i.e., music without words or program, the principle of organization works in a similar way. The composer will start either with an over-all structural idea or with a detail which suggests to him a certain kind of structure. He may want his piece to be simple or complex, dramatic or calm, dynamic or static; he may want to have his piece proceed synthetically or analytically; that is, either by building up a melodic line gradually from short fragments or by taking apart a complete musical statement into its components; he may produce a musical conflict and then resolve it, conclude peacefully, or with a question mark, and so forth. That all these effects may be achieved without a story or pictures as the stimulus may be gathered from the existence of "abstract art." Forms, lines, colors, textures, motion, may exist by themselves; they do not necessarily have to be embodied in the portrait of a beautiful girl, a landscape, or horses.

283.

HORIZONTAL VARIETY AND VERTICAL UNITY

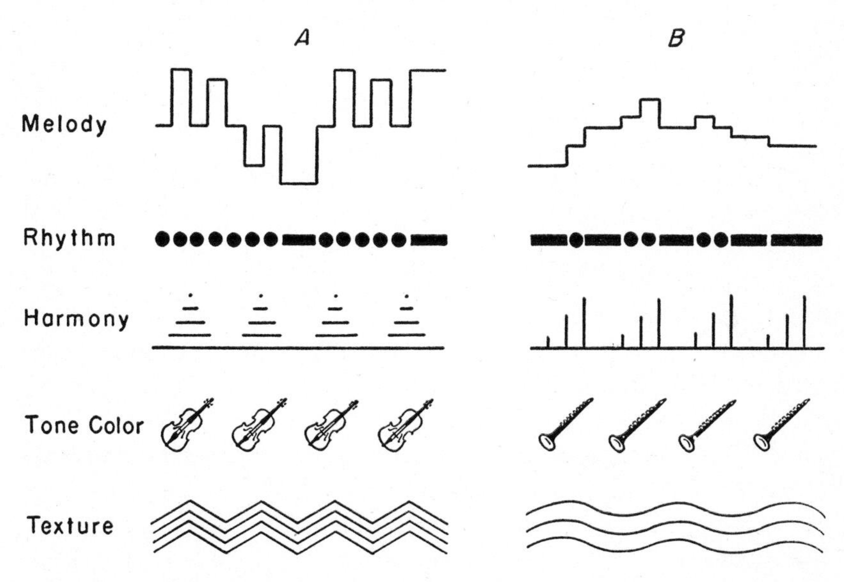

It seems strange at first that all structural principles of music may be described by the two terms *unity* and *variety*. However, if we realize how many factors are operating in music and that one or all may produce unity or variety, either successively or simultaneously, we may grasp the endless possibilities which are inherent in music. Let us imagine a clearly stated melody which has a specific and unified expressive character, with a beginning, a middle or climax, and a definite ending. If the composer supports this melody with harmonies, rhythms, tone color, and texture which form a homogeneous whole, we will have unity both horizontally and vertically. A different kind of melody may follow, again, with all other elements supporting and serving the new melody and its character. If we call the first melody and its accompaniment *A*, and the second melody *B*, we will have (horizontal) variety in going from *A* to *B* and (vertical) unity throughout each melody (see Figure 283).

If, on the other hand, we add to the *A* and *B* sections a *counter*-melody with its own distinct rhythm, we will obtain unity through these contrasting additions; we will thus link together the two diverse musical excerpts. Here, then, we have contrasting elements—a counter melody and rhythm—serving as vertical contrast and horizontal unification at the same time.

284.

Horizontal Unity and Vertical Variety

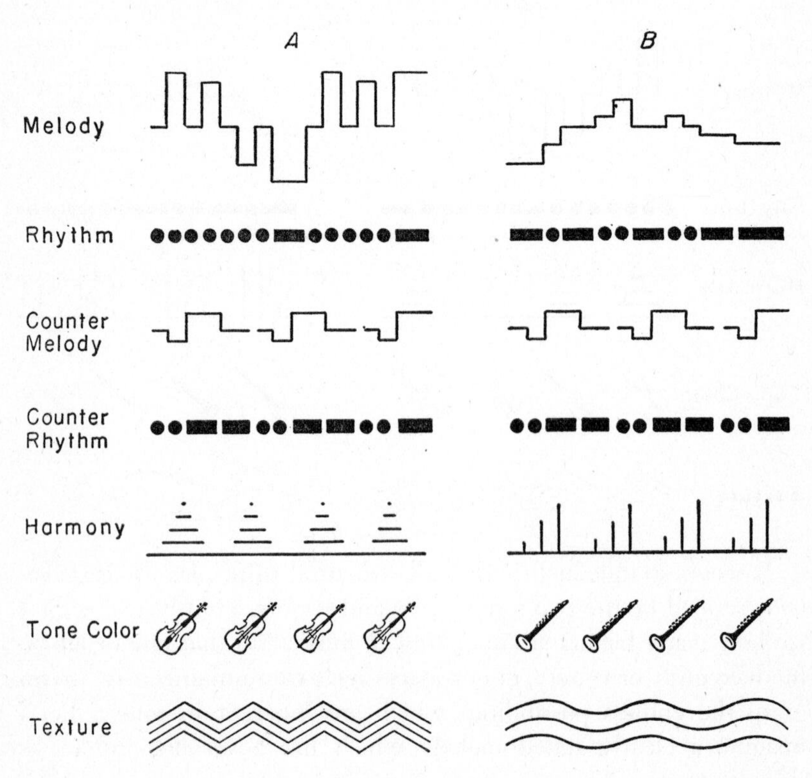

Let us remember now that meter, tempo, dynamics, etc., may all play a similarly helpful or contradictory role, creating vertical or horizontal unity or variety. The possibilities are so tremendous that it becomes clear that to preserve unity is more of a problem in music than to create variety. If we map a "score" for the various factors involved in a piece of music and name each element and factor by numbers or letters, a change in letters or numbers indicating a change in rhythm, melody, etc., we will create a chaos of unrelated pieces unless we introduce measures of stability and symmetry.

A Formless Conglomeration of Musical Elements
Within a "Piece" of Seven Sections

	Section 1	Section 2	Section 3	Section 4	Section 5	Section 6	Section 7
Meter	I	I	I	I	I	I	I
Rhythm	1	1	1	3	1	1	1
Melody	a	b	c	d	e	f	g
Harmony	*A*	*A*	D	*A*	E	*A*	*A*
Tone Color	Strings	Fl.	Cl.	Ob.	Br.	WW.	Strings
Dynamics	f	pp	p	p	f	mf	p
Texture	H	M	M	M	P	H	P
Tempo	t	t	t	t	t	t	t

	Symbols for Identical Musical Elements	Symbols for Changing Musical Elements
Meter	I	(None)
Rhythm	1	3
Melody	a	b, c, d, e, f, g
Harmony	*A*	*D, E*
Tone Color	Strings	Fl., Cl., Ob., Br., WW.
Dynamics	f	p, pp, mf
Texture	H	M, P
Tempo	t	(None)

Key to symbols: *Harmony,* A major, etc.; *Tone Color,* Strings, Flutes, etc.; *Dynamics,* forte, piano, pianissimo, etc.; *Texture,* Homophonic, Monophonic, Polyphonic.

While a piece of this kind would have a stable meter and tempo, and while the harmony provides a certain symmetry, the tone colors, dynamics, and texture change entirely too frequently. Worst of all, the melodies change continuously and are possibly held together only by a rather monotonous rhythmical design. This example of nonsensical fragments of musical matter may show us that the elements of music cannot always proceed independently; they have instead to serve or dominate at various times. Simplicity and stability as well as symmetry are indispensable in music. A typical piece in two successive sections (*A* and *B*) would be more likely to turn out as follows:

	A	*B*
Meter	I	I
Rhythm	1, 3	3, 1
Melody	a, b	b, a
Harmony	*A, E*	*E, A*
Tone Color	Strings	Strings
Dynamics	f, p	p, f
Texture	M, P	M, P

A three-section piece might appear with this structure:

	A	*B*	*A*
Meter	I	I	I
Rhythm	1, 3	2, 4	1, 3
Melody	a, b	c, d	a, b
Harmony	*A, E*	*D, G*	*A, E*
Tone Color	Strings	WW.	Strings
Dynamics	f, p	p, p	f, p
Texture	M, P	H	M, P

Let us not forget that we have dealt in the preceding examples with *one* principal melody only (the countermelodies and their rhythms, which are implied at times in the polyphonic texture, are not even inserted). If we now attempt a similar graph for a truly polyphonic piece, a three-voiced fugue, let us say, we will have three independent "streams" of rhythm, melody, and tone color. They are diagonally connected or unified, but vertically contrasted: stable and simplifying elements must therefore counteract these complications and hold the structure horizontally together. It is for this reason that, in the case of fugues, tempo and meter remain always, and dynamics usually, stable and that the harmonic progressions are relatively simple. It is not difficult to see that the retaining of stable elements will result in unity and that the literal repetition of entire sections after an intervening change of musical material will serve to produce a symmetrical structure which tends to act as a stabilizing frame. On the other hand, the role played by those sections which provide (horizontal) variety is not as simple to define. In a piece which consists of three sections, *A–B–A*, for example, the middle part may bring a complete change in meter, rhythm, melody, tonality, tone color, and texture, let us say. In this case, the purpose is one of contrast, relief, diversity. If, however, the middle section brings about a gradual or partial change from what went on in section *A*, we speak of a development, spinning out, expansion, elaboration, variation, permutation, transformation, etc. New material may be introduced in section *B* as a contrast and an antithesis to what went before, and later in the course of the piece this contrasting musical matter may be merged with elements of section *A*. Or vertical or horizontal additions may add new light to a repeated musical thought.

It is unfortunate that the term *development* has been reserved for the middle section of a "sonata-allegro" (see p. 301) only. The expansion and contraction of melodies of the Baroque, for instance; any kind of variation in rhythm, harmony, tone color, dynamics; any addition of a counterpoint; the inversion of melodies or other polyphonic devices—all these represent equally a *development* of a musical idea in the truest sense of the word. Let us think of the "Bolero" by Ravel for a moment. Here a melody and a rhythm are repeated without change; however, the dynamics and the orchestration (tone color) produce a gradual change, variations which *develop* the piece toward a dramatic climax. At other times a development may "thin out" a melody, dissect it in playful ornamentation, or circumscribe its rhythmic, melodic, and harmonic elements in fragmentary outlines.

Because of the countless applications of the organizing principle of unity and variety which the many factors involved in music make possible, the listener frequently gets lost during the course of an extensive piece. A keen perception for what is most important at any one moment has to be developed, and a musical memory which facilitates the recognition of repetitions and partial changes. It should be of considerable help in this connection if we become acquainted with some of the specific formative devices which are commonly used in pieces of particular eras and in "form" categories.

Formative Devices

SEQUENCES.—One of the most common devices used for the "spinning out" or expanding of musical phrases is the *sequence*. If we apply the polyphonic device of imitation (p. 270) to one single voice, that is, if we convert a vertical device into a horizontal one, we obtain the repetition of a motive or melody in a different pitch.

285. SYMPHONY NO. 40 IN G MINOR, K. 550 (Minuet)

Wolfgang Amadeus Mozart (1756–1791)

Flute

In the device of the sequence, which is also found in repeated harmonic progressions or in rhythms, we find simultaneously incorporated the two basic laws of organization: unity and variety.

A look at the full score of the Minuet from Mozart's great G Minor Symphony (Fig. 287) will show us that while the violins and flute play their sequences, bassoons (fagotti), celli, and contrabasses play different ones:

286. SYMPHONY NO. 40 IN G MINOR, K. 550 (Minuet)

Mozart

Sequences are rarely literal repetitions. For reasons of harmonic requirements, voice leading, or simply for variety's sake, the second link of a sequence usually adjusts or even inverts the intervals of the first link. (Compare, e.g., in the foregoing excerpt, measures two and five.) More sequences are found in the oboe, clarinet and viola parts of our example, and a literal repetition of a motive in the horns.

287. SYMPHONY NO. 40 IN G MINOR, K. 550 (Minuet)

Wolfgang Amadeus Mozart (1756–1791)

Bb
Fl.
Obs.
Cls.
Bssns.
Hns.
Vln. I
Vln. 2
Vla.
Vcl. B.
a 2
15
20

Fl.
Obs.
Cls.
Bssns.
Hns.
Vln. I
Vln. 2
Vla.
Vcl. B.
a
25

Fl.
Obs.
Cls.
Bssns.
Hns.
Vln. 1
Vln. 2
Vla.
Vcl. B.
30
35
p
40

Binary Form. Let us now observe in this piece (which shall serve as our Exhibit A for form) the rhythm and the harmony. Allowing one line for each separate rhythm, we find in the first 14 measures the following picture: [2]

288.

By comparing each line with the others, we find that this section of the piece begins with four different rhythms and ends with two: the rhythmical procedure tends from complexity toward simplicity. This tendency is also emphasized by the fact that the syncopation ("the swallowing up" of the first beat in measures 2, 5, 8) gradually disappears.

Harmonically, this is what happens: the piece begins in G minor and modulates towards D minor, or in other words, the dominant (d) of the original key (g) becomes tonic just before the *double bar,* which latter indicates the end of a movement or, as in this case, of a section of a piece. The double dots which are placed immediately before the double bar indicate that the preceding section is to be repeated for reasons of proportional balance and in order to let the listener grasp more details at the repetition than he did at the first time.

[2] There is a slight divergence in the viola and bassoon parts—an extra syncopation—and the flute pauses for a measure and a half; otherwise the various instruments play "unison rhythms" as indicated.

We have now inspected fairly carefully what happened in the first "*A*" section of this minuet. The second or "*B*" section brings first of all a further "development," "spinning out," or "treatment" of the musical material of part *A*.

Flute, oboe, clarinet, viola, cello, and bass bring the main (syncopated) melody or theme three times in sequence. To this the bassoons and violins add a seemingly entirely new counterpoint. Seemingly, we must say, because a look at the bass rhythm at the seventh and eighth measures of part *A* (Figure 288) reveals that the rhythm ♩ ♩ ♩ | 𝅗𝅥. is not new, and that its continuation in the countermelody of part *B* is but a rhythmic inversion of the repeated ♩ ♫♫ rhythm in part *A* (measures 9 and 10, or measures 2, 5, and 8 if we disregard the syncopation.)

In measures 23–25 the inversion becomes the original rhythm again, to which viola, cello, bass, flute, oboe, and clarinet add a new syncopated counterrhythm (a rhythmic inversion of measures 1, 2, 4, and 5 in the oboe and clarinet). In measure 26 the two rhythms are interchanged between two instrumental groups. Wood winds (except bassoon) and basses and violas which had ♩ 𝅗𝅥 continue with ♩ ♫♫ and the violins, bassoons, and horns end their ♩ ♫♫ sequence with ♩ 𝅗𝅥.

With the last beat of measure 27 we have reached home ground again; we are back in G minor and the first violins, oboe, clarinet, and bassoon recapitulate the main theme. However, there is a difference from the original version: these instruments get no farther than the first two measures, which they repeat (slightly varied) three times. The flute, second violins, second oboe, clarinet, and bassoon follow in the manner of a canon a fourth above. Finally, in measures 34 and 35 a definite cadence and unified rhythm lead to a close in G minor. There follows now what is called a *coda*. In the manner of an epilogue or afterthought, as if something had been forgotten, the flute plays the main theme in its complete (if unexpanded) version. One bassoon and the clarinets help a little with chromatic countermelodies, and in the last three measures the entire orchestra (except for oboes) marks an authentic cadence.

Part *B*, which is longer than *A*, is also repeated in order to round out the form and because much went on in it which must escape the hearer the first time. Harmonically, we move from B♭ major (the relative major of G minor) back to G minor, and we touch in passing (without confirming these tonalities through cadences) E♭ major, and C minor. Noteworthy also is the dissonance in the second measure of section *B* (measure 16), where the minor seventh jump from F to the E♭ above, in the violins and bassoons, clashes with the syncopated D of the main theme. The rhythmical device of the syncopation is here underlined by making of the (metrically) held over note a (harmonic) suspension as well: i.e., a dissonance serves as accentuation of the syncopation.

If we now want to summarize in general terms what happened in these one and a half minutes of music, we might say:

1. Proportionally, the piece has two sections, *A* and *B*. Section *B* consists of two subdivisions, *b* and *a*.
2. Harmonically, *A* moves from the tonality of the tonic of the piece to that of the dominant. Section *B* moves via several tonalities back to the tonic.
3. Thematically, the piece derives all motives, rhythms, and melodies from the principal material which is stated in the first three measures. While the theme is developed, added to, modulated, its basic expressive character does not change.
4. The formative devices used are those of Mozart's time, e.g.: (*a*) sequences, (*b*) melodic and rhythmic inversions, (*c*) syncopations, (*d*) counterpoints and counterrhythms, (*e*) underlining of basic harmonies and rhythms by the horns.
5. The texture remains unchanged.
6. The musical events may be described by explaining that first the thematic material is presented or "exposed" in part *A*, and then *developed* further and *recapitulated* and brought to its close in part *B*.

Here, then, we have the famous *binary* or *bipartite*[3] form of a piece of music, which is used in countless dances of the preclassical and classical era and which is at the same time a miniature edition of the so-called sonata-allegro form, as we shall see later.

Ternary Form Categories. The polarity of principles of organization—unity and variety, continuity and separation, similarity and change, etc.—will work in short fragments of music as well as in extensive musical structures. The composer will link together small

[3] The reader is advised to reserve the term *two-* or *three-part piece* for a piece for two or three voices and to use *binary* and *ternary* or *bipartite* and *tripartite* for the description of two- and three-section pieces.

particles or large quantities of material, and the degree of closeness or separation depends on our frame of reference. In the minuet which we have considered, for example, we conceive a unity of purpose and character when we think of the whole piece. Taking the principal theme, on the other hand, as our point of departure, we will detect many changes which occur during the course of the piece.

Let us assume now that the composer wants to continue his minuet so as to prolong the composition. The material presented is exhausted so that an entirely new theme is needed. A change of key and tone color would also be advisable for reasons of variety. Yet together with these changes in the melodic and harmonic character of the new piece, factors of unity are also needed. They will come forth if the continuation is another minuet, built again in binary fashion. Because of the demand for a change of tone color, such a second minuet was frequently played by three wood winds only, and thus became known as a *trio*.[4] This name has been retained even where more than three players are involved.

A comparison between the trio (see Figure 289) and the minuet of Mozart's G Minor Symphony will disclose the following differences:

1. The trio is in G major.
2. The texture is "lighter," i.e., no polyphony, and fewer instruments, are involved. Single melodies are portioned out to various instruments in "broken fashion" (p. 277).
3. Fewer tonalities are "visited."
4. There are more changes in dynamics.
5. The articulation is predominantly legato (while the minuet was staccato throughout.)

The similarities, on the other hand, between the trio and the minuet lie in these factors which may be found in both pieces:

1. The tempo and meter are the same.
2. Part *A* moves from G major to D major (from the key of the tonic to that of the dominant), and Part *B* from D back to G major.
3. A unified theme is exposed in *A* and developed and recapitulated in *B*.
4. There is a little coda, fashioned from material of the theme ending both parts A and B.

[4] The term *trio* may mean three things: (1) the trio of a minuet, (2) a composition for three instruments, and (3) the three persons who play such a composition.

289. SYMPHONY NO. 40 IN G MINOR, K. 550 (Trio)

Wolfgang Amadeus Mozart (1756–1791)

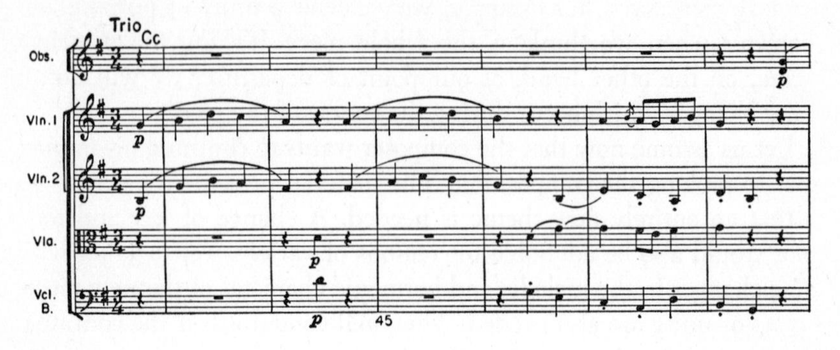

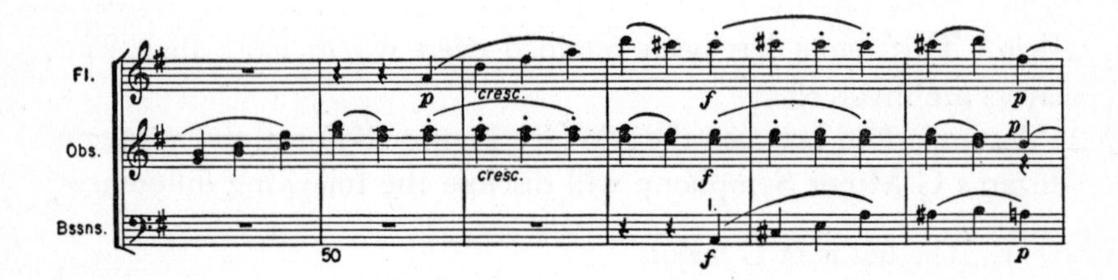

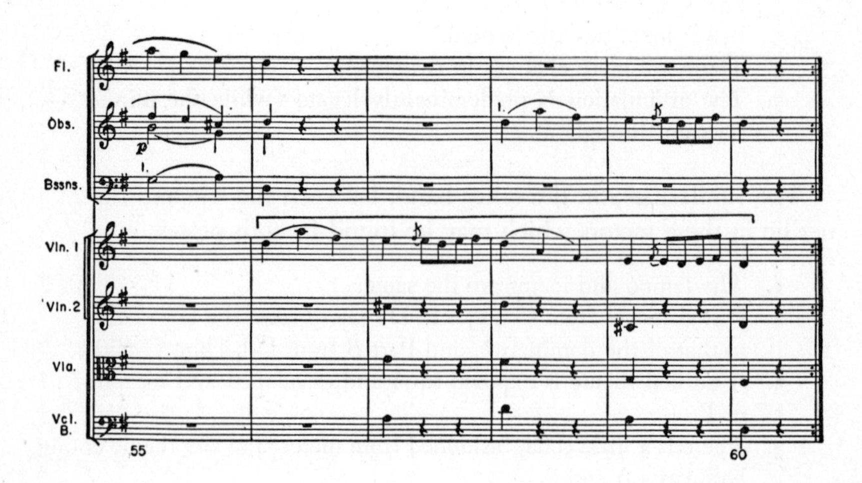

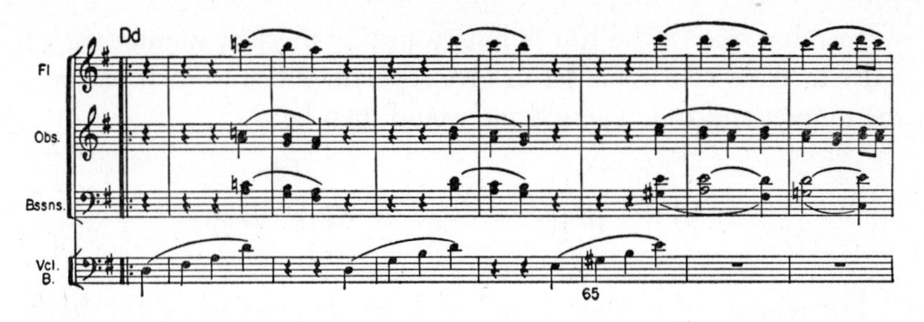
Dd
Fl
Obs.
Bssns.
Vcl. B.
65

C
Fl.
Obs.
Bssns.
cresc.
Hns.
p
cresc.
Vln. 1
Vln. 2
div.
Vla.
Vcl. B.
70
75

Fl.
f
p
Obs.
Bssns.
Hns.
Vln. 1
Vln. 2
div.
Vla.
Vcl. B.
80
Menuetto da capo

In other words, the trio is binary just as the first minuet was. In order to avoid confusion, let us give separate letters to each section of the minuet and trio. The scheme would then be:

Minuet		Trio	
|*A* :|[5]	|*B* :|	|*C* :|	|*D* :|
(*a*)	(*ba*)	(*c*)	(*dc*)

For reasons of symmetry and perhaps also to enclose the lighter texture of the trio with the steady frame of a full orchestra sound, it has been customary for a long time to repeat the minuet after the trio. This is indicated by the direction *da capo* (abbreviated *D.C.* = from the head of the piece). This repetition is literal except for the fact that *A* and *B* are only played once each the last time they are heard. The design then becomes:

Minuet	Trio	Minuet
AA BB	*CC DD*	*A B*

If we dispense with the naming of internal sections, we might call the entire minuet *A* and the entire trio *B* and thus arrive at the ternary or tripartite scheme:

A	*B*	*A*
Minuet	Trio	Minuet

This form category may again be found in a very great number of compositions. Above all, every minuet and scherzo of a symphony, sonata, quartet, etc., is written so as to include a contrasting (trio) part. In speaking of a minuet, we nowadays mean not only the minuet proper but the entire complex of minuet–trio–minuet.

Da capo arias, preclassical overtures, and some nocturnes, ballads, waltzes, songs, and slow instrumental pieces may also be described by the scheme *A–B–A*. However, all they have in common is that they repeat a section after a contrasting middle part. Obviously the contrast will be provided by different factors in each individual piece, and the listener will fail to discover the scheme *A–B–A* unless he becomes aware of the endless shades of unity and diversity through repeated hearing and studying of a musical composition.[6]

[5] Or, *AA*.

[6] The choice of collateral listening for this and the remaining chapters is left to the reader, inasmuch as any one piece from the entire musical literature may serve as an example for "form" and "style."

18

Form
(*Continued*)

Sonata-Allegro Form

WHAT IS commonly called sonata-allegro form or first-movement form or simply sonata form frequently adds another case to the many mistaken identities which the hazy terminology of music creates.

First of all, the term *sonata form* applies to the form of one or several *parts* or *movements* of a sonata, not to the entire piece. Secondly, a movement in sonata form is not always an allegro (nor, by any means, is every allegro in sonata form); and finally, sonata form is frequently found in other movements besides the first, of a sonata, symphony, string quartet, etc. Inasmuch as the so-called development section is more extensive and characteristic in these movements than in others, we might perhaps substitute *development form* for the term *sonata-allegro form*. However, because the device of development is also to be found in binary and ternary forms and, as we shall see, in rondos, variations, and fugues—let us rather adhere to the traditional term *sonata-allegro*.

The sonata-allegro form has been the most common structural procedure since the classic era. It is basically a binary form. The main difference from the minuet, allemande, courante, etc., is that two tonalities and themes, instead of one, are presented and developed. Eventually composers expanded the two principal themes further into two thematic groups or complexes, each standing in a different tonality. Much has been made of the contrasting character of the two thematic groups; the first is supposed to be energetic, dramatic, and the second (sometimes also called the "subsidiary theme"), more lyrical. There are many cases, however, where these descriptions do not fit and where the second theme is even derived from the first. The various themes are repeatedly presented in the *A*, or *exposition*, section of the development form. Frequently the exposition ends with a third or closing theme, and it is usual for the composer to request that the exposition section be repeated. If that is done (frequently our craving for the saving of time and money prevents it!) the hearer has a chance to engrave in his memory the various thematic groups and the two principal tonalities.

The first half of the *B* section literally defies description. Here, anything goes—themes are dissected, telescoped, contrasted, inverted, diminished, augmented, and formerly unimportant rhythmic or melodic fragments come into an entirely unexpected prominence. In other words, everything—melodies, rhythms, harmonies, tonalities, orchestration, texture, expression—is subjected to an extensive "development" treatment. When the composer has explored all inherent possibilities of his themes in the development subdivision of *B*, the second part of section *B* occurs—the *recapitulation,* which is usually introduced dramatically or at least unexpectedly. During the recapitulation all principal themes recur, and this time they all stand in the basic tonality of the piece. Many changes in orchestration occur; shortening or expanding of the themes is frequent (sometimes one can speak of a new "development" in the recapitulation section), but almost everything is said in the basic tonality. A coda rounds out the movement, bringing for the last time the gist of the first thematic group (here again, composers—Beethoven especially—have introduced and "developed" new themes).

Through the development which they undergo, themes occur finally in a new light in the recapitulation and in the coda. Furthermore, the composer, by shortening or changing them when they recur, acts as if to say, "You know what I mean." Therefore, the recapitulation, even aside from the change in the tonality of the second thematic group, is anything but a literal repetition of part *A*. The development section, on the other hand, is by no means a contrasting *B* section, as is the case in ternary *A–B–A* form categories; it simply transforms previously stated materials. Our scheme for the *sonata-allegro* form then must read:

A	*B*		
a, b, c, (two or three thematic groups). Two basic tonalities.	(1) Development of thematic material of *A*. Many modulations.	(2) Recapitulation of basic thematic materials in one tonality.	(3) Coda.

It should be clear that, in program as well as in absolute music, this scheme provides for the statement, clash, and resolution of conflicting ideas; for contrast, gradual and sudden changes; surprising developments and solutions, unrest and peace, etc., etc.

If the reader will spend the time and energy to study the scores and to hear repeatedly recordings and performances of movements in the sonata-allegro form, if he will analyze and coordinate the smallest details, as exemplified in the section which follows, he will find an inexhaustible treasure of great music revealing itself gradually to him.

An Analysis of the First Movement of Beethoven's Symphony No. 1 in C Major, Op. 21

We shall ignore here the short Introduction (Adagio molto) and observe only the sonata form proper which begins with the Allegro con brio (measure 13 in the score). Because so much happens at the same time in a sonata-allegro movement it seems advisable to follow at first the course of a single theme only throughout the entire movement. Let us see for example what happens to *the first principal theme* (I_1) with which the exposition starts.

290.

The theme is repeated in D minor (measures 19–22), then abbreviated to:

291.

Measure 3 of the principal theme is used as a modulating sequence beginning in measure 41:

292.

Measure 4 of the principal theme occurs as counterpoint to the "second theme" (to be discussed later):

293.

The entire theme recurs in a varied form (compare the tonality, the first two imitative measures and measures 3 and 4 with the original), and divided between higher and lower strings, at the end of the exposition:

294.

In the development section (starting at measure 110), measures 2 and 3 of our theme recur with changed dynamics three times in sequence.

295.

Next, measure 4 of the principal theme appears in many different tonalities (measures 122–135); and the typical 𝅘𝅥𝅮. 𝅘𝅥𝅯 𝅘𝅥 rhythm of the first two measures of the original theme wanders in imitative fashion through all the wood winds and strings (measures 144–159). At measure 160, the initial theme is further varied:

296.

The recapitulation (starting at measure 178) brings no new versions of our theme. But in the coda (starting at measure 259) there appears a mixture of measures 15, 90, and 88:

297.

And finally, at measure 277, the theme is again varied. The first bar occurs only once (see also measures 25, 110, etc.), and the brass and wood winds expand the fourth measure and convert it into a fanfare.

So far, we have only followed what happened to the first four bars of the principal theme. However, its continuation—the fifth and sixth bars—also plays an important part during the course of this movement. The chord progression and the chromatic line of the flute:

298.

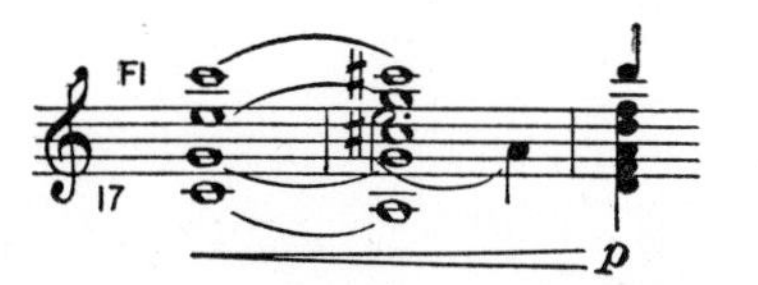

(see also measures 92–94) are expanded greatly in the recapitulation (measures 188–98). And the run of sixteenth notes, which seems at first nothing but a conventional connecting link:

299.

becomes eventually an important thematic factor. In the exposition it reappears as part of another theme of the first thematic group:

300.

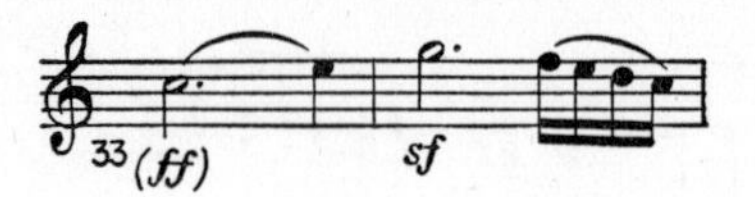

In the development section we find its inversion:

301.

And finally, in the recapitulation (measures 189–201) it gradually rises to a prominent position:

302.

The second theme of the first thematic group (I_2), which was just mentioned, is divided between strings and wood winds:

303.

and is immediately repeated in a varied version:

304.

The second measure of its original version

becomes, a little later, in the exposition

and recurs as a short canon between first and second violins in the development section:

305.

Additional Thematic Material. Because the remainder of the thematic material recurs unchanged—except for its tonality—in the recapitulation section, we will remember and recognize it with greater ease, once we have analyzed closely its first occurrence.

The first part of the *second thematic group* (II_1) is divided between oboe and flute at first

306.

and later concluded by a syncopated "tutti" phrase (see Figure 308).

The theme is "exposed" again in G minor a little later (measure 77) in a varied form: the characteristic scale figure is inverted at times, an extra bar is inserted:

(a reminder of bar 37), and the oboe adds a melody which is repeated in sequence fashion by oboe and bassoon:

307.

The syncopated ending of the first theme of the second thematic group:

308.

may be recognized faintly in the rhythm of the beginning of the development:

309.

(Compare the bass with wood winds and violins in bar 95.)

It remains now to mention (1) the second theme of the second thematic group (II_2):

310.

(2) the closing (or third thematic) group:

311.

both of which recur in the recapitulation, and (3) the transitional passage (T) which leads first back to C major and the exposition:

312.

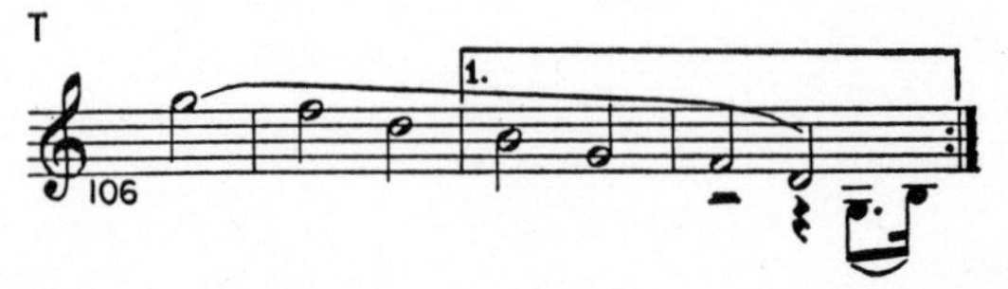

and the second time, after the repetition of the exposition, to a deceptive cadence and the development section:

313.

This transition passage recurs immediately before the recapitulation in augmentation:

and again, expanded to a sequence, at the beginning of the coda (measures 259–70).

One more melodic fragment needs mentioning before we can summarize our findings. At measure 146 the wood winds bind together the fragments of theme I_1 with:

314.

This phrase (derived from the closing theme, Figure 311) is repeated several times and finally expanded to:

315.

Let us now look at the tonalities which are employed.

Exposition

I_1 in C major, D minor, C major
I_2 in C major
II_1 in G major
II_2 in G major
II_1 (varied) in G minor
I_1 (varied) in G major
III in G major

Development

Fragments of I_1 in A major, D major, G major, C minor, F minor, B♭ major, E♭ major, F minor, G minor, D minor, A minor.

RECAPITULATION

I_1 in C major; D minor; fragments of I_1 in F major, G major, A minor, B♭ major, C major, D minor, F major, C major.
II_1 in C major
II_2 in C major
II_1 (varied) in C minor
I_1 in C major
III in C major

CODA

T in F major, D minor, C major
I in C major

It will become clear from a mere reading of the above list of tonalities that C major wins out. It would also seem to be a fair generalization to say that (1) the main thematic material is first presented in the exposition in two principal and closely related tonalities (here C and G); (2) the development contains many thematic fragments and a great number of modulations; (3) the recapitulation starts with the statement of the first principal theme in its totality and in its original key and mode, followed by the remainder of the principal thematic material also in its totality, but this time in the principal key (C major) of the movement; (4) the coda starts when all themes have been recapitulated and dwells mostly on an aphorism which is derived from the first principal theme. However, we must also remember that (1) modulations occur; and (2) themes are stated, repeated, expanded, dissected, combined, and "developed" in *every* section of the sonata form, not only in the development section; and (3) the recapitulation is not an exact repetition.

The Rondo

If we think of a refrain, repeated at regular intervals, but rather at the beginning instead of at the end of each verse, we have a good idea of the formative structure of the rondo. Just as a refrain repeats the gist of a story, so the rondo theme in music provides the basic links in a chain of diverse, that is, contrasting or related musical events. The scheme *A–B–A–C–A–B–A* gives a rough outline of what might happen in a rondo. The interspersed links might be contrasting material or they might derive from or lead over into the rondo theme (*A*). The rondo theme might be literally repeated in the same or in a different tonality, slightly varied rhythmically or melodically, and so forth. Sometimes in the so-called sonata or development rondo, the first section *B* contains the exposition of several themes which are developed in *C* and recapitulated in the last *B* section. Many last movements of concerti, string quartets, sonatas, and symphonies from the Classic Era demonstrate the boundless ingenuity of composers in the use of the rondo.

Variations

Variations are the oldest "developing" device or principle known in music. Again, this device may be applied to short stretches or to lengthy pieces. In the latter case we speak of a *variation form.* A complete musical idea is stated and then expressed in a different manner. The change may occur in the melody, the rhythm, the harmony, etc. The purpose is to exploit all inherent possibilities of an original or borrowed theme and to preserve the sense of continuity and accumulative development in spite of all variety. The means employed in this procedure are innumerable.

Nowhere may we understand better than in the case of the variation form-category that we are at a loss if we try to schematize the formal procedure of great composers into the straitjacket of so-called typical "molds." Here is a well-defined task for the composer: to vary the appearance, the character, the meaning of a theme, and yet the thousands of ways and means and methods used by various composers cannot be summarized by generalities but only with the help of many detailed analyses of pieces or movements which are constructed according to the principle of variation.

The term *variation* does not always appear in the title of a piece or movement. Nevertheless, musicians and analysts usually agree whenever a variation form is employed. The criterion here is that we may speak of variations whenever a *complete* melody is taken as a point of departure, and whenever the successive order of the original components is preserved: that is to say, whenever the theme consists of 16 measures, the "strict" variation will also consist of 16 measures. And if the theme consists of two sections, *A* and *B,* they will be varied in the same order, not first *B* and then *A.* Whenever there are interpolations, substantial interludes, separate developments, etc., contained within a chain of variations, we call this kind of organization *free variation form.*

The slow movements of Beethoven's Fifth and Haydn's "Surprise" Symphonies are at first difficult to follow at times, for this very reason of interpolated transitions or reiterations. We do well, then, to investigate some of the innumerable variations proper first, so as to be ready to recognize later the free use of the variation principle as well.

Let us take first a few cases where the (soprano) melody is the essential element of the theme and where the variations consist in the changing of the melody. Later we will enumerate other possibilities.

A. *Melodic Theme and Melodic Variations*

1. The melody is broken up into shorter note values, thus giving the illusion of a faster tempo.

316. SYMPHONY NO. 94 IN G MAJOR ("Surprise," Second movement)

Joseph Haydn (1732–1809)

2. The melody is embellished or circumscribed. (See Figure 109.)

317. THE QUEENES COMMAND

Orlando Gibbons (1583–1625)

Whenever the process of increasing the number of notes and thus outlining the shape of the melody (and harmony) is applied to an entire dance movement, the variation is called a *double* (see Figure 269).

3. The melody is divided between various parts of the texture.

318. SEPTET, OP. 20 (Fourth movement)

Ludwig van Beethoven (1770–1827)

4. Only a shadow (a figure, a rhythm, an interval) remains of the melody of the theme, or of its accompaniment.

319. DIABELLI VARIATIONS, OP. 120

Ludwig van Beethoven (1770–1827)

(See also Figure 322.)

5. Sometimes we will find a negative melodic variation, so to speak. The melody disappears and only the harmony of the theme is indicated. (Cf. Variation No. 4 of the *Diabelli Variations* by Beethoven.)

B. *Variations of Rhythm, Meter, and Tempo*

1. The rhythm of the melody is changed (with or without a simultaneous change of meter).

320. SYMPHONY NO. 9 IN D MINOR, OP. 125 (Finale)

Ludwig van Beethoven (1770–1827)

2. The meter is changed (see Figures 319 and 320).
3. The tempo is changed (see Figure 319).

C. *Harmonic Variations*

1. The mode is changed, i.e., major (*maggiore*) becomes minor (*minore*).

321. SYMPHONY NO. 94 IN G MAJOR

Joseph Haydn (1732–1809)

2. The tonality is changed.

322. STRING QUARTET IN B♭ MAJOR, OP. 67

Johannes Brahms (1833–1897)

D. *Contrapuntal Variations*

The principle of counterpoint applied to the variation form creates variations which are different from those we have dealt with so far. The many devices which we have observed, change a theme as a whole generally, using one musical element first as a reminder of the theme and later as the changing agent, in a continuing process of give and take. The roles in contrapuntal variation technique, on the other hand, are set and not fluid. One element remains fixed throughout the entire complex of variations and new elements are added vertically. New interpretations are provided above, around, and within a constantly recurring melodic or harmonic progression. The idea is the same as that used in contemporary jazz when improvisations are executed above a relentlessly repeated bass (boogie-woogie). In musical terminology, the recurring bass figure is called *basso ostinato* ("obstinate bass").[1] Its most famous application occurs in the "Lament of Dido" by Purcell:

323. DIDO AND AENEAS ("Lament of Dido")

Henry Purcell (*c.* 1659–1695)

and in the Crucifixus of Bach's B Minor Mass (see Figure 246). When the recurring figure becomes a full-grown melody or a harmonic progression, we speak of a *passacaglia* or *chaconne.* The two terms have been used interchangeably throughout history. However, taking the two celebrated works in these variation forms by Bach as a point of

[1] The combination of a basso ostinato with the doubling device (Figure 316) is called "Divisions on a Ground."

departure, the following distinction might be made: the passacaglia variations are based on a reiterated melody which occurs at first as bass line and may later wander into the soprano range, for example. The chaconne variations are based on a fixed chord progression which is filled out melodically, used as harmonic frame or "accompaniment" for melodies and their counterpoints during the course of the variations. Because a harmonic progression may also be implied by a single bass line, chaconnes have, during many of their variations, not chords but a bass melody only as the recurring figure, just as the passacaglia has, according to its above definition.

324. PASSACAGLIA IN C MINOR FOR ORGAN

Johann Sebastian Bach (1685–1750)

325. CHACONNE IN D MINOR FOR VIOLIN SOLO

Johann Sebastian Bach (1685–1750)

Another variation work of Bach, the *Goldberg Variations* (written for a pupil and friend named Goldberg) might be called a sort of huge chaconne or passacaglia. Throughout 30 variations on an "aria" of 32 measures, not the melody of the theme but its harmonic framework, or rather its bass line, is used as the basic fixed element.

326. GOLDBERG VARIATIONS

Johann Sebastian Bach (1685–1750)

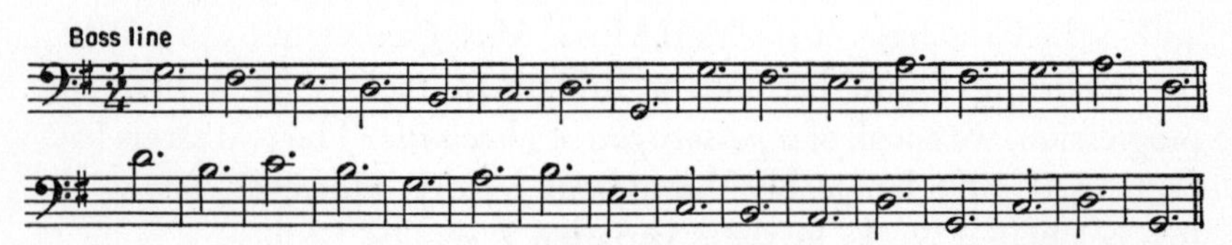

The idea and the various techniques of variation are the gist of all music. Whenever a single musical thought is spun out, elaborated, and developed, we will find a more or less strictly employed variation technique. Because in the strict variation form the composer's thought and work process can be most intimately traced back to the theme in the case of each variation, nothing is more rewarding in music than to study the variations left us as an inheritance by countless great composers of the past.

The Fugue

The fugue is another "form" with a given task and innumerable ways of fulfilling it. A single theme, called *subject* in this case, is to be repeated in various voices (parts) and "developed" through added counterpoints and a certain amount of modulation. Some or all of the polyphonic devices (p. 269) are used in reaching this goal. There is only one rule which all fugues follow—the subject is to be stated by one voice alone first and it is to be restated by all other voices successively as promptly as possible. The second entrance of the subject (also called the "answer") brings the subject a fifth higher. This might involve modulation or slight adjustments in the melodic intervals. In the meantime the first voice continues with a countersubject. There are "episodes" between various sections of the fugue where all voices continue in a somewhat freer manner, with fragments of the subject, the countersubjects, or diverse new musical thoughts.

The diagram of the beginning of a four-voiced fugue might look as follows:

327.

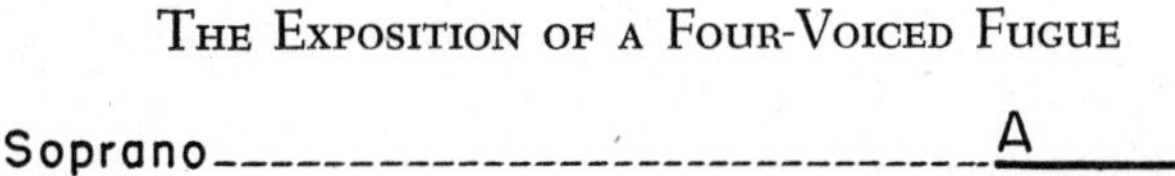

THE EXPOSITION OF A FOUR-VOICED FUGUE

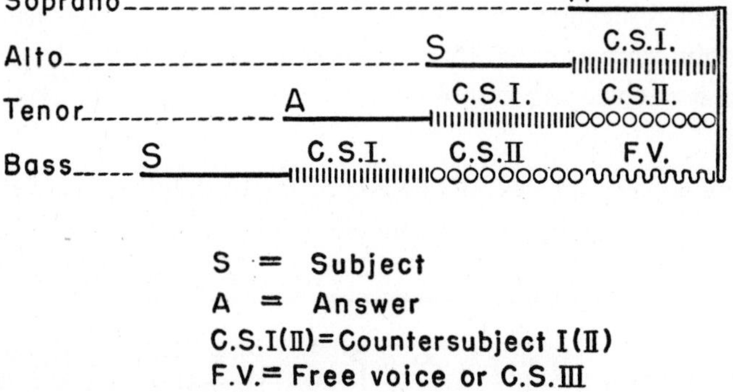

This first part of a fugue is also called the exposition. After an episode, a second or development section follows with modulations, strettos, and a less restricted order of multiple subject entries.

Finally, a recapitulation section will bring back subject and answer in the original tonality.

Double fugues are those fugues which have two subjects, either stated simultaneously (as in the final fugue of Bach's *C Minor Passacaglia*) or successively first, and later combined (as in the double and triple fugues of Bach's *Art of the Fugue*). The reader is urged by all means to study as many fugues as possible, by Bach especially, and to concentrate not only on the subject of a fugue, but also on the countersubjects, as shown in the section which follows.

Analysis of the E Major Fugue No. 9 from the Second Book of the Well-tempered Clavier by J. S. Bach

The first step in analyzing a fugue for a keyboard instrument is to copy the piece in score form so that each voice occupies one staff only. The very process of copying will make us better aware of the relationship among the various strands of melody. To sing or play one single voice at a time will produce a still more vivid picture of the melodic material which is used and varied by the composer. Next should come the playing and singing of two, then three, and in the case of a four-voiced fugue, all four parts.

In order to acquire a more intimate knowledge of the vertical combination of voices it is revealing to combine first soprano and bass only, then soprano and alto, next alto and tenor, etc. This done, we will experience a considerable improvement in our aural perception when we hear a phonograph reproduction or an actual performance.

We will achieve the greatest pleasure in listening, however, if we analyze our score as carefully as possible in regard to the development and the ever-changing combinations of the thematic material of our fugue.

THE SUBJECT. The Ninth Fugue of Bach's *Well-tempered Clavier* (Book II, in E major) has the following subject:

328.

Let us follow this melody and its many permutations throughout the entire piece. In the exposition (measures 1–6½) it is first stated as Subject–Answer–Subject–Answer successively by the bass, tenor, alto, and soprano.

After a short episode it is used in the following stretto:

329.

Another episode follows and in measure 16 a second stretto is started by the alto:

330.

After a third episode, a third stretto starts which brings the subject in diminution in the order soprano, alto, tenor, bass.

331.

In measures 30 and 31 the stretto continues and becomes still more exciting and concentrated because of the astonishing fact that the subject appears simultaneously in three different versions. The bass brings it in diminution:

332.

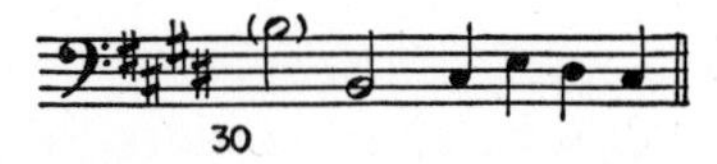

the alto in the original form:

333.

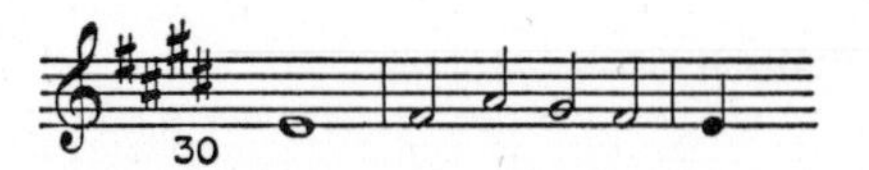

and tenor and soprano present the inversion in diminution. The inversion is literal, except for the first note; instead of

334.

we have:

335.

and

336.

A similar stretto occurs—after a three-bar episode—at measure 35:

337.

And finally, from measure 36 to the end, we hear the subject three more times in its original form: twice it is brought by the bass (measures 36 and 40) and once by the soprano (measure 37).

The Countersubjects. So far, our analysis may have helped us recognize the subject better, whenever it appears in its original form or in any of its many "disguises." The various countersubjects, on the other hand, which are set against the subject play every bit as important a part in the texture and development of a fugue as the subject. One could almost say that it is more helpful to concentrate on the countersubjects rather than on the subject, as a fugue unfolds, inasmuch as the subject through its many repetitions is more firmly embedded in our musical consciousness anyway. Because a countersubject has two functions, namely to continue the subject horizontally and at the same time to "accompany" the answer to the subject vertically, a great many changes will be noticed in a countersubject during the course of a fugue. These changes may be occasioned by rhythmic, melodic, or harmonic considerations.

We might find the basic form or gist of a countersubject by observing and enumerating those features which are most frequently repeated. Thus we might call the following phrase (*A*), countersubject I, and its continuation (*B*) (because it occurs frequently by itself), countersubject II:

338.

It will help us to recognize the many versions of the first two countersubjects if we give an account of what is characteristic of them. In countersubject I three factors are outstanding: (1) the initial interval of an ascending fourth; (2) the ascending scale fragment; and (3) the descending interval of a fourth in eighth notes.

The outstanding factors in countersubject II are: (1) the syncopation; (2) the descending scale fragment; and (3) the rhythm . Keeping these basic details in mind we will be able to detect countersubjects I and II in the endless variations they undergo throughout the fugue.

Countersubject I, for example, occurs in the following measures, either in its original version or with the changes which are here indicated:

In measure 3 in the bass; in measure 4 in the tenor:

339.

In measure 6 in the alto; in measure 8 in the tenor:

340.

In measure 11 in the tenor;

341.

And in measures 13 and 14, in the alto, tenor, and bass voices, respectively:

342.

In the middle of the piece countersubject I disappears—other countersubjects and the variously changed subject are presented instead. Only at measure 36 does it reappear telescoped into the diminutive version of the inverted subject:

343.

And from there on to the end it appears three more times in the following variants:

344.

Countersubject II occurs at first only as the completion of countersubject I. In measure 16, however, the characteristic interval of the initial fourth of countersubject I is combined with the syncopation and the ♫𝅗𝅥 rhythm of countersubject II into a phrase which we might call countersubject III.

345.

The same countersubject III appears again in measure 17 in the alto part and in measure 19 in the soprano as a direct continuation of the fugue subject.

346.

A fourth countersubject occurs first in the bass:

347.

and then varied and as a continuation of countersubject III in the tenor:

348.

and in the alto:

349.

The Episodes. Let us now recall the exact moments where episodes occur.

Episode I enters in the seventh measure and lasts through measure 8.
Episode II starts in the middle of measure 12 and lasts through measure 15.

Episode III begins in measure 22 and ends at measure 26.
Episode IV lasts from measure 32 to measure 35.
Episode V consists of one measure only, measure 39.

If we want to describe the functions of the five episodes in this fugue we might say that (1) all of them (except the last) introduce a stretto; (2) three episodes modulate, II to C♯ minor, III to F♯ minor, and IV to G♯ minor. The thematic material of Episodes I, II, and V is mostly derived from countersubjects I and II. Episode IV uses the inverted and diminished version of the subject (Figure 335) as point of departure; and Episode III, a seemingly new melody which is presented in the form of a stretto.

350.

Let us look somewhat closer at the above melody. The fact that it sounds vaguely familiar may be explained by its close relationship to the subject of our fugue. Suppose we started the subject in its original form on the same tone as the above episode-melody:

351.

Once we have compared these two melodies our vagueness disappears and we discover with certainty that the episode is derived from the subject and incorporates in it the syncopation feature of countersubject II.[2] In other words, we are able to follow more closely the

[2] It is for these reasons that the episode in question is sometimes also labeled "an incomplete development" (Riemann) or a "variation stretto" (Tovey).

thinking process of the composer if we interpolate once in a while on paper and in singing and playing certain links of a musical "equation." Because the composer is more apt to think in long and complicated chains of musical thought, he may keep intermediate permutations in his mind without putting them down, where the layman must "figure out" the intervening stages of a musical thinking process.

Let us close our analysis with a careful observation—in reading and listening—of the two final measures. No more perfect example exists of a concluding cadence, that is to say, the final falling in line of four independent voices toward the inevitable gravity point of the final E-major chord!

Summary

Once we have attained a certain facility in recognizing formative principles and devices, we will be able to follow the procedures of composers in their free and conjunctive use of the resulting forms. An overture may be in development or in ternary form (cf. overtures by Beethoven and Bach); a rondo theme may consist of a canon (see the last movement of the César Franck Violin Sonata); a *finale* may be written as a sonata-allegro in fugal style (e.g., the Finale of Mozart's "Jupiter" Symphony in C Major, K. 551).

A large complex of music, as, for instance, an opera, an oratorio, a cantata, a suite or symphony, a sonata, a string quartet, etc., may consist of any number of distinct movements, each of which makes use of different formal devices. To recognize the musical intentions of the composer at any one moment will only be possible if we abandon the notion of form as something restrictive and prescriptive. It is true that classical sonatas, symphonies, or string quartets will always contain three or four movements which are different in tempo and character. The slow movement will be in a different basic tonality from the rest. As far as forms are concerned, we will find in most cases that the first movement is in sonata-allegro form, and the second in ternary or in variation form. The third movement will usually be a minuet or scherzo, and the finale a rondo. These are general indications of what a great number of composers have found practicable and desirable in constructing an extended instrumental piece. Our own detailed study and listening will have to educate us gradually to recognize exceptions to these traditions and to perceive and evaluate the factors which produce the specific form in question. Usually, the theme for a fugue will have properties different from those of a theme for a sonata-allegro. Binary, ternary, and rondo form categories will each require still other kinds of basic material. The composer, then, when he has a theme will have to find a logical formative organization for it. Or, if he thinks in terms of a fugue, rondo, etc., initially, his choice of basic material will be influenced by the treatment which he has in mind for it. During the history of music, themes and forms have undergone certain further modifications, as we shall see in the following chapter.

19

Style

WE HAVE now reached a point, in our discussion of the elements and factors which are the components of music, where we have to consider the total effect and aspect of a complete piece of music from a distance, so to speak. In the preceding chapters we tried to explore the various component parts of music separately, as far as possible. And yet we observed that a change in melody may bring a change in rhythm and tonality, that a change in texture may educe a different tone color or new dynamics or harmonies, and that expressiveness and form are affected by the slightest change in the employment of musical elements. Furthermore, while we tried to perceive the content of music through the music itself, and while we had said that the life of a composer is not mirrored accurately in his music, nor great music chained forever to its original function or a temporary fashion, we nevertheless had to admit that the outer world enters into the specialized workshop of a composer. Thus, we found it would be best for the listener to try to acquaint himself with the philosophical outlook of a composer, with the cultural patterns of his time, with his social milieu, and with whatever special forces may have influenced the creation of a composition. A close interpenetration of all musical elements, then, and of extramusical factors, has been apparent all along. We shall now have to attempt what we mentioned in our introductory chapter as the final, the historical, approach to music. And while this is neither a world history book nor one about the history of music, we might attempt to see, in principle at least, the connection between the world at large and the music which it produces.

The agent which acts as the connection between musical and extramusical components is called *style*. We have here to deal with a force which embraces and pervades all those musical details which we have analyzed previously. Because the word derives from the ancient writing utensil, *stilus*, style is usually explained as the "handwriting" of eras, nations, individuals, etc. Perhaps this analogy is too narrow and we should rather include as components of style, in addition to the appearance and character of a handwritten message, the writing material (medium), the choice of words, and the connotation of phrases.

Let us assume that we receive a written invitation to the house of a friend. The form of the invitation may be formal or informal, while the content, an invitation, remains the same in either case. Beyond this we will observe what paper is chosen, what ink, what words are used and—the handwriting.

If we now imagine someone who 2,000 years from today finds our invitation, we can see that without any knowledge of our way of life he might arrive at entirely wrong conclusions. Suppose the invitation is written in green ink, the address is 12½ Harbor Terrace, and the note ends with "Love, Mary," and an R.S.V.P. It is likely that our historian of the future would grasp the content of the message and its form fairly accurately. Beyond these simple elements, however, he might come to entirely wrong conclusions about the "style" of our life and the individuals involved. He might declare that in 1952: (1) invitations were always written in green ink; (2) houses were cut in half and put upon terraces near the harbor; (3) the invitation was addressed to a lover; and (4) everybody (or at least all lovers in America) spoke French to each other.

Considering the more complicated messages conveyed in music and the involved style elements inherent in an international art, we must admit that our contemporary evaluations of the music of the past may frequently be further from the truth and would seem more ridiculous to the composer (if he could hear them) than the performance of our imaginary historian.

Nevertheless, we must attempt unceasingly to perceive that over-all guiding, controlling, and forming agent in music which supersedes all other musical elements—style. In order to express its supreme significance and its flexibility we might call style not the handwriting nor the static stamp, but rather the living gesture in music. This human gesture is brought forth by circumstances and tendencies which are determined and influenced by history, human institutions, philosophies, fashions, and by the individual composer—who is himself again a product of his society, his ancestry, his schooling, etc.

Therefore, if we want to perceive a complete work of art, we will have to conceive it as a living document (not a dead monument) of a human spirit and soul which has its own past, present, and future at any one moment of its lifetime. If we want to grasp the significance of a work of art both in its temporary as well as in its timeless role, we will indeed have to consider the time and place of its origin and its historical function: that is to say, its ancestry and its progeny. The physical and psychological circumstances of its inception will certainly help us gain a perspective and place our emphasis where it belongs.

Music of a particular era or by an individual composer produces particular phenomena: certain textures, rhythms, forms, etc. However, these style elements or musical "gestures" have to be familiar *before* we consider the extramusical social and spiritual forces which activated them. The statement that at the time of Monteverdi the desire for a heightened individual expressiveness produced an abundance of chromatics, dissonances (of the seventeenth-century variety), and a homophonic texture remains meaningless until the terms *chromatics, dissonances, homophony*, are clear in the mind and familiar to the ears of the listener.

Assuming that the reader has at this point attained a measure of familiarity with the fundamentals of music, supplemented by intensive and extensive listening, there remains no more nor less to be done than to become familiar with: (1) the history of the world; (2) the history of individual composers; (3) the history of each particular composition within the composer's life.

We have here the reason why it is utterly impossible ever to "understand" music completely, or to know all there is to know even about a single composition. Claiming to "understand" music is as absurd as pretending to "understand" nature or science. However, it is never too late to embark on an unending search along these lines—nor will it ever prove to be without interest.

History and Style

Let us in a very few broad outlines and simplified examples try to recognize in what way extramusical factors may influence the style and therefore any one or all elements of music. We might for clarity's sake distinguish between: (*a*) historical, (*b*) functional, and (*c*) expressive causes, although all these will overlap.

A. Historical. The time and place where a composer is born will produce:

1. Either Oriental or Occidental music: decidedly Oriental or else Occidental rhythms, melodies, tone colors, etc.; however, Western music might be influenced and attracted by the tone ideals and rhythms of Oriental music, and vice versa.
2. National music, if he was born after the birth and before the destruction of nations. National tunes may preclude by their very nature certain kinds of development treatment, and they may require particular harmonizations and instrumentation. His national origin will force him—
3. To write music for aristocracies, democracies, or dictatorships. Aristocracies may demand chamber music and operas; democracies, big orchestras and choruses; and dictatorships, noisy marches.
4. Or it will place him in either a conservative, progressive, or revolutionary period in history. Depending on his own personality, the composer will either conform to the prevailing progressive or conservative tendencies or else oppose them in his music. He may stay within the customary orbit of consonances and dissonances, and use "proper" texts for his songs, or else he may "shock" his contemporaries with unusual dissonances, opera librettos, etc.

B. Functional. Among the functional causes of style we must mention above all: (1) the churches; then, (2) secular functions like the dance; (3) the desire to transmit a "message" of a spiritual, religious, or political character; and (4) the motoric or sensual impetus destined to produce a certain artistic playfulness (art for art's sake or simply "entertainment"). In musical terms this might mean, respectively: (1) the use of Gregorian chant or the Protestant chorale; (2) the use of more or less stylized dance meters and rhythms influenced by the manners and the dress of a particular period; (3) the use of dramatic, shocking, or suggestive musical materials for purposes of propagating an extramusical idea; and (4) the employment of virtuoso singing or playing and the catering to contemporary taste in the use of tone colors, dynamics, harmonies, etc.

C. Expressive. Finally, the expressive cause of a particular style may be: (1) the choice of the medium (instruments, voices, or both, combined either in large or in small numbers); (2) the dramatic or lyrical character of a piece; (3) an emphasis on certain "isms," as nationalism, naturalism, impressionism, neoclassicism, neopreclassicism, etc.; (4) the predominance of either the words over the music or the music over the words in operas and choral works.

It would be superfluous to continue this catalogue of possibilities and their realization in actual music. The point should be clear that outer and inner circumstances, tendencies, and desires may influence essentially any or all details of the music of a particular era and of a composer who lives during that time.

Every piece of music, then, has to be comprehended as placed and as moving in the stream of time. Any consideration of music as a thing in itself will be one-sided, and any omission of music, in the study of the history of a period, will leave an important area unexplored.

In recognition of this fact, it has become customary to transfer historical terms from one art category to another. We speak, for example, of the music of the Renaissance, the Baroque, the Rococo, etc. If these terms are only employed in lieu of figures (*ca.* 1400–1600, *ca.* 1600–1750, *ca.* 1725–1775) or in order to elicit the association ". . . that is to say, the music which is contemporary with the art and life during the Italian Renaissance," etc., a useful purpose is served. We must not, however, assume that what was significant for the architecture of the Renaissance is also necessarily reflected in all the music of that time. Frequently, the arts and music supplement each other, but just as often they tend in opposite directions.

As far as music is concerned, for example, one of the principal ideas of the Renaissance, the revival of antique culture, did not make its appearance in the music of the Renaissance period at all but only with the beginning of the Baroque, as we shall see in a moment. It also happens that one period or even one composer comprises several diverse style elements. The music of Bach, for example, has been called at various times, and in different contexts, Gothic, Baroque, Rococo—and there is a measure of truth in all of these statements.

In order, then, to avoid sweeping comparisons and misleading generalizations, it seems best for those concerned with music to start with an actual piece of music, comparing it with other contemporary, preceding, and succeeding compositions, and subsequently to branch out into a consideration of relevant arts, ideas, and sociological and historical backgrounds and causes. As soon as we have gained a precise impression of the style of a piece of music, that is to say, once we have recognized musically well-defined tendencies, principles, expressive factors, by observing and analyzing the musical components and the "gesture" of a certain composition, the art historians, sociologists, etc., will be able to point out to us where a parallel or opposing style occurs in the contemporary world of art and literature, where mutual influences or a cause and effect connection may be discerned, and so forth.

Musical Styles

A consideration of a few well-defined examples of the evolution of musical style will show us how many different causes may produce a style in music, and it may also train us to recognize the essential "gesture" in a musical composition.

Palestrina or *Roman* or *a capella style* are terms used for the church music of G. Palestrina (1525–1594), L. Victoria (1540–1613), and Orlando di Lasso (1525–1594), and their congenial followers. This style grew out of a reaction to the florid lines of complicated polyphony which obscured the liturgical text and had introduced too many secular melodies into the church, in the opinion of the Council of Trent (1545–1563). A simpler texture, that is, attention to a logical, clearly understandable and meaningful setting of the text, was one of the prime considerations of the Counter-reformation. This precluded in the minds of the Roman School the use of "worldly" instruments, and of "disturbing, undignified, noisy" dissonances. Thus the solution was to be unaccompanied, *a capella* choral singing and a careful consideration of harmonic progressions—a preoccupation with vertical as well as with horizontal forces. This, and the attempt to make the text understood, is exemplified in many works of Palestrina which use a *chordal* or *familiar style*, i.e., the hymnlike simultaneous progression of all voices from one chord and syllable to the next.

352. MISSA *AETERNA CHRISTI MUNERA*

Giovanni da Palestrina (1525–1594)

Familiar or Chordal Style

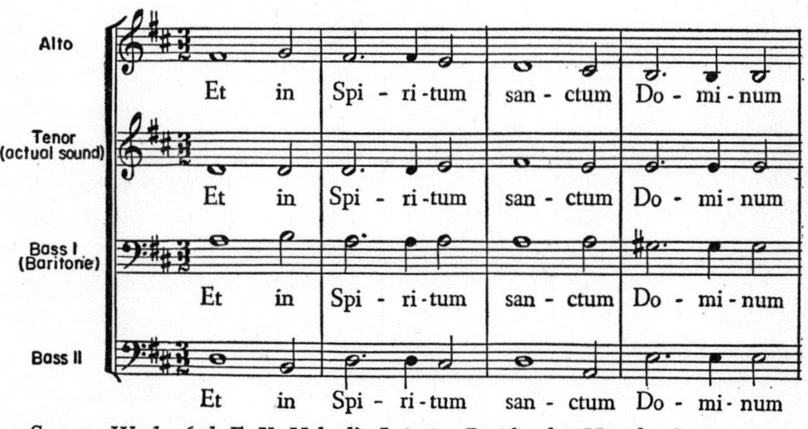

Source: *Werke* (ed. F. X. Haberl). Leipzig: Breitkopf & Härtel, 1874–1907.

True polyphony—that is to say, a texture which contains voices which are independent rhythmically as well as melodically—is apparent in the (contrapuntal) *motet style* of Palestrina's time. Here, successive sections of the text are imitated throughout all voices as in the exposition or *stretto* of a fugue. If the melodies chosen for the imitative treatment are not too florid, a clearly discernible diagonally orientated texture will result—as distinguished from the florid text-obscuring counterpoint and the *hocket*-distortions (Figure 282) of the text which were common in medieval polyphony.

353. MISSA *AETERNA CHRISTI MUNERA*

Giovanni da Palestrina (1525–1594)

MOTET STYLE

Source: *Werke* (edition of F. X. Haberl).

The more expressive, less "contrived" treatment of the text of masses and motets in Palestrina's time was achieved with the help of the secular, so-called *madrigal style* of the 16th century. In the madrigal, worldly poetry of a refined and sensitive character was set to music which stressed through its melodic line, its rhythm and harmony, the meaning of the poem, as well as of single words. The madrigal of the Age of Palestrina was just like the motet, either homophonic or contrapuntal in texture. The difference between these two Renaissance "forms" lies solely in the fact that the motet uses exclusively Latin sacred texts while the madrigal (except for a few spiritual madrigals of Palestrina, for example) is vocal chamber music (*Musica Reservata*) based on worldly, pastoral, amorous, sentimental, playful, dainty poetry.

Finally, we must mention as an important contributing tendency in the Palestrina style the custom of having two choruses, placed at a distance from each other, sing in echolike antiphony, or combine at other times and thus produce rich and colorful sonorities. This style, which was later also extended to instruments by Giovanni Gabrieli (1557–1612), is called *Venetian style* because it was introduced in St. Mark's of Venice by the Flemish chapel master, Willaert (*ca.* 1485–1562).

While the Roman style continued throughout the seventeenth century and even further as the conservative, "old-fashioned" style (*stile antico*), the *Nuove Musiche* of the seventeenth century created new styles for voices and instruments. In the *stile nuovo* (or *expressivo, rappresentativo, recitativo*), the urge for a natural expression of words and feelings made use of a single flexible melodic line which was underlined and punctuated by harmonic progressions and cadences played by a basso continuo accompaniment. The resulting *recitativo* had an additional source in the attempt to re-create the heightened speech of the Greek drama by reciting poetry and drama in free rhythms and inflections, halfway between recitation and song. The demand for dramatic expression and for the full use of the melodic and harmonic means of the Baroque Era led eventually to the creation of the *aria*, an extensive lyric or dramatic musical elaboration inserted at a moment when the action of a drama calls for a highly individualized commentary. Once the vocal and instrumental expressive means had been developed in arias, the recitative took on two forms: the recitativo *secco* (= dry), which served mainly as a narrative device, rapidly telling the story or presenting a dialogue accompanied by punctuating basso continuo chords; and the *recitativo accompagnato* [1] (accompanied by a larger and more independent group of instruments), which occurred at the most important moments of the action (e.g., for the part of Christ or as the immediate introduction to an extended aria in Bach's *St. Matthew Passion*).

With the dramatic recitative, the expressive and sometimes brilliant aria, and the use of homophonic or polyphonic choruses, the Baroque stage was set for the opera, the oratorio (a dramatic musical retelling of a biblical story in the manner of an opera, only without costumes and scenic action), and the cantata (a small oratorio).

Stile moderno or *stile concertante* describes the brilliant instrumental concerti of the preclassical era. Here the principle of contrast and of "question and answer" which G. Gabrieli had already used for instrumental choirs at St. Mark's was extended to a continuous "discussion" between an orchestra and his "concert master" who serves as soloist and elaborates in brilliant and expressive accompanied passages on what the total orchestra, the *tutti* (= all), state initially. In the course of a concerto the soloist and orchestra will interrupt each other, contend (= *concertare*) for the "last word," and finally join forces. In the case of the *concerto grosso* the "solo" role is played by several players who, as the *concertino*, take off from the rest for expressive and brilliant solo passages and combine with their colleagues again for the tutti sections.

During the late Baroque, operatic and instrumental style invaded the church, so that in the so-called cantata-mass we find overtures, arias, concerti grossi, and sonatas *da chiesa* (church sonatas), besides the traditional a capella settings. The outcome of this "mixed" style (= *stile misto*) we find in many of the masses by composers of the Classic and Romantic Eras.

With *Rococo* we describe that late Baroque period which dissolved (in architecture) broad, dramatic, and rich mass effects into pleasant miniature decorations and into "nice" scrolls and shells (*rocaille* = shell). It was the time when the ladies and gentlemen of the French court went "slumming" by pretending to be farmers and farmerettes, shepherds and shepherdesses, at Marie Antoinette's Haineau Castle.

The expressiveness which music had achieved in dramatic operas

[1] Sometimes also called *arioso*.

and oratorios, the flexibility of melodies and the suggestiveness of harmonic progressions which it had attained in virtuoso arias and intimate chamber music, ended in an elegant and individualistic style which is called the *gallant style.* The deficiency of the harpsichord, its lack of a sustaining sound and of powerful sonorities, was made into a Rococo virtue by breaking up the melodic line and the chords into a rich chain of embellishments, scale runs, and arpeggios in the fashion of the lute idiom of bygone days and in imitation of the violin virtuosity of the Baroque.

It was furthermore the ideal of this style to become "sensitive," to let instruments express various emotions (affects) as suggestively and accurately as sung poetry. And as a tribute to the rationalism of the eighteenth century, theories were compounded which, as "doctrine of affects," (*Affektenlehre*) "regulated" the spectrum of emotions and explained how certain musical figures, intervals, harmonies, and tonalities expressed definite "affects" (see also p. 244). The gallant style of the Rococo found its first great realization in the harpsichord works of François Couperin (1668–1733) and later in Telemann (1681–1767), D. Scarlatti (1685–1757), and others. The traditional order of the preclassical dance suite or *sonata da camera* (chamber sonata), which had usually consisted of four movements, *Allemande, Courante, Sarabande, Gigue,* was at this time expanded so as to include additional, more elegant and fashionable dances—for example, the *Minuet, Bourrée, Gavotte, Musette* (a French bagpipe and the shepherd dance for which it is used), *Polonaise,* etc. These "extra" dances, which were usually inserted before the final Gigue, were frequently called "gallantries" (*Galanterien*).

The sensitive side of the gallant style was designated "sensitive style" (*Empfindsamer Stil*) and cultivated especially by two sons of J. S. Bach, W. F. (1710–1784) and K. P. E. Bach (1714–1788). In the desire of this period to arrive at a true and natural expression of feelings in instrumental music, without the necessity of adding words, we may detect the sources of the symphonies and chamber music of the Classic Era. In the intimacy of the Rococo chamber music, on the other hand, especially in the sensitive touch which could be cultivated on the clavichord (the favored instrument of K. P. E. Bach), we sense the sources of the Romantic piano music and the Schubert *Lied* which were to come in the 19th century.

Conclusions and Examples

In the foregoing, we have traced the connection between specific musical idioms, that is to say, melodies, harmonies, textures, media (chosen instruments or voices), "forms," and extramusical contemporary, traditional, or progressive causes. A church dogma, the architecture of a church (St. Mark's in Venice), a "romantic" striving for expressiveness and virtuosity, an archeological urge, dramatic and lyrical literary tendencies, a society "fad," a philosophy, and the idiom of instruments—all these we found reproduced in precise musical symbols, in suggestive musical gestures. In a similar manner, the current events and their roots, which lie in the past and in the contemporary scene, and mankind's longing and grasping for a future, if not for eternity, have been transformed into music by composers at all times.

It would seem, then, that a thorough knowledge of history would lead directly into the heart of music and provide the safest guidance for those who want to become more sensitive to music. This, however, proves to be a common fallacy, as was mentioned before. Only if every human being were a composer would events and tendencies of the extramusical world translate themselves into music in the minds and ears of everybody. Because this is not the case, we find highly cultivated, sensitive, erudite historians whose historical knowledge fails to bring them any nearer to music than others who know little of history.

For similar reasons, "program music" is a poor road to a more intimate acquaintance with music. Unless a piece of program music is a mere narration with sound effects and primitive *Leitmotifs,* the transforming of a story, an idea, a painting, into music presupposes that the listener nearly equals the *musical* imagination of the composer, who transposes into music and elaborates in tones an extramusical impetus. Whenever we stress the "story" of the music in children's concerts, we expect our children to be composers who can think and feel in terms of music where others need pictures, landscapes, stories, the theater. Good program music presupposes a far from elementary stage in the perception of the music, namely a thorough acquaintance with the symbols and gestures of music so that the "story" may not interfere with the hearing of the music, so that the listener may perceive the gist of the composition which is the *musical crystallization* of an outside event or an extramusical idea or story. Children and many adults will be disturbed rather than helped in listening to Richard Strauss' *Till Eulenspiegel* if they are told in detail the historical pranks which, as the composer reluctantly confessed, nourished his musical imagination. The fact that Strauss gave in to a pedantic and musically unimaginative critic in labeling his score, after it was completed, with descriptions of detailed "episodes" has become a distraction and despair for many listeners. Instead of enjoying the music and the spirit, the sarcastic and yet lovable atmosphere spread by the medieval rascal, our program-note-reading audiences struggle in "spotting" the exact moment where Till disturbs the pots and pans of the market women with his horse. And because the piece is loud and dramatic in many places, the over-zealous listener is worried for quite a while whether "these" are the dishpan noises, whether he has missed them, or whether they are still to come.

In order to arrive at a clearer perception of the relationship between the listener and the "gist" of a piece of music, let us try to analyze the reaction toward an unknown piece of music on the part of an untrained average layman. Suppose we were to hear two pieces which never were performed before, for example, a "newly discovered" Rhapsody by Gershwin and another one by Brahms (unfortunately, this assumption is fictitious in both cases). The inexperienced listener of today would spot the Gershwin Rhapsody immediately and the Brahms indirectly by elimination. Not only would the Gershwin composition remind him of the "language" of the "Rhapsody in Blue" but it would also revive, more or less unconsciously, memories of Negro jazz bands, a far-distant New Orleans flavor, metropolitan dances and musicals. If the listener is middle-aged, it will recall memories of the hectic, carefree 1920's and the postwar frantic desires for "a good time." The harmonies of Gershwin, his rhythms, and the impact of his melodies will revive a complex of nebulous subconscious thoughts, emotions, and more or less hazy dreams. We hear more than mere tones; our whole being is affected by the ring of a familiar note. There is no doubt that "this is Gershwin"; it is the music with which we grew up, the echo of which still surrounds us through many contemporary imitative or related musical pieces.

Now, let us imagine somebody, today or a century later, who never lived in America or in the "jazz-crazy" Europe of the 1920's. Would the most detailed description of our society and life make him hear in his mind music in the Gershwin style? Would our historical, sociological, etc., analysis inevitably induce a composer who is distant in time and space to write a Gershwin rhapsody? It seems safe to assume that a composer who is removed from the world and time of Gershwin, even if he has the same talent and a similar personality, will create a different type of music.

If, on the other hand, we study the music of Gershwin meticulously by comparing it with authentic jazz and with Debussy, Ravel, Stravinsky, we can obtain through his music an intimate glance at the society and the time which were instrumental in producing its style, even if we live outside that society and in another era.

The same procedure will work with the Brahms Rhapsody. The listener who has heard other works of Brahms will recognize the "handwriting," he will hear harmonies, melodies, counterrhythms, "inner" voices, which are "typical" Brahms. By comparisons with Schubert and Beethoven, he will detect the romantic and the neoclassical traces, and, if he is conversant with the music and the world history of the nineteenth century he will, through the music, detect humanism, national and mystical varieties of romanticism, conservative anti-Wagnerianism, liberal Protestantism, and the German polyphonic inheritance, mixed with a longing for the southern melos.

Familiarity, then, with the music of a composer and with an era may disclose the life of a master of music, his artistic ancestry, and the contemporary currents of his lifetime. To proceed in the opposite direction, to conclude from history and from the life of a composer what his music intends to say to us, is a hopeless undertaking unless we all claim to be equal in musical imagination to Bach, Mozart, Beethoven, and to all other great composers.

It is fortunate, therefore, that even a slight acquaintance with the language of music and its symbols, its grammar, and its typical "behavior patterns," leads us into the realm of more accurate discrimination of musical styles. Our concluding examples are excerpts from two minuets, one by J. S. Bach and the other by Schubert. They remain unidentified and the reader is invited to decide for himself which piece is written in the style of Schubert and which in that of Bach.

It will be obvious that facts of the "human interest story" variety will not be of much help here. The incessantly repeated facts that Bach had twenty children and that Schubert died young, poor, and unmarried will be of no avail in our task of evaluating what is typical for one and what for the other great composer. Even the most detailed biography of the lives of Schubert and Bach will not furnish us with the slightest clue for a more intimate acquaintance with their music, that part which made them immortal.

354.

MINUET A

355.

MINUET B

Familiarity with the history of music, on the other hand, with the varying use of its elements, its texture, style, instrumentation, etc., will lead us immediately into the music itself.

Comparing the excerpts of these two minuets, we discover these instances of external and internal differences in style:

	Minuet A (Fig. 354)	Minuet B (Fig. 355)
Range	Wider	Narrower
Dynamic signs	Many	None
Harmony	Unexpected progression in measure 5 (deceptive cadence followed by modulations)	Built on logical bass line
Texture	Varies	Remains the same; wide jumps in melody occasionally suggest a hidden polyphony
Melody	Set in octaves; with dynamics, this produces greater sonority and a more "personal" or dramatic expressiveness	More figurative
Tempo	Fast (allegro); thus this "minuet" approaches the character of a Beethoven scherzo	Slower
Phrases	3 + 2 + 2 + 2 + 3	More regular: 2 + 2 + 2 + 2

If we compare the above points, we will have no doubt about the respective composers. The second composition is written for the harpsichord, in basso continuo style, and with a "busy" melodic line somewhat reminiscent of D. Scarlatti and Couperin, and the first is romantic in the choice of harmonies, dynamics, texture, form—nearer to Beethoven than to Bach.

If we had been satisfied with generalities, we would have described one composition as "flowing, emotional, tuneful," and the other as "angular, ornamental, geometrical," etc. However, it would remain for the listener to decide what these terms mean in the language of music, and what they mean in the case of Schubert and in that of Bach. Furthermore, any finer distinction of compositions which are more extended and more closely related in time and style would become increasingly nebulous in a procedure of this kind.

Let us not forget, then, that only with a basic knowledge of the elements of music and their historical development and use may we analyze the place of any piece of music in the total work of a composer, and in comparison with the work of his contemporaries, predecessors, and successors in music. To do so we must hear and think in terms of melodies, harmonies, etc., not in literary descriptive terms.

20

Music Today

If it is true that the spirit of a time may be detected in its music, it seems strange that music by contemporary composers has so frequently puzzled audiences throughout history. The judgment that a certain piece sounds unpleasant, ugly, contrived, shocking, and that a composer is breaking "rules" of beauty, common sense, and tradition, has been made by competent and well-meaning listeners and critics against many now-recognized composers. The layman will find again and again that what he thinks about Schoenberg today was thought and written at one time or another about Monteverdi, Haydn, Mozart, Beethoven, Berlioz, Wagner, Brahms, Debussy, Stravinsky, and Hindemith. This does not mean, of course, that condemning or praising two composers in identical terms makes them equal in stature for all times. We may, however, conclude that if a man like Beethoven, who expressed himself so masterfully in his music, was misunderstood by his contemporaries, this same danger of misjudging a man's work is even greater in the case of a lesser genius.

The time gap between the creation and the assimilation of a new composition has frequently been explained by the statement that a genius is ahead of his time. Rather than to accept this convenient alibi and to continue in our lagging appreciation of the great men of our own time, we might confess that we, the audience, are behind our time and have repeatedly, through our passive resistance, lost sight of our most significant cultural exponents. The reason for these conditions and at the same time the remedy may be found in three interrelated factors: (1) our mental attitude toward the task and work of a composer, (2) the status of the world, and (3) the deficiency of our musical life.

Audience and Composer

It has been mentioned previously that it is a common error to assume that all music has to be pleasant or even beautiful. The listener who expects forever to be entertained, mildly stimulated, but not *bothered* by music will miss just the most essential and the largest part of the world's greatest music.

All art aspires to express experiences of our world in a crystallized and organized man-made creation which searches deeper, and thus makes us perceive a more significant and truer picture of our fears and aspirations than the daily life struggle permits us to see. The artistic result may not always be a pleasant and playful fairytale excursion, but just as frequently an elation such as is felt at the end of a steep and arduous climb or a fantastic nightmare and unresolved sadness, even an unmitigated shock. If we want to continue calling the art of Dante, Shakespeare, Michelangelo, El Greco, and Beethoven beautiful, we will have to redefine the term. In the sense of the pleasant, harmonious, undisturbing, Olympian, the word "beautiful" will not suffice as a description of the masterworks of these great men. We should rather add the possibility that beautiful may also mean moving, logical, true in a special sense known at first only to the creative artist.

In their excursions into unconquered territory, artists of all times have used new materials and means in reaching their artistic goal. Their method of travel has often seemed to be risky, impractical, and uncomfortable to people who did not know beforehand the destination or the condition of the road. Think of the difference in our emotional experience when we were told that Lindbergh had crossed the ocean in an airplane, and today when someone tells us that he is flying to Europe. And let us imagine the contrast between the thoughts and feelings of Lindbergh and those of today's casual air passenger.

Returning to earth and to music, we may well understand from this comparison that some of Beethoven's more daring music, when first performed, elicited puzzled surprise and even doubts about whether he knew what he was doing.

> All impartial experts and music lovers have unanimously been of the opinion that never has such incoherent, shrill, confused, ear-shocking music been written. The most cutting dissonances follow each other in really horrible harmony.[1]

[1] A critique of Beethoven's *Fidelio,* by the critic of *Der Freimüthige,* September 11, 1806. Quoted in Max Graf, *Composer and Critic,* p. 155.

To us today Beethoven seems less dissonant, less abrupt and shocking, for two obvious reasons: we have heard more of his music, and more composers have followed his path. Consequently his music is accepted as the rule and that of contemporary innovators in comparison appears to some as an "inconsequential" exception. However, if and when we become similarly acquainted with contemporary composers by hearing their music repeatedly, we will be able to approximate their musical thoughts and intentions just as well as Beethoven's.

In this case we will make up for the time lost during which the composer prepared and created his composition without our being able to follow his mental and actual musical progress. This time lag between the inception of a piece of music and the final completion and performance is inevitable unless the audience is let in on "work in progress." More reason, then, to grab each newly written composition and hear it as often as the composer heard it in his mind while composing it.

Even so, it needs repeating that to do justice to a new piece is almost impossible for the layman. His praise might be just as unfounded as his condemnation. Many great composers were overshadowed by contemporaries whose names we hardly recognize today. And there are also the cases where cantatas by Bach or operas by Mozart were hardly recognized as more than common products of a custom or fashion rampant in those days.

Let us beware, then, of snap judgments about any music and rather clear the air for an unprejudiced reception of the message of composers of all times. Every good composer expresses in his own way the spirit of his time, and the artistic truth of his work can open up for us vistas of our own time as well as those of the past and the future.

A great deal of tolerance, mental flexibility, and active imagination is demanded of an intelligent audience which wants music to remain a living art rather than have it relegated to the function of a storeroom in a museum of music of the past. The time may not be far when the latest composition by an honor student of the conservatory of a city will arouse as much interest among its population as an exhibition of the latest Diesel engine.

The Composer and the World

The composer of today finds himself in the same difficulties as the statesman, the educator, the scientist. We have the know-how but are ignorant of the know-what, as Norbert Wiener says.

A young composer can acquire an excellent musical education, his knowledge of the music of the past can be immensely greater than was the case among former generations, and he may even be able to earn a living, after a fashion. He will have the urgent desire to express himself in a message—but what this message shall be and where the spiritual stimulus for it shall come from is his great problem. He feels himself inescapably drawn into a world where Christian and democratic ideas are making little progress. Two inconclusive wars of the immediate past and the possibility of an impending third one give little hope for lasting peace. And while hardly any historical era has been without wars or other public calamities, today there is no South Sea island nor any other calm and peaceful spot left on earth for those who might, in order to create a work of art, prefer to escape into a physical or mental hiding place. Romantic egotism and nationalistic preoccupations seem to have little place in an age that struggles in a rather hazardous way to become One World. The dawn of a happy age seems to be as far removed from reality as is the Hollywood "happy ending." How is the composer to find a distinct style for himself, a personal language which mirrors at the same time the spirit of the time?

His music may consist of violent clashes, bitter struggles—or else he may deceive himself and his audience in vague sweet dreams. He may also concern himself with musical technology, inventing new devices and musical combinations which fascinate as gadgets do. Or he may revert to ideologies of the past: eternal classical beauty, romantic dreams of the Superman, sensual pleasures of tone paintings, folkloristic imitations, etc., etc. In musical terms he may produce polytonality, antitonality, polyrhythm, new sonorities, or he may revert to an eighteenth-century musical rationalism or to medieval modes, neoclassicism, chromaticism, jazz, Oriental tone color; in other words, the music picture of today is just as violent, puzzling, divergent, obscure, and interesting as the world.

And sometimes a modern master will succeed so well in his music in creating a bridge between the past and the future that we can regain hope and lose our fear temporarily in daring and courageous musical excursions which show us in a momentary flash the potential of life. It is for these few gratifying and spiritually strengthening moments that we must keep an active generation of contemporary composers at work.

Our Musical Life

Let us now by way of conclusion investigate whether the musical climate of our days is favorable to our aspirations toward a healthy general musical culture which includes and encourages new music and new musicians as well as uncontested masterpieces and artists.

To appraise and to predict the musical atmosphere in America is as difficult as to predict the weather in New England. The old saying, "If you don't like the weather, just wait a minute," could apply to our musical life as well. It is hard to believe that seventeen years ago the suggestion to broadcast concerts conducted by Toscanini was greeted with derisive laughter, followed by the "experts'" explanation that the man who buys a high-priced car does not care for "that highbrow stuff." Or, let us remember that not so long ago a then and now world-famous composer could not perform his music in the auditorium of one of our greatest educational institutions because the music department disapproved of his music. That it is possible today to hear good music on the air, at least with FM sets, and that a great number of prominent composers are teaching in our colleges today—these are gratifying facts. We may add that never has there been a country outside of the United States where more time and money was spent on music education in the grade and high schools and in colleges.

However, it is also true that recently a great modern composer had an exceedingly hard time earning a living and that only after his death were his compositions suddenly performed everywhere, thus bringing an avalanche of royalties to his heirs.

The sad truth that our musical life is unstable is also indicated by the facts that music education in schools and colleges is pushed into the background whenever the times are critical; that our finest orchestras, the envy of the world, and our only permanent opera have to go begging every few years; and that the big radio networks act like timid souls as soon as television offers wrestling instead of concert music.

What is needed most in the face of these unpredictable and freakish fluctuations of our musical surroundings seem to be a fair and clearly defined attitude on the part of the audience toward the potentialities and functions of music.

It is customary either to praise our music indiscriminately by calling it bigger and better than ever, or to condemn it roundly, praising in comparison the musical life of olden times or of the Old World. Both these attitudes are unjustified and ineffective as far as planning and realizing a healthy musical life for our communities is concerned. Whenever we are disturbed by finding dolls, cigarette boxes, Easter bunnies, in a music store rather than music, let us remember that in 1887 there was presented to Queen Victoria "a musical bustle so designed as to provide a performance of the national anthem (God Save the Queen) whenever the wearer sat down."[2]

Today, whenever a soloist strikes us as more of a circus acrobat than a musician, let us ponder the fact that Beethoven's Violin Concerto had its world première under the following circumstances: The soloist, Mr. Clement, after the first movement of the concerto, "played them one of his own sonatas on one string and with the violin upside down. . . . Then, in the second part of the program, he continued with the last two movements of the concerto."[3]

The holding of a competition for composers to "complete" Schubert's Unfinished Symphony and "jazzing up" the classics seem to many connoisseurs typical of our uncultured and decadent times. However, in 1820, William Gardiner, a stocking manufacturer and amateur composer from Leicester, sent Beethoven an opus entitled "Sacred Melodies," explaining in an accompanying letter that these "contain your divine adagios appropriated to the British Church." Mr. Gardiner continued:

> I am now engaged upon a work entitled "The Oratorio of Judah," giving a history of that peculiar people from the Jewish Scriptures. The object of this letter is to express a hope that I may induce you to compose an Overture for this work, upon which you can bring all the force of your sublime imagination (if it please you) in the key of D minor.[4]

The same gentleman sent Haydn six pairs of cotton stockings adorned with quotations from Haydn's quartets.[5] We see, then, that there can be found a precedent for everything in history—even for the connection between haberdashery and music.

[2] Apel, *Harvard Dictionary of Music,* p. 432.

[3] Abraham Veinus, *Victor Book of Concertos,* p. 66.

[4] F. H. Shera, *The Amateur in Music,* p. 57. New York: Oxford University Press, 1939.

[5] *Ibid.,* p. 55.

The real danger to our music of today seems rather to lie in our famous flair for specialization and centralization, and the commercial attitude which is both the cause and effect of our time dis-ease. While there probably is no book on the appreciation of baseball, everybody knows and likes the game. The finer points of this sport are valued by a vast public because everybody has tried his hand at it on a sandlot in his early youth. From there to the major leagues a continuous flow of players, as well as a public of all stages of skill and appreciation, is kept alive. In music we have the sandlot and the major leagues but nothing in between. The two extremes—amateurs and professionals—are constantly driven further apart by reason of this very cleavage, as we shall see.

The predilection for methods and procedures over subject matter in our training of teachers is well known. The results are that music teachers are frequently comparable to dietitians who are told how to feed people but not what to feed them. One can realize this by looking over catalogues of music for school bands, orchestras, and choruses: hardly any names of well-known old or modern composers appear, only arrangements and "original" educational music by bandmasters and orchestra and chorus leaders. Poor and dull imitations of music *à la* Mendelssohn, Tchaikovsky, and Brahms are the rule, and the pioneer work of A. T. Davison, who showed with his Harvard Glee Club editions that young people of today might just as well sing Palestrina, Lassus, Bach, and Brahms in the original, remains the exception after forty years.

The young professional music student, on the other hand, shies away from a music teaching profession which stresses teaching rather than music; he specializes in his own field to the exclusion of a general and pedagogical education, especially since there are no "minor leagues" available for him. He must make the major leagues or starve—more reason then to study his violin or clarinet and nothing else. We do find many of these aspiring young musicians later in teaching positions. They are unequipped to teach and forever bitter over their professional musical failure.

Specialization is also evident in conductors who neither play nor sing nor compose, players and singers who do not compose, composers who do nothing but compose, teachers who do nothing but teach, dance bands which play for dances only, musicians who only improvise, others who only read, orchestras which play only classical music, quartets which play only modern music, etc. Type-casting in the field of music, in other words, has done as much damage as it did to the theater and the moving pictures. It is a fact that all great performers of the past were also composers, teachers, and improvisers, and so on.

It has been said that the modern music student is familiar with more music than his predecessors of former generations. However, while it is true that an immense and varied literature is available to him through records, this very multitude of "perfect" performances on ice is also a danger. When Bach had to hitchhike 300 miles in order to hear the greatest organ masters and composers of his time in North Germany, this trip was more of a revelation to him than the avalanche of music at our fingertips is today for us. When there was no master-recording of every famous piece available, and when the young aspiring future musicians had to grapple for themselves with dormant masterpieces, there was more occasion for discoveries and originality in conception among players, singers, and conductors than there is today.

Limiting our good orchestras, choruses, and opera companies to a few big cities has deprived our future musicians and audiences of a valuable training ground. Intimacy with music is attained much better by observing work in progress in rehearsals and throughout the stages of gradual improvement than by endlessly repeated "flawless" phonograph records. The few highly developed orchestras are to the majority of our audiences what a high-powered automobile is in the hands of a bicycle rider who is not used to such high speed and intricacy and is really unable to judge the highly complicated machine from where he sits. To expect our young musicians to graduate from a conservatory to the Metropolitan Opera or one of the major orchestras is as unreasonable as to expect a college graduate to become, upon graduation, a senior executive.

We do not provide a chance for our musicians and our audiences to work their way up through the "sticks" and through "in-service training." The fact that so many foreigners still occupy prominent posts in our musical life is explained by their more extensive training, by their good luck which allowed them to gain experience outside America and to arrive at the top not suddenly but gradually.

Commercially, our few monopolized concert agencies and radio networks operate under an economy of scarcity. If an agent gets 20 per cent commission, why should he be interested in young artists who might get only $100–$200 for a performance? His life and business will be better if he claims that there are only three pianists worth hearing—and advises the public to save up for a fee of $4,000 and not to bother with any of the smaller fry. Radio networks pride themselves in piping a few high-powered musical "entertainments" across the country rather than encouraging local talent. At the moment, a great deal of American musical talent which goes wasted in our country is snatched up by opera companies in Europe.

It is, then, clearly up to the audiences to create gradually the many musical minor leagues which are still missing in America. Once we have a permanent opera company and an opera and symphony orchestra in every city of more than fifty thousand inhabitants, we will create employment and proving grounds for our composers and musicians. Audiences will grow in quantity and quality because they will watch the development of an indigenous musical culture and participate in it.

The majority of our musical masterpieces has been first performed by amateurs. The world premières of Haydn's, Mozart's, Beethoven's, and Brahms' quartets were frequently played by amateurs, and every oratorio, opera, and much of the symphonic literature allows for amateur participation. If it seems utopian that every city should have an opera and orchestra—partly amateur but always under professional direction—let us remember that college dance bands, orchestras, and choruses are doing valuable work even now, comparable to and sometimes in co-operation with professionals. Instead of waiting for the great virtuoso or the famous orchestra or opera company which comes to town once a year, let us prepare for that visit by arranging for and participating in "minor league" activities throughout the year.

Our great problem will be, Who pays the piper? The sponsorship of kings and dukes has passed on to a few public-spirited and far-sighted individuals and to colleges and universities. But we cannot always trust that there will be an Elizabeth Sprague Coolidge (who has done more for chamber music and young composers in America than any other person). We cannot trust that there will be conductors like Stokowsky, Koussevitzky, Mitropoulos, who have successfully battled with their board of directors for the inclusion of contemporary music in conventional symphony concert programs for ancient subscribers. We cannot even trust that industrial magnates will see that their only chance for immortality lies in sponsoring many composers one of whom might turn out to be a Beethoven. Radio and big phonograph companies are out because they aim for the lowest common denominator of musical taste. Colleges, on the other hand, often are preoccupied with the sometimes rarefied atmosphere of the upper 15 per cent who attend or teach in colleges.

It is rather in our communities that the future of music lies. Every year hundreds of well-equipped musicians and potential musical leaders graduate from colleges and conservatories. They are qualified and eager to bring chamber music and symphony concerts, opera and oratorio performances, to thousands of American communities in a way which might make music a daily occurrence like radio or television, a way of living rather than a luxurious pastime for a certain leisure class. There are now two or three states of the Union and several cities which sponsor musical activities for their citizens. This seems to point the way for our future music. There might come the time when we all will pay gladly not only for street cleaning and defense expenditures, but also for what, among other things, we all should strive to defend and to keep alive as an active force for the good: the speaking and the understanding of the language of music.

Bibliography

Note: Only books which are referred to in the text are listed in this bibliography.

ABERT HERMANN. *W. A. Mozart, Neubearbeitete und erweiterte Ausgabe von Otto Jahns' Mozart*. Leipzig: Breitkopf & Härtel, 1923.

American Standard Acoustical Terminology, American Standards Association, Inc., 1951.

APEL, WILLI (ed.). *Harvard Dictionary of Music*. Cambridge: Harvard University Press, 1947.

BACH, K. P. E. *Essay on the True Art of Playing Keyboard Instruments*. W. J. Mitchell, translator and editor. New York: W. W. Norton & Co., Inc., 1949.

BARTHOLOMEW, WILMER T. *Acoustics of Music*. New York: Prentice-Hall, Inc., 1942.

BERLIOZ, HECTOR. *Treatise on Instrumentation*. Enlarged and revised by Richard Strauss; translated by Theodore Trout. New York: E. F. Kalmus, 1948.

BODKY, ERWIN. *Der Vortrag alter Klaviermusik*. Berlin: Max Hesse, 1932.

DAVISON, A. T., and APEL, W. *Historical Anthology of Music*. 2 vols. Cambridge: Harvard University Press, 1946, 1950.

DRINKER, HENRY S., JR. *The Chamber Music of Johannes Brahms*. Philadelphia: Elkan-Vogel, 1932.

EINSTEIN, ALFRED. *The Italian Madrigal*. Princeton: Princeton University Press, 1949.

GEIRINGER, KARL. *Musical Instruments*. New York: Oxford University Press, 1937.

GRAF, MAX. *Composer and Critic*. New York: W. W. Norton & Co., Inc., 1946.

JEANS, SIR JAMES HOPWOOD. *Science and Music*. New York: The Macmillan Co., 1937.

LANG, P. H. *Music in Western Civilization*. New York: W. W. Norton & Co., 1941.

MCGINNIS, C. S., and GALLAGHER, C. "The Mode of Vibration of a Clarinet Reed," *Journal of the Acoustical Society of America*, XII (1941), 529.

MCGINNIS, C. S., HAWKINS, H., and SHER, N. "Experimental Study of Tone Quality of Boehm Clarinets," *Journal of the Acoustical Society of America*, XIV (1943), 228.

MOZART, LEOPOLD. *A Treatise on the Fundamental Principles of Violin Playing*. Translated by Editha Knocker. New York: Oxford University Press, 1948.

Musical Quarterly, Vol. XXXVI, No. 2 (April, 1950). New York: G. Schirmer, Inc.

NETTL, PAUL. *The Story of Dance Music*. New York: Philosophical Library, Inc., 1947.

PARKER, S. E. "Analyses of the Tone of Wooden and Metal Clarinets." *Journal of the Acoustical Society of America*, XIX (1947), 417.

PISTON, WALTER. *Harmony*. New York: W. W. Norton & Co., Inc., 1941.

POWERS, STEPHEN. "Tribes of California," Dept. of the Interior, *North American Ethnology* (III). Government Printing Office, Washington, 1877.

PRUNIÈRES, HENRY. *A New History of Music*. Translated by Edward Lockspeiser. New York: Macmillan Co., 1946.

ROLLAND, ROMAIN. *Ludwig van Beethoven*. Zürich: Max Rascher Verlag, 1921.

ROSCOE, JOHN. *The Banyankole*. Cambridge: Harvard University Press, 1923.

SACHS, CURT. *The History of Musical Instruments*. New York: W. W. Norton & Co., Inc., 1940.

SCHWARTZ, H. W. *The Story of Musical Instruments*. Elkart, Ind.: Pan-American Band Instruments, Division of C. G. Conn Ltd., 1938.

SCHWEITZER, ALBERT. *J. S. Bach.* 2 vols. London: Breitkopf and Härtel, 1911.
SHERA, F. H. *The Amateur in Music.* New York: Oxford University Press, 1939.
SPITTA, PHILIPP. *Johann Sebastian Bach.* 3 vols. Translated by Clara Bell and J. A. Fuller-Maitland. New York: Dover Publications, 1951.
STRAVINSKY, IGOR. *Histoire du Soldat.* Wien: Wiener philharmonischer Verlag A.G., c. 1924.
STRUNK, OLIVER. *Source Readings in Music History.* New York: W. W. Norton & Co., Inc., 1950.
TERRY, C. S. *Bach, A Biography,* 2d ed. London: Oxford University Press, 1933.
THAYER, A. W., and KREHBIEL, H. E. *The Life of Ludwig van Beethoven.* 3 vols. New York: The Beethoven Association (G. Schirmer, printers), 1921.
VEINUS, ABRAHAM. *Victor Book of Concertos.* New York: Simon & Schuster, 1948.
WOOLDRIDGE, H. E. "The Polyphonic Period, Part I." In *The Oxford History of Music,* 2d ed., Vol. I. London: Oxford University Press, 1929.

INDEX

Note: Figures in **boldface** type refer to pages on which musical examples, tables, diagrams, etc., appear. Only plates are identified by Figure numbers.